Information Security: Principles and New Concepts

Volume II

Information Security: Principles and New Concepts
Volume II

Edited by **Fiona Hobbs**

New Jersey

Published by Clanrye International,
55 Van Reypen Street,
Jersey City, NJ 07306, USA
www.clanryeinternational.com

Information Security: Principles and New Concepts
Volume II
Edited by Fiona Hobbs

International Standard Book Number: 978-1-63240-307-0 (Hardback)

Printed in the United States of America.

Contents

Preface

In contemporary times, there is no dearth of information. In fact, since the advent of technology and the World Wide Web, there has been an overload of information. All data needs to be recorded, saved and stored. However, some information is more crucial as compared to others. And this is where the concept of Information Security comes in. The origins of Information Security can be traced to the times of Julius Caesar in 50 B.C, when he invented the Caesar cipher. This mechanism was used to protect the confidentiality of correspondence and provided a means of detecting tampering, in case any. Regardless of the form that the data may take, electronic or physical, Information Security is a must in present times.

Information Security has grown and evolved significantly in recent years. Numerous occurrences of international terrorism, through disruption of data fuelled the need for better methods of Information Security. Today, it is an indispensable part of all the business operations across different domains. Protecting information has also become an ethical and legal requirement in many cases. Essentially, the practice of defending information from unauthorized access, use, disclosure and destruction is referred to as Information Security. The CIA triad of confidentiality, integrity and availability is one of the core principles of information security.

There are two important aspects to Information Security. These are Information Technology Security, which is concerned with technology security and Information Assurance, whose aim is to ensure that data is not lost during critical times.

I would like to thank all the contributors who have shared their knowledge in this book. I would also like to thank my family for their constant trust and support.

Editor

1

A Robust Method to Detect Hidden Data from Digital Images

Romany F. Mansour[1], W. F. Awwad[1], A. A. Mohammed[2]
[1]Department of Computer Science, Faculty of Science, Northern Borders Univeristy, Arar, KSA
[2]Department of Computer Science, Faculty of Science, South Valley University, Qena, Egypt

ABSTRACT

Recently, numerous novel algorithms have been proposed in the fields of steganography and visual cryptography with the goals of improving security, reliability, and efficiency. Steganography detection is a technique to tell whether there are secret messages hidden in images. The performance of a steganalysis system is mainly determined by the method of feature extraction and the architecture selection of the classifier. In this paper, we present a new method *Visual Pixel Detection VPD* for extract data from a color or a grayscale images. Because the human eye can recognize the hidden information in the image after using this detection. The experimental results show that the proposed method provides a better performance on testing images in comparison with the existing method in attacking Steghide, Outguess and F5.

Keywords: Data Hiding; Steganography; Steganalysis; Attack; Color Image Hiding; Stego-Image

1. Introduction

Steganography is the art, science, or practice in which messages, images, or files are hidden inside other messages, images, or files. The concept of steganography is not a new one; it dates back many millennia when messages used to be hidden on things of everyday use such as watermarks on letters, carvings on bottom sides of tables, and other objects. The more recent use of this concept emerged with the dawn of the digital world. Experiments have shown that data can be hidden in many ways inside different types of digital files. The main benefit of steganography is that the payload is not expected by the investigators who get to examine the computer data. The person sending the hidden data and the person meant to receive the data are the only ones who know about it; but to everyone else, the object containing the hidden data just seems like an everyday normal object. A classification of information hiding techniques is described in [1].

Generally, steganographic methods proposed in the past few years can be categorized into two types. The methods of the first type employ the spatial domain of a host image to hide secret data. In other words, secret data are directly embedded into the pixels of the host image [2-5].

Steganographic methods of the second type employ the transformed domain of a host image to hide secret data [6-10]. Transformation functions like the discrete cosine transform (DCT) or discrete wavelet transform (DWT) are first exploited to transform the pixel values in the spatial domain to coefficients in the frequency domain. Then the secret data are embedded in the coefficients.

Recently, the scheme proposed in [11] hid large amounts of data in the pixels of a true color image, which used 8 bits to represent each color component of a color pixel. The secret image can be both a grayscale and a true color image. However, the quality of the extracted color secret image is not good in terms of the peak signal-to-noise ratio (PSNR) value and visual observation. In this paper, we propose a steganographic method which hides a color or a grayscale image in a true color image.

The detection of hidden data presents a big challenge to investigators and individuals looking for hidden data. For images only, there are hundreds of billions of images on the web and looking through all of them would be a very time consuming and computationally challenging task; let alone the other types of files that data can possibly be hidden in. Even if someone manages to go through all the current images on the web, what if some new algorithm for hiding data in images emerges? Is the application used to scan the images for hidden data suitable for and capable of uncovering the hidden data? And is it feasible to go back and rescan all the images all over again with the same or other software updated to detect the hidden data by the new algorithm? The answer to the above questions is that it's close to impossible to be able to accurately scan or attempt to detect hidden data on such a wide scope of suspect images. It is somewhat easier for investigators to scan for hidden data on a smaller scale such as an image of a hard drive, but they are still faced with the same software inaccuracy and the possibility of encountering unknown data-hiding algorithms.

In our proposed method, the local color information of an image can be preserved well because the technique of color quantization in the proposed method is image-dependent and adaptive color quantization [12]. The extracted color secret image is perceptibly almost identical to the original image, and its PSNR value is very high Moreover, the hiding capacity of the host image and the quality of the stego-image in the proposed method are also superior to that of the scheme in [11].

The remainder of this paper is organized as follows. In Section 2, a brief description of the scheme related to this paper will be given. In Section 3, we shall present our proposed method. The overall algorithm for the proposed method will be provided in Section 4. Finally, the experiments and conclusions shall be given in Sections 5 and 6.

2. Color Quantization

Color quantization is the process that drastically reduces the number of colors used in a digital color image by approximating the original pixels with their nearest representative colors. The true color image is usually quantized to reduce the size of the image to be stored or transmitted. This means the 224 colors of a true color image have to be greatly reduced to a limited number of representative colors, which is called a color table (palette).

Typically, a color table consists of 256 entries where each entry represents a color containing red, green, and blue components. In general, a palette-based image mainly consists of a color table and some image data, which contain indices corresponding to the color table entries.

Bitmap images consist of matrices of numbered points with two dimensions for grayscale and three dimensions for RGB color images. The grayscale images, also called intensity images, contain numbered values at these points, called pixels, between 0 for black and 255 for white, which can be represented as 8-bit binary strings (2^8 = 256). The numbers between represent gradient gray values between black and white. The RGB, abbreviated for Red, Green and Blue, images are actually three two-dimension image layers, a red, a green and a blue layer, that are combined to produce the full color image. Each layer of a color image also contains values from 0 for black to 255 for the lightest shade of the color. The RGB color scheme is referred to as an additive scheme because adding the effective value of the three layers usually produces a lighter color at that pixel.

For instance if all three values that comprise a pixel are 0, *i.e.* (0, 0, 0) for (red, green, blue), they produce the color black. If the three are 255, *i.e.* (255, 255, 255) they add to produce a much lighter shade, white. The product of these three layers can produce over 16 million different colors and is called 24-bit color because $256^3 = (2^8)^3 = 2^{24}$ = 16,777,216, in which three 8-bit binary strings represent pixel colors. They are intensity, color, red layer, green layer and blue layer, from left to right. Notice that the vertical white line that appears in the center of the intensity and color images is lighter than that in the RGB layers and that the blackish colors appear black in all images. This demonstrates the additive nature of RGB color images with respect to intensity.

Messages are hidden in the least significant bits of the 8-bit binary strings representing the color numbers; hence the abbreviated name for this method is "lsb" steganography. Each character in a message has a binary representation under the ASCII (American Standard Code for Information Interchange) character system, which assigns characters with integer values between 0 and 255. This system represents a way to express all necessary single character letters, numbers, punctuations, symbols, etc. for general communication purposes. The pixel is capable of representing 2^{24} or 16,777,216 color values. If we use the lower 2 bits of each color channel to hide data as shown in **Figure 1**.

3. The Proposed Scheme

In this section, we shall present the proposed the VDX method for extracting hiding a color or a grayscale secret image in a true color host image.

The proposed method is described below.

3.1. Requirements of Hiding Information Digitally

There are many different protocols and embedding techniques that enable us to hide data in a given object. However, all of the protocols and techniques must satisfy a number of requirements so that steganography can be applied correctly. The following is a list of main requirements that steganography techniques must satisfy:

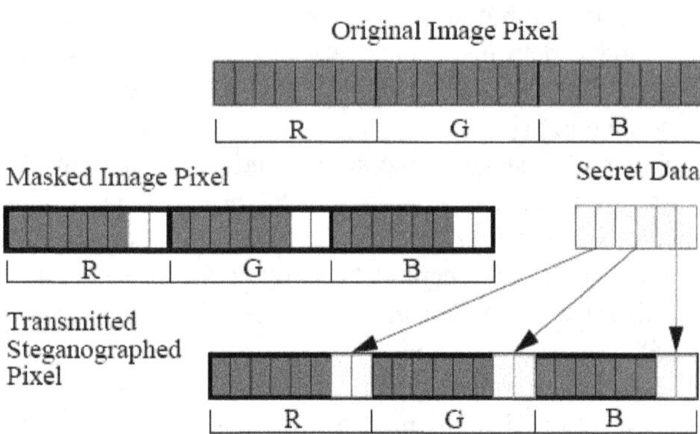

Figure 1. Illustrated representing the pixel values used the lower 2 bits of each color channel to hide data.

- The integrity of the hidden information after it has been embedded inside the stego object must be correct. The secret message must not change in any way, such as additional information being added, loss of information or changes to the secret information after it has been hidden. If secret information is changed during steganography, it would defeat the whole point of the process.
- The stego object must remain unchanged or almost unchanged to the naked eye. If the stego object changes significantly and can be noticed, a third party may see that information is being hidden and therefore could attempt to extract or to destroy it.
- In watermarking, changes in the stego object must have no effect on the watermark. Imagine if you had an illegal copy of an image that you would like to manipulate in various ways. These manipulations can be simple processes such as resizing, trimming or rotating the image. The watermark inside the image must survive these manipulations, otherwise the attackers can very easily remove the watermark and the point of steganography will be broken.
- Finally, we always assume that the attacker knows that there is hidden information inside the stego object.

3.2. Embedding and Detecting a Mark

Figure 2 shows a simple representation of the generic embedding and decoding process in steganography. In this example, a secret image is being embedded inside a cover image to produce the stego image. The first step in embedding and hiding information is to pass both the secret message and the cover message into the encoder. Inside the encoder, one or several protocols will be implemented to embed the secret information into the cover message. The type of protocol will depend on what information you are trying to embed and what you are embedding it in. For example, you will use an image protocol to embed information inside images.

4. The Overall Proposed System Is Designed to Extract the Hidden Data

Hiding information in digital media requires alterations of the media properties, which may introduce some form of degradation or unusual characteristics. The degradation, at times, may become perceptible [1]. These characteristics may act as signatures that broadcast the existence of the embedded message and steganography tools used, thus defeating the purpose of stenography, which is hiding the existence of a message.

The passive attacks of steganalysis involve the detection of these characteristics and signatures. Manipulating digital media in an effort to disable or remove the embedded messages is a simpler task than detecting the messages. Any image can be manipulated with the intent of destroying some hidden information whether an embedded message exists or not. Detecting the existence of a hidden message will save time in the activity to disable or remove messages by guiding the analyst to process only the media that contain hidden information [2].

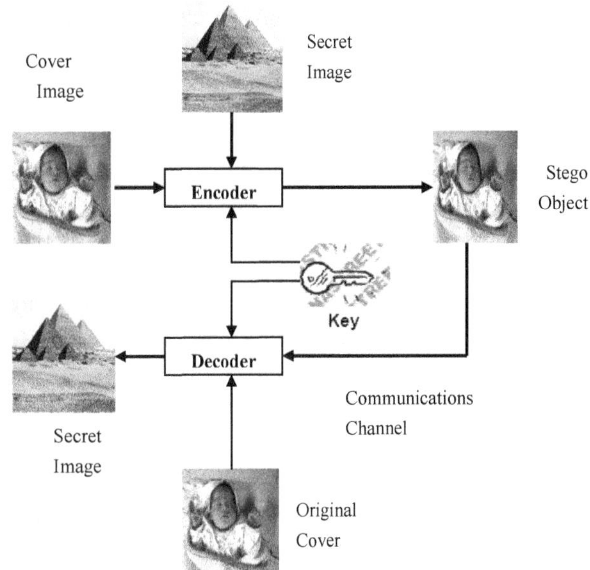

Figure 2. Generic processes of encoding and decoding.

4.1. Visual Pixel Detection

Some steganographic algorithms are embedded data in the media by replacing some bits of media with bits of data. For images, these algorithms will replace the bits of pixels by bits of data needed to hide it or changing the palette of image that depends on the value of data. The changing or replacing in values of pixels will be in most cases not sense or seeing by human eyes and will have effect in relation between pixels by increasing the amount of difference between the neighborhood pixels in the same level.

Any pixels have the same color or equal to the neighborhood pixels in the same portion or object in image. When we measure the difference between the pixels in the same portion, and evaluate the relation between these pixels, we can represent the image by these differences or relations.

The image that has no noise changing in the portions will have a good view for user. A user can see the most edge of object in this image, and the user has the ability to distinguish the details of the image. For some case the image will appear with a good efficient viewing. Some images have a bad image pattern details viewing, but have a number of edges and with details clear. When the image has some noise or hidden data in it, the looking will not be clear. Most edges will be destroyed and the image details will not be clear and this depends on the amount of noise or hidden data and the algorithms that are used to hide data.

The visual pixel detection takes the relation between the pixels in images. It deals with BMP and GIF image file format only. The visual pixel detection works as a filter. Its filtering the pixels depends on its information and relation between other neighborhood pixels. This filter can remove from image pixels 1, 2, 3, 4 or 5 bits then re-drew the image depends on these bits.

4.2. Visual Pixel Detection Algorithm

Step1: Load Images.

Step2: Get color of pixels (Red, Green, Blue).

Step3: Calculate the relation between pixels in the same portion.

Step4: Compare between the values of pixel with the neighborhood pixels (4-neighborhood, 8-neighborhood).

Step5: Cut one bit from the pixels then re-draw the image which depends on these bits of pixels and the relation between the pixel and pixels in the neighborhood.

Step6: Repeat Step5 by changing the number of bits from 2 to 5 bit cut from the pixels and re-draw the images.

Step7: End.

The output images will help user to see the amount of hidden data noise. When original image pixels change by 1-bit the output images after filter are follows:

1) When the filter cut 1-bit from suspected image pixels, image output will be destroyed by amount of hidden data.

2) When the filter cut 2-bit from pixels, image output will be approximately clear (have some noise).

3) When the filter cut 3, 4, 5 bits from pixels, images output will be clear 3, 4, 5 bit or have a few noises. If the image has hidden information in two bits (1-2 bits), the output images from the filter will be:

- For 1, 2-bit images not clear.
- For 3, 4, 5-bits image approximately clear.

This filter will be very sensitive to any change in the first five bits of pixels in any BMP or GIF file format images. The number of color levels will not affect the filter results. The filter has the ability to deal with color level, it works in 256, 16-bit high color and true color for BMP images type. This filter also gives good results when used on GIF images; this is due to the fact that GIF file format has a maximum of 256 colors.

5. Experimental

To evaluate the effectiveness of the proposed method, we apply the proposed method "VPD" on deferent three types of secret images, hiding a color secret image, hiding a palette-based 256-color secret image, and hiding a grayscale image in a true color image the VPD Method will detect the stego objects from the different image that contain the stego objects as shown in **Figures 3** and **4** in the first both types but it fail in the third type.

The proposed method also is compared with Fridrich's method [13], Y. Q. Shi's method [14] and Z. M. He's method [15]. The averaged results of four independent runs for different steganographic embedding techniques are shown in **Tables 1-3**.

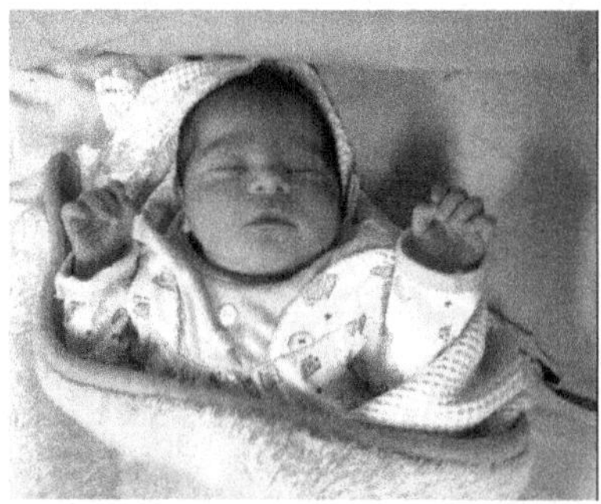

Figure 3. Original image with secret image.

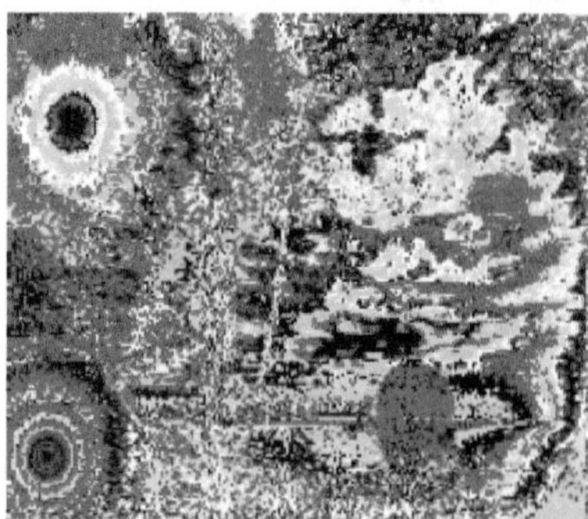

Figure 4. After using visual pixel detection.

Table 1. Detection accuracy for OutGuess.

bpc	Fridrich's	Y.Q.Shi's	Z.M. He's	proposed
0.05	74.65	88.00	89.60	91.65
0.1	92.00	98.00	99.70	99.86
0.2	99.25	99.85	100.00	100.00

Table 2. Detection accuracy for F5.

bpc	Fridrich's	Y.Q.Shi's	Z.M. He's	proposed
0.05	69.15	57.65	69.70	77.30
0.1	88.45	77.00	90.90	92.70
0.2	99.20	97.10	99.25	99.10

Table 3. Detection accuracy for Steghide.

bpc	Fridrich's	Y.Q.Shi's	Z.M. He's	proposed
0.05	71.80	86.70	86.95	87.10
0.1	79.45	96.60	96.05	96.00
0.2	89.20	99.70	99.90	98.90

The proposed method outperforms the Fridrich's method and the Y. Q. Shi's method in attacking all three types of steganographic embedding techniques. Experimental results show that Fridrich's and He's methods perform well for F5 while the Shi's and He's methods perform well for OutGuess and Steghide. In contrast, the proposed method performs the best on attacking all three types of steganographic embedding techniques. Overall, the proposed method provides good performance on steganalysis and outperforms current methods.

6. Conclusion

It is very difficult to extract a secret message from image due to the numerous methods of hiding in images. In this paper , we apply VPD method on deferent types of secret images to extract the hidden information. Some of these types need stego-image and stego-key, others need stego-image only, and the paper has extracted the secret data that has been hidden by deferent tools. The final conclusion is very difficult to apply one general method for extraction because there are different techniques such as encryption (block and stream), colors and filters could be used for embedding and each one needs special way to solve it (find the hidden information). In feature works, we will also try to select features using the localized generalization error model to reduce the system complexity.

REFERENCES

[1] C.-C. Thien and J.-C. Lin, "A Simple and High-Hiding Capacity Method for Hiding Digit-by-Digit Data in Images Based on Modulus Function," *Pattern Recognition*, Vol. 36, No. 12, 2003, pp. 2875-2881.

[2] C.-K. Chan and L. M. Cheng, "Hiding Data in Images by Simple LSB Substitution," *Pattern Recognition*, Vol. 37, No. 3, 2004, pp. 469-474.

[3] C.-C. Chang, J.-Y. Hsiao and C.-S. Chan, "Finding Optimal Least-Significant Bit Substitution in Image Hiding by Dynamic Programming Strategy," *Pattern Recognition*, Vol. 36, No. 7, 2003, pp. 1583-1595.

[4] C.-C. Thien and J.-C. Lin, "A Simple and High-Hiding Capacity Method for Hiding Digit-by-Digit Data in Images Based on Modulus Function," *Pattern Recognition*, Vol. 36, No. 12, 2003, pp. 2875-2881.

[5] R.-Z. Wang, C.-F. Lin and J.-C. Lin, "Image Hiding by Optimal LSB Substitution and Genetic Algorithm," *Pattern Recognition*, Vol. 34, No. 3, 2001, pp. 671-683.

[6] C.-C. Chang, T.-S. Chen and L.-Z. Chung, "A Steganographic Method Based upon JPEG and Quantization Table Modification," *Information Sciences*, Vol. 141, No. 1-2, 2002, pp. 123-138.

[7] M. Iwata, K. Miyake and A. Shiozaki, "Digital Steganography Utilizing Features of JPEG Images," *IEICE Transactions on Fundamentals of Electronics, Communications and Computer Sciences*, Vol. E87-A, No. 4, 2004, pp. 929-936.

[8] H. Noda, J. Spaulding, M. N. Shirazi and E. Kawaguchi, "Application of Bit-Plane Decomposition Steganography to JPEG2000 Encoded Images," *IEEE Transactions on Signal Processing Letters*, Vol. 9, No. 12, 2002, pp. 410-413.

[9] T. Liu and Z.-D. Qiu, "A DWT-Based Color Image Steganography Scheme," *Proceedings of the International Conference on Signal Processing*, Beijing, 26-30 August 2002, pp. 1568-1571.

[10] R. R. Ni and Q. Q. Ruan, "Embedding Information into Color Images Using Wavelet," *Proceedings of the International Conference on Computers, Communications, Control and Power Engineering of the IEEE TENCON*, Beijing, 28-31 October 2002, pp. 598-601.

[11] M.-H. Lin, Y.-C. Hu and C.-C. Chang, "Both Color and Gray Scale Secret Images Hiding in a Color Image," *International Journal of Pattern Recognition and Artificial Intelligence*, Vol. 16, No. 6, 2002, pp. 697-713.

[12] W.-S. Kim and R.-H. Park, "Color Image Palette Construction Based on the HSI Color System for Minimizing the Reconstruction Error," *Proceedings of the International Conference on Image Processing of the IEEE*, Lausanne, 16-19 September 1996, pp. 1041-1044.

[13] J. Fridrich, "Feature-Based Steganalysis for JPEG Images and Its Implications for Future Design of Steganographic Schemes," *Proceedings of the 6th International Conference on Information Hiding*, Toronto, 23-25 May 2004, pp. 67-81.

[14] Y. Q. Shi, C. C. Chen and W. Chen, "A Markov Process Based Approach to Effective Attacking JPEG Steganography," *Proceedings of the 8th International Conference on Information Hiding*, Alexandria, 10-12 July 2006, pp. 249-264.

[15] Z.-M. He, W. W. Y. Ng, P. P. K. Chan and D. S. Yeung, "Steganography Detection Using Localized Generalization Error Model," *Proceedings of the International Conference on Systems Man and Cybernetics of the IEEE SMC*, Istanbul, 10-13 October 2010, pp. 1544-1549.

2

A Visual Cryptography Based Digital Image Copyright Protection

Adel Hammad Abusitta
College of Engeenering & IT, Al Ain University of Science and Technology, Al Ain, UAE

ABSTRACT

A method for creating digital image copyright protection is proposed in this paper. The proposed method in this paper is based on visual cryptography defined by Noor and Shamir. The proposed method is working on selection of random pixels from the original digital image instead of specific selection of pixels. The new method proposed does not require that the watermark pattern to be embedded in to the original digital image. Instead of that, verification information is generated which will be used to verify the ownership of the image. This leaves the marked image equal to the original image. The method is based on the relationship between randomly selected pixels and their 8-neighbors' pixels. This relationship keeps the marked image coherent against diverse attacks even if the most significant bits of randomly selected pixels have been changed by attacker as we will see later in this paper. Experimental results show the proposed method can recover the watermark pattern from the marked image even if major changes are made to the original digital image.

Keywords: Image Watermark; Pattern; Visual Cryptography; Digital Image; Copyright

1. Introduction

The proliferation of digitized images has made the digital images to be modified, distributed, duplicated and accessed easily. It is creating a pressing need to develop copyright protection methods. A watermarking technology is now providing highly attention as a desired method and technology for protecting copyrights for digital data [1-7]. A watermarking has been defined as the practice of embedding identification information in an image, audio, video or other digital media element to provide privacy protecttion from attackers [8-9]. The identification information is called "watermark pattern" and the original digital image that contains watermark pattern is named "marked image". The embedding takes place by manipulating the contents of the digital image [10]. Also, a secret key is given to embed "watermark pattern" and to retrieve it as well. **Figure 1** gives summarize of standard watermarking embedding scheme.

Basically, if the owner wants to protect his/her image, the owner of an image has to register the image with the copyright office by sending a copy to them. The copyright office archives the image, together with information about the rightful owner. When dispute occurs, the real owner contacts the copyright office to obtain proof that he is the rightful owner. If he did not register the image, then he should at least be able to show the film negative. However, with the rapid acceptance of digital photography, there might never have been a negative. Theoretically, it is possible for the owner to use a watermark embedded in the image to prove that he/she owns it [11].

A typical image watermark algorithm must satisfy the following two properties: transparency and robustness. Transparency means that the embedded watermark pattern does not visually spoil the original image fidelity and should be invisible. Robustness means the watermark pattern is not easy to detect and remove illegally. Moreover, any modifications of the image values have to be invisible, and the watermark method has to be robust or fragile in order to provide protection against attackers.

In 1994, Noor-Shamir proposed the concept of visual cryptography [12]. The concept nowadays is being developed and/or improved several times for different purposes of applications by authors [13-24]. A good survey on visual cryptography can be found in [25]. Actually, Visual cryptography is describing as a secret sharing scheme extended of digital images, this will be discussed in the next section. Hwang [26] is the first author proposed

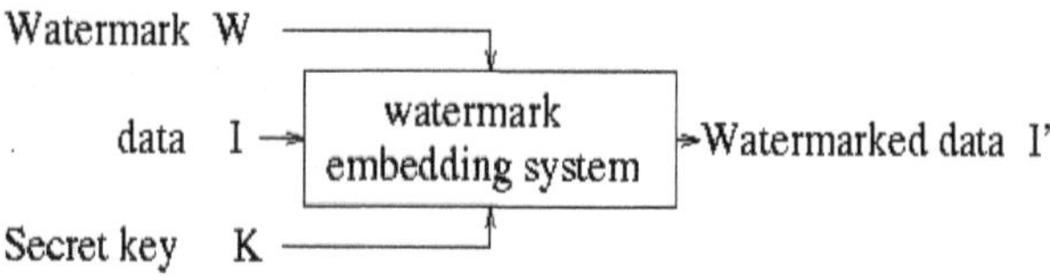

Figure 1. Watermarking embedding scheme.

a method of how to take a benefit of visual cryptography to create digital image copyright protection. According to Hwang method, the watermark pattern does not have to be embedded into the original image directly, which makes it harder to detect or recover from the marked image in an illegal way. [27-30] improved different methods to overcome Hwang method's shortcomings. We will come to these shortcomings in Section 3.

This paper proposes new digital images copyright protection based on Hwang method. The proposed method is based on visual cryptography defined by Noor-Shamir and Hwang method. Marking images will be conducted without embedding patterns into images. This leaves marked images unchanged with sizes exactly equal to the original ones. This paper is organized as follows. Section 2 reviews the concept of visual cryptography and digital image copyright protection. Section 3 presents our proposed digital image copyright protection method. Section 4 reports some experimental results and makes some discussions concerning our method. Finally, conclusions appear in Section 5.

2. Visual Cryptography and related Digital Image Copyright Protection

Naor and Shamir in 1994 proposed the concept of visual cryptography during EUROCRYPT 94. **Figure 2** from [31] demonstrates a simple version of visual cryptography. In their method, they introduced encoding scheme to share a binary image into two shares Share 1 and Share 2. A pixel P is divided into two subpixels in each of the two shares. If P is white one of two rows above in **Figure 2** is selected to create Share 1 and Share 2. But, if P is black one of two rows below in **Figure 2** is selected to create Share 1 and Share 2. A binary image at the end becomes secret image or invisible unless both shares are superposition.

Hwang created the first and typical idea for a digital image copyright protection based on the visual cryptography. The method use a simple (2, 2) visual threshold scheme defined by Naor-Shamir. Referring to Hwang's algorithm, the owner must select h × n black/white image as his/her watermark pattern P and a key S which must be kept securely. Then, verification information V is generated from the original k × 1 image M and the watermark pattern P using the key S; as follows:

1) Use S (the secret key) as the seed to generate h x n different random numbers over the interval [0, k × 1]. (Ri represents the i-th random number).

2) Assign the i-th pair (Vi1, Vi2) of the verificatin on information V based on the following **Table 1**:

Collect all the (Vi1, Vi2) pairs to construct the verification information V. This verification information must be kept by neutral organization. When the owner of an image M wants to claim the ownership of an image M' as

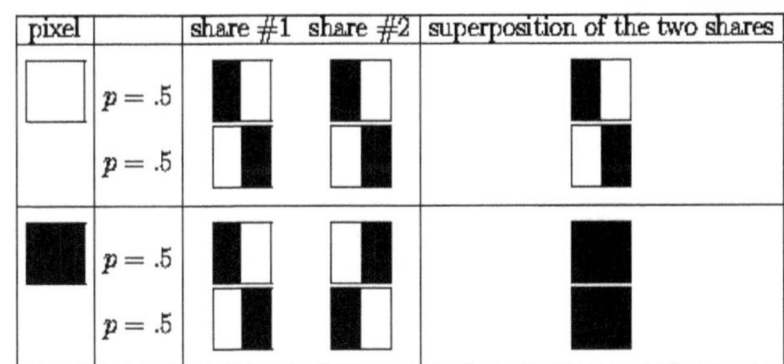

Figure 2. Naor and Shamir's scheme.

Table 1. The rules to assign the value of verification information.

The color of the i-th pixel in watermark pattern is	The left most bit of the Ri-th pixel of Image M is	Assign the i-th pair, (vi1, vi2), of *verification information V* to be
Black	"1"	(0,1)
Black	"0"	(1,0)
White	"1"	(1,0)
White	"0"	(0,1)

a copy of the original image M, the owner has to provide the secret key S, and the watermark pattern P is restored using the image M' and verification information V as follows:

1) Use S as a seed to generate h × n different random numbers over the interval [0, k × 1]. (Ri represents the i-th random number).

2) Assign the color of the i-th pixel of the watermark pattern P' based on the image M' as follows:

Get the left-most bit, b, of the Ri-th pixel of image M', and if b is 1 then, assign fi = (1, 0); otherwise assign fi = (0, 1).

If fi is equal to i-th pair of V then assigns the color of the i-th pixel of P' to be white; otherwise, assign it to be black.

3) If P' can be recognized as P through the human, the neutral organization shall adjudge that the image M' is a copy of M.

According to the previous method and also the related methods, these methods are strongly related to the values of the most significant bits of pixels selected randomly from the original digital image; therefore, if the most significant bit to some pixels selected randomly has been changed, the modified image M' will fail to retrieve the watermark pattern P successfully. Also, since the method does not consider the relationship between pixels and its neighbors, the watermark pattern would not be retrieved, if part of image has been cropped. Moreover, if we have an image X with some similarities with the original image M. The watermark pattern P might be restored successfully, despite the image X is not the same as the image M.

3. The Proposed Digital Image Copyright Protection

In this section, we present the proposed watermark method. The method acctually use the relationship between 8-neighbours pixels of pixel P(x, y) as a base of embedding algorithm as you will see later. **Figure 3** shows the 8-neighbours of pixel P(x, y).

We assume that the owner wants to embed the h × n watermark pattern into the image M that is a k × l 256 gray-leveled image. The owner embeds the watermark pattern P into the image M by generating the secret key, S, and the verification information, V, as the following steps.

Step Embedding-1. Select number S randomly as the secret key of the image M.

Step Embedding-2. Use S as the seed to generate h × n different random numbers over the interval [0, k × l]. Where Ri is the i-th random number.)

Step Embedding-3. Calculate the number of Ri-th pixel's neighbours pixels from its 8-nieghbours pixels that are less than or equal to the Ri-th pixel, this number named, Number_of_neighbors_less_or_equal_Ri-th_pixel. Also, calculte the number of Ri-th pixel's nieghbour pixels from its 8-nieghbour pixels that are greater than Ri-th pixel, this number named Number_of_ neighbor_greater_ Ri-th_pixel.

For example, as in **Figure 4**, the Number_of_neighbors_ less_or_equal_Ri-th_pixel = 3, because we have three pixels {97, 98, 100} less or equal the Ri-th pixel, which equals 100. Also, Number_of_neighbors_greater_Ri-th_ pixel = 5, because we have 5 pixels in the following set {101, 103, 101,105,111} greater than Ri-th pixel.

It is obvious, in case the Ri-th pixel is a border pixel, this pixel do not have a full 8-nighbours. In this case, the available nighbours should be considerd and calculate Number_of_neighbors_less_or_equal_Ri-th_pixel and Number_of_neighbors_greater_Ri-th_pixel same as in step Embedding-3.

Step Embedding-4. Find the i-th pair (vi1, vi2) of the verification information V based on **Table 2**.

Step Embedding-5. Assemble all the (vi1, vi2) pairs to create the verification information V.

Note that Step Embedding-5 constructs the verification Information V based on the watermark pattern P and the relationship result between Number_of_neighbors_ less_ or_equal_Ri-th_pixel and Number_of_neighbors_ greater_ Ri-th_pixel as shown in **Table 2**, and moreover the proposed method does not make any change into image M or alter any pixel of image M.

The verification information V genrated from Step Embedding-5 must be given to the notarial organization. If an image M is appropriated by somebody as the image M', The owner of an image has to provide the secret key S to the notarial organization. The notarial organization retrives the verification information V and the watermark pattern P, which the owner has registered, and verifies the ownership of the image M' as follows:

X − 1, y − 1	X − 1, y	X − 1, y + 1
x, y − 1	x, y	x, y + 1
X + 1, y − 1	X + 1, y	X + 1, y + 1

Figure 3. 8 Neighbours pixels of pixel P(x, y).

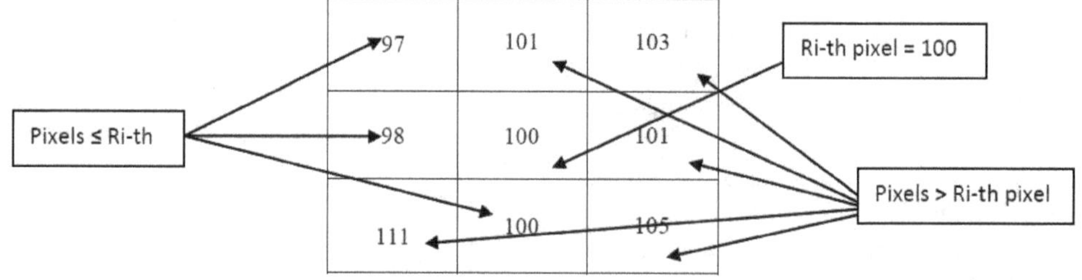

Figure 4. Example of Ri-th pixel's neighbors.

Table 2. The proposed method's rules to assign the value of verification.

The Color of the i-th pixel in watermark pattern is	The relationship between *Number_of_neighbors_less_or_equal_Ri-th_pixel* and *Number_of_ neighbors _ greater_Ri-th_pixel*	Assign the i-th pair, (vi1, vi2), of *verification information V* to be
Black	*Number_of_neighbors_less_or_equal_Ri-th_pixel* ≤ *Number_of_neighbors_greater_Ri-th_pixel*	(0,1)
Black	*Number_of_neighbors_less_or_equal_Ri-th_pixel* > *Number_of_neighbors_greater_Ri-th_pixel*	(1,0)
White	*Number_of_neighbors_less_or_equal_Ri-th_pixel* ≤ *Number_of_neighbor_greater_Ri-th_pixel*	(1,0)
White	*Number_of_neighbors_less_or_equal_Ri-th_pixel* > *Number_of_neighbors_greater_Ri-th_pixel*	(0,1)

Step Verification-1. Use S as the seed to generate h × n different random numbers over the interval [0, k × 1]. Where Ri is the i-th random number.)

Step Verification-2. Assign the color of the i-th pixel of the watermark pattern based on image M' as follows:

If (*Number_of_neighbors_less_or_equal_Ri-th_pixel ≤ Number_of_neighbors_greater_Ri-th_pixel*) **AND** (the i-th pair, (vi1, vi2), of verification information V = (0,1)) **then**

Assign the color of the i-th pixel of P' to be <u>white</u>

Else If (*Number_of_neighbors_less_or_equal_Ri-th_pixel ≤ Number_of_neighbors_greater_Ri-th_pixel*) **AND** (the i-th pair, (vi1, vi2), of verification information V = (1,0)) **then**

Assign the color of the i-th pixel of P' to be <u>black</u>

Else If (*Number_of_neighbors_less_or_equal_Ri-th_pixel>Number_of_neighbors_greater_Ri-th_pixel*) **AND** (the i-th pair, (vi1, vi2), of verification information V = (1,0)) **then**

Assign the color of the i-th pixel of P' to be <u>white</u>

Else If (*Number_of_neighbors_less_or_equal_Ri-th_pixel > Number_of_neighbors_greater_Ri-th_pixel*) **AND** (the i-th pair, (vi1, vi2), of verification information V = (0,1)) **then**

Assign the color of the i-th pixel of P' to be <u>black</u>.

Step Verification-3. If P' equals the original watermark pattern P or can be recognized as it, then the notarial organization can conclude that image M' is a copy of M.

Note that the code written in Step Verification-2 can be concluded directly from **Table 2** which displays the proposed method's rules to assign the value of verification information.

The security of the proposed method is based on the relationship of pixels selected randomly and their 8-neighbor's pixels. This happened because whenever a change is applied into original digital image pixels, the result of the relationship mostly becomes the same. In other words, the relationships between Number_of_neighbors_less_or_equal_Ri-th_pixel and Number_of_neighbors_greater_Ri-th_pixel will not be affected by some majer changes in image pixels' bits. Experimental results in the next section will reflect that fact.

4. Experimental Results

The proposed algorithms are studied using Matlab 7. Images used are 256 × 256 pixels images Lina, Baboon and F-16 (shown in **Figure 6**). In Matlab 7, we made some changes in the three images before applying the proposed method. The changes are applied in the most significant bits of randomly selected pixels. Also, we did make changes in images quality using Adobe Photoshop CS 5 by applying diverse compressions in the three images. The watermark pattern used in the experiment is "cheng" in **Figure 5**. From the results shown in **Table 3**, we find that the watermark pattern "cheng" get some noise but still can be recognized even if the three images have been compressed and the size of those files is changed.

5. Conclusion

This paper presents a digital image copyright protection method using watermarking technology. The method proposed in this paper does not require that the watermark pattern to be embedded in to the original digital image. Instead, Verification information is generated which will be used to verify the ownership of the image. This leaves the marked image equal to the original image. The proposed method is tested and shows that a watermark pattern can be retrieved easily from marked image even the image is attacked by major changes in pixels bits.

Figure 5. The watermark pattern "cheng".

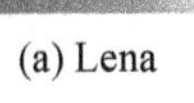
(a) Lena

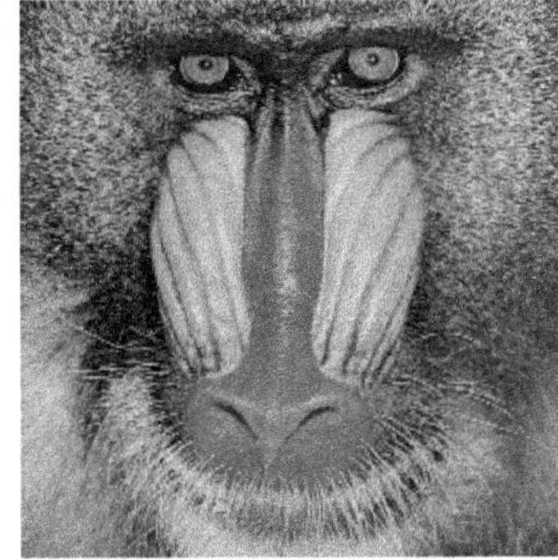

(b) Baboon

(c) F-16

Figure 6. Three images of our Experiments.

Table 3. Experimental results.

(a) Use the proposed method to embed "Cheng" into "Lena"

The Marked Image	The Digital Image Quality with Adobe Photoshop CS 5	The Recovered Watermark Pattern "Cheng"
	0/low (the size of compressed file is 10,463 Bytes)	
	1/low (the size of compressed file is 12,501 Bytes)	
	2/low (the size of compressed file is 13,830 Bytes)	
	3/middle (the size of compressed file is 15,643 Bytes)	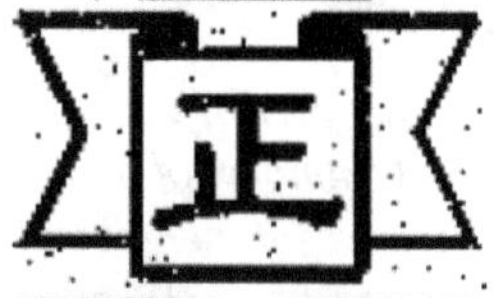
	4/middle (the size of compressed file is 17,344 Bytes)	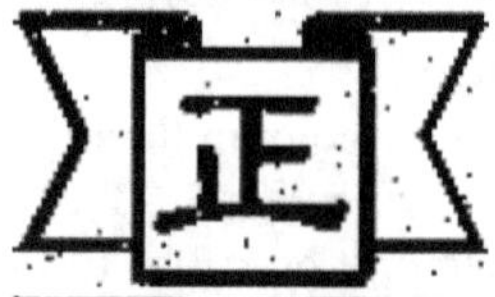
Marked Image = Original Image	5/middle (the size of compressed file is 17,139 Bytes)	
	6/high (the size of compressed file is 19,113 Bytes)	
	7/high (the size of compressed file is 24,385 Bytes)	
	8/maximal (the size of compressed file is 30,930 Bytes)	
	9/maximal (the size of compressed file is 39,177 Bytes)	
	10/maximal (the size of compressed file is 48,199 Bytes)	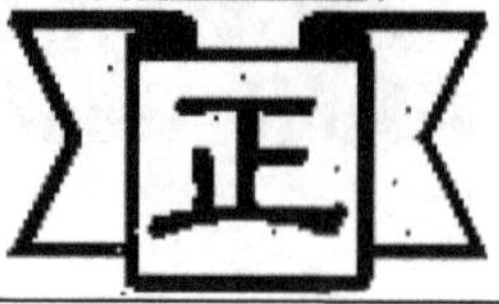

(b) Use the proposed method to embed "Cheng" into "Baboon"

The Marked Image	The Digital Image Quality with Adobe Photoshop CS 5	The Recovered Watermark Pattern "Cheng"
	0/low (the size of compressed file is 17,930 Bytes)	
	1/low (the size of compressed file is 22,112 Bytes)	
	2/low (the size of compressed file is 23,856 Bytes)	
	3/middle (the size of compressed file is 27,115 Bytes)	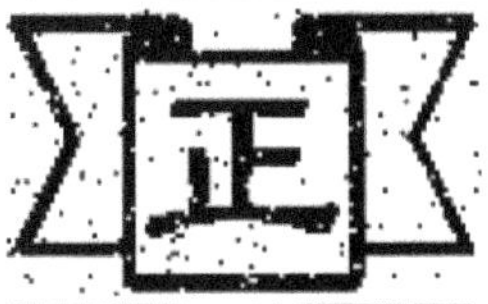
	4/middle (the size of compressed file is 30,103 Bytes)	
Marked Image = Original Image	5/middle (the size of compressed file is 27,992 Bytes)	
	6/high (the size of compressed file is 33,120 Bytes)	
	7/high (the size of compressed file is 38,004 Bytes)	
	8/maximal (the size of compressed file is 44,759 Bytes)	
	9/maximal (the size of compressed file is 53,992 Bytes)	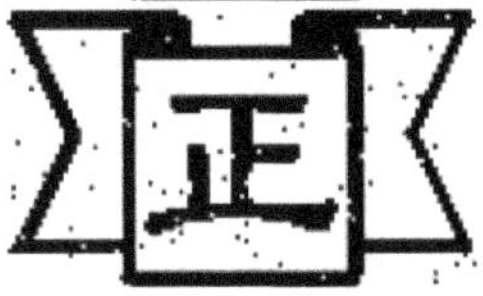
	10/maximal (the size of compressed file is 62,951 Bytes)	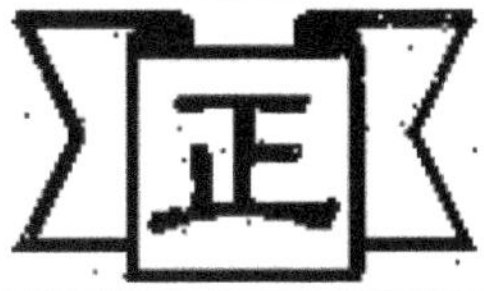

(c) Use the proposed method to embed "Cheng" into "F-16"

The Marked Image	The Digital Image Quality with Adobe Photoshop CS 5	The Recovered Watermark Pattern "Cheng"
	0/low (the size of compressed file is 9850 Bytes)	
	1/low (the size of compressed file is 11,451 Bytes)	
	2/low (the size of compressed file is 12,344 Bytes)	
	3/middle (the size of compressed file is 13,949 Bytes)	
	4/middle (the size of compressed file is 16,278 Bytes)	
Marked Image = Original Image	5/middle (the size of compressed file is 14,929 Bytes)	
	6/high (the size of compressed file is 17,930 Bytes)	
	7/high (the size of compressed file is 21,125 Bytes)	
	8/maximal (the size of compressed file is 25,920 Bytes)	
	9/maximal (the size of compressed file is 32,852 Bytes)	
	10/maximal (the size of compressed file is 40,877 Bytes)	

The watermark pattern cannot be retrieved from the marked image unless the key is given, and the key is only known by the owner. Also, the watermark pattern cannot be retrieved from the marked image unless the secret key and the verification information are given.

REFERENCES

[1] B. Surekha and G. N. Swamy, "A Spatial Domain Public Image Watermarking," *International Journal of Security and Its Applications*, Vol. 5, No. 1, 2011, 12 p.

[2] R. J. Anderson, "Information Hiding," *First International Workshop*, Vol. 1174, 1996, pp. 1-7.

[3] I. J. Cox, M. L. Miller and J. A. Bloom, "Digital Watermarking," Morgan Kaufmann Publishers Inc., San Fransisco, 2002.

[4] M. Kutter and F. A. P. Petitcolas, "Fair Benchmark for Image Watermarking Systems," *Proceedings of the Conference on Security and Watermarking of Multimedia Contents*, San Jose, 25 January 1999, pp. 226-239.

[5] G. C. Langelaar, J. C. A. van der Lubbe and J. Biemond, "Copy Protection for Multimedia Data Based on Labelling Techniques," *Proceedings of the* 17*th Symposium on Information Theory in the Benelux*, Enschede, May 1996, pp. 33-39.

[6] M. S. Fu and O. C. Au, "Joint Visual Cryptography and Watermarking," *Proceedings of the IEEE International Conference on Multimedia and Expo*, Taipei, 30 June 2004, pp. 975-978.

[7] R.-H. Hwang, "A Digital Image Copyright Protection Scheme Based on Visual Cryptography," *Tamkang Journal of science and Engineering*, Vol. 3, No. 2, 2002, pp. 97-106.

[8] H. Inoue, A. Miyazaki, A. Yamamoto and T. Katsura, "A Digital Watermark Technique Based on the Wavelet Transform and Its Robustness on Image Compression and Transformation," *IEICE Transactions on Fundamentals of Electronics, Communications and Computer Sciences*, Vol. 82, No. 1, 1999, pp. 2-10.

[9] G. W. Braudaway, K. A. Magerlein and F. C. Mintzer, "Protecting Publicly Available Images with a Visible Image Watermark," *Proceedings of the SPIE*, San Jose, 1 February 1996, pp. 126-133.

[10] L. Hawkes, A. Yasinsac and C. Cline, "An Application of Visual Cryptography to Financial Documents," *Technical Report TR*001001, Florida State University, Tallahassee, 2000.

[11] C.-N. Yang, "A Note on Efficient Color Visual Encryption," *Journal of Information Science and Engineering*, Vol. 18, 2002, pp. 367-372.

[12] M. Noar and A. Shamir, "Visual Cryptography," *Advances in Cryptography Eurocrypt*'94, Vol. 950, 1995, pp. 1-12.

[13] W.-P. Fang, "Non-Expansion Visual Secret Sharing in Reversible Style," *International Journal of Computer Science and Network Security*, Vol. 9, No. 2, 2009, pp. 204-208.

[14] J. Weir and W.-Q. Yan, "Sharing Multiple Secrets Using Visual Cryptography," *Proceedings of the IEEE International Symposium on Circuits and Systems*, Taipei, 24-27 May 2009, pp. 509-512.

[15] Z. X. Fu and B. Yu, "Research on Rotation Visual Cryptography Scheme," *Proceedings of the International Symposium on Information Engineering and Electronic Commerce*, Ternopil, 16-17 May 2009, pp. 533-536.

[16] X.-Q. Tan, "Two Kinds of Ideal Contrast Visual Cryptography Schemes," *Proceedings of the* 2009 *International Conference on Signal Processing Systems*, Singapore, 15-17 May 2009, pp. 450-453.

[17] H. B. Zhang, X. F. Wang, W. H. Cao and Y. P. Huang, "Visual Cryptography for General Access Structure by Multi-Pixel Encoding with Variable Block Size," *Proceedings of the International Symposium on Knowledge Acquisition and Modeling*, Wuhan, 21-22 December 2008, pp. 340-344.

[18] M. Heidarinejad, A. A. Yazdi and K. N. Plataniotis, "Algebraic Visual Cryptography Scheme for Color Images," *Proceedings of the IEEE International Conference on Acoustics, Speech and Signal Processing*, Las Vegas, 31 March-4 April 2008, pp. 1761-1764.

[19] F. Liu1, C. K. Wu and X. J. Lin, "Colour Visual Cryptography Schemes," *IET Information Security*, Vol. 2, No. 4, 2008, pp. 151-165.

[20] W. Qiao, H. D. Yin and H. Q. Liang, "A Kind of Visual Cryptography Scheme for Color Images Based on Halftone Technique," *Proceedings of the International Conference on Measuring Technology and Mechatronics Automation*, Zhangjiajie, 11-12 April 2009, pp. 393-395.

[21] L. M. E. Bakrawy, N. I. Ghali, A. E. Hassanien and A. Abraham, "An Associative Watermarking Based Image Authentication Scheme," *Proceedings of the* 10*th International Conference on Intelligent Systems Design and Applications* (*ISDA* 2010), Cairo, 29 November-1 December 2010, pp. 823-828.

[22] V. V. R. Prasad and R. Kurupati, "Secure Image Watermarking in Frequency Domain Using Arnold Scrambling and Filtering," *Advances in Computational Sciences and Technology*, Vol. 3, No. 2, 2010, pp. 236-244.

[23] P. Fakhari, E. Vahedi and C. Lucas, "Protecting Patient Privacy from Unauthorized Release of Medical Images Using a Bio-Inspired Wavelet-Based Watermarking Approach," *Digital Signal Processing*, Vol. 21, No. 3, 2011, pp. 433-446.

[24] A. De Bonnis and A. De Santis, "Randomness in Secret Sharing and Visual Cryptography Schemes," *Theoretical Computer Science*, Vol. 314, No. 3, 2004, pp. 351-374.

[25] P. S. Revenkar, A. Anium and Z. Gandhare, "Survey of Visual Cryptography Schemes," *International Journal of Security and Its Applications*, Vol. 4, No. 2, 2010, pp. 49-56.

[26] R. Hwang, "A Digital Image Copyright Protection Scheme Based on Visual Cryptography," *Tamkang Journal of*

science and Engineering, Vol. 3, No. 2, 2002, pp. 97-106.

[27] M. A. Hassan and M. A. Khalili, "Self Watermarking Based on Visual Cryptography," *Proceedings of the World Academy of Science, Engineering and Technology*, October 2005, pp. 159-162.

[28] A. Sleit and A. Abusitta, "A Visual Cryptography Based Watermark Technology for Individual and Group Images," *Journal of Systemics, Cybernetics and Informatics*, Vol. 5, No. 2, 2008, pp. 24-32.

[29] A. Sleit and A. Abusitta, "A Watermark Technology Based on Visual Cryptography," *Proceeding of the 10th World Multi Conference on Systemic, Cybernetics and Informatics*, 2006, pp. 227-238.

[30] A. Sleit and A. Abusitta, "Advancedd Digital Image Copyright Protection Based on Visual Cryptography," *Proceeding of the 4th International Multi Conference on Computer Science & Information Technology*, Amman, 5-7 April 2006, pp. 365-375.

[31] D. Stinson, "Doug Stinson's Visual Cryptography Page," 2003. http://www.cacr.math.uwaterloo.ca/~dstinson/visual.html

Effect of Network Traffic on IPS Performance

Shahriar Mohammadi, Vahid Allahvakil, Mojtaba Khaghani
Department of IT, Khajeh Nasir University, Tehran, Iran

ABSTRACT

The importance of network security has grown tremendously and intrusion prevention/detection systems (IPS/IDS) have been widely developed to insure the security of network against suspicious threat. Computer network intrusion detection and prevention system consist of collecting traffic data, analyzing them based on detection rules and generate alerts or dropping them if necessary. However IPS has problems such as accuracy signature, the traffic volume, topology design, monitoring sensors. In this paper, we practically examine the traffic effect on performance of IPS. We first examine the detection of DOS attack on a web server by IPS and then we generate network traffic to see how the behavior of IPS has influenced on detection of DOS attack.

Keywords: Network Security; Network Intrusion Detection and Prevention System; DOS Attack; Network Traffic Generation

1. Introduction

Over the past few years, computer security has become a great concern in computer science. Intrusion detection and prevention system has become important tools in network security. Operation of intrusion detection/prevention system can be divided into five modules, as given in **Figure 1** [1,2]. First, the sensor module gathers data for processing. This module can be categorized into two classes, Network IPS and Host IPS. The former captures network traffic in promiscuous mode (Network IPS), while the latter gathers characteristics of hosts (Host IPS). The second module is the decoder which identifies each layer header. Third module is responsible to look for abnormality in packet header or host information and organizes data and information to be further analyzed by detection engine. The Fourth module is the detection engine which detects attacks and threats base on misuse and anomaly detection. In the former, detection is occurred base on comparing the packet to known pattern attacks, while in the latter, detection is occurred base on normal profile that defines normal activity and anything that doesn't have that behavior considered as a threat. The final module is responsible for taking care of identified attacks. Dropping the packets and generating alerts for administrator is the main configuration for this module.

The structure of these modules can be changed on demands; For Example sensor module can act as centralized or distributed module. There has been much progress in detection engine and algorithms used in misuse detection and anomaly detection; however, there are many challenges to overcome in this field. The main issues in IPS are accuracy signature, the traffic volume, topology design, quota usage logging, monitoring sensor and protecting intrusion detection and prevention system, more discussion on this issues can be found on [3].

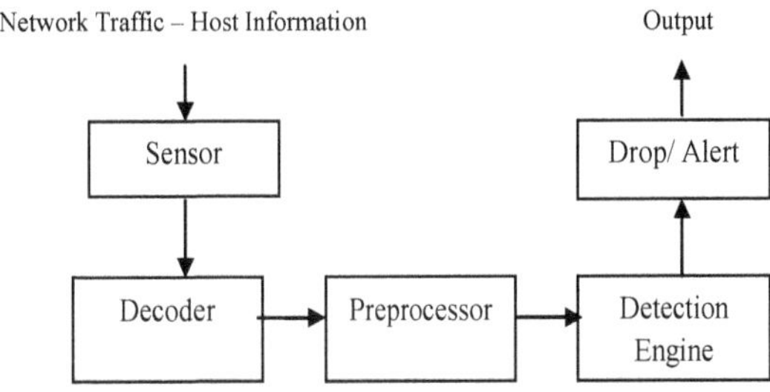

Figure 1. Operation of intrusion prevention system.

In this paper, we want to study the effect of traffic volume on performance of IPS. In the previous works which has been done on IPS, metrics such as TP, TN, FP and FN has been introduced for measuring the performance of IPS [3,4]. These metrics evaluate the accuracy of detection engine module in IPS, for example TP (True Positive) points to the number of attacks which IPS correctly identified related to the number of packets that IPS analyzed. In this paper, we measure the performance of IPS base on number of packets that IPS captures but cannot be analyzed because of resource limitation. If intrusion prevention system cannot analyze the packets, the probability of happening attack, without IPS/IDS knowledge, increase and this is a great risk to our network security. According to Murphy's Law, attacks are happening when IPS/IDS is overloaded [5].

The rest of this paper is structured as follow. In Section 2, we go over the related works in this area, in Section 3 we explains our approach and the tools which we use in our network scenario. In Section 4, we evaluate IPS performance and result of each step in test, Section 5 we explain our results from the experiments performed in this paper, and finally we conclude our paper results and future works.

2. Related Works

In this section, we points to some of the previous works which has been done on IDS/IPS performance; we give the main idea in each of them and compare our works with them.

The subject of Master thesis in [6] is about the performance testing of intrusion detection server. In this thesis, the writer specifically concentrates on snort as IDS and measures the delay which snort puts in network traffic. He talks about the modules in snort and focuses more on the preprocessing modules in snort. As the final results of his work, he mentions that the flow and stream4 preprocessing are the most expensive modules of snort in detection of intrusions; however, he doesn't examine attacks while monitoring the network traffic. The main contribution of this thesis is about the effect of IDS in network performance.

In paper [3], the writers count the trends of IPS which are accuracy signature, the traffic volume, topology design, quota usage logging, protecting intrusion prevention system, monitoring sensor, and collaboration of UTM. This paper explains these issues and gives some solutions to minimize these effects; however, the writers don't statistically reason these trends and only give a summery about these problems. In this paper, we focus on traffic volume and logging issue and examine them in IPS.

In paper [1], the writers analyze the strengths and weaknesses of different types of IDS. They introduce four metrics for their comparison which are false positive, false negative, true positive and true negative. These metrics evaluate the accuracy of detection engine module in IPS but we focus on number of packets that IPS captures but can't be analyzed because of resource limitation. They also didn't consider the complexity of the environment and the overload of network traffic in their experiment.

There is a good survey on [7] which categorized intrusion detection systems based on data source, processing, time of detection, environment, reaction and alert. The architecture of intrusion detection system is perfectly explained in this paper which we use as the basic understanding for IPS modules.

All of these above articles didn't consider the effect of network traffic on performance of IPS in identifying attacks. The main contribution of this paper is to analyze the performance of IPS in controlled environment base on network traffic. In the next section, we explain the tools which we use in this experiment.

3. Approach

We want to scrutinize the effect of network traffic on IPS performance. To evaluate IPS performance, we use an attacker in our network. IPS should detect this attacker and prevent it from disturbing the network; here we focus on attacks to a web server. Then we generate network traffic to see if the performance of IPS in detection of attack will change. We consider two types of traffic, normal traffic and provocative traffic. Normal traffic doesn't trigger any IPS rules as an attack; however, provocative traffic triggers one of IPS rules and IPS alert this traffic as an attack. Our hypothesis is as follow:

1) Normal traffic doesn't have an effect in detection of attacker in the network;

2) Provocative traffic will exhaust IPS resources and decrease the performance of IPS in detection of attacker in the network.

Before we continue to the evaluation part; we should determine the tools which we are using in our approach. We need to choose an intrusion prevention system, network traffic generation tool and network attack type and the specification of our network environment.

3.1. IPS Choice

In this paper, we focus on centralized network intrusion prevention system. We choose Snort for IPS in this experiment because it is lightweight, open source network intrusion detection-prevention system [8]. Snort modules are shown in **Figure 1**.

We use WinCap library for capturing the network traffic. Preprocessor module has several plug-ins that can be turned on or off. They perform a variety of transformations, makes the data easier for Snort to digest such as session management, detect abnormality, http inspecting [8]. In this experiment, we use Stream5, Frag3, sfPortScan, performance monitor, http inspect plug-ins. Detection engine of Snort takes information from the packet decoder and preprocessor modules and operates on it at the transport and application layer, comparing the packet to its rule-based database .When a rule is triggered, an alert is generated and logged. Snort logging module supports a variety of output plug-ins, including text, database and csv formats [9].We use output plugin in text format, storing alerts in files on hard disk. We use Snort 2.9 on windows server 2003 SP2. The default rule database is used in this experiment. Snort also is configured to be used in IPS mode.

3.2. Network Traffic Generation Tools

In our approach to examine the effect of network traffic on IPS performance, we need a controlled environment; therefore we need a way to control the network traffic in our test environment. There are two general approaches for traffic generation. The first approach is to capture traffic from some usual network and then reply it in our test network. The second approach is to generate the network traffic. In this paper, we use D-ITG (Distributed Internet Traffic Generator) which is capable of generating network traffic at packet level. The main components of D-ITG are: 1) Internet Traffic Generator Sender (ITG-Sender); 2) Internet Traffic Generator Receiver (ITG-Recv); 3) Internet Traffic Generator Log Server (ITG-Log); 4) ITG Send Manager (ITGManager) [10-11].

We use only ITG-Send, for sending generated traffic, and ITG-Recv, for receiving generated traffic. ITG-Send generates multiple flows of data which every flow has its own manager thread and can be configured separately.

3.3. Network Attack Type

In this paper, we use DOS attack, which tries to slow down or completely shut down the web server denying the legitimate and authorized users to access it. There are a number of different kinds of DOS attack such as flaw exploitation DOS attack, flooding DOS attack, and penetration attack; here we use flooding DOS attack.

In flooding attack, an attacker simply sends more requests to a target than it can handle. Such attacks can either exhaust the processing capability of the target or exhaust the network bandwidth of the target, either way leading to a denial of service to other users. This attack is one of the most common attacks nowadays and this is the reason why we choose the flooding DOS attack.

In this experiment, we develop a web site on IIS 6.0 in windows server 2003 SP2. In flooding attack to the website, we create multiple concurrent connection and exhaust web server processing capability and unable it to service to other users.

3.4. Network Environment

Our network environment contains five elements consist of a web server, the victim of flooding DOS attack, an attacker, performs flooding DOS attack, an intrusion prevention server, a D-ITS Send, which is the sender of generated traffics, a D-ITS Recv, which is the receiver of generated traffics. Each of these components are deployed on separate PC, you can see the hardware configuration of these PCs on **Table 1**.

Our network architecture is a traditional LAN, where an attacker, access the web server through IPS. Range of internal network IP is 192.168.1.0/24 and range of external network IP is 192.168.2.0/24.

4. Evaluation

Our approach to evaluate the performance of IPS contains four phases, in each of them; we declare the purpose of the phase, Accomplishment and conclusion of it. Before we continue to the phases, we must define our evaluation method.

4.1. IPS Evaluation Criteria

In previous works done on IPS, some metric such as true negative, true positive, false negative and false positive has been introduced for IPS evaluation. These metrics point out to the correctness or incorrectness of IPS's decision in identifying of attacks, however, in addition to these factors, we care about the percentage of packets that IPS will analyze whether IPS will identify the attacks or not.

The limitation in IPS is its resources such as CPU, memory, etc. In this paper, we use analyze rate -AR- as determined in (1). AR determines the relation between number of packets that detection engine module analyze and number of packets that sensor module capture. If IPS can't analyze the packets, the probability of happening attack without IPS knowledge will increase, therefore lower AR points to lower IPS performance.

Table 1. Hardware configuration of PCS.

Component	CPU	RAM	OS	IP
Web Server	Intel® Core™2 Duo Processor E7500	2 GB DDRII	Windows Server 2003 SP2	192.168.1.218
IPS	Intel® Core™2 Duo Processor E7500	2 GB DDRII	Windows Server 2003 SP2	192.168.1.214 192.168.2.1
D-ITS Send	Intel® Core™2 Duo Processor E7500	2 GB DDRII	Windows XP SP2	192.168.1.217
D-ITS Receiver	Intel® Core™2 Duo Processor E7500	2 GB DDRII	Windows XP SP2	192.168.2.2
Attacker	Intel® Core™2 Duo Processor P8800	4 GB DDRII	Windows 7 ultimate	192.168.2.216

$$AR = \frac{\text{Number of Packets Analyzed}}{\text{Number of Packets Captured}} \quad (1)$$

4.2. Deployment of an Attack on a Web Server

In this phase, we only deploy an attacker and a web server which connected through direct link, without IPS Interface as shown in **Figure 2**.

Purpose: To examine flooding DOS attack and how it will affect the web server performance. We measure the performance of the web server based on http request lost which returns http response code 408 (http request timeout).

Accomplishment: In this phase, we attack the web server with flooding DOS from attacker. We use concurrent connections to send http request to the web server. We change the concurrent connection to see the performance change in http request lost. The data that acquired during this phase has been summarized in **Table 2** and **Figure 3**.

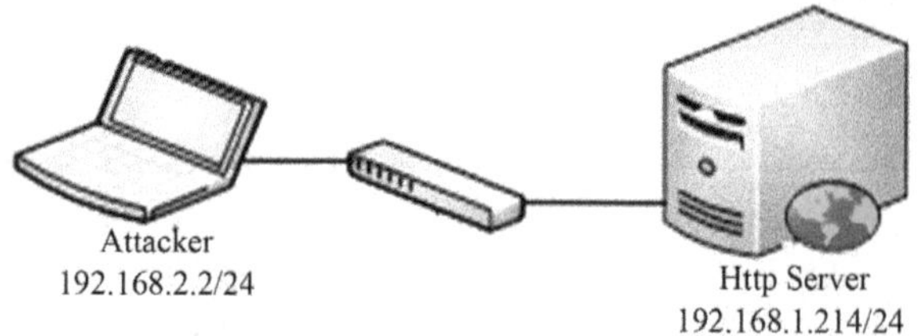

Figure 2. Network test scenario of phase I consists of an attacker and a web server.

Table 2. Result of phase I.

Concurrent Connection	Http Request Sent	Http Request Lost
10	2389	0.42%
50	3133	1.63%
200	2746	80%
300	3821	89.71%
850	4334	95.43%

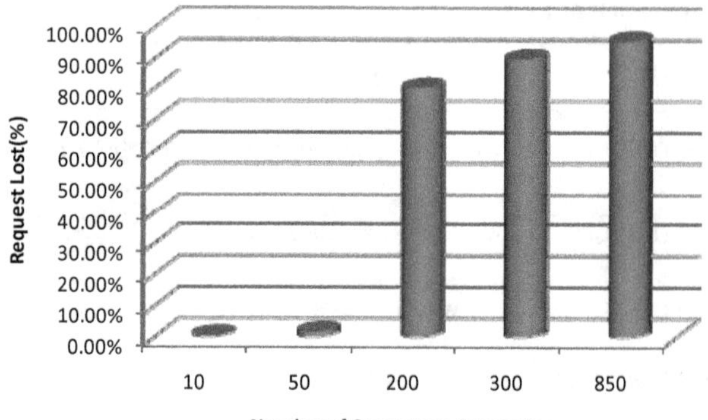

Figure 3. Results of Phase I.

Conclusion: In this phase, we've performed flooding DOS attack that result in process exhaustion of the web server. As the number of concurrent connection increased, the more resources of web server have been used to respond to requests until the web server resources have been used completely, after this point, we've see that the http request lost increased tremendously. As you can see in the results, flooding DOS attack is successful in disturbing the web server. For other phases of this paper, we choose 200 concurrent connections that result in 80% request lost, in this situation the web server is completely down and we can say that the DOS flooding attack is successful.

4.3. Phase II: Deployment of IPS

In this phase, we deploy Snort as IPS in addition to the web server and attacker as shown in **Figure 4**. The communication and connection of the web server and attacker is through the IPS.

Purpose: To examine the efficiency of IPS in detection and prevention of flooding DOS attack.

Accomplishment: In this phase, we perform flooding DOS attack to the web Server with 200 concurrent connections. Snort detects and prevents this attack and the analyze rate is equal to 98%. You can see the alert record which has been generate for flood DOS attack as Potentially Bad Traffic in **Figure 5**.

Conclusion: When snort has deployed as IPS in network, snort has identified flooding DOS attack with AR = 98%. This shows the normal performance of IPS without presence of any traffic. In the following phases, we generate traffics to see how it affects IPS performance and analyze rate.

4.4. Deployment of Network Traffic Generation

In this phase, we deploy network traffic generation tool, D-ITS Send, D-ITS Recv and IPS as shown in **Figure 6**.

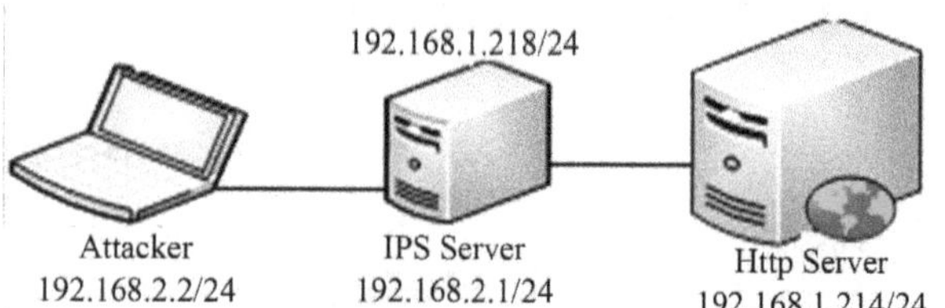

Figure 4. Network test scenario of Phase II, consists of attacker and web server and IPS.

```
[**] [129:15:1] Reset outside window [**]
[Classification: Potentially Bad Traffic] [Priority: 2]
01/05-12:07:10.947614 192.168.2.2:1803 -> 192.168.1.214:80
TCP TTL:127 TOS:0x0 ID:19690 IpLen:20 DgmLen:40 DF
***A*R** Seq: 0x4C588E57 Ack: 0x46525FEC Win: 0x0 TcpLen: 20
```

Figure 5. The alert record in snort for detection of flooding DOS attack as potentially bad traffic.

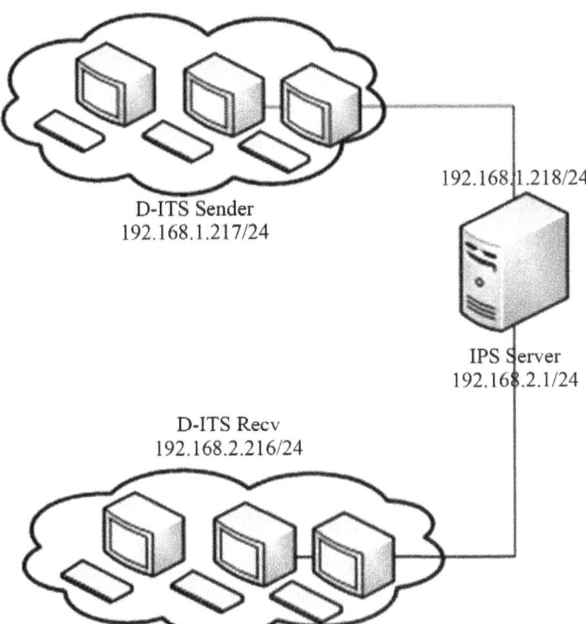

Figure 6. Network test scenario of Phase III, consists of IPS and network traffic generation tools.

Purpose: This is the main phase of our experiment. In this phase, we examine the effect of network traffic on analyze rate of IPS. In this paper, we consider two types of traffic, normal traffic, provocative Traffic. Normal traffic doesn't provoke any IPS rules as an attack, however, provocative traffic triggers one of IPS rules and IPS alert this traffic as an attack.

Accomplishment: We want to examine the effect of normal traffic and provocative traffic on IPS. For normal traffic, we generate UDP packet which doesn't provoke any Snort rules; we use one flow of data between D-ITS Send and D-ITS Recv. We increase the packet per second, run the traffic for 30 second and then calculate AR according to Equation (1). Based on our bandwidth limit, we increase the rate of packet per second to 140,000. The analyze rate of IPS report remains at 100% according the reports in Snort. (The report shows equality between number of packets captured and number of packets analyzed).

For provocative traffic, we use packet ICMP with type echo reply. Alert that Snort generates for this traffic is shown in **Figure 7**.

To compare these two traffics, we use two flows of data between D-ITS Send and D-ITS Recv. One contains UDP packet (normal traffic) and the other contains ICMP packet (provocative traffic). We change packet per second rate of provocative traffic to examine the effect of pro- vocative traffic on snort. The data that acquired during this phase has been summarized in **Table 3** and **Figure 8**. In each stage, we generate traffic for 30 seconds and then we calculate analyze rate of Snort.

```
[**] [1:408:5] ICMP Echo Reply [**]
[Classification: Misc activity] [Priority: 3]
01/05-12:21:51.805109 192.168.2.216 -> 192.168.1.215
ICMP TTL: 127 TOS:0x0 ID: 19925 IpLen: 20 DgmLen: 29
Type: 0 Code: 0 ID: 0 Seq: 0 ECHO REPLY
```

Figure 7. The alert record in Snort for Provocative traffic.

Table 3. Result of phase III.

Normal Traffic UDP[a]	Provocative Traffic ICMP[a]	Number of Packets Snort Captured	Analyze Rate
70,000	0	2,989,572	100%
70,000	1000	2,129,044	100%
70,000	5000	2,250,065	100%
70,000	10,000	2,399,349	100%
70,000	15,000	2,510,819	63.015%
70,000	18,000	2,590,347	56.782%
70,000	20,000	2,638,594	52.235%
70,000	50,000	3,142,679	28.673%

[a]Unit traffic icmp and traffic udp are packet per second and for calculation of analyze rate, we use snort reports based on generated traffic for 30 seconds.

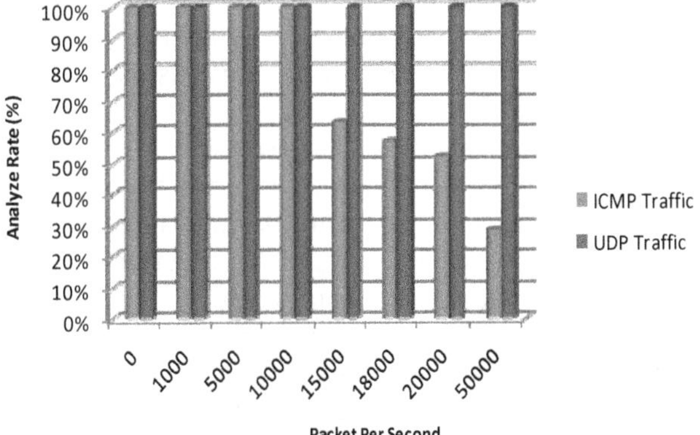

Figure 8. Difference between ICMP and UDP traffic.

Conclusion: In this phase, we've examined the effect of network traffic on IPS analyze rate. In normal traffic, IPS analyze rate didn't change noticeably, but if we combine normal traffic with provocative, we face the reduction of analyze rate. As mentioned in previous sections, there is a direct relation between analyze rate reduction and reduction of IPS performance. The main reason for reduction of analyze rate was a large amounts of alerts that has been generated for provocative traffic, for example with ICMP rate 20,000 packet per second , for 30 seconds, 700 MB alerts have been generated which consumed IPS resources.

In the next phase, we examine the effect of analyze rate reduction in detection of attacks by IPS.

4.5. Phase IV: Effect Of Network Traffic on IPS

In this phase, we accumulate all of the previous phases as shown in **Figure 9**.

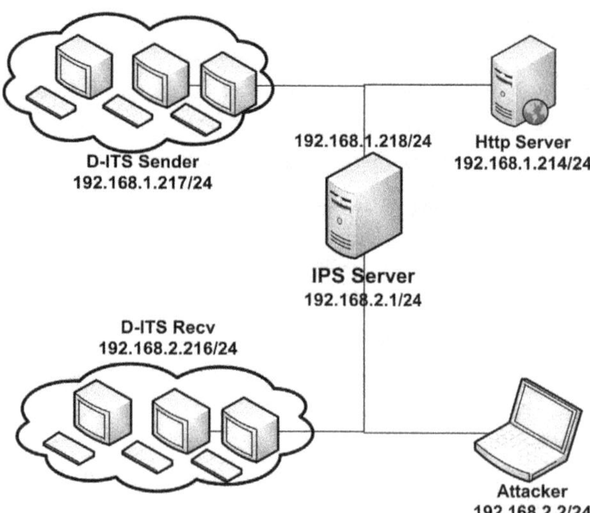

Figure 9. Network test scenario of Phase IV, consists of web server, attacker, IPS and network traffic generation tools.

Purpose: To examine the effect of network traffic on IPS in detection and prevention of flooding DOS attack to the web server. In the previous phase, we face with the reduction of analyze rate in presence of provocative traffic. In this section, we see the result of this reduction in IPS performance.

Accomplishment: As we have seen in Phase II, Snort detects and prevents flooding DOS attack completely without presence of any other traffic. In this phase, while we attack to the web server with 200 concurrent connections; we generate normal and provocative traffic.

For normal traffic, we have used UDP with 70,000 packet per second; Snort has detected and prevented flooding DOS attack with AR = 100%. The results were the same as phase II. This concludes that normal traffic doesn't have an effect of IPS performance.

For provocative traffic, we have chosen ICMP with 20,000 packets per second from Phase III. By analyzing the alert file of snort, we find out that only 19% of flooding DOS attack was Detected and Prevented by Snort. In this stage, flooding DOS attack has performed successfully on web server in the presence of IPS.

Conclusion: In this phase, we've examined the effect of network traffic on detection of flooding DOS attack. Normal traffic didn't have any effect on IPS performance in detection and prevention of the attack, however, in provocative traffic, Snort couldn't perform his job in detection and preventing of the attack and efficiency of Snort has been undermined. Overusing of resources in any module in IPS even the alert module could result in the reduction of the analyze rate and IPS performance. Provocative traffic uses this weakness and decreases the performance of IPS by forcing IPS to overuse its logging module and consume its resources completely. As a result, IPS can't prevent flooding DOS attack from disturbing the web server.

5. Conclusions & Future Work

In this paper, we've examined the effect of network traffic on IPS performance. In the previous works that has been done on IPS, metrics such as TP, TN, FP and FN has been introduced for measuring the efficiency of IPS but in this paper, we've measured the performance of IPS base on the packets that IPS capture but cannot analyze as a consequence of resource shortage. If intrusion prevention system can't analyze the network packets, the probability of happening attack, without IPS/IDS awareness, increase and this is a great risk to our network security.

First, we've attacked a web server with flooding DOS attack without presence of any traffic, which caused unavailability of the web server, and then we've developed Snort as IPS which has detected and prevented flooding DOS attack completely.

Next, we examined the effects of network traffic on analyze rate of IPS by considering two types of traffic, normal and provocative traffic. Normal traffic, which doesn't trigger any IPS rules, didn't have any affect in analyze rate and performance of IPS whereas provocative traffic, which triggers IPS rules, reduced the analyze rate of IPS considerably. Provocative traffic decreases the performance of IPS by forcing IPS to overuse its logging module and consume its resources completely. Overusing of resources in any module in IPS even the alert module could result in the reduction of the analyze rate and IPS performance. The analyze rate reduction decreased snort's functionality in detection and prevention of flooding DOS attack. Although in this paper, we only consider flooding DOS attack, but the result of this experiment can be applied to any attack.

In our future work, we want to improve the analyze rate of IPS by implementing a preprocessor module for Snort which log only the summery of traffic packets and not details of every packets .This will cause the reduction of alerts and effective usage of process and memory in IPS and make sure that no traffic can abuse the alert and logging module.

REFERENCES

[1] D. Padilla, Y. Colorado and E. Guillen, "Weaknesses and Strengths Analysis over Network-Based Intrusion Detection and Prevention Systems," *Proceedings of the Latin-American Conference on Communications of the IEEE LATINCOM* 09, Medellin, 11-19 September 2009, pp. 1-5.

[2] M. Beheshti, K. Kowalski, J. Ortiz and J. Tomelden, "Component-Based Software Architecture Design for Network Intrusion Detection and Prevention System," *Proceedings of the 6th International Conference on Information Tec-*

hnology: New Generations (*IEEE ITNG* 09), Las Vegas, 27-29 April 2009, pp. 248-253.

[3] A. H. Abdullah, M. Y. Idris and D. Stiawan, "The Trends of Intrusion Prevention System Network," *Proceedings of the 2nd International Conference on Education Technology and Computer of the IEEE ICETC*, Shanghai, 22-24 June 2010, pp. 217-221.

[4] A. Movaghar and F. Sabahi, "Intrusion Detection: A Survey," *Proceedings of the 3rd International Conference on Systems and Networks Communications of the IEEE ICSNC*, Sliema, 26-31 October 2008, pp. 23-36.

[5] P. Wolfe, B. Hayes and C. Scott, "Snort for Dummies," 1st Edition, Willey, Indianapolis, 2004.

[6] R. Wagoner, "Performance Testing an Inline Network Intrusion Detection System Using Snort," Master's Thesis, Morehead State University, Morehead, 2007.

[7] S. Kumar, "Survey of Current Network Intrusion Detection Techniques," 2007, pp. 1-18.

[8] Z. W. Chen, T. C. Zhou, X. H. Guan and Z. M. Zhou "The Study on Network Intrusion Detection System of Snort," *Proceedings of the 2nd International Conference on Networking and Digital Society of the IEEE ICNDS*, Wenzhou, 30-31 May 2010, pp. 194-196.

[9] http://www.snort.org
http://www.snort.org/assets/156/snort_manual.pdf
http://www.snort.org/assets/156/snort_manual.pdf

[10] D. Emma, A. Pescapè, G. Ventre and S. Avallone, "A Distributed Multiplatform Architecture for Traffic Generation," *Proceedings of the Symposium on Performance Evaluation of Computer and Telecommunication Systems* (*SPECTS*), Philadelphia, 24-28 July 2004, pp. 659-670.

[11] A. M. Faizal, *et al.*, "Threshold Verification Technique for Network Intrusion Detection System," *International Journal of Computer Science and Information Security*, Vol. 2, No. 1, 2009, pp. 1-8.

4

Digital Evidence for Database Tamper Detection

Shweta Tripathi[1], Bandu Baburao Meshram[2]
[1]Department of Computer Engineering, Fr. Agnel Institute of Technology, Navi Mumbai, India
[2]Head Department of Computer Technology, Veermata Jijabai Technological Institute, Mumbai, India

ABSTRACT

Most secure database is the one you know the most. Tamper detection compares the past and present status of the system and produces digital evidence for forensic analysis. Our focus is on different methods or identification of different locations in an oracle database for collecting the digital evidence for database tamper detection. Starting with the basics of oracle architecture, continuing with the basic steps of forensic analysis the paper elaborates the extraction of suspicious locations in oracle. As a forensic examiner, collecting digital evidence in a database is a key factor. Planned and a modelled way of examination will lead to a valid detection. Based on the literature survey conducted on different aspects of collecting digital evidence for database tamper detection, the paper proposes a block diagram which may guide a database forensic examiner to obtain the evidences.

Keywords: Tamper Detection; Log Files; Forensics; Oracle Database

1. Introduction

Database security is not a new buzz. But identifying the reasons of security violation in a database is a recent point of discussion. To understand how, when and what was tampered in a database the thorough knowledge of the architecture of database is required. To bind the vast information about architectures of different databases the architecture of oracle 10g is considered.

Database Forensics is a branch of digital forensic science relating to the forensic study of databases and their related metadata. For the forensic examination of a database, it has to be related to the timestamps that apply to the update time of a row in a relational table being inspected and tested for validity in order to verify the actions of a database user. Alternatively, a forensic examination may focus on identifying transactions within a database system or application that indicate evidence of wrong doing, such as fraud. Hence forth identifying who, when and how modified or tampered the data.

There are many approaches towards forensics of database defined by different researchers. A structured model to collect the evidence is a need of database forensics which has been proposed in this paper as the initial step of examining the database after the tamper.

The organisation of rest of the paper is as follows: Section 2 gives the literature survey. Based on basic concepts, section 3 is devoted for process to collect evidence. Section 4 gives the conclusion.

2. Literature Survey

The literature survey explores from the basics of architecture of oracle 10g to the vulnerabilities in oracle, digital forensics analysis and database tamper detection.

2.1. Basics of Oracle Architecture

In this section the basics of oracle 10g is explained highlighting few **Figure 1** [1]. Oracle physical storage and memory structure is explained in brief. Since these locations may guide us to locate and analyse the tamper in the database.

2.1.1. Oracle Physical Storage Structures

The Oracle database uses a number of physical storage structures on disk to hold and manage the data from user transactions. Some of these storage structures, such as the datafiles, redo log files, and archived redo log files, hold actual user data; other structures, such as control files, maintain the state of the database objects, and text-based alert and trace files contain logging information for both routine events and error conditions in the database. **Figure 1** [1] shows the relationship between these physical structures and the logical storage structures.

2.1.2. Datafiles

One Oracle datafile corresponds to one physical operating system file on disk [1].

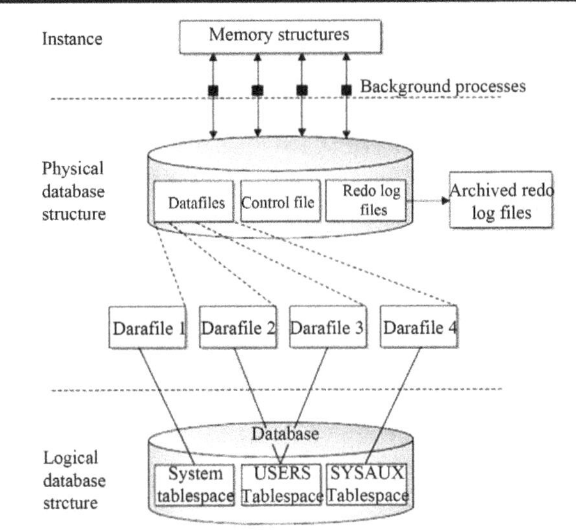

Figure 1. Oracle physical storage structures.

2.1.3. Redo Log Files

Whenever data is added, removed, or changed in a table, index, or other Oracle object, an entry is written to the current redo log file [1].

2.1.4. Control Files

Every Oracle database has at least one control file that maintains the metadata of the database (in other words, data about the physical structure of the database itself) [1].

2.1.5. Archived Log Files

An Oracle database can operate in one of two modes: archivelog or noarchivelog mode. When the database is in noarchivelog mode, the circular reuse of the redo log files is no longer available in case of a failure to a disk drive. Archivelog mode sends a filled redo log file to one or more specified destinations and can be available to reconstruct the database at any given point in time in the event that a database media failure occurs [1].

2.1.6. Alert and Trace Log Files

When things go wrong, Oracle can and often does write messages to the alert log and, in the case of background processes or user sessions, trace log files [1].

2.1.7. Backup Files

Backup files can originate from a number of sources, such as operating system copy commands or Oracle Recovery Manager (RMAN) [1].

2.2. Vulnerabilities in Oracle

To collect the evidences for data tamper detection one should have a brief knowledge of the suspicious location in the database. This part of the paper summarizes the vulnerabilities in oracle 10g with the [2].

The author mentions there are three areas an attacker can exploit to break in to a given system. Firstly, they can exploit the trust already given to them in the case of an inside attacker or in a social engineering attack; secondly, an attacker can exploit a weakness in the configuration of the server and third and last, an attacker can exploit a vulnerability in the software. Social engineering attacks are beyond the scope of this paper. We have highlighted few weaknesses in server configurations and software vulnerabilities. Some of the common configuration weaknesses that can be exploited to break in are listed below.

2.2.1. Exploiting Configuration Vulnerabilities

Exploiting configuration vulnerabilities is an easy task of an attacker due to following vulnerable configuration [2].

Default Usernames and Passwords Prior to 10g, Oracle was renowned for the number of default user accounts that have default passwords after an install. Some common accounts with their password include [2].

Username	Password
SYS	CHANGE_ON_INSTALL
SYSTEM	MANAGER
DBSNMP	DBSNMP
MDSYS	MDSYS
CTXSYS	CTXSYS
WKSYS	WKSYS
SCOTT	TIGER

Files: After installing 10g, both release 1 and 2, there are a number of files that contain the password selected by the DBA during installation. Whilst the passwords are obfuscated it is trivial to recover the clear text password from these files. If an attacker can gain access to these files then they have the keys to the kingdom. These files include:

CONFIGTOOLS.XML
CONFIGTOOLSINSTALLDATE.LOG
IAS.PROPERTIES
TARGETS.XML [2]

Reflections on default passwords Many times we often hear a DBA protest that they block direct connections to the database with a firewall rule setting—this generally means blocking access to port 1521—so they don't need to worry about default user IDs and passwords. However, they often forget to block ports 2100 and (less so) 8080 which means that, if the Oracle server is running the XML Database (XDB), then attacker can log in over these ports. An FTP service in XDB listens on TCP port 2100 and a web server on port 8080 [2].

Unnecessary Services Here is a simple chain of logic: the more services that are running, the greater the size of the attack surface; the greater the attack surface; the greater the likelihood of a flaw existing, the greater the likelihood of a successful break in. If there is no strict business requirement for something to be running, if it doesn't serve an active role in any business processes then it should be turned off [2].

The TNS Listener Prior to Oracle 10g the TNS Listener was installed without a password set for it. This means that, unless a password was set at a later time, anybody with access to port 1521, or whatever the port the server is listening on, could remotely administer the Listener. One of ways in which an attacker could exploit this was to set the listener's log file to a set location such as ~/.rhosts on a *nix system or a batch file in the Startup folder of the administrator on a Windows system. Once the location is set then the attacker can write content to the file such as "+ +" in the case of .rhosts or a command to execute in the case of a batch file in the Startup folder [2].

2.2.2. Exploiting Software Vulnerabilities

There are many different classes of software vulnerability and every so often new classes are discovered. Oracle has suffered from most at some point or continues to and these provide an attacker with a way into the server [2].

Buffer Overflow Vulnerabilities

A buffer overflow vulnerability is conceptually easy to understand. The programmer sets aside some memory to hold some data and they make some assumptions about the size of that data. Along comes an attacker however and stuffs too much data into the buffer. The buffer overflows and the data overwrites other "stuff" in memory—some of which may be crucial to the running of the program or the program's flow of execution. With this now under the control of the attacker they can get the program to do their bidding as opposed to what the program was supposed to do [2].

Format String Vulnerabilities

Format string vulnerability arises when a programmer uses one of the functions in the printf family of functions without specifying the format string. This, in effect, allows the attacker to present the format string instead [2].

PL/SQL Injection

PL/SQL injection vulnerabilities are one of the more common types of Oracle security flaw. Oracle stored procedures are known as packages. These packages contain data, procedures and functions. They also have the ability to execute dynamic SQL statements. By default, when a PL/SQL package executes it does so with the privileges of the owner and so, if the package suffers from a security vulnerability, it presents the attacker with the ability to run SQL as the owner of the package [2].

Trigger Abuse

Not only are packages, procedures and functions vulnerable to PL/SQL injection but triggers can be too. A trigger is a piece of PL/SQL code that fires when a specific event occurs—for example a user performs a DML operation such as an INSERT. A number of triggers have been found to contain security weaknesses. These include the SDO_LRS_TRIG_INS, SDO_GEOM_TRIG_INS1 and SDO_DROP_USER_BEFORE triggers owned by MDSYS and the CDC_DROP_CTABLE_BEFORE trigger [2].

Attacks via Oracle Application Server

Attacks from the outside of the network, particularly where the database server is properly protected by a firewall, typically originate from the web server—more often than not in the form of SQL injection attacks in the custom JSP, PHP or ASP application [2].

2.3. Digital Forensic Analysis Methodology

The entire investigation process can be divided into four phases [3].

1) Identification: in this phase it collects the information of the compromised system. System Configuration, software loaded, User profiles etc.

2) Collection Phase: collects the evidence from the compromised system. Evidence is most commonly found in files and Databases that are stored on hard drives and storage devices and media. If file deleted, recovering data from the deleted files and also collects evidence file deleted files.

3) Analysis phase: analyse the collecting data/files and finding out the actual evidence.

4) Report phase: the audience will be able to understand the evidence data which has been acquired from the evidence collection and analysis phases. The report generation phase records the evidence data found out by each analysis component. Additionally, it records the time and provides hash values of the collected evidence for the chain-of-custody.

2.4. Database Tampering

Maintaining data integrity is an important aspect of security in a database. The basics of database tampering can be explained better with the case study.

2.4.1. Example of Data Tampering

Any business cannot afford the risk of an unauthorized user observing or changing the data in their databases. There are several types of concerns that are realized about database security. They are "unauthorized data observation, incorrect data modification, and data unavailability". An example of unauthorized data observation would be a database user accessing information that they are not authorized to view. Incorrect data modification can be intentional or unintentional. Intentional data modification could be a student changing their grade or a data entry clerk accidentally entering the price of a line item incorrectly for an order. Data unavailability exists when "information crucial for the proper functioning of the organization is not readily available when needed." [4].

A data breach in a bank information system [5] was an unauthorized access to clients banking accounts which has resulted with money problems to a certain number of clients. Somehow, they have a minus on credit card accounts. Bank personnel are unable to identify the culprit. Persecution department send a team of digital forensics. They have a task to collect all evidence about suspicious transactions, examine them and make a report to the court of low. The team needs to follow a precisely defined procedure to provide valid court evidence (**Figure 2**).

Different kinds of log files are available in oracle 10g. To identify who had got the unauthorized access, when he had got the access and how he had tampered the data in the accounts database, a forensic examiner should collect the relative log files and perform the analysis to gain the information about the criminal.

2.4.2. Detection Methods

Different methods to detect tampering can be based on the identification of violation of the integrity of the database. The threats to integrity are [6] authentication and access control, application integration, database extensions, inherited OS vulnerabilities, privileged parties.

A novel relational hash tree [6] can be designed for efficient database processing, and evaluate the performance penalty for integrity guarantees. Such implementation does not require modification of system internals and can therefore easily be applied to any conventional DBMS.

Database provenance chronicles the history of updates and modifications to data [7]. Without additional protecttions, provenance records are vulnerable to accidental corruption, and even malicious forgery, a problem that is most pronounced in the loosely-coupled multi-user environments often found in scientific research. The problem of providing integrity and tamper-detection for database provenance can be solved by a checksum-based approach, is well-suited to the unique characteristics of database provenance, including non-linear provenance objects and provenance associated with multiple fine granularities of data [7].

The Enterprise Resource Planning system (ERP system) manages database through application on the database top layer [8]. The investigation of the corporate frauds, gives output as investigation data from application software, which cannot be trusted. The database design in the form of dual-book may be used for hiding data; hence

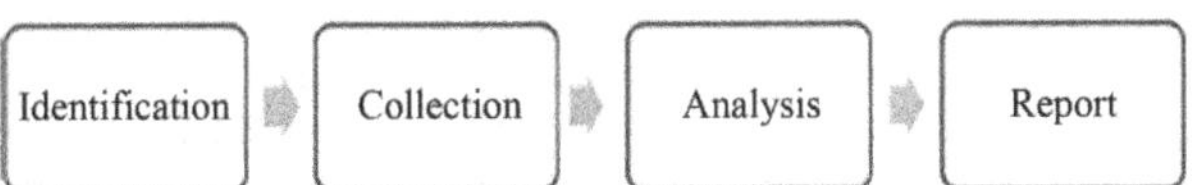

Figure 2. Investigation processes.

investigation data cannot be obtained from these systems. In such case the data is not only provided in the application software in the database, but there is additional data which is related with investigation. Therefore, the investtigators must verify what investigation data exists on the database. These fields are based on the database and application. The attribute information of these fields are stored in a database schema, through the DBRE (database reverse engineering), it is possible to determine the table relationship by extracting schema information. The DBRE largely divide two parts: data structure extraction and data structure conceptualization. Improving the DBRE process and hence analyzing the table relationship of database and data extraction method is useful from the view of the digital forensics.

There are different mechanisms within a database management system (DBMS), based on cryptographically strong one-way hash functions, which prevent an intruder, including an auditor or an employee or even an unknown bug within the DBMS itself, from silently corrupting the audit log [9]. DBMS transparently store the audit log as a transaction-time database, so that it is available to the application if needed. The DBMS should also store a small amount of addition information in the database to enable a separate *audit log validator* (to be referred to simply as the *validator*) to examine the database along with this extra information and state conclusively whether the audit log has been compromised. The DBMS periodically send a short document (a hash value) to an off-site *digital notarization service*, to bind when changes were made to a database [10].

The above methods have discussed about the models to identify the threat and hence detect the evidences in the vulnerable database. But our problem as a database forensic examiner to analyse the data to identify who, where and how tampered the data, is still not solved. With above methods we cannot gather the data for analysis. The later part of the paper summarizers the work of the researchers in the field of identifying locations for collecting the evidences.

2.4.3. Sources for Evidences

The author of [11] has listed the main source of evidence as follows:

1) Listener log—logs connections to the listener, use lsnrctl to administrate it. It Can be found in /u01/app/oracle/oracle/product/10.2.0/db_4/network/listener.log.

2) Alert log—system alerts important to DB e.g. processes starting and stopping. It Can be found in /u01/app/oracle/admin/orcl/bdump

3) Sqlnet.log—some failed connection attempts such as "Fatal NI connect error 12170".

4) Redo logs—current changes that have not been checkpointed into the datafiles (.dbf).

/u01/app/oracle/oradata/orcl/redo02.log
/u01/app/oracle/oradata/orcl/redo01.log
/u01/app/oracle/oradata/orcl/redo03.log

5) Archived redo logs—previous redo logs that can be applied to bring back the data in the db to a previous state using SCN as the main sequential identifier. This can be mapped to timestamp.

6) Fine-Grained Auditing audit logs viewable from FGA_LOG$ and DBA_FGA_AUDIT_TRAIL VIEW.

7) Oracle database audit SYS.AUD$ table and DBA_AUDIT_TRAIL VIEW.

8) Oracle mandatory and OS audit /u01/app/oracle/admin/orcl/adump

9) Home-made trigger audit trails—bespoke to the system.

10) Agntsrvc.log—contains logs about the Oracle Intelligent agent.

11) IDS, Web server and firewall logs should also be integrated to the incident handling timeline. This will rely heavily on well synchronised time in the network as previously mentioned.

Different locations [12] to find forensics data is listed below:

- TNS listener log
- Many types of trace files
- Sqlnet logs (server and clients)
- Sysdba audit logs
- Datafiles for deleted data
- Redo (and archive) logs
- SGA (v$sql etc)
- Apache access logs
- v$db_object_cache
- Wrh$%% views
- Wri$ views
- Statspack views
- col_usage$
- Audit trails –
  - AUD$, FGA_LOG$
  - Application audit (who/when, triggers, other)
- Flashback, recycle bin

The capabilities of LogMiners can be evaluated as a Forensics investigation tool. Its general applicability can be assessed for its forensics by testing how well it can create a timeline and copy of past database actions. LogMiner proves itself to be very useful for this purpose. The interpretation of the TIMESTAMP data types is also done by The LogMiners. Databases are excellent reporting mechanisms and LogMiner allows the analyst to use a database SQL interface to the redo logs of Oracle which are separate from the database itself.

At minimum this can provide verification of information found through normal database Auditing and at maximum could be the main source of information in an investigation and allow subsequent recovery of lost data [13].

3. Proposed System

Our proposed system is based on two basic steps in identifying the location, that is summarizes the flow of processes for collecting the evidences and we have also designed the block diagram summarizing the vulnerable locations in the database.

3.1. Identifying Locations for Evidence

A series of papers on performing a forensic analysis of a compromised Oracle database server is published by Mr. Litchfield. Based on these papers we have identified the locations where we may obtain the evidences for tamper detection.

Redo Logs

A Redo Entry, otherwise known as a Redo Record, contains all changes for a given SCN [14]. The entry has a header and one or more "change vectors". There may be one or more change vectors for a given event. For example, if a user performs an INSERT on a table that has an index then several change vectors are created. There will be a redo and undo vector for the INSERT and then an insert leaf row for the index and a commit. Each change vector has its own operation code that can be used to differentiate between change vectors. The table below lists some of the more common ones:

5.1 Undo Record
5.4 Commit
11.2 INSERT on single row
11.3 DELETE
11.5 UPDATE single row
11.11 INSERT multiple rows
11.19 UPDATE multiple rows
10.2 INSERT LEAF ROW
10.4 DELETE LEAF ROW
13.1 Allocate space [e.g. after CREATE TABLE]
24.1 DDL

The forensic examiner must go through each redo entry and work out what has happened and attempt to separate those which are "normal" and those which are part of an attack.

Data Blocks

The second paper [15] in this series is dedicated on Locating dropped objects. When the block is filled up, the server starts filling a new block. Each row in the block has a three byte header. The first byte is a marker and contains a set of flags to indicate the row's state. For example, if the row has been deleted the 5th bit of the byte is set. For example, a common set of flags value for a marker is 0 × 2C—which becomes 0 × 3C when the "deleted" flag is set. This is an important point to remember as it is a key indicator when looking for dropped objects. The second byte of the row header is used to determine lock status and the third byte indicates the total amount of data in the row. If the total amount is greater than 255 bytes then the row header is four bytes allowing for up to 65,536 bytes. After the row header is the data itself. Each column of the row data is preceded with a byte indicating the size. If there is no data for a given column, in other words it is null, then it is represented with a 0 × FF.

TNS Listener's log file and the audit trail

To be able to log into the RDBMS an attacker [16] needs to know the Service Identifier or SID for the database. Before Oracle 10g this could be extracted from the TNS Listener with the SERVICES or STATUS command.

Here's something to be careful of with the audit trail. When a user successfully logs on a row is created in the audit trail. This has an ACTION# number of 100 (LOGON) and the TIMESTAMP# column reflects when the logon occurred.

In building a timeline of events this is important. This effectively hides when the user actually logged on. However, if we describe the AUD$ table we can see a LOGOFF$TIME column. If we then query this column, too, we can reconcile the logon and logoff times:

Live Response

When the database is shutdown cleanly this would wipe the audit trail making the task of the forensic examiner that little bit harder [17]. Of course, the attacker could do more than just wiped the audit trail in such a trigger. Due to issues like this and the loss of volatile information, some organizations prefer to perform an analysis on the system whilst it's still powered on and connected to the network. This is called a Live Response. Live Response is all about recovering and safely storing volatile data for later analysis, in other words, all the information that will disappear when the machine is disconnected from the network and switched off. Further, Live Response gives the forensic examiner the chance to collect non-volatile evidence in a "humanreadable" format that's easier to peruse than its stored binary version—for example event logs.

Views

There are a number of virtual tables and views that Oracle maintains for performance purposes [18]. These views are accessible to DBAs and can often contain evidence of attacks. Two of these views are of particular interest—V$SQL and V$DB_OBJECT_CACHE. The V$SQL fixed view contains a list of recently executed SQL. Evidence of an attacker's activities may be found in this fixed view and careful examination of the SQL_TEXT should reveal this. It must be stressed that if an attacker can find a way to execute arbitrary SQL as DBA, of which there are many, then they can clear the SQL from this view by executing "ALTER SYSTEM FLUSH SHARED_POOL". V$DB_OBJECT_CACHE contains details about objects in the library cache.

Oracle Recycle Bin

Whenever a table is dropped, the table and any [19] dependent objects such as indexes and triggers are moved to the Recycle Bin. This way, if it is decided that the table has been dropped in error, it can be recovered from the Recycle Bin using the UNDROP statement.

System Change Number

During a forensic examination of a compromised [20] Oracle database server the SCN and its timestamp can help tell the investigator whether a block of data has been changed. This is especially useful in those cases where there is an absence of other evidence such as the redo logs or audit trail. As with all forensic examinations it's critical not to change any evidence so any investigation should take place on a cold data file and not a live data file.

3.2. Steps to Collect the Evidence

With the help of the above study we have identified the steps which are useful in collecting the evidences [17].

1) Setup the evidence collection server by the following ways:

- firstly by mapping a drive if the system is running on Windows or has Samba and then using file redirection: D:\>listdlls.exe > z:\case-0001-listdlls.txt
  Using file redirection can be prone to error—for example the incident responder could type C instead of Z—which would be disastrous.
- The second method is to pipe output over the network using netcat or cryptcat.

2) Perform the following general steps to get basic information like [17].

***System time and date*:**

The incident responder should first record the system time and date of system that they're investigating.

***Logged on users*:**

The list of users that are currently logged on to the system and from where and for how long is extremely useful.

***List all users and groups*:**

Obtain a list of all users, gathering details on when they last logged in, and groups on the server and group membership.

***List open ports and connections* :**

All open and connected TCP ports should be collected as well as listening UDP ports.

***List running processes*:**

A list of all running processes should be obtained. Close attention should be paid to suspicious looking entries and also any shells such as cmd.exe or /bin/sh—indeed keep an eye out for //bin/sh (note two slashes) as this may indicate an overflow or format string exploit has been launched. The forensic examiner should also get a list of each process's parent process.

***List of DLLs or shared objects*:**

A list of the DLLs or shared objects that are loaded by each process should be obtained. Keep an eye out for odd looking names; on Windows look out for DLLs that are loaded via a UNC path across the network.

***List of open handles*:**

As well as what file handles a process has open a list of other handles should be obtained as well. Whilst this can reveal what an attacker may have been doing it can also help identify "parentless" processes.

***Perform memory dumps*:**

Memory dumps of all running process should be gathered even in what appear to be "normal" looking processes. The reason for this is to catch cloaking attacks—an attacker may launch a benign process like "notepad" and using CreateRemoteThread() load code into its address space.

***Perform system memory dump* :**

A dump of all system memory should be performed. This will cover those bit of memory not dumped when dumping each process.

***Get file names and MACTimes*:**

The incident responder should perform a full recursive directory list of every disk and get file and directory names as well as their creation, access and modification times. They should also gather information about each file's owner and any special attributes such as whether the read only, system or hidden attributes are set.

***Dump registry information*:**

On Windows all registry information should be dumped.

***Locate and take copies of log files and message logs*:**

All of the servers log files and event and message logs should be copied to the collection server for analysis. These logs will vary from system to system depending upon what services are running.

3) Collect the Oracle files of Interest

The Oracle specific log, trace and control files can be located in various places [17]. Firstly we need to know where each instance of Oracle is installed this can be extracted from the ORACLE_HOME environment variable if set. On Windows the HKEY_LOCAL_MACHINE\Software\Oracle Registry key stores information about each Oracle home For each Oracle home the incident responder should locate the server's start up parameter file. This will be found in the "database" directory on a Windows system or the "dbs" directory on a *nix system. Generally the filename is "spfilesid.ora" where "sid" is the database service identifier. This file contains information about where log and trace files etc are written to:

- audit_file_dest
- background_dump_dest
- core_dump_dest
- db_recovery_file_dest
- user_dump_dest
- utl_file_dir
- control_files
- db_create_file_dest
- db_create_online_log_dest_n
- log_archive_dest
- log_archive_dest_n

The incident responder should also be aware that what is listed in the start up file may not actually be what settings the Oracle server is actually using

4) Get the previously executed SQL [17].

- Get a copy of the most recently executed SQL. This can be retrieved from the V$SQL fixed view.
  On Oracle 10g the query should be:
  SQL> SELECT LAST_ACTIVE_TIME, PARSING_USER_ID, SQL_TEXT FROM V$SQL ORDER BY LAST_ACTIVE_TIME ASC;
  This will list the SQL that was executed by who and when from the V$SQL fixed view.
- Next in line should be the audit log. Everything should be selected from this table for later consumption and analysis.
  SQL > SELECT * FROM AUD$;

5) Getting a list of users and roles [17].

The incident responder should get a complete listing of all users on the system.

SQL > SELECT USER#, NAME, ASTATUS, PASS WORD, CTIME, PTIME, LTIME FROM

SYS.USER$ WHERE TYPE# = 1;

6) Getting a list of dropped tables [17].

In 10g, if a user has dropped any tables and they have not been purged from the recyclebin then a list of dropped tables should be present. This may indicate evidence of an attack:

SQL > SELECT U.NAME, R.ORIGINAL_NAME, R.OBJ#, R.DROPTIME, R.DROPSCN

FROM SYS.RECYCLEBIN$ R, SYS.USER$ U WHERE R.OWNER# = U.USER#;

7) Getting information about PL/SQL objects [17].

The source of PL/SQL objects should be retrieved and analyzed. Much of the source is encrypted or "wrapped" to use the Oracle term. The incident responder should obtain an "unwrapper" to examine the clear text as an attacker can modify a PL/SQL object and re-encrypt it to hide their attack.

8) Finishing up [17].

Once all queries have been executed the spool file should be closed and sqlplus can be closed.

SQL > SPOOL OFF

SQL > QUIT

Disconnected from Oracle Database 10g Enterprise Edition Release 10.2.0.2.0—Production with the Partitioning, OLAP and Data Mining options

C:\oracle\product\10.2.0\db_1\BIN>

Once disconnected from the server an md5 checksum should be made of the spool file and recorded with a witness present.

3.3. Block Diagram

The proposed process flow has been shown in **Figure 3**. This diagram summarizes the different methods explained above. We have considered a database server which has been tampered by an unauthorized user. To detect the tamper the forensic analyzer has to focus and collect information from the specified locations such as redo logs, data blocks, audit trails, live response, views, oracle recycle bin, and system change number. Different sql commands and tools are available to retrieve the information. The obtained information should be stored in a server and a comparative analysis should be performed on the basis of different kinds of users and their grant roles, role membership, object privileges, system privileges, authentication and authorizations of each and every user of the database. The analysis should be performed in the presence of an in charge and reliable authority of the organisation or the database. A graph should be produced to show the variations in the expected performance. The graph can be considered as the summarized output of the digital evidences collected for detecting the tampering in the database. Hence using this output forensic analysis of the database server can be performed which can be used to identify who, when and where tampered the data.

The locations defined in the proposed block diagram shown in **Figure 4** can be useful to get information about the system and its user and hence will give guidance to process the flow shown in **Figure 4**. Analyzing the flow may give us the desired information.

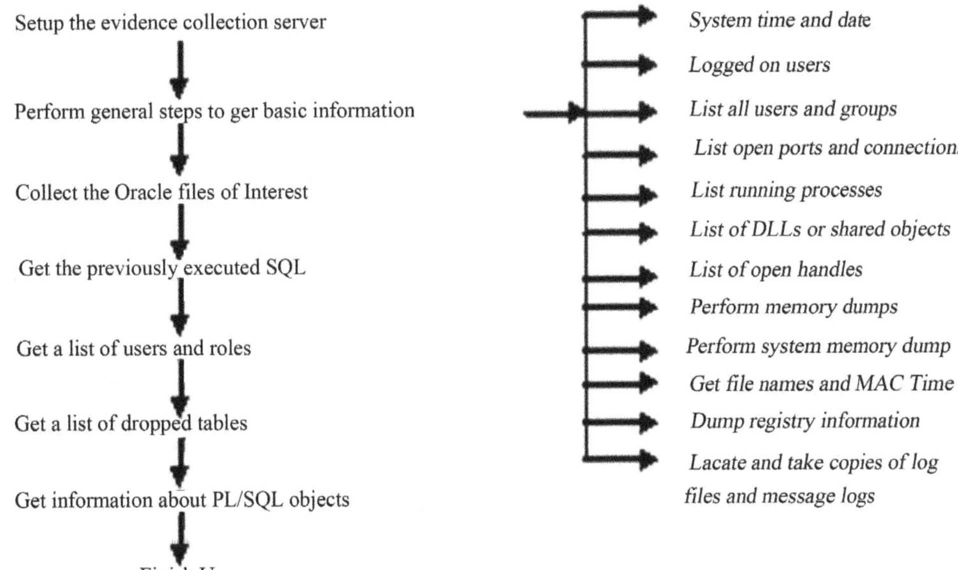

Figure 3. Process Flow.

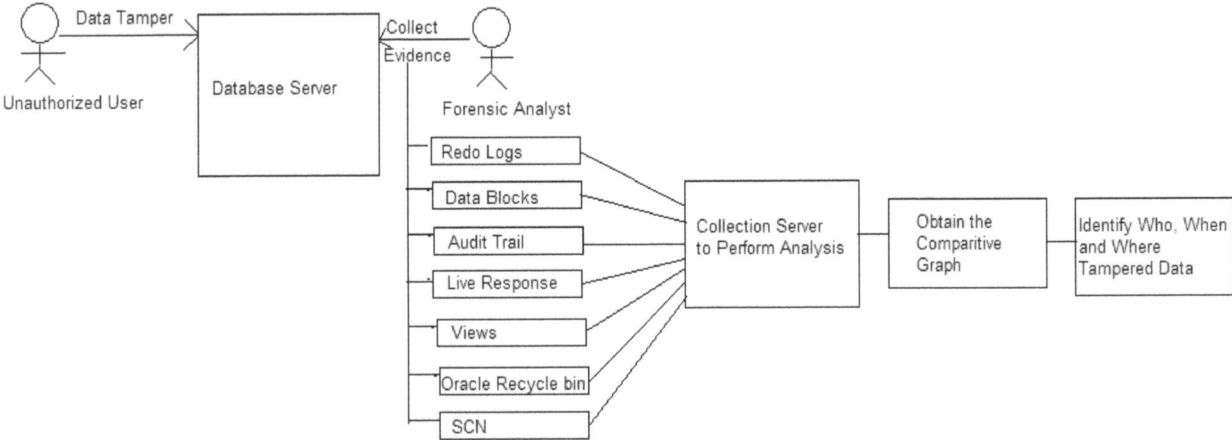

Figure 4. Proposed block diagram.

4. Conclusion

There are many ways of securing the database. The attackers have the methods to violate the security. Then comes the role of forensic analyst who should have a thorough knowledge of the basics of a database and also the information about the database on which he is going to perform the analysis. The forensic analyst should also be able to think from the attacker's point of view. Based on different cases, the digital evidences can be collected from the specified locations. If the intensions of the attacker are known identifying the attacked location may be easier. Thinking from the attacker's point of view this paper gives a contribution towards the identification of the general locations in a database for collecting the digital evidences.

REFERENCES

[1] K. Loney and B. Bryla, "Oracle Database 10g DBA Handbook," McGraw-Hill, New York, 2005.

[2] D. Litchfield, "Book on 'Oracle Forensics'," Wiley, Hoboken, 2008.

[3] O. L. Carroll, S. K. Brannon and T. Song, "Computer Forensics: Digital Forensic Analysis Methodology," *Computer*, Vol. 56, 2008, pp. 1-8.

[4] N. Aaron, "Oracle Database Security," *ICTN* 4040, Spring, 2006.

[5] J. Azemović and D. Mušić, "Efficient Model for Detection Data and Data Scheme Tempering with Purpose of Valid Forensic Analysis," *Proceedings of the* 2009 *International Conference on Computer Engineering and Applications*, Manila, 6-8 June 2009.

[6] G. Miklaul and D. Suciu, "Implementing a Tamper-Evident Database System," University of Massachusetts & University of Washington, Amherst & Washington DC, 2005.

[7] J. Zhang, A. Chapman and K. LeFevre, "Do You Know-Where Your Data's Been?—Tamper-Evident Database Provenance," *Proceedings of the* 6*th VLDB Workshop on Secure Data Management*, Lyon, 28 August 2009.

[8] D. C. Lee, J. M. Choi and S. J. Lee, "Database Forensic Investigation Based on Table Relationship Analysis Techniques," *Proceedings of the* 2*nd International Conference on Computer Science and Its Applications of the IEEE SCA*, Jeju, 10-12 December 2009, pp. 1-5.

[9] M. J. Malmgren, "An Infrastructure for Database Tamper Detection and Forensic Analysis," Bachelor's Thesis, University of Arizona, Tucson, 2007.

[10] R. T. Snodgrass, S. S. Yao and C. Collberg, "Tamper Detection in Audit Logs," *Proceedings of the* 30*th International Conference on Very Large Data Bases*, Toronto, 31 August-3 September 2004.

[11] "Oracle Forensics In a Nutshell 25/03/2007," 2007.

[12] P. Finnigan, "Oracle Forensics," OUG Scotland, DBA SIG, 30 April 2008.

[13] P. M. Wright, "Oracle Database Forensics Using LogMiner Option 3—Perform Forensic Tool Validation," *Proceedings of the GCFA Assignment—GSEC, GCFW, and GCIH*, London, 10 January 2005.

[14] D. Litchfield, "Oracle Forensics Part 1: Dissecting the Redo Logs," *NGSSoftware Insight Security Research* (*NISR*), Next Generation Security Software Ltd., Sutton, 2007.

[15] D. Litchfield, "Oracle Forensics Part 2: Locating Dropped Objects," *NGSSoftware Insight Security Research* (*NISR*), Next Generation Security Software Ltd., Sutton, 2007.

[16] D. Litchfield, "Oracle Forensics Part 3: Isolating Evidence of Attacks against the Authentication Mechanism," *NGSSoftware Insight Security Research* (*NISR*), Next Generation Security Software Ltd., Sutton, 2007.

[17] D. Litchfield, "Oracle Forensics Part 4: Live Response," *NGSSoftware Insight Security Research* (*NISR*), Next Generation Security Software Ltd., Sutton, 2007.

[18] D. Litchfield, "Oracle Forensics Part 5: Finding Evidence of Data Theft in the Absence of Auditing," *NGSSoftware Insight Security Research* (*NISR*), Next Generation Security Software Ltd., Sutton, 2007.

[19] D. Litchfield "Oracle Forensics Part 6: Examining Undo Segments, Flashback and the Oracle Recycle Bin," *NGSSoftware Insight Security Research* (*NISR*), Next Generation Security Software Ltd., Sutton, 2007.

[20] D. Litchfield, "Oracle Forensics Part 7: Using the Oracle System Change Number in Forensic Investigations," *NGSSoftware Insight Security Research* (*NISR*), Next Generation Security Software Ltd., Sutton, 2008.

5

Experimental Evaluation of Cisco ASA-5510 Intrusion Prevention System against Denial of Service Attacks

Raja Sekhar Reddy Gade, Sanjeev Kumar
Networking Research Lab, Department of Electrical/Computer Engineering, The University of Texas-Pan American, Edinburg, USA

ABSTRACT

Cyber attacks are continuing to hamper working of Internet services despite increase in the use of network security systems such as, firewalls and Intrusion protection systems (IPS). Recent Denial of Service (DoS) attack on Independence Day weekend, on July 4th, 2009 launched to debilitate the US and South Korean governments' websites is indicative of the fact that the security systems may not have been adequately deployed to counteract such attacks. IPS is a vital security device which is commonly used as a front line defense mechanism to defend against such DoS attacks. Before deploying a firewall or an IPS device for network protection, in many deployments, the performance of firewalls is seldom evaluated for their effectiveness. Many times, these IPS's can become bottleneck to the network performance and they may not be effective in stopping DoS attacks. In this paper, we intend to drive the point that deploying IPS may not always be effective in stopping harmful effects of DoS attacks. It is important to evaluate the capability of IPS before they are deployed to protect a network or a server against DoS attacks. In this paper, we evaluate performance of a commercial grade IPS Cisco ASA-5510 IPS to measure its effectiveness in stopping a DoS attacks namely TCP-SYN, UDP Flood, Ping Flood and ICMP Land Attacks. This IPS comes with features to counteract and provide security against these attacks. Performance of the IPS is measured under these attacks protection and compared with its performance when these protection features were not available (*i.e.* disabled). It was found that the IPS was unable to provide satisfactory protection despite the availability of the protection features against these flooding attacks. It is important for the network managers to measure the actual capabilities of an IPS system before its deployment to protect critical information infrastructure.

Keywords: Denial of Service (DoS); SYN Flood Attack; Proxy Protection; Firewall Security; Availability

1. Introduction

Exchange of Information in Government organizations, Educational institutions, corporate offices, and for each and every individual mostly depends on Internet. Today everyone, who are using the Internet as media for transferring valuable information, are worrying about securing their systems or networks from attacks on Internet. On August 6th 2009, servers like Twitter, Facebook, Live journal, Google's Blogger and Youtube were under DoS attack, where Twitter was down for several hours [1]. According to "2008 CSI Computer and Security Survey", Firewall type of security technology was used by 94% of the organizations to secure their networks [2]. Many manufacturers are designing firewalls to provide complete protection for their consumers from different types of attacks and at the same time provide availability for good communication between protected private network and public network of the legitimate users. Despite widespread use of firewalls to protect the private networks, the damage caused by the denial of service attacks does not seem to have mitigated. The recent Independence Day Denial of Service attack on July 4th, 2009 launched against US and South Korean government websites [3,4] has caused significant interruption in their operation and now it is prompting many to question the performance of firewalls in defending against such DoS attacks.

In this paper, we evaluate performance of Cisco ASA-5510 Intrusion Prevention System in preventing DDoS attacks. This system provides security to the private networks from many threats on the Internet that already exist and also from the zero day threats. The Denial of Services attacks are over Internet from many years, and there is a lot of research work going on in defending against these attacks. Cisco claims as they are a step forward in defending against these Denials of service attacks. In this paper, we measure the impact of Denial of Service Attack (DoS) on Cisco ASA 5510 Intrusion Prevention System, protecting a Web server (HTTP server) deploying

Windows server 2003. Because of its stateful features, Cisco ASA maintain sessions for each and every packet passing through it. This may cause stateful firewall to consume more resource when compared with a stateless firewall. However it may provide more security than the other techniques [5-9]. Despite of security systems installed to provide security to the private networks, servers have been compromised due to DoS attacks [10-12]. The availability and security provided by the Cisco IPS when it is defending against the DoS attacks explains the performance of the IPS.

The rest of the paper is organized as follows: Section II gives some background about Layer-3 attacks, Ping Flood and ICMP Land Attacks. Section 3 explains the protection techniques used by Netscreen in defending against such attacks. Section 4 explains the Experimental Setup whereas; Section 5 is Results and discussions. Section 6 concludes our findings from this experimental evaluation. Section 7 is Acknowledgments followed by References in Section 8.

2. Dos Attacks

2.1. Layer-4 Denial of Service Attacks

2.1.1. Transmission Control Protocol-SYN Attack

The Transmission Control Protocol (TCP) is a connection oriented protocol. TCP connections are formed between source and the destination hosts before transferring of data. During TCP connection, information is maintained for sockets, sequence numbers and window size. TCP layer provides reliability, flow control, and congestion control, when the connect ion is formed between two hosts. Depending on the Sequence number, Acknowledgment number and the Window size options that are part of TCP header (**Figure 1**). Because of the reason that the connection should be established between unreliable hosts through unreliable Internet, 3-Way Handshake method is used to establish a TCP connection between two applications of the hosts (**Figure 2**).

2.1.1.1 Three-Way Handshake

3-Way Handshake is the connection mechanism used in the Transport Control Protocol. From the **Figure 2**, we can see the connection established between the HTTP client and HTTP server [13]. The process for this connection is given below:

Step 1: Connection was initialized by client, by sending Synchronize Packet (SYN packet) to the server;

Step 2: Server responds to the client by sending SYN_ ACK (Synchronize and Acknowledgment messages);

Step 3: After client receives the SYN_ACK, it replies with final ACK (Acknowledgment message).

When the final ACK is received by the server, the TCP connection is established between the two hosts.

2.1.1.2. Half Open Connections

TCP connections are called Half Open connections when the third step of the 3-Way handshake sending final ACK to the server fails (**Figure 3**), or if one of the hosts closes the connection without acknowledging the other [14]. Half Open connection process is given below:

Step 1: Client initializes the request by sending SYN packet;

Step 2: Server replies to the client with SYN_ACK, and at this point server reserves some resource for the client and waits for the final ACK to arrive (Acknowledgment message);

Step 3: However, the client does not respond to the server with final Ack.

The reason can be that the request initialized by the client could be a spoofed source IP address where that IP address may not exist as the real TCP source.

At this point server waits up to timeout and if it does not receive the final acknowledgment from client, then it releases the resources reserved for the client.

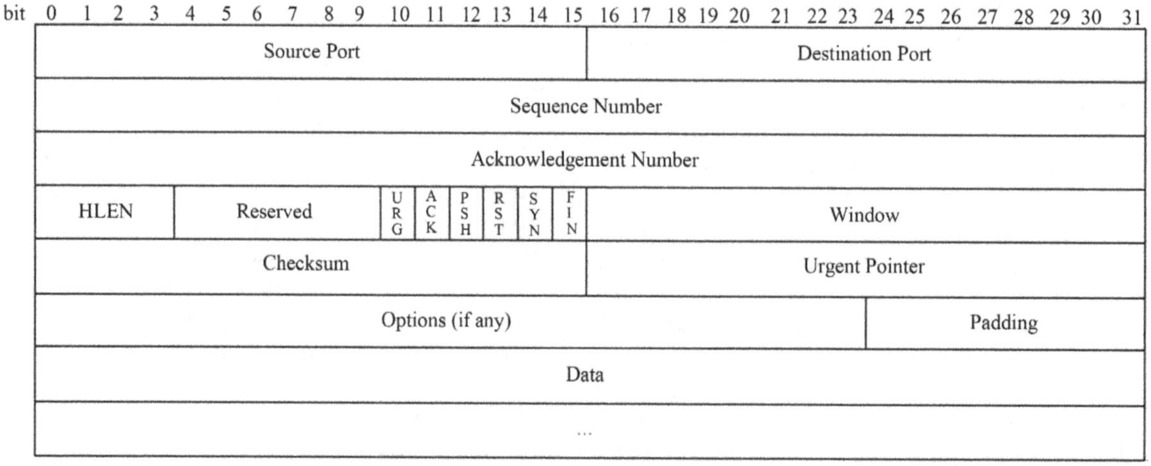

bit 0–3	4–9	10	11	12	13	14	15	16–31
Source Port								Destination Port
Sequence Number								
Acknowledgement Number								
HLEN	Reserved	URG	ACK	PSH	RST	SYN	FIN	Window
Checksum								Urgent Pointer
Options (if any)								Padding
Data								
...								

Figure 1. Transmission control protocol.

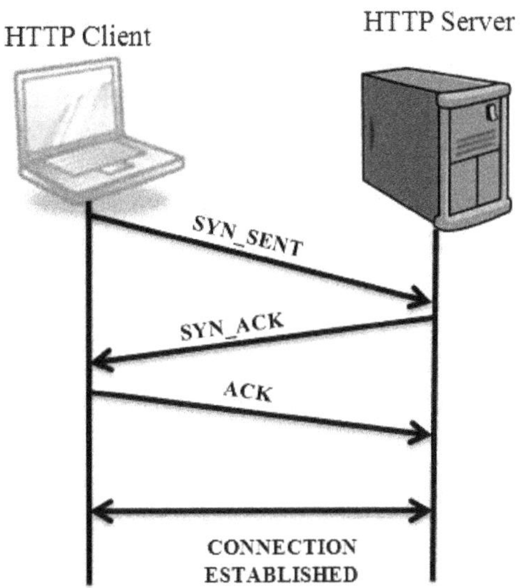

Figure 2. Three-way handshake.

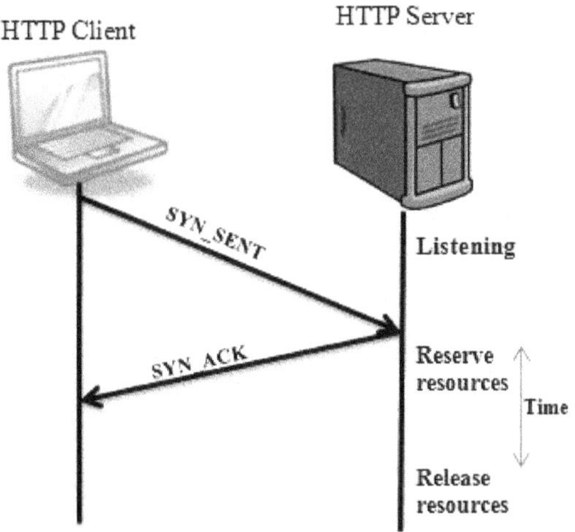

Figure 3. TCP half open connections.

2.1.1.3. TCP SYN Flood Attack

From the **Figure 4**, when the server receives a SYN segment from Internet that was initialized using a spoofed source IP address, it replies to the spoofed IP with a SYN_ACK reserving some resources for the client and waits for final ACK from the client [15]. As the address was a spoofed one, which may not available on Internet temporarily or permanently, the server waits up to timeout and releases the resources.

What happens if the server receives a flood of SYN packets from the Internet with a spoofed source IP address? Resources of the server were consumed totally deceiving the legitimate user from getting the services provided by the server. This Denial of Service attack is called TCP-SYN Flood Attack.

UDP Flood attack is simple, common and famous Layer-4 attack DoS attack. UDP Flood vulnerabilities have been discovered during the year 1998-2000. In this attack a barrage of UDP packets are sent to the victim computer either on selected UDP port or on random port (**Figure 5**). The targeted system processes the incoming datagram to determine which application it has requested on that system by refereeing the port number and in case if the requested application is not present on the system or the requested port was not opened on the targeted system, an ICMP Destination Unreachable message was to the source address from which it receives the datagram, where attackers use spoofed IP address as source address to avoid their identification. If flood of these UDP requests are sent to the targeted system, then it results in Denial of Service attack on the targeted system or the targeted network where victim needs to process all the request and needs to send ICMP Destination Unreachable messages in case if the application was not present on the system, which consumes all the resources of victim [16].

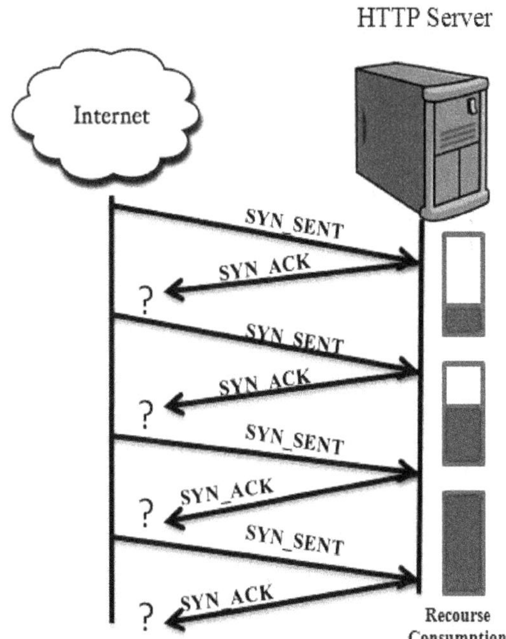

Figure 4. TCP syn flood.

2.2. Internet Control Message Protocol Based Denial of Service attacks

In this DoS attack, attacker takes advantage of ICMP protocol (**Figure 6**) in launching an attack. Internet Control message Protocol (ICMP) is used to diagnose and report any error in a network and which is of Internet Protocol (IP) suit defined in RFC 792 [17]. For example, "Destination Unreachable" is an ICMP message which is generated towards source at the time when the packet is not able to reach the destination, where source can resend the packet to the destination which is a type of error reporting message. "Ping" is an ICMP message used for checking host availability in a network.

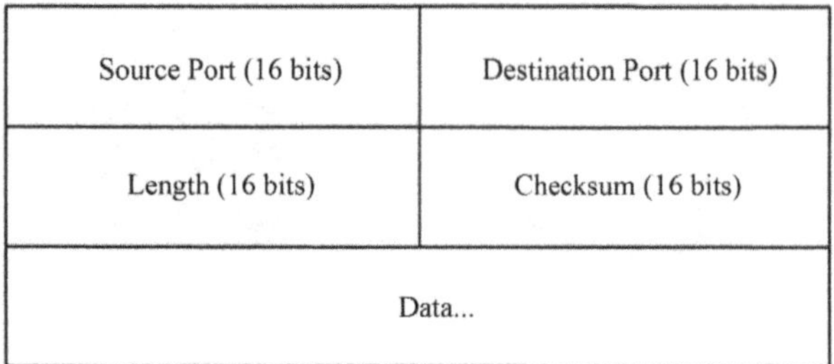

Source Port (16 bits)	Destination Port (16 bits)
Length (16 bits)	Checksum (16 bits)
Data...	

Figure 5. UDP header format.

TYPE	CODE (0)	CHECKSUM
IDENTIFER		SEQUENCE NUMBER
OPTIONNAL DATA		
....		

Figure 6. ICMP header format.

ICMP Ping is used by a user to verify the end-to-end Internet path operation, where ICMP Echo Request packet is send to the host and waits for the ICMP Echo Reply packet to confirm that the host is alive in the network [17].

The **Figure 7** shows that host "A" sends the Echo request to host "B" with source address as its own IP address and destination address as host "B" IP address. Then host "B" sends Echo reply confirming host "A" about its presence in the network, by changing the IP address of the source into an echo request as the destination address in the echo reply message. The Type code (**Figure 1**) in Echo Request is 8, and in Echo Reply is 0.

Basing on ICMP, there are so many attacks were ICMP based Ping attack and ICMP based Land attack were used in this thesis.

ICMP Ping DoS Attack

ICMP Ping DoS attack instigate from ping command line which is used to diagnose the network. As DoS attack is flooding illegitimate traffic towards the victim host, in this attack ICMP echo request packet was send towards the victim host and as the host which receives the echo request should reply with the same data to the source host with Echo reply message, the attacker intention is to consume the resources of the victim host. ICMP echo requests when flood towards the victim host, consumes all the resources of the victim in performing the job of sending echo replies for all the echo requests resulted in Denial of Service attack [18,19].

An attacker, by finding the loophole of the network or the Operating system on the victim hosts uses that vulnerability to launch an attack; this will prevents the victim from severing the legitimate users.

ICMP Ping attack is very simple to launch and was the basic of the Denial of Service attacks. And this was also a common type of attack. Victim, who came across this type of attack in a network, thinks that there was some problem in the network, but it was difficult to identify the attack, because attack traffic was similar to the original traffic [18,19].

2.3. ICMP Based Land Attack

ICMP ping is used to sense whether the host is reachable on an IP network or not. However if the host is flooded with continuous Ping Packets with same source and destination IP addresses, result in a DoS attack called ICMP Land Attack [20-23].

When the victim is flooded with continuous ICMP Echo Request having identical source and destination IP address, it needs to reply for the all Echo requests that consumes a lot of resources. As, the echo requests are having source and destination IP address identical, all the Echo replies sent by the victim are received at the victim and eventually dropped, consumes more resources then the earlier as shown in **Figure 8**.

3. Protection Features in Cisco ASA Intrusion Prevention System towards the Denial of Service Attacks

3.1. TCP-SYN Proxy Protection

Layer-4 TCP SYN attack is a well-known DoS attack. Any service that binds to TCP socket is probably vulnerable to TCP SYN flooding attacks. This includes popular web server applications for browsing, file storage and e-mail services on Internet. Protection against this attack is an important for network security.

Cisco ASA provides the SYN-Proxy protection technique to defend the TCP-SYN attack traffic. Maximum connections and maximum embryonic connections are configured, where number is an integer between 0 and 65,535. The default is 0, which means no limit on connections. The following command is used to set the number of connections on the Cisco IOS:

```
hostname(config-pmap-c)#set connection
{[conn-max number] [embryonic-conn-max number]
[per-client-embryonic-max number]
[per-client-max number]
[random-sequence-number {enable | disable}}
```

If the embryonic connection limit reaches, then the Cisco IPS responds to every SYN packet sent to the web server with a SYN-ACK, and does not pass the SYN packet to the internal web server. If the external device responds with an ACK packet, then the security appliance knows it is a valid request. The IPS then establishes

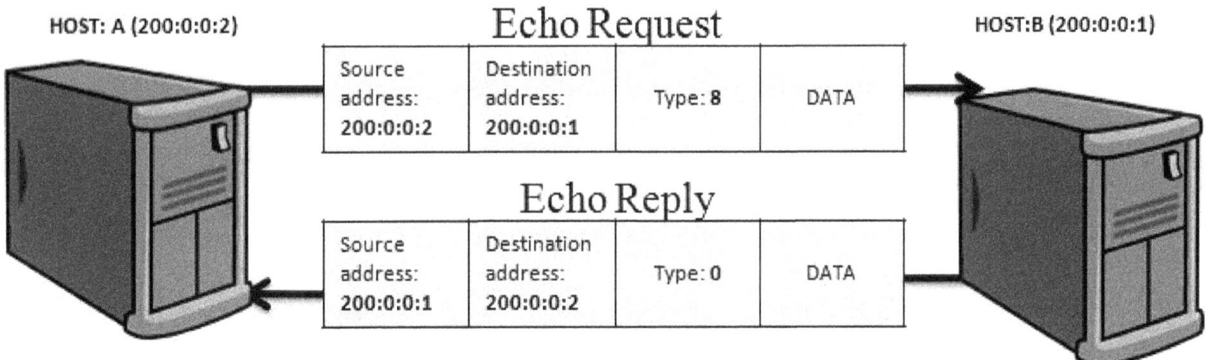

Figure 7. Ping utility.

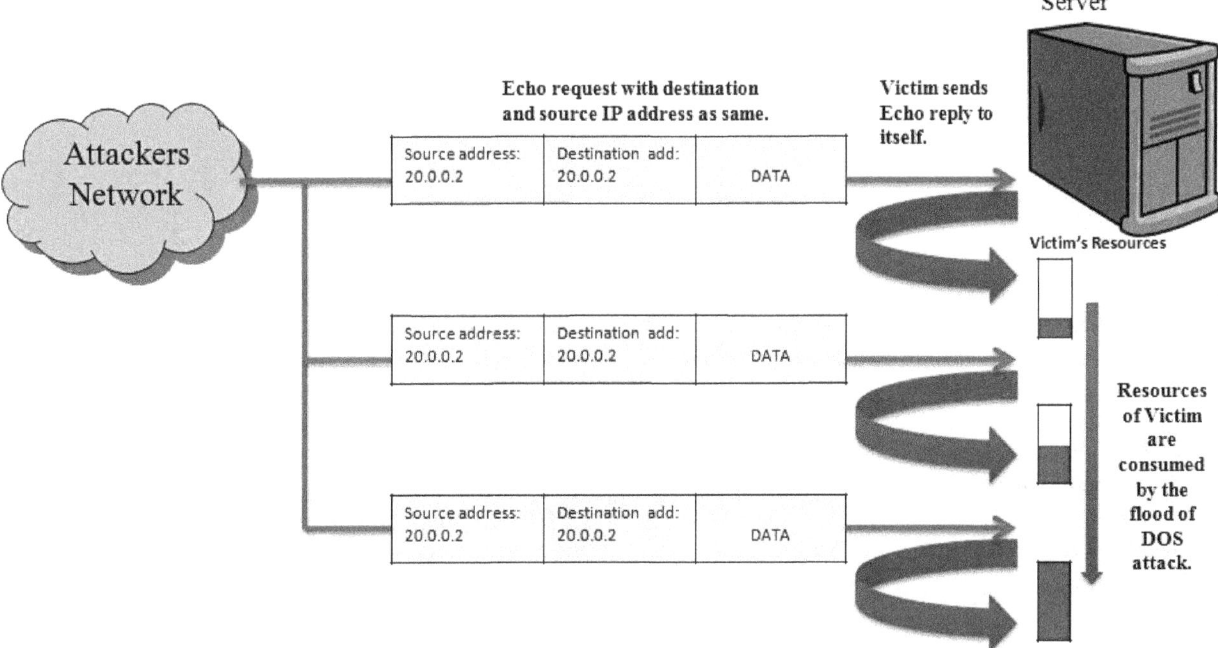

Figure 8. ICMP land attack.

a connection with the web server and joins the connections together. If it does not get an ACK back from the client, it times out that embryonic connection (**Figure 9**).

3.2. UDP Flood Protection

Flood of large number of raw UDP packets targeted at router, firewalls, IPS, IDS and end systems lead to UDP Flood denial of service attack. Many attackers use UDP based attacks, which have a capability to bring the whole network down. This can happen by attacking the Root DNS web servers, which are mainly based on UDP traffic [24-26].

Cisco ASA 5510 has a feature for UDP flood protection, which helps in defending the UDP-flood attacks by setting the threshold limit on the UDP packets. After enableing the UDP flood protection feature, once threshold level is exceeded, it invokes the UDP flood attack protection feature. If the number of UDP datagrams from one or more sources to a single destination exceeds this threshold, the security device ignores further UDP datagrams sent to that destination for the remainder of that second plus the next second as well.

3.3. ICMP Ping Attack Protection

Any IP packet that can be sent across the network can be used to execute a flooding DoS attack. Flood of ICMP echo requests toward the routers, firewalls, Web servers, IPS, IDS and End systems, that are useful for diagnoses, stresses their performance in serving the legitimate users. This stress on the systems due to illegitimate users lead to ICMP Ping flood attack.

Cisco ASA 5510, has inbuilt protection features to

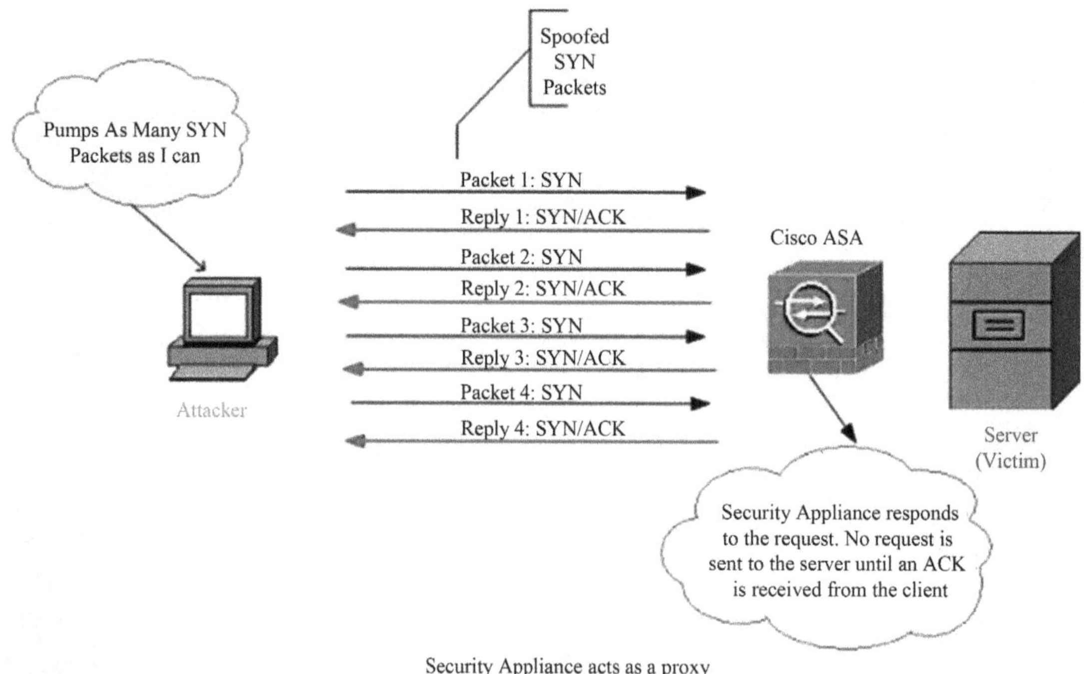

Figure 9. SYN proxy protection in Cisco ASA 5510.

protect against the Layer-3 attacks namely, Ping Flood. When enabling the ICMP flood protection feature in Cisco IPS, one can set a threshold that once exceeded invokes the ICMP flood attack protection feature. If the threshold is exceeded, the Cisco IPS ignores further ICMP echo requests for the remainder of that second plus the next second as well.

3.4. ICMP Land Attack Protection

When the victim is flooded with continuous ICMP Echo Request having identical source and destination IP address, it needs to reply for the all Echo requests that may consumes a lot of resources. As, the echo requests are having source and destination IP address identical, all the echo replies sent by the victim are received at the victim and eventually dropped. This consumes more resources. Flooding a system with such packets can overwhelm the system, causing a denial of service.

On Cisco IPS the Land attack protection was enabled by default, where it blocks the packets with same source and destination IP address as the destination IP address. In Internet, there is no possibility of facing packets with same source and destination IP address. Configuring this protection by default will helps in providing safer communication by preventing illegitimate traffic with spoofed addresses.

4. Experimental Setup

In the Networking Research Lab (NRL) at The University of Texas-Pan American, in a secured network environment we launched different types of DoS attacks on to Cisco ASA-5510. The performance of the in build protection techniques of Cisco ASA in defending the DoS attacks are observed. For this experiment the Cisco ASA—5510 IPS and Windows Web server 2003 on Intel® XeonTM 3 GHz Processor with 4 GB RAM are considered (**Figure 10**).

The maximum number of stable TCP connections that the web server can form with the legitimate users were 20,000 connections per second. The maximum number of stable legitimate TCP connections formed through the Cisco ASA 5510 IPS are 3000 connections per second. In this case, no attack traffic (illegitimate traffic) is sent towards the web server and also there is no protection (allowing all type of connections) configured on the Cisco ASA IPS.

Two cases are compared in each section; one without protection enabled on IPS and other with protection enabled on IPS, for each and every type of DoS attack. When the protection is not enabled on the IPS, it allows all the incoming connections both illegitimate and legitimate traffic. However when the protection on the IPS is enabled, IPS only allows the legitimate traffic and defend the illegitimate traffic.

3000 stable HTTP (TCP-Port 80) successful connections are maintained throughout the test period and attack traffic was applied in the range of 1 Mbps to 100 Mbps towards the web server. While executing the whole process the number of successful connections that are formed with the web server at different loads of attack traffic, amount of attack traffic reaches the web server

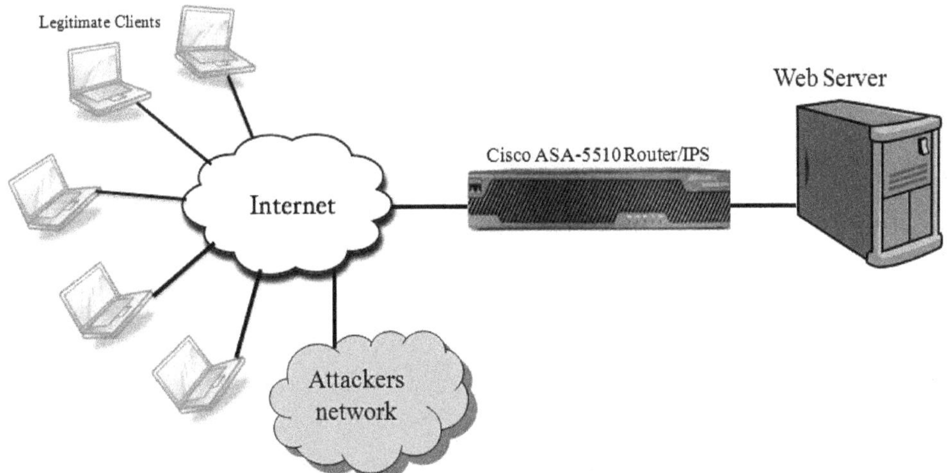

Figure 10. Experimental setup for DoS attacks on web server with Cisco ASA 5510 IPS in between.

and the replies sent by the web server for the corresponding attack load is observed and plotted.

To analyze the results more clearly, before testing the IPS along with the legitimate traffic, the resources consumed by IPS in the absence of legitimate traffic under different attack loads is recorded. These results explain the way the IPS is stressed due to the attack traffic. And these results help us in analyzing the performance of IPS with and without protection in the real time.

Analyzing all these results will help us in providing the defensive capability of Cisco ASA 5510 IPS in defending the common DoS attacks in the Internet.

5. Results and Discussions

5.1. Performance of Cisco ASA 5510 IPS under TCP-SYN Flood Attack

5.1.1. Processor Consumption by IPS under TCP-SYN without Legitimate Traffic

From the **Figures 4** and **3**, it is observed that the processor consumption increases exponentially to 30% at 60 Mbps TCP-SYN attack load and then 50% at 100 Mbps attack load. The exponential increase in the processor consumption along with the attack traffic may lead the legitimate users to denial of service. To observe the effect of this attack load in real time, the results that state the influence of attack on the number of legitimate connections are in the fallow section.

5.1.2. Performance of Cisco IPS under TCP-SYN Attack Along with the Legitimate Connections

From this experiment, it is observed that the legitimate connections are brought down to 66 per second, under TCP-SYN flood attack load of 100 Mbps without protection enabled on the ASA. When the TCP protection was enabled on the ASA it performs better compare to the case when there is no protection. In this case the connections at 100 Mbps TCP-SYN attack load are 1012 per second. When there is no protection on the ASA, at 10 Mbps attack load, successful connections recorded are 2394, and with protection the number improved to 2809. At 60 Mbps attack load, without protection successful connections are brought down to 1103 per second, which is improved by setting the threshold limit for embryonic connections records as 1821 connections per second (**Figure 11**).

The decrease of successful connections can be due to the consumption of resources on the ASA, such as processor, memory or even the bandwidth of the network. By observing the total number of received datagrams by the web server, which are the sum of legitimate packets and the attack packets, the reason behind the decrease in the successful connection rate along with the increase in attack load can be explained.

From **Figures 4** and **5**, it was observed that the number of datagram's received by the web server in the case of no protection on the ASA, are 10,000 per second at 1 Mbps attack load. The datagrams are exponentially increases and reaches to 29,000 at 10 Mbps attack load, and then to the maximum of 77,000 datagrams at 70 Mbps attack load. However at 1 Mbps attack load, the web server is forming 3000 connections per second (**Figure 12**) where 10,000 datagram's per second is recorded. The datagram's increasing with the increase in attack load are attack packets where legitimate packets are less than 10,000 per second. So, without having protection all the attack packets which may initiate the half open connections on the web server by consuming the resources are reaching the web server. Processing all these packets and maintain sessions for all these packets, may consume lot of resources (**Figure 13**).

In case, with the TCP protection enabled on the Cisco ASA, when the attack traffic reaches the threshold limit

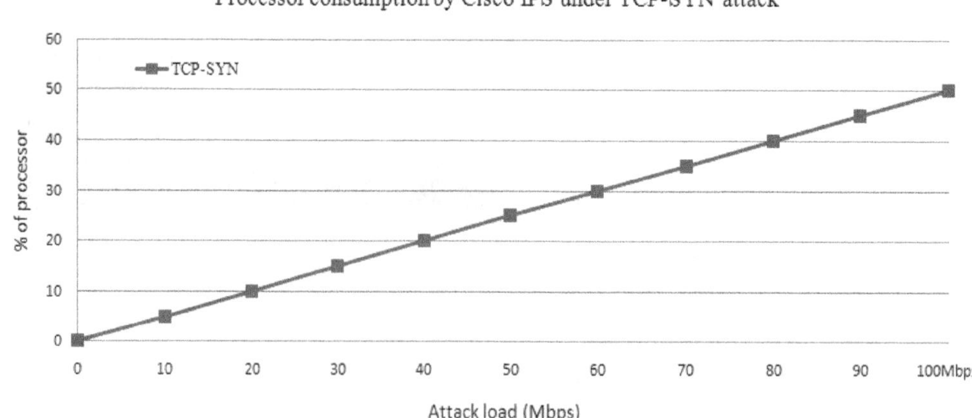

Figure 11. Processor consumption by Cisco IPS under TCP-SYN attack.

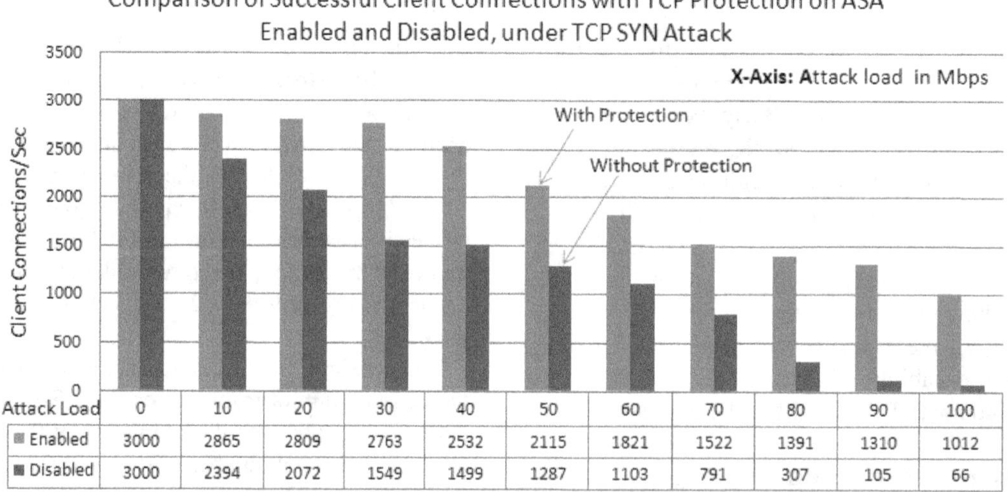

Attack Load	0	10	20	30	40	50	60	70	80	90	100
Enabled	3000	2865	2809	2763	2532	2115	1821	1522	1391	1310	1012
Disabled	3000	2394	2072	1549	1499	1287	1103	791	307	105	66

Figure 12. Successful TCP connections formed with web server under TCP-SYN flood attack, at different attack loads, compared at the time of TCP-SYN protection enabled and with the protection disabled the Cisco ASA.

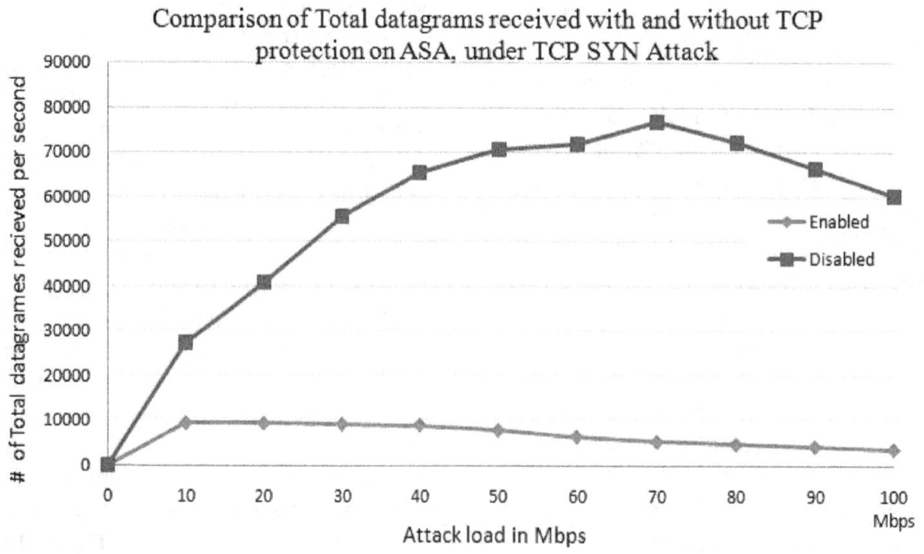

Figure 13. Comparison between total number of datagram's received by the web server at the time of ICMP protection enabled and disabled on the web server.

of 100 half-open connections, then the SYN proxy protection was enabled on the web server. This protection blocks the further SYN packets and acts as proxy. From results, (**Figure 12**) it is observed that only 10,000 datagrams are received by the IPS stably upto 10 Mbps attack load. Then, the received packets are dropped with the increasing of attack load. This explains that, processing the attack packets and protecting the web server by acting as a proxy may consumes resources on the IPS that may leaves limited resources for all the legitimate users. This results in only 1012 connections per second at 100 Mbps attack load.

5.2. Performance of Cisco ASA 5510 IPS under UDP Flood Attack

5.2.1. Processor Consumption by IPS under UDP Flood Attack without Legitimate Traffic

From the **Figure 14**, it is observed that the processor consumption reaches to 96% at 100 Mbps UDP-Flood attack load. It is exponentially increasing, with 65% at 40 Mbps attack load to 85% at 80 Mps attack load. The exponential increase in the processor consumption along with the attack traffic may lead the legitimate users to denial of service.

5.2.2. Performance of Cisco IPS under UDP-Flood Attack Along with the Legitimate Connections

From this experiment (**Figure 15**), it is observed that the legitimate connections are drops to almost zero (less than 50 connections) under UDP flood attack load of 50 Mbps without protection enabled on the ASA. With protection enabled on the ASA, it performs well compare to the case when there is no protection. However in this case the successful connections are brought down to 973 at 100 Mbps attack load. This shows that the protection on the ASA is able to serve better than the case without protection. But still, this protection on the ASA was not able to withstand the higher amounts of UDP Flood attack loads. This results in preventing 70% of the legitimate users from receiving service, from the web server at 100 Mbps attack load (**Figure 15**).

The number of attacks packets received by the web server, number of legitimate traffic received by the web server and also packets sent by the web server in reply to the received packets are observed.

From **Figures 16** and **17**, it is observed that when the UDP protection is not enabled on the ASA, maximum of 140,000 UDP attack packets reach the web server. And web server replies to all the packets received by it with Destination Unreachable messages. On the other hand when the protection is enabled on the ASA, the IPS blocks all the UDP packets that are targeted to bring down the web server and just allows the legitimate traffic. From **Figures 16** and **17**, the number of UDP packets received by the web server at the time of UDP protection enabled are zero. The replies sent by the web server to the received UDP packets are also zero because of this protection.

From **Figure 18**, it is observed that the maximum number of total datagrams received by the web server are 140,000 per second at the time of without protection enabled on it. The total datagram's indicates the sum of legitimate and attack packets. However with the protection enabled it is only 10,000 packets which are only legitimate packets. Processing all the legitimate and attack packets with no protection, and maintaining sessions for all of the packets may consume more resources than the case with protection. Even with dropping the attack packets, in order to provide protection, IPS may consume some resources when a large flood of attack packets reaches the IPS.

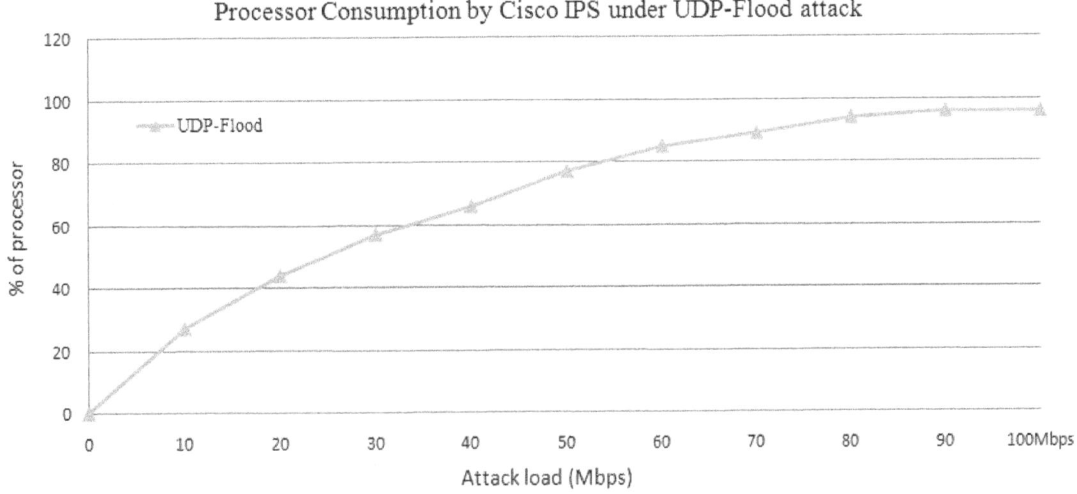

Figure 14. Processor consumption by Cisco IPS under UDP flood attack.

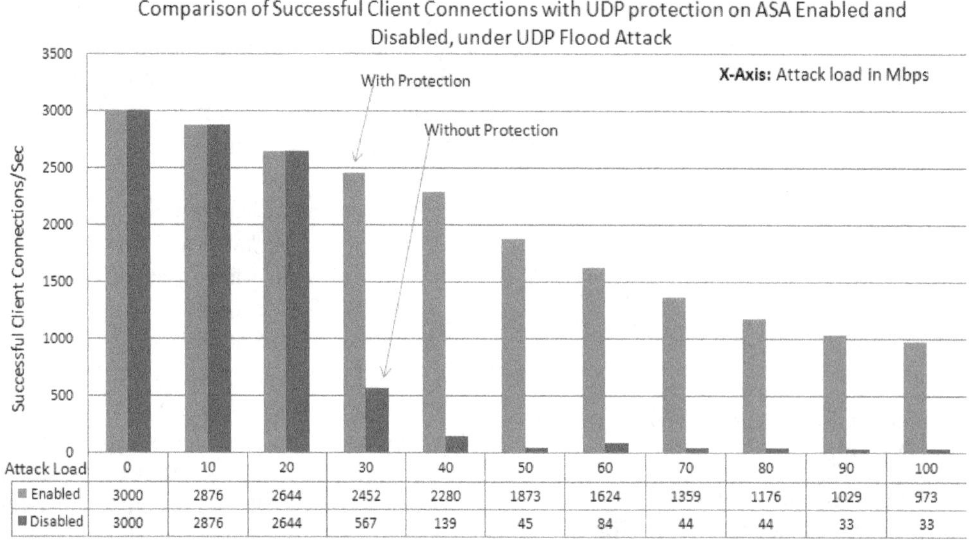

Figure 15. Successful TCP connections formed with web server under UDP flood attack, at different attack loads, compared at the time of UDP security enabled with UDP security disabled on the Cisco ASA.

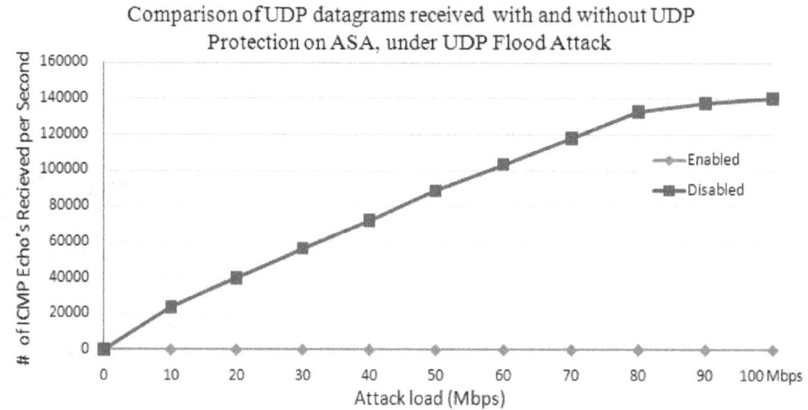

Figure 16. Comparison of UDP datagrams received by web server at the time of UDP flood protection enabled and disabled on the Cisco ASA.

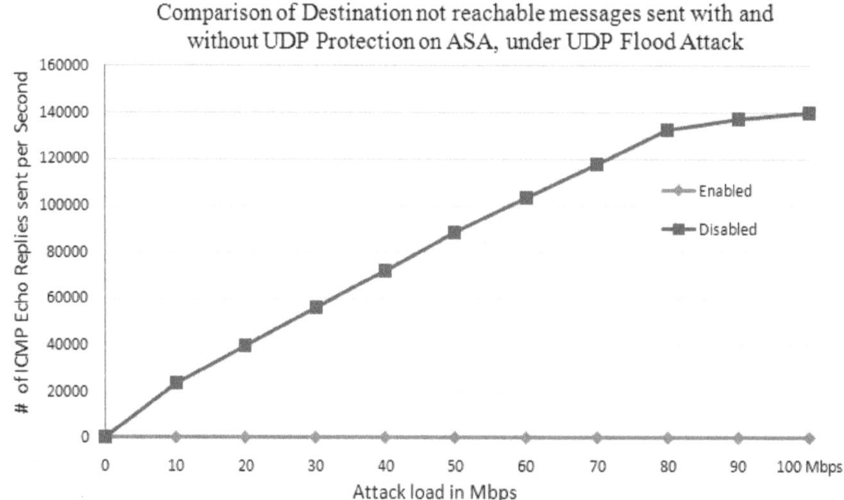

Figure 17. Comparison of Destination not reachable messages sent by web server at the time of UDP flood protection enabled and disabled on Cisco ASA.

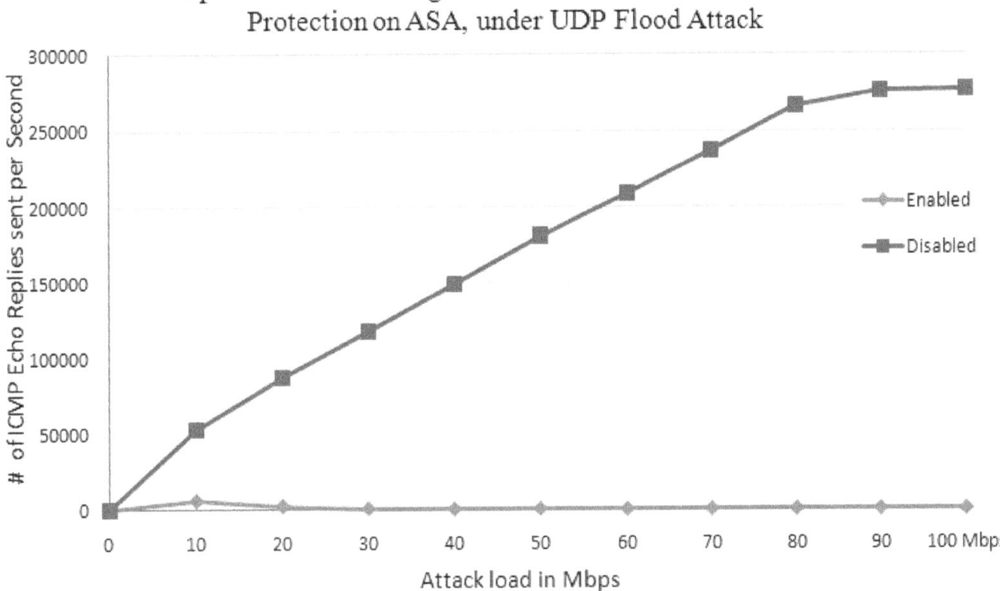

Figure 18. Comparison between total number of datagrams received by the web server at the time of ICMP protection enabled and disabled on the web server.

5.3. Performance of Cisco ASA 5510 IPS under ICMP PING Attack

5.3.1. Processor Consumption by IPS under ICMP-PING Attack without Legitimate Traffic

From the **Figure 19**, it is observed that the processor consumption reaches to 97% at 30 Mbps Ping attack load. The processor consumption of 97% by the attack traffic may lead the legitimate traffic to denial of service. To observe the effect of this attack load in real time, the influence of attack traffic on the performance of Cisco IPS is observed under stable simulated legitimate users.

5.3.2. Performance of Cisco IPS under ICMP-PING Attack Along with the Legitimate Connections

From these results (**Figure 20**), it is observed that the legitimate connections are brought down to almost zero (less than 30 connections) under ICMP Ping flood attack at attack load of 20 Mbps without protection enabled on the ASA. At the time when the protection is enabled on the ASA, it is performing better compare to the case when there is no protection. However in this case, the successful connections drops to 176 connections at 40 Mbps attack load. And at 90 Mbps attack load the successful connections are almost drops to zero. This shows that, the protection on the ASA was able to serve better than the case without protection but still this protection on the ASA was not able to withstand the higher amounts of ICMP Ping flood attack load. This still results in denial of service preventing the illegitimate users from getting service from the web server (**Figure 20**).

The decrease of successful connections can be due to the consumption of resources on the ASA, such as processor, memory or even the bandwidth of the network. These may cause the ASA to drop the legitimate users or even take more time to process the packets. The number of attack packets (Illegitimate packets) received by the web server.

From **Figures 21** and **22**, it is observed that when the ICMP protection is disabled on the ASA, maximum of 10,500 ICMP attack packets (Echo's) reaches the web server. Web server replies to all the ICMP packets received by it with echo replies. On the other hand, when the protection is enabled on the Cisco IPS, the IPS blocks all the ICMP packets that are sent to bring down the web server and just allows the legitimate traffic. So, it is observed from the **Figures 21** and **22**, the number of ICMP packets received by the web server at the time of security enable are zero. So the replies sent by the web server to the received echo's are also zero.

From **Figure 23**, it is observed that the number of total datagrams received by the web server are stable after 20 Mbps attack load at 11,000 connections per second without ICMP protection. However from **Figure 21**, the total ICMP echo's received by the web server, which are attack packets, are around 10,500 after 20 Mbps of attack load. This explains that the packets reaching the serve after the 20 Mbps of attack traffic is only the attack traffic. In case with protection enable, the total number of datagram's received by the web server decreases with increase in the attack load. And all the datagram's received by the web server are only legitimate packets, which are brought down rapidly with increase in the attack load.

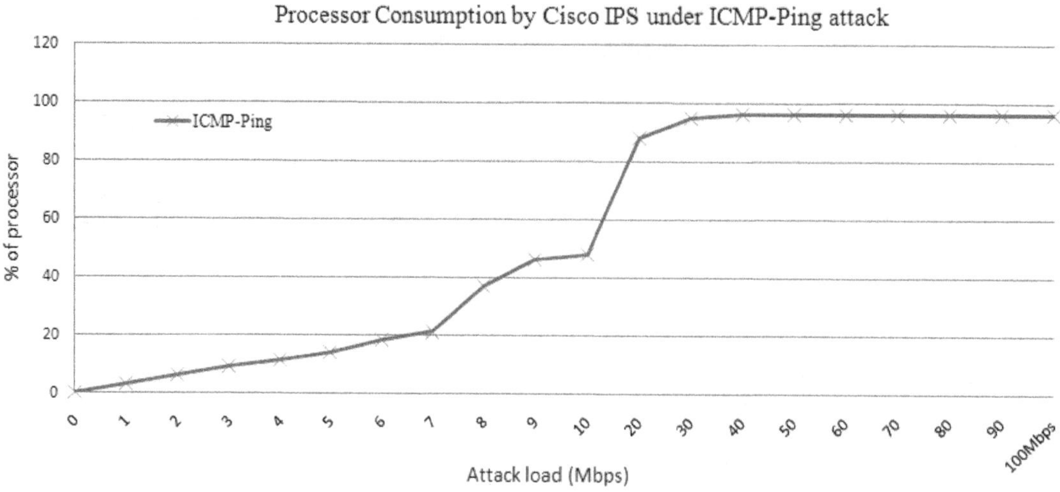

Figure 19. Processor consumption by Cisco IPS under ICMP ping attack.

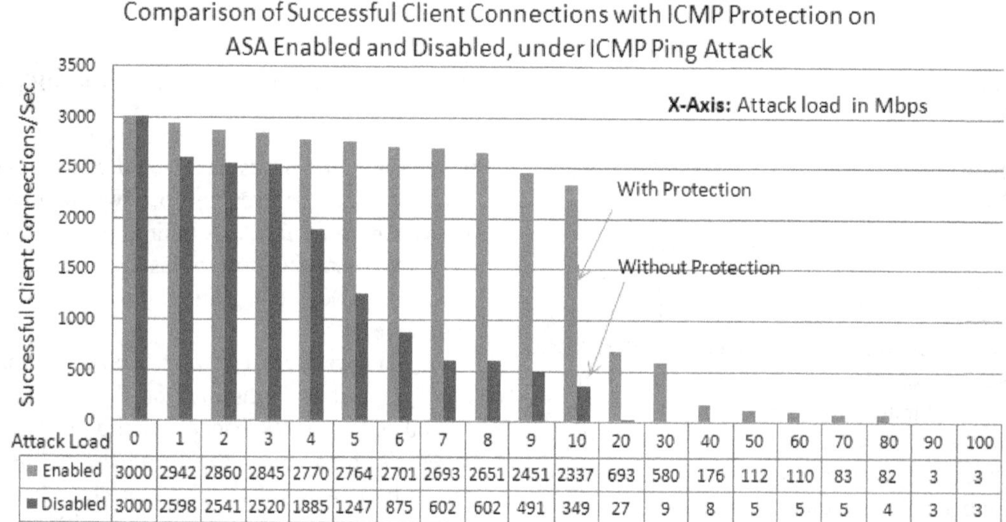

Attack Load	0	1	2	3	4	5	6	7	8	9	10	20	30	40	50	60	70	80	90	100
Enabled	3000	2942	2860	2845	2770	2764	2701	2693	2651	2451	2337	693	580	176	112	110	83	82	3	3
Disabled	3000	2598	2541	2520	1885	1247	875	602	602	491	349	27	9	8	5	5	5	4	3	3

Figure 20. Successful TCP connections formed with web server under ICMP ping flood attack, at different attack loads, compared at the time of ICMP security enabled and disabled on the Cisco ASA.

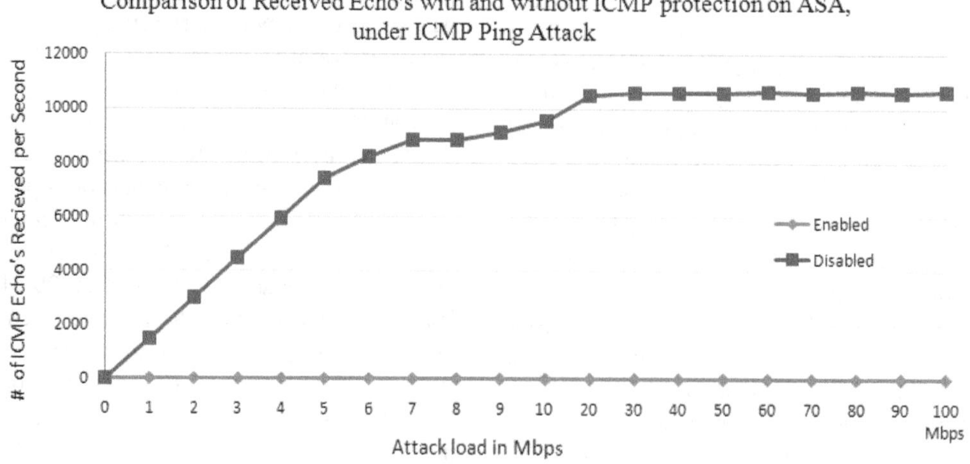

Figure 21. Number of ICMP echo's requests received by the web server with and without of ICMP protection on the Cisco ASA-IPS.

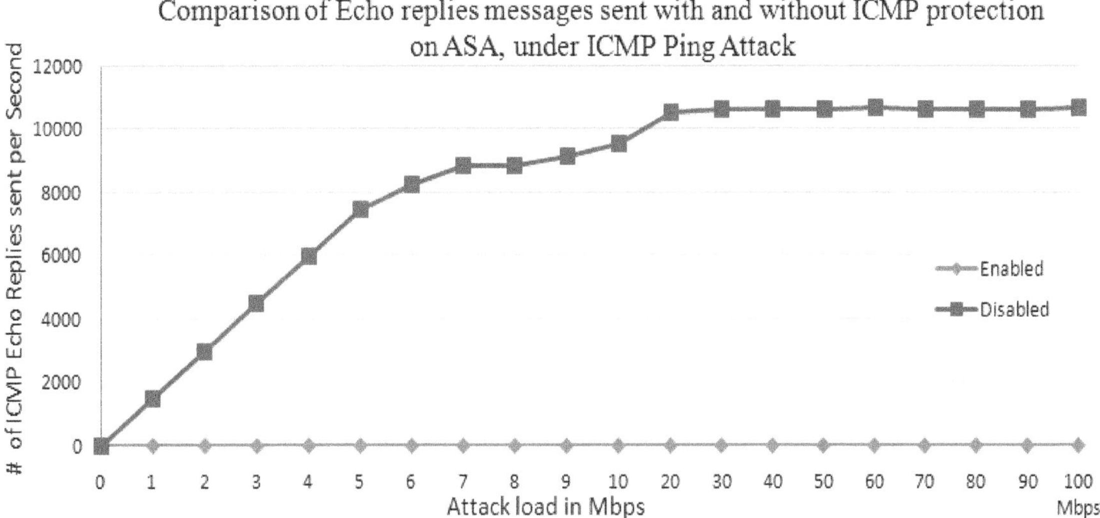

Figure 22. Number of ICMP echo's replies sent by the web server with and without of ICMP protection on the Cisco ASA-IPS.

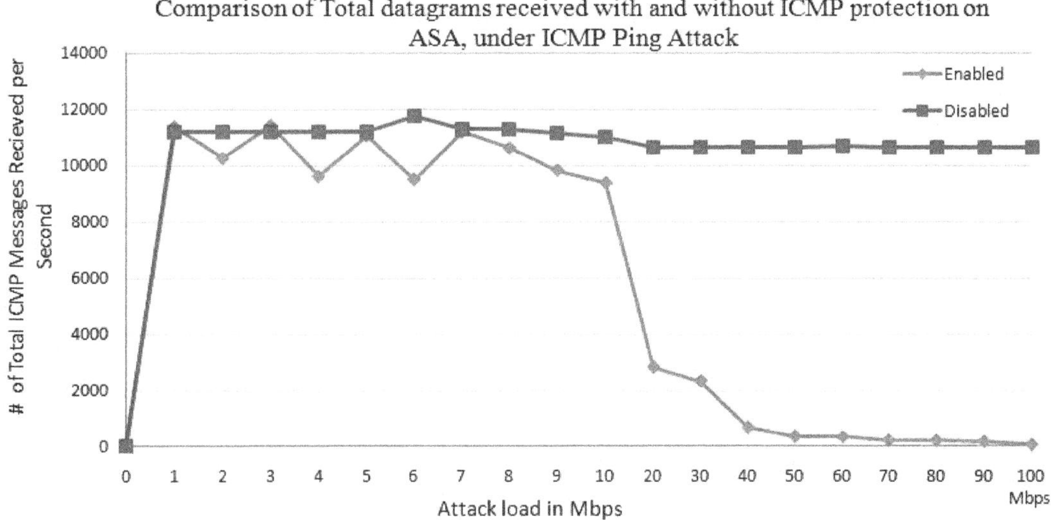

Figure 23. Total number of datagrams received by the web server with and without ICMP protection enabled on Cisco IPS.

5.4. Performance of Cisco ASA 5510 IPS under ICMP Land Attack

5.4.1. Processor Consumption by IPS under Land Attack without Legitimate Traffic

From **Figure 24**, it is observed that the processor consumption reaches to 97% at 30 Mbps Land attack load. The processor consumption of 97% by the attack traffic may lead the legitimate users to denial of service. To observe the effect of this attack load in real time, the influence of attack traffic on the performance of Cisco IPS is observed under stable simulated legitimate users.

5.4.2. Performance of Cisco IPS under ICMP-Land Attack Along with the Legitimate Connections

From this experiment (**Figure 25**), it is observed that the legitimate connections are brought down to 700 under ICMP Land attack load of 40 Mbps with default Land Attack protection enabled on the ASA. The number of connections are brought down to 633 at land attack load of 60 Mbps, and at 100 Mbps attack load total connections are 177 per second. This shows that the Land attack protection on the ASA was not able to withstand the higher amounts of ICMP Land DoS attack load. This results in preventing the maximum number of legitimate users from getting service, from the web server.

Successful TCP Connections formed with web server under ICMP Land attack, at different attack loads, with ICMP Land attack security enabled by default on the Cisco ASA.

The number of attack packets and legitimate packets received by the web server and also the packets sent by the web server in reply to the received packets are observed. It is observed that the default ICMP Land Attack

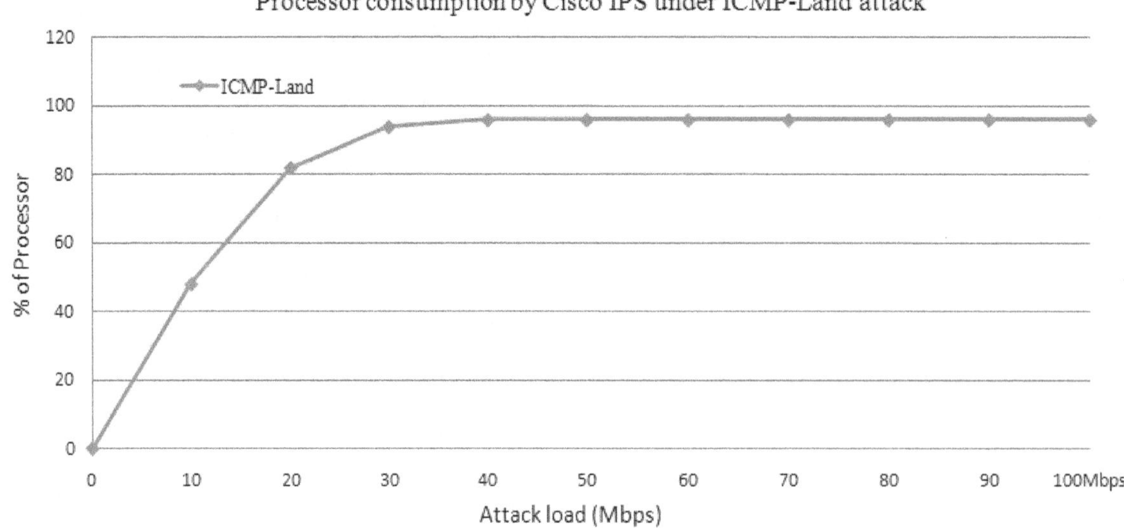

Figure 24. Processor consumption by Cisco IPS under ICMP land attack.

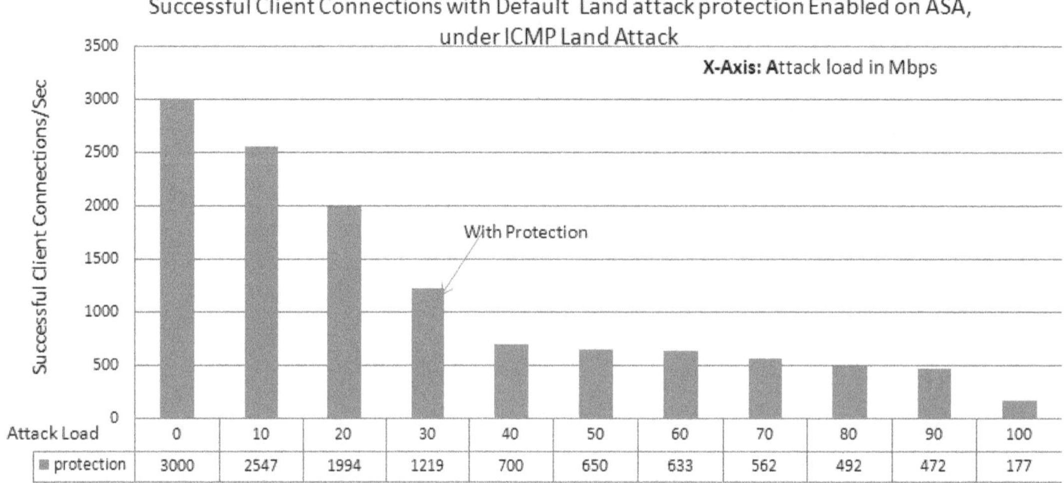

Attack Load	0	10	20	30	40	50	60	70	80	90	100
protection	3000	2547	1994	1219	700	650	633	562	492	472	177

Figure 25. Successful TCP Connections formed with web server under ICMP land attack, at different attack loads, with ICMP Land attack security enabled by default on the Cisco ASA.

protection enabled on the ASA blocks all the Land attack packets which are having the source and destination IP addresses, same as the targeted victim address. On the web server, no ICMP Echo packets are received and no Echo replies are sent by the web server.

From **Figure 26**, it is observed that the number of total datagrams received by the web server are almost 12,000 per second upto the 20 Mbps of Land attack load, with the default ICMP Land attack protection enabled on the Cisco IPS. As, the total attack packets received by the web server are zero, which explains that the packets reaching the web server are only legitimates packets (TCP-Segments). The total datagram's received by the web server from 40 Mbps of attack load are 200 datagrams per second, is may be due to the resources consumed by the Land attack packets. Where Cisco ASA needs to processes the received land attack packets and then drop them when if finds them as land attack traffic. Dropping the land attack packets helps in not allowing the land attack traffic reaching the web server and consuming resources on the web server. However processing such a huge amount of packets and allowing the legitimate traffic at the same time left the IPS with limited resources (**Figure 24**) for the legitimate traffic. This lead to no service for most of the clients, after reaching 40 Mbps attack traffic (**Figure 25**).

6. Conclusions

The evaluation of popular Cisco ASA-5510 intrusion prevention system, which is a latest technology and has built in security features for Denial of Service attacks. This was stressed under DoS attacks and the performance

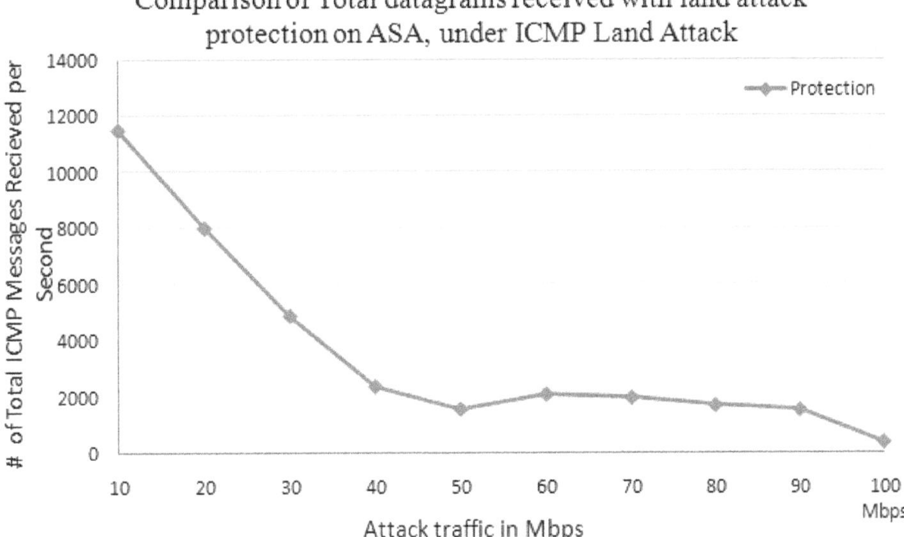

Figure 26. Comparison between total number of datagrams received by the web server at the time of ICMP protection enabled and disabled on the web server.

in defending them was observed in the paper. As Cisco is one of the leading manufacturers in security systems we selected this for our experiments. It was tested against DoS attacks such as TCP-SYN Flood, ICMP-Ping Flood, ICMP-Land and UDP-Flood attacks. The IPS is used to secure the Web server installed on Windows web server 2003. The maximum number of successful stable TCP connection rate formed with the web server was 3000 per second. We had two cases for each type of DoS attack traffic, with the protection on ASA enabled and disabled.

When the ICMP-Ping flood attack was sent towards the web server through IPS, without any protection enabled on the IPS, it was observed as almost zero connections at 20 Mbps attack load. And at 10 Mbps attack load 349 successful connections were observed and at low amount of 5 Mbps attack load the connections were brought down to 1247 per second. However, with ICMP protection enabled on the IPS, it resulted in 2337 connections at 10 Mbps attack load. And at 90 Mbps attack load the connections drops to zero. This shows improvement with the protection on the IPS, but after 40 Mbps attack load, no legitimate users were able to use the services. In the case of Land attack, Cisco ASA has the protection by default, because of the attack packets structure. The packets with same source and destination IP addresses were identified as land attack packets and were blocked. Under this attack, the connections were recorded as 1219 at attack load of 30 Mbps and at 90 Mbps it was recorded as 472 connections per second. This may be due to the overhead created by the land attack packets on the IPS in processing those packets and verifying with the default security features. This may utilizes more resources at higher attack loads. Under TCP-SYN attack without protection, the connections were brought down to 50% of the total legitimate connections at attack load of 40 Mbps, and at 80 Mbps attack load, it was recorded as less than 307 connections. However by enabling SYN protection with threshold limit for embryonic connections as 100, there was an improvement in the number of connections. At 40 Mbps the recorded connections were 2500 and at 80 Mbps they were 1300. Under UDP flood attack without protection, the number of successful connections were around 500. And with protection it was improved to around 2500. At 90 Mbps UDP flood attack traffic without protection, the connections observed were 33, with protection this was improved to 1000 connections per second.

REFERENCES

[1] CNET News, "Twitter Crippled by Denial-of-Service Attack," 2009. http://news.cnet.com/8301-13577_3-10304633-36.html

[2] R. Richardson and CSI Diretor, "2008 CSI Computer Crime & Security Survey," SCI, 2008.

[3] IBN Live World, "US Suspects N Korea Launched Internet Attack," 2009. http://ibnlive.in.com/news/us-suspects-n-korea-launched-internetattack-on-%20%20%20%20%20july-4/96715-2.html

[4] R. S. R. Gade, A. S. S, Leonel and S. Kumar, "Are Microsoft Windows Servers' Capable of Defending against Security Attacks?" *Poster Presentation of HESTEC Science Symposium*, The University of Texas-Pan American, Edinburg, 2010.

[5] "Defeating DDoS Attacks," 2010. http://www.ciscosystems.net/en/US/prod/collateral/vpndevc/ps5879/ps6264/ps5888/prod_white_paper0900aecd8011e927.html

[6] "Strategies to Protect against Distributed Denial of Ser-

vice (DDoS) Attacks," 2010. http://www.cisco.com/en/US/tech/tk59/technologies_white_paper09186a0080174a5b.shtml

[7] "DDoS Protection Solution Builds on Cisco Managed Service Leadership," 2010. http://newsroom.cisco.com/dlls/2005/prod_060605b.html

[8] "Using CAR during DOS Attacks," 2010. http://www.cisco.com/en/US/products/sw/iosswrel/ps1835/products_tech_note09186a00800fb50a.shtml

[9] Cisco Visual Networking Index Forecast, "Ascending the Managed Services Value Chain," 2008. http://www.cisco.com/en/US/solutions/collateral/ns341/ns524/ns546/white_paper_c11-5540

[10] R. Richardson, "2008 CSI Computer Crime and Security Survey," 2008. http://i.cmpnet.com/v2.gocsi.com/pdf/CSIsurvey2008.pdf

[11] The FBI Federal Bureau of Investigation, "Mafiaboy Pleads Guilty," 2010. http://www.fbi.gov/pressrel/pressrel01/mafiaboy.htm

[12] "FBI Ranks Cyber Attacks Third Most Dangerous behind Nuclear War and Weapons of Mass Destructions," 2010. http://www.tgdaily.com/security-features/40861-fbi-ranks-cyber-attacks-third-most-dangerous-behind-nuclear-war-and-wmds

[13] S. Kumar and E. Petana, "Mitigation of TCP-SYN Attacks with Microsoft's Windows XP Service Pack2 (SP2) Software," *Proceedings of the 7th International Conference on Networking of IEEE*, New York, 13-18 April 2008.

[14] P.-E. Liu and Z.-H. Sheng, "Defending against TCP SYN Flooding with a New Kind of SYN-Agent," *Proceedings of the* 2008 *International Conference on Machine Learning and Cybernetics,* Kunming, 12-15 July 2008, pp. 1218-1221.

[15] R. K. C. Chang, "Defending against Flood-Based Distributed Denial-of-Service Attack: A Tutorial," *IEEE Transactions on Communication Magazine*, Vol. 40, No. 10, 2002, pp. 42-51.

[16] W. Chen, D.-Y. Yeung and P.-E. Liu, "Defending against TCP SYN Flooding Attacks under Different Types of IP Spoofing," *Proceedings of the International Conference on Networking, International Conference on Systems and International Conference on Mobile Communications and Learning Technologies*, (*ICN/ICONS/MCL* 2006), Wuhan, 23-29 April 2006, p. 38.

[17] J. Postel, "Internet Control Message Protocol," 2010. http://www.faqs.org/rfcs/rfc792.html

[18] S. Sirisha and S. Kumar, "Is McAfee SecurityCenter/Firewall Software Providing Complete Security for Your Computer?" *Proceedings of the International Conference on Digital Society of the IEEE ICDS*, St. Maarten, 10-16 February 2010, pp. 178-181.

[19] S. Kumar, "PING Attack—How Bad Is It?" *Computers & Security Journal*, Vol. 25, No. 5, 2006, pp. 332-337.

[20] R. S. R. Gade, H. Vellalacheruvu and S. Kumar, "Performance of Windows XP, Windows Vista and Apple's Leopard Computers under a Denial of Service Attack," *Proceedings of the* 4*th International Conference on Digital Society of the IEEE ICDS*, St. Maarten, 10-16 February 2010, pp. 188-191.

[21] R. S. R. Gade, S. Sirisha, H. Vellalacheruvu and S. Kumar, "Impact of Land attack Compared for Windows XP, Vista and Apple's Leopard," *Poster Presentation of the HESTEC Science Symposium*, The University of Texas-Pan American, Edinburg, 2009.

[22] S. Kumar, *et al.*, "Can Microsoft's Service Pack2 (SP2) Security Software Prevents Smurf Attacks?" *Proceedings of the International Conference on Internet and Web Applications and Services*/*Advanced International Conference on Telecommunications of the IEEE AICT-ICIW*'06, 19-25 February 2006, p. 89.

[23] S. Kumar, "Smurf-Based Distributed Denial of Service (DDoS) Attack Amplification in Internet," *Proceedings of the* 2*nd International Conference on Internet Monitoring and Protection of the IEEE ICIMP* 2007, San Jose, 1-5 July 2007, p. 25.

[24] D. K. Y. Yau, J. C. S. Lui, L. Feng, and Y. Yeung, "Defending against Distributed Denial of Service Attacks with Max-Min Fair Server-Centric Router Throttles," *Journal of IEEE*/*ACM Transactions on Networking*, Vol. 13, No. 1, 2005, pp. 29-42.

[25] R. K. C. Chang, "Defending against Flood-Based Distributed Denial-of-Service Attack: A Tutorial," *IEEE Transactions on Communication Magazine*, Vol. 40, No. 10, 2002, pp. 42-51.

[26] Y. Xu, "Statistically Countering Denial of Service Attacks," *Proceedings of the International Conference on Communications of the IEEE ICC* 2005, Seoul, 16-20 May 2005, pp. 844-849.

6

New Video Watermark Scheme Resistant to Super Strong Cropping Attacks

Ming Tong, Tao Chen, Wei Zhang, Linna Dong
School of Electronic Engineerin, Xidian University, Xi'an, China

ABSTRACT

Firstly, the nonnegative matrix factorization with sparseness constraints on parts of the basis matrix (NMFSCPBM) method is proposed in this paper. Secondly, the encrypted watermark is embedded into the big coefficients of the basis matrix that the host video is decomposed into by NMFSCPBM. At the same time, the watermark embedding strength is adaptively adjusted by the video motion characteristic coefficients extracted by NMFSCPBM method. On watermark detection, as long as the residual video contains the numbers of the least remaining sub-blocks, the complete basis matrix can be completely recovered through the decomposition of the nonnegative matrix of the least remaining sub-blocks in residual videos by NMFSCPBM, and then the complete watermark can be extracted. The experimental results show that the average intensity resistant to the various regular cropping of this scheme is up to 95.97% and that the average intensity resistant to the various irregular cropping of this scheme is up to 95.55%. The bit correct rate (BCR) values of the extracted watermark are always 100% under all of the above situations. It is proved that the watermark extraction is not limited by the cropping position and type in this scheme. Compared with other similar methods, the performance of resisting strong cropping is improved greatly.

Keywords: Digital Watermarking; Cropping Attack; Geometric Attacks; Nonnegative Matrix Factorization (NMF); Sparseness Constrain

1. Introduction

The watermarking robustness has been a focus in multimedia research field, and how to resist geometric attacks is the hotspot and difficulty of the study [1]. Geometric attacks destroy the synchronization between the watermark and the videos, which seriously affect the robustness of the watermarking and pose a deadly threat to the watermarking security. At the same time, with the appearance and maturity of a variety of video signal processing tools, the video data can be cropped, copied and tampered in various forms and different degrees much more conveniently, faster and more casually. Especially to strong cropping, the embedded watermark information is cropped directly and enormously and the copyright of digital video products is facing serious challenges. How to extract and recover the complete watermark in residual videos has always troubled researchers [2]. Consequently, the research on video watermark methods resisting to strong cropping attacks can help strengthening the copyright authentication and management, standardizing the market of video products, and solving the technology bottleneck problem of commercializing watermark, which has important academic research value and extensive market application prospect.

A four-level dual-tree complex wavelet transform (DT CWT) is applied to every video frame of the host video in [3], which embeds the watermark in the coefficients of low frequency sub-band. This method takes the advantage of perfect reconstruction, shift invariance, and good directional selectivity of DT CWT, and can resist the cropping attacks with a certain strength. In [4], the watermark is embedded into 8 × 8 sub-blocks of each I-frame, which is robust to row and column cropping attacks with small strength. Since the geometrical distortions operations for every frame along the time axis in a video sequence are the same [5], the watermark is embedded into the same position in the video frame by modifying the pixels of texture complex or sports intense area. But the information of the watermarks embedded by this method is less, and the robustness is greatly influenced by host carrier characteristics. So this method cannot resist cropping attacks. In [6], the watermark is embedded into the singular value of the coefficient matrix of nonnegative matrix factorization (NMF). This method is robust to noise, filtering and other general attacks, but cannot resist strong cropping attacks. Theoretical analysis and experimental results show that most existing video watermarking methods [2-7] resisting to geometric attack can resist cropping attacks with smaller strength, but are sensitive to strong cropping attacks.

Nonnegative matrix factorization (NMF) is a matrix factorization method under the condition that all the elements of the matrix are nonnegative, which can greatly reduce the dimensions of the data. The decomposition characteristics meet the experience of human visual perception, and the decomposition results have interpretability and clear physical meaning. Since it is proposed, NMF has been paid to great attentions, and it succeeds in the application to pattern recognition, computer vision and image engineering etc [8-11].

This paper proposes a new video watermarking scheme based on nonnegative matrix factorization with sparseness constraints on parts of the basis matrix (NMFSCPBM), in which the watermark is embedded into the basis matrix of NMFSCPBM. It uses video motion coefficients to adaptively control the watermark embedding strength. This scheme can resist various high-intensity cropping attack, and experimental results show the effectiveness of this scheme.

2. Complete Basis Matrix Recovery and Video Motion Components Extraction Based on NMFSCPBM

The NMF with sparseness constraints (NMFSC) method is proposed in [12], which uses a nonlinear projection operator to achieve the precise control of the sparseness by adding sparseness constraints in all basis vectors. But the data is described insufficiently under higher sparseness constraints. A NMFSCPBM method is proposed in this paper, in which controllable sparseness constraints are added in the part of basis vectors. Not only can the NMFSCPBM method extract video motion components quickly and correctly, and filter out the static background interference completely, but also solve the problems of the NMFSC method under higher sparseness constraints. Meanwhile it reduces the decomposition error and speeds up the convergence rate.

2.1. NMFSCPBM Model Construction

Sparse matrix is the matrix that most of the elements are zero or approach to zero and only a few are nonzero. The sparse degree of a vector is defined as Equation (1).

$$\text{sparseness}(y) = \frac{\sqrt{n} - \left(\sum |y_i|\right) / \sqrt{\sum y_i^2}}{\sqrt{n} - 1} \quad (1)$$

where n is the dimension of y [12].

So the NMFSCPBM can be transformed into the following constrained optimization problem that given a nonnegative matrix B of size $m \times n$, solve the basis matrix W of size $m \times r$ and coefficient matrix H of size $r \times n$, where r is the decomposition dimension of B.

If squared Euclidean distance D of primitive matrix and reconstructed matrix is defined as the target evaluation function, shown as Equation (2), which is used to describe the error between primitive matrix B and reconstructed matrix WH, W and H should satisfy the condition of Equation (3).

$$D(B,\ WH) = \sum_{ij} \left[B_{ij} - (WH)_{ij} \right]^2 \quad (2)$$

$$\begin{cases} \min\ \ D(B,\ WH), W \ge 0, H \ge 0 \\ \text{sparseness}(w_i) = s_i, \quad i = 1,\ 2,\ \cdots,\ z(z < r) \end{cases} \quad (3)$$

where w_i is the ith column of the basis matrix I, and s_i is the expected sparseness of w_i.

The iteration rules of NMFSCPBM are described as follows:

1) Basis matrix W:

$$\begin{cases} W_{ij} = W_{ij} - \lambda \sum_k (WH - B)_{ik} H_{jk} \\ W_{ij} = \begin{cases} W_{ij}, if\ W_{ij} \ge 0 \\ 0,\ else \end{cases} \\ w_i = L(w_i) \end{cases} \quad (4)$$

where $L(w_i)$ is performing nonlinear projection operation to w_i [12].

2) Coefficient matrix H:

$$H_{kj} \leftarrow H_{kj} \frac{\left(W^T B\right)_{kj}}{\left(W^T WH\right)_{kj}} \quad (5)$$

Firstly, the definitions of some parameters used in iterative process are given. L is iterations. s is sparseness degree. W_{new} is the sparse constraint matrix to be added. w_k is the kth column of W_{new}. $\text{sparseness}(w_k, s)$ is the adding sparseness constraints with the sparseness degree s for w_k. w_k is the column vector after the sparse constraint. W_{newj} is sparseness constraints matrix. dw is intermediate variable, λ is penalty factor. β is penalty factor threshold. τ' is the convergence error threshold of objective function. T is transpose operation. Therefore, the iterative steps of NMFSCPBM can be described below. The algorithm input is B, r, and L. The output is W and H.

Step 1. Initialize β, set the loop variable I = 1, and initialize W and H to random positive matrices.

Step 2. $H = H \otimes \dfrac{\left(W^T B\right)}{\left(W^T WH\right)}, D(B,\ WH) = \|B - WH\|^2$.

Step 3. $dw = (WH - B)H^T,\ \lambda = 1/2,\ j = 1$.

Step 4. Add partly sparseness constraints to W and start the iteration.

(a) $W_{new} = W - \lambda \times dw$.

(b) $w_k' = \text{sparseness}(w_k,\ s), k = 1,\ \cdots,\ z.\ (z < r)$.

(c) $D(B,\ W_{newj}H) = \|B - W_{newj}H\|^2$.

(d) If $D(B,\ W_{newj}H) < D(B,\ WH)$ or $\lambda < \beta$, then $W = W_{newj}$, turn to Step 5. Otherwise, return to Step 4(a), and set $\lambda = \lambda/2,\ j = j+1$.

Step 5. If $\|B - WH\|_F^2 < \tau'$ or $i = L$, then exit. Otherwise, return to Step 2, and set $i = i+1$.

2.2. Complete Basis Matrix Recovery Based on the Least Remaining Sub-Blocks

First of all, the definition of least remaining sub-blocks is given, followed by the **Theorem 1** and its proof, which is the theoretical basis of resisting strong cropping attack of this scheme. Here, the residual video is defined as the remaining of the watermarked video after it is suffered from cropping attacks.

The number of least remaining sub-blocks is defined as the number of the least complete video sub-blocks needed to recover the complete basis matrix from the residual video.

Set the basic NMF model $B_{m\times n} = W_{m\times r} \times H_{r\times n}$. b_i is the ith column of *B*. h_i is the ith column of *H*. $B_{m\times n} = [b_1,\ b_2,\ \cdots,\ b_n]$ and $H_{r\times n} = [h_1,\ h_2,\ \cdots,\ h_n]$ are substituted in the basic model of NMF, then:

$$[b_1,\ b_2,\ \cdots,\ b_n] = W_{m\times r} \times [h_1,\ h_2,\ \cdots,\ h_n] \tag{6}$$

Outspread Equation (6), then Equation (7) is obtained.

$$b_i = W_{m\times r} \times h_i \quad i \in [1, n] \tag{7}$$

Firstly, perform blocking preprocessing to video, shown as **Figure 1**. The rules of blocking are as follows. Divide original video *V* into sub-blocks with size of $a \times a \times K$ along the temporal axis, and outspread each sub-block as one column of nonnegative matrix *B*. Let C_j be the jth sub-block of *V*, then:

See the Equation (8).

where $\lceil\ \rceil$ denotes rounding operation toward 0, mod() denotes modulus operation, *K* is the number of video frames, $i = 1,\ 2,\ \cdots,\ Ka^2$, and $k = 1, 2, \cdots, K$.

Actually, cropping attacks may occur in anywhere of the video. If video sub-blocks at its position suffer from cropping attacks, the corresponding data in the data matrix directly set to 0, shown as **Figure 2**. Let *c* denote the number of remaining complete sub-blocks after strong cropping attacks. For convenience, the remaining complete sub-blocks are rearranged from 1, 2, ⋯, *c* according to blocking order. Then the data matrix B', the coefficient matrix H' and the base matrix W corresponding to the remaining sub-blocks are as follows:

$$B' = \begin{bmatrix} b_{11} & b_{12} & \cdots & b_{1c} \\ b_{21} & b_{22} & \cdots & b_{2c} \\ \vdots & \vdots & & \vdots \\ b_{m1} & b_{m2} & \cdots & b_{mc} \end{bmatrix},\quad H' = \begin{bmatrix} h_{11} & h_{12} & \cdots & h_{1c} \\ h_{21} & h_{22} & \cdots & h_{2c} \\ \vdots & \vdots & & \vdots \\ h_{r1} & h_{r2} & \cdots & h_{rc} \end{bmatrix},$$

$$W = \begin{bmatrix} w_{11} & w_{12} & \cdots & w_{1r} \\ w_{21} & w_{22} & \cdots & w_{2r} \\ \vdots & \vdots & & \vdots \\ w_{m1} & w_{m2} & \cdots & w_{mr} \end{bmatrix},$$ where r is the dimension of nonnegative matrix factorization. According to Equation (7), Equation (9) is obtained.

$$B' = W \cdot H' \tag{9}$$

Equation (9) shows that after the video suffers strong cropping attacks, B' is obtained by Equation (8) and H' and complete matrix W can be obtained by the iteration rules of NMFSCPBM. Therefore, the following **Theorem 1** is established.

Theorem 1: When the watermarked video suffers from strong cropping attacks, as long as the residual video contains the number of least remaining sub-blocks and meets $c \ge r$, the complete basis matrix W can be recovered from residual video uniquely and correctly.

Theorem 1 is proved as follows. Transpose Equation (9) to obtain Equation (10).

$$H'^T \cdot W^T = B'^T \tag{10}$$

Take B', H' and W into Equation (10), then Equation (11) is obtained.

See the Equation (11).

Let $w_1 = [w_{11}\ w_{12}\ \cdots\ w_{1r}]^T, w_2 = [w_{21}\ w_{22}\ \cdots\ w_{2r}]^T$, $\cdots,\ w_m = [w_{m1}\ w_{m2}\ \cdots\ w_{mr}]^T, b_1 = [b_{11}\ b_{12}\ \cdots\ b_{1c}]^T$, $b_2 = [b_{21}\ b_{22}\ \cdots\ b_{2c}]^T,\ \cdots,\ b_m = [b_{m1}\ b_{m2}\ \cdots\ b_{mc}]^T$, then Equation (11) is converted into:

$$B(i, j) = \begin{cases} C_j(\text{mod}(i,\ a), \lceil i/a \rceil - a\times(k-1),\ k) & \text{if } \text{mod}(i,\ a) \ne 0 \\ C_j(a, \lceil i/a \rceil - a\times(k-1), k) & \text{if } \text{mod}(i,\ a) = 0 \end{cases} \tag{8}$$

$$\begin{bmatrix} h_{11} & h_{21} & \cdots & h_{r1} \\ h_{12} & h_{22} & \cdots & h_{r2} \\ \vdots & \vdots & & \vdots \\ h_{1c} & h_{2c} & \cdots & h_{rc} \end{bmatrix} \cdot \begin{bmatrix} w_{11} & w_{21} & \cdots & w_{m1} \\ w_{12} & w_{22} & \cdots & w_{m2} \\ \vdots & \vdots & & \vdots \\ w_{1r} & w_{2r} & \cdots & w_{mr} \end{bmatrix} = \begin{bmatrix} b_{11} & b_{21} & \cdots & b_{m1} \\ b_{12} & b_{22} & \cdots & b_{m2} \\ \vdots & \vdots & & \vdots \\ b_{1c} & b_{2c} & \cdots & b_{mc} \end{bmatrix} \tag{11}$$

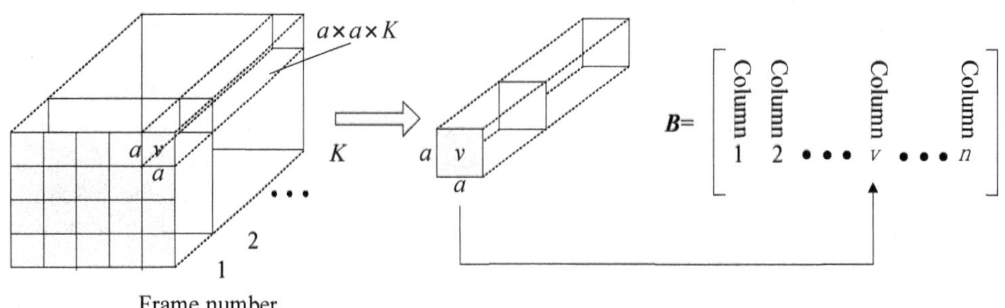

Figure 1. Video blocking of this paper.

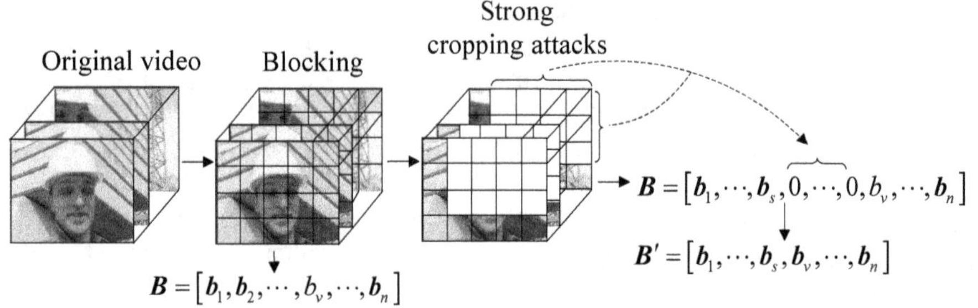

Figure 2. Vide suffer from strong cropping.

$$H'^{T}\cdot[w_1 \quad w_2 \quad \cdots \quad w_m]=[b_1 \quad b_2 \quad \cdots \quad b_m] \quad (12)$$

Let $A = H'^{T}$, then Equation (12) can be converted to the following linear equations, shown as Equation (13), where A is the coefficient matrix of each equations and $W^T = [w_1 \quad w_2 \quad \cdots \quad w_m]$ is the unsolved unknown vectors.

$$\begin{cases} Aw_1 = b_1 \\ Aw_2 = b_2 \\ \quad \vdots \\ Aw_m = b_m \end{cases} \quad (13)$$

What follows is: taking the linear equation $Aw_1 = b_1$ as example, the existence and uniqueness of its solution is discussed. By the uniqueness of nonnegative matrix decomposition results, we know that, $Aw_1 = b_1$ is solvable and has a unique solution. In fact, the necessary and sufficient conditions of r-dimensional homogeneous linear equations are $R(A)=R(\overline{A})=r$, where $\overline{A}=[A \quad b_1]=[H'^{T} \quad b_1]$ is the augmented matrix of A, $R(A)$ and $R(\overline{A})$ are the rank of A and $\overline{A}$ respectively, $R(A)\le \min(r,c)$, and $R(\overline{A})\le \min(r+1,c)$. It can be divided into three cases. 1) If $c<r$ and $R(A)=R(\overline{A})\le c<r$, $Aw_1 = b_1$ has infinite solutions; 2) If $c\ge r$ and $R(A)=R(\overline{A})<r$, $Aw_1 = b_1$ has infinite solutions. The above two cases violate to uniqueness of the nonnegative matrix factorizing results, the solutions are rejected. 3) If $c\ge r$ and $R(A)=R(\overline{A})=r$, $Aw_1 = b_1$ has the unique solution. Similarly, other equations have the same conclusions.

We can see from the above solution process, if $c\ge r$ and $R(A)=R(\overline{A})=r$, w_1, w_2, $\cdots$, w_m separately has unique solution, or the base matrix W has a unique solution. In other words, when the watermarked video suffers from strong cropping attacks, as long as the residual video contains complete video sub-blocks and the number meets $c\ge r$, the complete basis matrix W can be recovered from residual video uniquely and correctly. Namely, **Theorem 1** is established. Experimental results of this paper verify the correctness of theoretical analysis.

2.3. Video Motion Components Extraction Based on NMFSCPBM

The basis matrix and coefficient matrix can be obtained by nonnegative matrix factorizing. Basis matrix represents the major features of video. Coefficient matrix is the linear projection of nonnegative matrix to basis matrix and represents the local feature weights of video. Video frames can be seen as linear weighted sum of the static components and motion components. In general, the static components are nonsparse, while the motion components are sparse. So motion component can be separated from the static background by controlling sparseness constrains of the basis matrix, and then extract the motion components. The motion component extraction processes based on NMFSCPBM includes:

1) Video pre-processing. Take the target frame of the movement components to be extracted as the center for the original video $V(m_x \times m_y \times K)$ and choose the forward and the next l frames separately. Let the total $2l+1$ frames compose of a video frame group V'. Outspread V' one-dimensionally as one column of non-

negative matrix *B*, shown as Equation (14), where the size of video frame is $m_x \times m_y$, $i = 1, 2, \cdots, m_x m_y$, $j = 1, 2, \cdots, 2l+1$. The parameter l needs a reasonable choice. If l is chosen too large, calculation is risen significantly. If l is chosen too small, there have no obvious motion information between video frames.

$$B(i, j) = V'(\lceil i/m_x \rceil, \ \mathrm{mod}(i, m_x), j) \tag{14}$$

2) NMFSCPBM factorization. Perform NMFSCPBM to matrix *B*, and set *r* as the factorization dimension. Add sparseness constraints to the $(r-1)$ basis vectors, so the basis vectors constrained sparseness $w_i \ (i = 1, 2, \cdots, r-1)$ represents the motion components of video [12].

3) Solving Video motion components. Motion components M of target frame can be obtained by weighting and summing to the $(r-1)$ motion components, shown as Equation (15).

$$M = \sum_{l=1}^{r-1} w_i H_{i,l+1} \tag{15}$$

where, $H_{i,l+1}$ is the weighting coefficient of basis vectors w_i corresponding to target frame. For each pixels of the target frame, there is one element in M which is corresponding to it, M has the same size with target frame, the bigger of the element in M, the more intensity of the corresponding pixels moving in target frame.

Motion components extracted by the NMFSCPBM and other similar methods are shown in **Figure 3**. It can be seen that, the motion components in **Figure 3(b)** extracted by the proposed method filter out the static background interference completely, and show the trajectory clearly compared with **Figure 3(a)**. **Figure 3(c)** cannot distinguish the moving target from static background and cannot show the trajectory. **Figure 3(d)** has improved a little compared with **Figure 3(c)**, but still cannot separate the moving target from static background completely. To quantitatively assessment the effectiveness of the motion components extraction of this paper, the matching rate [13] τ is defined to evaluate as follows:

$$\tau = \frac{\sum_{x,y \in R} I(x,y) \times \mathrm{SMD}(x,y)}{\sqrt{\sum_{x,y \in R} I(x,y) \times I(x,y)} \cdot \sqrt{\sum_{x,y \in R} \mathrm{SMD}(x,y) \times \mathrm{SMD}(x,y)}} \tag{16}$$

where $\mathrm{SMD}(x,y)$ is the motion components extracted, $I(x,y)$ is the manually specified target motion area, and R is the target frame. The more the τ is close to 1, the more matching of the extracted motion features compared with the features specified motion area. When the extracted motion features are exactly the same with the features specified motion area, $\tau = 1$.

The experiment chooses "hall", "stefan" and "tennis" as test videos. (http://trace.eas.asu.edu/yuv/index.html).

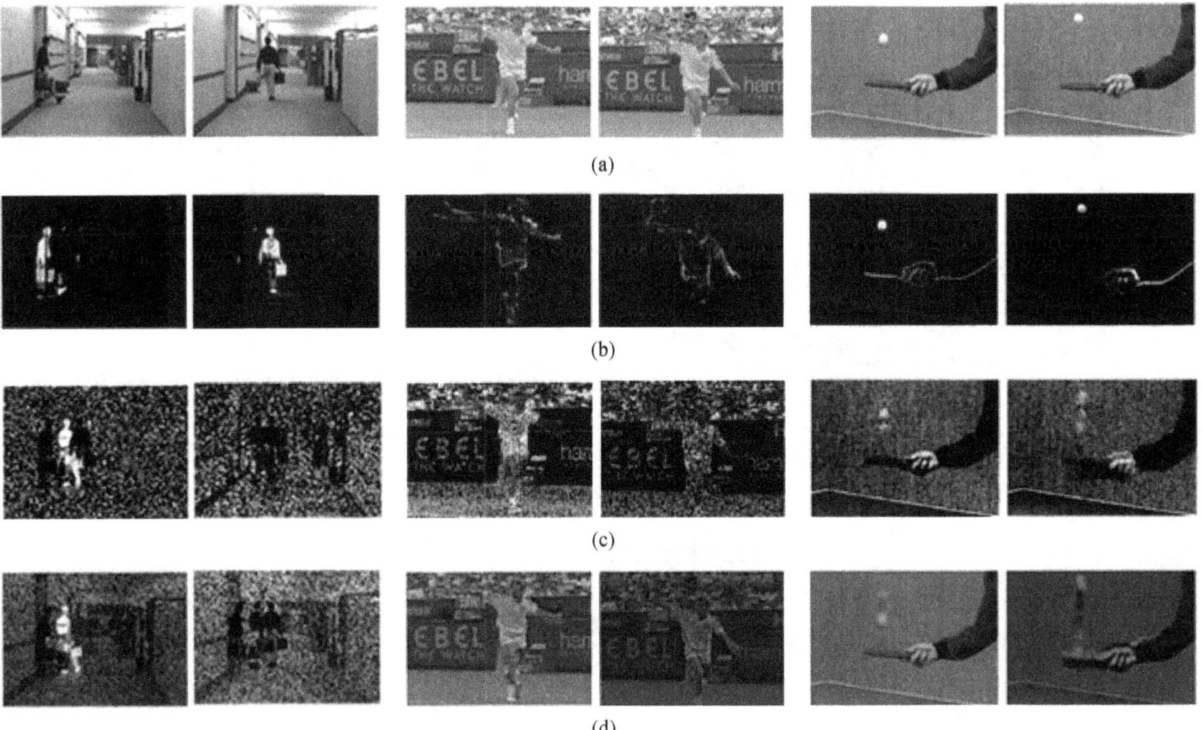

Figure 3. Motion components extraction results obtained by NMFSCPBM method and other similar methods. (a) Original video; (b) Motion components extraction results obtained by NMFSCPBM; (c) Motion components extraction results obtained by NMFSC; (d) Motion components extraction results obtained by NMF.

Compute the matching rate of the 25th fame and the 55th frame in "hall", the 26th frame and the 30th frame in "stefan", and the 16th frame and the 18th frame in "tennis", respectively. The experiment sets $l=5$, and experimental results are shown in **Figure 4**. It can be seen that the matching rates of this paper are more close to 1 compared with other methods. The average matching rate of this paper is 0.8907, NMF is 0.5371, and NMFSC is 0.4070.

3. Watermark Embedding and Extraction

Watermark embedding. The general watermark methods based on the NMF attempt to change the coefficient matrix by various signal processing operations to accomplish watermark embedding [6], but the robustness is subjected to comparative limitation. As a linear expression method, the significant advantage of NMF lies in that the basis matrix is changeable [10] and that is robust to cropping attack [9]. Therefore, this scheme embeds the watermark into the basis matrix that is decomposed into by NMFSCPBM. When the watermarked video suffers from strong cropping attacks, known by Chapter 2.2 of this paper, as long as the residual video contains the numbers of least remaining sub-blocks, the complete basis matrix W' can be completely recovered and then the complete watermark can be extracted. The watermark embedding schematic diagram of the proposed scheme is shown in **Figure 5.**

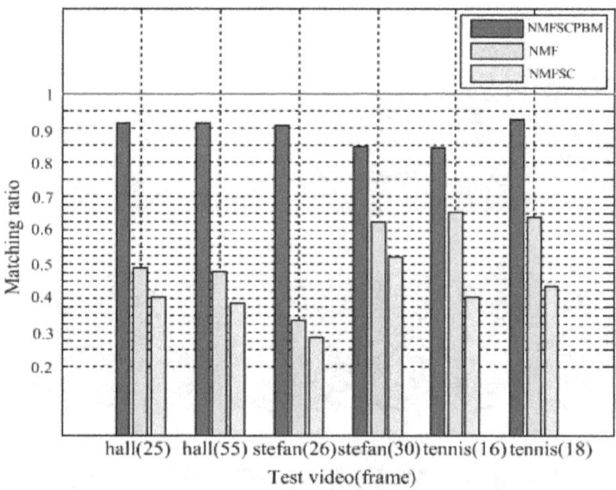

Figure 4. Comparative analysis of matching rate of the motion components obtained by NMFSCPBM method and other similar methods.

1) Video pre-processing. Perform blocking preprocessing to the original video $V(m_x \times m_y \times K)$. According to the blocking rules Chapter 2.2 of this paper, obtain the nonnegative matrix B.

2) Performing the NMFSCPBM decomposition to B. Calculate the decomposition error according to Equation (17), and retain W for watermark extraction.

$$E = B - WH \tag{17}$$

3) Watermark encryption. Select pseudo-random sequence U as the secret key, perform encryption to watermark signal S, and gain the secret information P, shown as Equation (18).

$$P(k) = \sum_{t=1}^{l} s_t(k) u_t(k), k = 1, 2, \cdots, N \tag{18}$$

4) Watermark embedding. The proposed scheme chooses the N biggest elements $w_1, w_2 \ldots w_N$ of the basis matrix W as the positions for watermark embedding, embeds watermark by Equation (19) multiplicative rules, and gains the watermarked basis matrix W'.

$$w_n' = w_n \cdot (1 + I \cdot p_n) \tag{19}$$

5) Watermark embedding strength adaptively adjustment. Perform the blocking processing to video according to Chapter 2.2 of this paper. Extract the video motion components M according to Chapter 2.3 of this paper. Calculate the motion feature coefficient $F(w_i)$ of the row where the ith coefficients locate according to Equation (20). Therefore, the watermark embedding strength of the ith coefficient is $I(w_i) = \alpha \cdot F(w_i)\ i = 1, 2, \cdots, N$, where α is the motion masking weighting factor and $\alpha = 0.013$ is selected by the experiments.

$$F(w_i) = \frac{a^2}{m_x m_y} \sum_j M(i, j) \tag{20}$$

6) Performing nonnegative matrix synthesis by NMFSCPBM. Perform nonnegative matrix synthesize to W', H, E as Equation (21).

$$B' = W'H + E \tag{21}$$

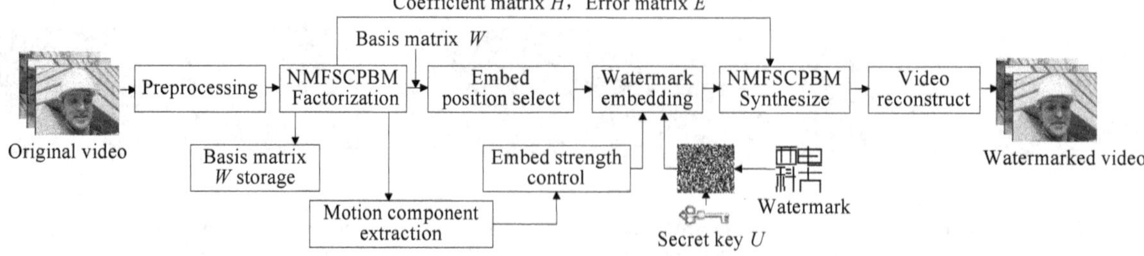

Figure 5. Watermark embedding scheme of this paper.

7) Video reconstruction. Reconstruct B' according to blocking rules, and then output the watermarked video finally.

Watermark extraction. The watermark extraction schematic diagram of the proposed scheme is shown in **Figure 6**. Firstly, perform the blocking preprocessing for the watermarked video that has been attacked according to Chapter 2.2 of this paper, obtaining the nonnegative matrix B'' constituted by the remaining complete sub-blocks in residual video. Secondly, perform the NMFSCPBM decomposition to B'', getting the watermarked complete basis matrix W' in residual video. Finally, by comparing W with W', the encrypted watermark is extracted as Equation (22), and then it is decrypted by the secret key U. From the process of watermark extraction, we know that the watermark extraction of this scheme does not need original video. So it is a blind watermark scheme.

$$p = \begin{cases} 0 & if\ w \geq w' \\ 1 & if\ w < w' \end{cases} \tag{22}$$

4. Experiment and Analysis

In order to verify the validity of this paper, the videos "football", "mother-daughter", "tempete", "mobile", "akiyo", "hall", "foreman" and "soccer" with the format of CIF and the length of 300, 260, 260, 300, 300, 300, 300 and 300 frames are selected as the host video for ex- periment respectively. A 64 × 64 binary image is selected as the watermark, the size of sub-block is 8 × 8, the decomposition dimension r of NMFSCPBM is 32, and the experimental software environment is matlab 7.2. The experiment conducts the test and analysis about the transparency, bit rate constancy, robustness, real-time property, and the algorithm efficiency etc. for this scheme respectively. Due to the length limitation of this paper, only a partial list of results are listed such as the transparency, bit rate constancy, and strong cropping attacks etc.

4.1. Transparency Tests

Figures 7(a) and **(b)** are the I-frame video captures of the original frame and watermarked frame from football sequence. It can be seen that there is no significant visual perceptive distortion before and after the watermark is embedded. From the quantization assessment data shown in **Table 1**, we also know that the difference value ΔPSNR of video coding before and after the watermark is embedded decreases only by average 0.025dB (PSNR, Peak Signal to Noise Ratio of video coding) and that there is no influence on visual perception. The reason is that the proposed scheme sufficiently considers the visual masking features for watermark embedding position selection and strength control, embeds the watermark into the big coefficients of the basis matrix, and meanwhile embeds comparatively strong strength watermark into the regions where the motion is intense [14], eliminating the flicker influence and guaranteeing the transparency of the method.

4.2. Bit Rate Constancy Tests

Table 2 shows the test results of the bit rate constancy of this paper. The experiment is assessed by the bit increased rate (BIR) before and after the watermark is embedded, as Equation (23).

$$\text{BIR} = \frac{watermarked\_BR - original\_BR}{original\_BR} \times 100\% \tag{23}$$

where *original_BR* is the bit rate before the watermark is embedded, and *watermarked_BR* is the bit rate after the watermark is embedded. It can be seen that the increase in video BIR after the watermark is embedded in this paper is under 0.15%, with a good bit rate constancy.

4.3. Strong Cropping Attacks Experiments

Strong cropping attacks include various regular and irregular cropping, such as row and column cropping, edge cropping, top right corner cropping and center cropping etc. The same type and intensity of cropping attacks are synchronously carried out to paper [3], and the comparative analysis is given. The experimental results are assessed by the bit correct rate (BCR) of the extracted watermark, as Equation (24).

$$\text{BCR} = \frac{e}{m} \times 100\% \tag{24}$$

where e is the number of correct bits of the extracted watermark, and m is the number of total bits of the extracted watermark. The more the BCR is close to 100%, the more higher of the correct rate. Let the threshold $T = 70.00\%$ that is determined by experiments. If $\text{BCR} > T$, the watermark is detected. Some figures and

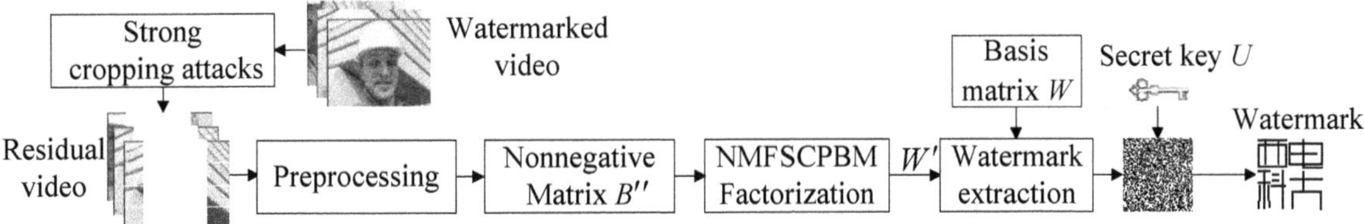

Figure 6. Watermark extraction scheme of this paper.

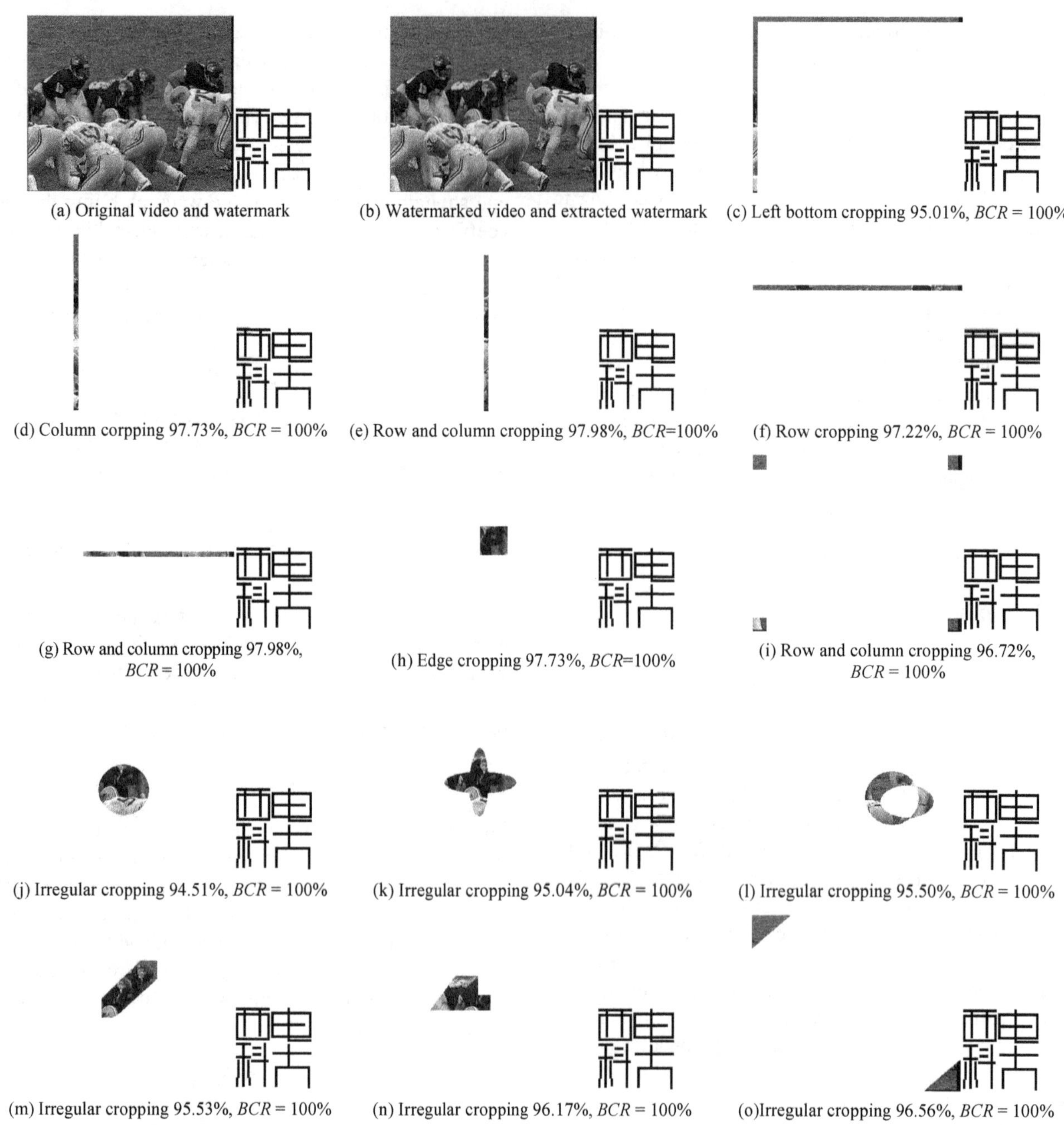

(a) Original video and watermark (b) Watermarked video and extracted watermark (c) Left bottom cropping 95.01%, *BCR* = 100%

(d) Column corpping 97.73%, *BCR* = 100% (e) Row and column cropping 97.98%, *BCR*=100% (f) Row cropping 97.22%, *BCR* = 100%

(g) Row and column cropping 97.98%, *BCR* = 100% (h) Edge cropping 97.73%, *BCR*=100% (i) Row and column cropping 96.72%, *BCR* = 100%

(j) Irregular cropping 94.51%, *BCR* = 100% (k) Irregular cropping 95.04%, *BCR* = 100% (l) Irregular cropping 95.50%, *BCR* = 100%

(m) Irregular cropping 95.53%, *BCR* = 100% (n) Irregular cropping 96.17%, *BCR* = 100% (o)Irregular cropping 96.56%, *BCR* = 100%

Figure 7. Strong cropping attacks test results of this paper.

Table 1. Transparency test results of this paper.

Test video	PSNR (dB)		△PSNR (dB)
	Without watermark	With watermark	
football	33.25	33.24	0.01
mother-daughter	37.90	37.87	0.03
tempete	32.92	32.88	0.04
mobile	32.22	32.17	0.05
akiyo	38.45	38.44	0.01
hall	36.31	36.28	0.03
foreman	35.15	35.14	0.01
soccer	34.31	34.29	0.02

Table 2. Bit rate constancy tests results of this paper.

Test video	Bit rate (kbps)		*BIR*
	watermarked_BR	*original_BR*	
football	1667.98	1668.89	0.0546%
mother-daughter	222.22	222.38	0.0720%
tempete	1101.06	1101.61	0.0500%
mobile	1651.80	1651.83	0.0018%
akiyo	226.49	226.52	0.0130%
hall	415.98	416.05	0.0168%
foreman	489.58	490.33	0.1500%
soccer	654.55	655.44	0.1400%

quantification assessment results of the robustness experiment are shown in **Figure** 7 and **Table 3.**

It can be seen from **Figure** 7 and **Table 3** that, 1) the BCRs of the proposed scheme are all 100% for various regular and irregular strong cropping attacks. The scheme can recover the complete watermark without any damage, and has a very strong ability to resist strong cropping attacks. Analysis of the main reasons is that, based on the strong robustness of basis matrix to cropping attacks, this scheme embeds the encrypted watermark into the big coefficients of the basis matrix that the host video is decomposed into by NMFSCPBM. When the watermarked video suffers from strong cropping attacks, the complete basis matrix can be completely recovered through decomposition of the residual video by NMFSCPBM, and then the complete watermark can be extracted. The selection of the big coefficients of the basis matrix and the adaptive control of the watermark embedding strength based on the video motion feature coefficients, further increase the watermark embedding strength and improve the robustness. The spread spectrum encryption processing for watermark also increases the robustness while increases the watermark invisibility. 2) About various regular and irregular cropping attacks listed in the experiment, with the same attack intensity compared with this paper, the BCRs of the paper [3] are completely not up to 70% of the threshold requirements. Take the example of the "football" test video, when the row regular cropping is 97.22%, the BCR of the paper [3] is 51.25%. When the edge cropping is 97.73%, the BCR of the paper [3] is 48.82%. For various irregular cropping attack, as **Figures 7(j)-(o)** shown, the BCRs of the paper [3] are between 47.07% - 56.35%, which can not meet the threshhold 70%. The same conclusion is obtained from the mother-daughter, tempete, mobile, akiyo, hall, foreman and soccer test videos.

Figure 8 shows the relation curve of BCRs of the proposed scheme with the cropping attack intensity. It can be seen that the inflexion where the BCR is less than 100% appears on the point with the cropping intensity 97.98%, while the cropping intensity is maximum and the number of the remaining complete sub-blocks in the residual video is $c = 32$, neither more nor less than equaling to the dimension of NMF $r = 32$. Further analysis shows that, with the further increase of the cropping intensity, the BCR decreases rapidly. It is mainly because the number of the remaining complete sub-blocks in the residual video c is less than 32, which indeed does not meet the least number of the remaining complete sub-blocks required in the **Theorem 1** of this paper. This fact makes e that is the number of correct bits of the extracted watermark decrease rapidly and causes the BCR decrease rapidly. The above analysis and results are fully consistent with the results of the theoretical analysis in Chapter 2.2 of this paper.

Table 3. Robustness comparison of this scheme and paper [3] for strong cropping attacks.

Attacks	BCR (%)															
	football		mother-daughter		tempete		mobile		akiyo		hall		foreman		soccer	
	Our	Paper [3]	Our	Paper [3]	Our	Paper [3]	Our	Paper [3]	Our	Paper [3]	Our	Paper [3]	Our	Paper [3]	Our	Paper [3]
No attacks	100	100	100	100	100	100	100	100	100	100	100	100	100	100	100	100
Row cropping 94.00%	100	56.30	100	57.38	100	59.07	100	55.48	100	52.86	100	56.21	100	54.40	100	55.03
Row cropping 97.22%	100	51.25	100	51.36	100	52.82	100	51.21	100	45.65	100	51.29	100	53.15	100	54.25
Column cropping 95.45%	100	59.76	100	57.23	100	57.15	100	56.32	100	52.80	100	51.25	100	50.53	100	53.29
Column cropping 97.73%	100	52.05	100	55.15	100	47.41	100	51.26	100	48.99	100	47.26	100	53.34	100	51.77
Row and column cropping 97.98%	100	52.55	100	52.58	100	49.09	100	52.10	100	51.67	100	46.54	100	48.55	100	49.85
Edge cropping 97.73%	100	48.82	100	50.06	100	50.15	100	50.23	100	52.27	100	49.36	100	47.73	100	47.76
Top corner cropping 95.01%	100	50.44	100	49.56	100	52.71	100	51.85	100	53.59	100	50.45	100	52.01	100	50.31
Bottom corner cropping 95.01%	100	47.85	100	49.98	100	51.64	100	50.36	100	52.52	100	43.56	100	53.19	100	52.24
Centre cropping 93.56%	100	53.55	100	50.25	100	50.39	100	50.85	100	49.86	100	51.19	100	54.05	100	49.12
Irregular cropping 94.51%	100	52.80	100	52.01	100	51.26	100	51.36	100	50.71	100	48.57	100	52.16	100	48.58
Irregular cropping 95.04%	100	51.89	100	52.54	100	54.55	100	49.95	100	51.45	100	51.26	100	53.15	100	51.36
Irregular cropping 95.50%	100	55.39	100	54.60	100	56.25	100	50.26	100	55.32	100	51.35	100	51.14	100	52.25
Irregular cropping 95.53%	100	50.85	100	50.76	100	52.35	100	51.25	100	48.07	100	49.68	100	51.65	100	54.33
Irregular cropping 96.17%	100	52.92	100	56.35	100	54.35	100	55.35	100	54.17	100	48.69	100	47.65	100	47.07
Irregular cropping 96.56%	100	51.31	100	52.16	100	53.63	100	52.86	100	50.95	100	50.25	100	51.23	100	48.25

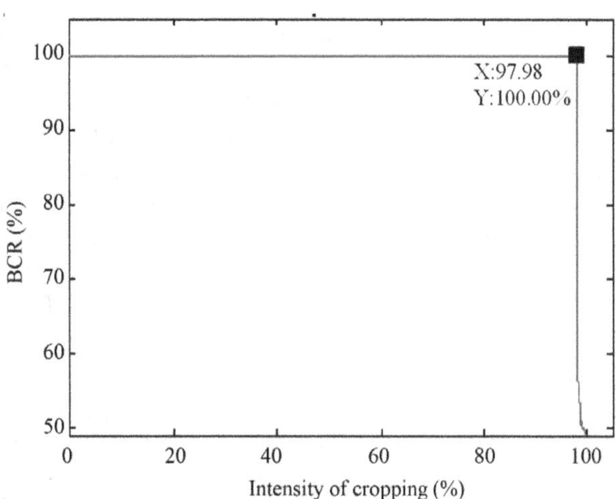

Figure 8. Relation curve of BCRs with the cropping attack intensity in the proposed scheme.

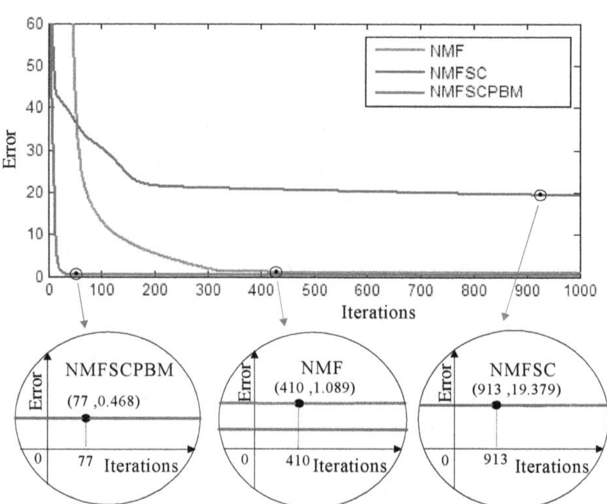

Figure 9. Decomposing errors and computational efficiencies of NMFSCPBM and other similar methods.

4.4. Computational Efficiency and Decomposing Errors Experiments of NMFSCPBM Methods

Figure 9 shows the convergence curves of decomposition error with the number of iterations of NMFSCPBM, NMF and NMFSC for different data sets. The sparseness constraint of NMFSC and NMFSCPBM is 0.6 respectively and the decomposition dimension is $r = 4$ respectively. Due to the length limitation of an article, **Figure 9** only shows the fore 1000 iterative results of the "football" test video. It can be seen that, 1) the convergence error of this paper is 0.468, 19.379 for the NMFSC and 1.809 for the NMF; 2) the convergence error comes up to the minimum after 77 iterations for NMFSCPBM, 913 for NMFSC, and 410 for NMF. Therefore, the decomposing error of this paper is the lowest in the similar methods, and the convergence rate is also obviously better than that of the similar methods. Other experimental data of the test videos give the same conclusion.

5. Conclusion

A novel video watermarking scheme robust to strong cropping is proposed in this paper. It is characterized as follows. 1) The improved NMFSCPBM method is proposed, which can extract the video motion features accurately, filter out the static background interference completely, and is simple and effective. Solve the problems of the similar methods that cannot describe the data sufficiently under higher sparseness constraints. Meanwhile, reduce the decomposition error and speed up convergence rate. 2) Based on the robustness of basis matrix for shearing attacks, this framework innovatively embeds the encrypted watermark into the big coefficients of the basis matrix that the host video is decomposed into by NMFSCPBM. To achieve the greatest strength of the watermark embedding with no visual perception, this scheme adaptively adjusts the watermark embedding strength by the video motion feature coefficients extracted by NMFSCPBM method, improving the robustness further. On watermark detection, as long as the residual video contains the numbers of least remaining sub-blocks, the complete basis matrix can be completely recovered through decomposition of the nonnegative matrix of the least remaining sub-blocks in residual videos by NMFSCPBM, and then the complete watermark can be extracted. The experimental results show that the performance of resisting strong cropping attacks of this scheme is improved greatly compared to existing methods, and that the scheme has good transparency, bit rate constancy and real-time property. It is a blind watermark scheme. How to extract and recover the complete watermark from the incomplete sub-blocks of the residual video will be as the further research content for authors.

REFERENCES

[1] H. Zhang, *et al.*, "Affine Legendre Moment Invariants for Image Watermarking Robust to Geometric Distortions," *IEEE Transactions on Image Processing*, Vol. 20, No. 8, 2010, pp. 2189-2199._

[2] C. V. Serdean, M. A. Ambroze, M. Tomlinso and J. G. Wade, "DWT-Based High-Capacity Blind Video Watermarking, Invariant to Geometrical Attacks," *IEEE Proceedings of the Vision, Image and Signal Processing*, Vol. 150, No. 1, 2003, pp. 51-58.

[3] L. E. Coria, M. R. Pickering, P. Nasiopoulos and R. K. Ward, "A Video Watermarking Scheme Based on the Dual-Tree Complex Wavelet Transform," *IEEE Transactions on Information Forensics and Security*, Vol. 3, No. 3, 2008, pp. 466-474.

[4] Y. L. Wang and A. Pearmain, "Blind MPEG-2 Video

Watermarking Robust against Geometric Attacks: A Set of Approaches in DCT Domain," *IEEE Transactions on Image Processing*, Vol. 15, No. 6, 2006, pp. 1536-1543.

[5] X. M. Niu, *et al.*, "A Video Watermarking against Geometrical Distortions," *Chinese Journal of Electronics*, Vol. 12, No. 4, 2003, pp. 548-552.

[6] M. Silja and K. Soman, "A Watermarking Algorithm based on Contourlet Transform and Nonnegative Matrix Factorization," *Proceedings of the International Conference on Advances in Recent Technologies in Communication and Computing*, Kottayam, 27-28 October 2009, pp. 279-281.

[7] A. D'Angelo, Z. P. Li and M. Barni, "A Full-Reference Quality Metric for Geometrically Distorted Images," *IEEE Transactions on Image Processing*, Vol. 19, No. 4, 2010, pp. 867-881.

[8] Z. Y. Yang, *et al.*, "Blind Spectral Unmixing Based on Sparse Nonnegative Matrix Factorization," *IEEE Transactions on Image Processing*, Vol. 20, No. 4, 2011, pp. 1112-1125.

[9] M. Tong, T. Yan and H.-B. Ji, "Strong Anti-Robust WaterMarking Algorithm," *Journal of Xidian University*, Vol. 36, No. 1, 2009, pp. 22-27.

[10] D. Gai, X. F. He, J. W. Han and T. S. Huang, "Graph Regularized Nonnegative Matrix Factorization for Data Representation," *IEEE Transactions on Pattern Analysis and Machine Intelligence*, Vol. 33, No. 1, 2011, pp. 1-13.

[11] T. Gao and M.-Y. He, "Using Improved Nonnegative Matrix Factorization with Projected Gradient for Single-Trial Feature Extraction," *Journal of Electronics & Information Technology*, Vol. 32, No. 5, 2010, pp. 1121-1125.

[12] P. O. Hoyer, "Nonnegative Matrix Factorization with Sparseness Constraints," *Journal of Machine Learning Research*, Vol. 5, 2004, pp. 1457-1469.

[13] T. K. Kim, *et al.*, "Video Object Segmentation and Its Salient Motion Detection Using Adaptive Background Generation," *Electronics Letters*, Vol. 45, No. 11, 2009, p. 542.

[14] S.-W. Kim, K. R. Rao, S. Suthaharan and H.-K. Lee, "Perceptually Tuned Robust Watermarking Scheme for Digital Video Using Motion Entropy Masking," *Proceedings of the International Conference on Consumer Electronics of the IEEE ICCE*, Los Angeles, 22-24 June 1999, pp. 104-105.

7

Detecting Threats of Acoustic Information Leakage through Fiber Optic Communications

Vladimir V. Grishachev
Russian State Geological Prospecting University (RSGPU), Moscow, Russia

ABSTRACT

Information leaks through regular fiber optic communications is possible in the form of eavesdropping on conversations, using standard fiber optic communications as illegal measuring network. The threat of leakage of audio information can create any kind of irregular light emission, as well as regular light beams modulated at acoustic frequencies. For information protection can be used a means of sound insulation, filtration and noising. This paper discusses the technical possibilities of countering threats by monitoring the optical radiation to detect eavesdropping.

Keywords: Fiber Optic Communications; Acoustic (Speech) Information Leakage Channel; Protection of Acoustic (Speech) Information

1. Introduction

Modern technologies of remote and local cable communication systems are based on optical data transmission systems due to the advantages of fiber optic cable over electrical cable as the transport medium. One of the main directions of development is to ensure the broadband subscriber access which is based on optical networks, completely passive (PON) in the future. Technologies such as fiber to the building/home/office/desk (FTTB/FTTH/FTTO/FTTD) lead to the fact that the fiber replaces wire technology in near environment of user [1]. In addition to communications technology fiber is actively used in measuring and security systems. Fiber optic distributed measuring network can control all the basic physical fields in real time with high sensitivity and accuracy [2,3]. One of the most active trends of fibers in the security systems is the application of optical interfaces for extension of special lines in Closed Circuit Television (CCTV), perimeter security system object.

Advancement of optical structured cable systems (SCS) closer to the man create new threats to information security circulating in building, office, workplace. One of the risks associated with possibility eavesdropping on confidential conversations, using influence of acoustic fields on transmission of light in the fiber. Optical fiber is successfully used to create sensors and distributed measuring networks. Hence regular optic structured cabling system in building is nothing short of a distributed measurement network, which can be used to measure various physical fields, including acoustic field.

Thus, in commercial and government buildings is necessary to protect confidential negotiations in office manager, office space, meeting rooms and other allocated areas of acoustic (speech) information leakage through the optic structured cabling systems. This problem is new, understudied in connection with what is very dangerous.

2. Physical Principles Eavesdropping

Covert obtain of acoustic (speech) information by using regular fiber optic communications for various purposes is one of the new methods of acoustic intelligence, which is called an acousto-optic (fiber) information leakage channel [4,5]. Forming leakage channel due to the fact that acoustic field from holder information affects the fiber of regular cable systems and causes a modulation of light passing through optical fiber, passive or active elements of optical equipment by acoustic frequencies, as well as reflection from a heterogeneities in them (**Figure 1**). Modulation of light in the optical fiber can take place in amplitude, phase, polarization and frequency of emission due to exposure on optical fiber of acoustic field. Light which has been modulated by sound can come out far beyond the protected premises through regular fiber optic communications. Then, attacker can gain access to functioning in the establishment of confidential information by demodulating.

On the principles of acousto-optic modulation implemented fiber optic sensor of acoustic field in sonar [6,7], vibration sensors [8,9], and other devices [2,3]. For example, in fiber optic perimeter security systems by vibration

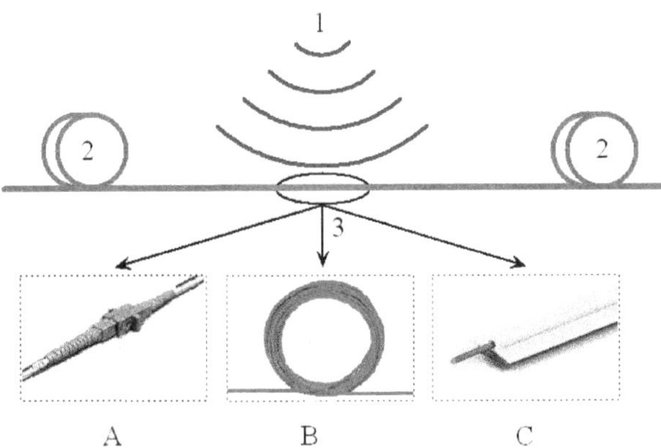

Figure 1. Model of acousto-optic (fiber) information leakage channels. 1: sound source, 2: optical cable, 3: element of optic cable system is subject to sound influence including optical plug contact (A), free optical cable (B), cable with vibro-acoustic contact with designs building (C).

acoustic effects of the intruder on fiber is registered penetration of object. Also, for a long time being developed fiber optic hydrophones, whose operation is similar to vibration sensors with various types of optical schemes. Thus, our research are supported by numerous practical work in neighboring areas. The intruder using various schemes to connect to fiber optic communications is able to conduct tapping conversations on securable.

The bases of channels leakage are light beams in an optical cable lines. All light beams can be divided into regular (legal), related to the physical implementation of data transmission protocol, and irregular (illegal), specially generated by an attacker to gain unauthorized output of the speech information. Regular light beams that are formed digital transmission techniques can create a leakage channel without disrupting the entire system, since level of acoustic action on a regular light beam reduces the signal/ noise is negligible. By irregular flows will be assigned any radiation, which generated by light sources with unauthorized connections to fiber optic communications.

Research on the effectiveness of speech leakage carried by the articulator method, which defines speech intelligibility W (%) as the number of words correctly understood at channel output to the number of words spoken at entrance channels leakage. They showed a high risk of new method of eavesdropping. Estimation of efficiency made for amplitude modulation of light passing flows in communication line, containing the basic elements of passive optical networks—fiber optic cable free and attached to the building design, detachable connections, attenuators, etc. This research on shared standard equipment was shown possibility eavesdropping of voice over fiber optic communications with the sound pressure level (SPL) of 60 dB in intelligibility of W up to 80%. The modulation depth of intensity of transmitted light reached saturation into 0.3% at an SPL of 90 dB in the surrounding space.

3. Script Eavesdropping Threats

We discuss the overall sequence of actions infringer to obtain acoustic information through fiber optic communications and give a general description used by special technical facilities (**Figure 2**). Formation of an acousto-optic

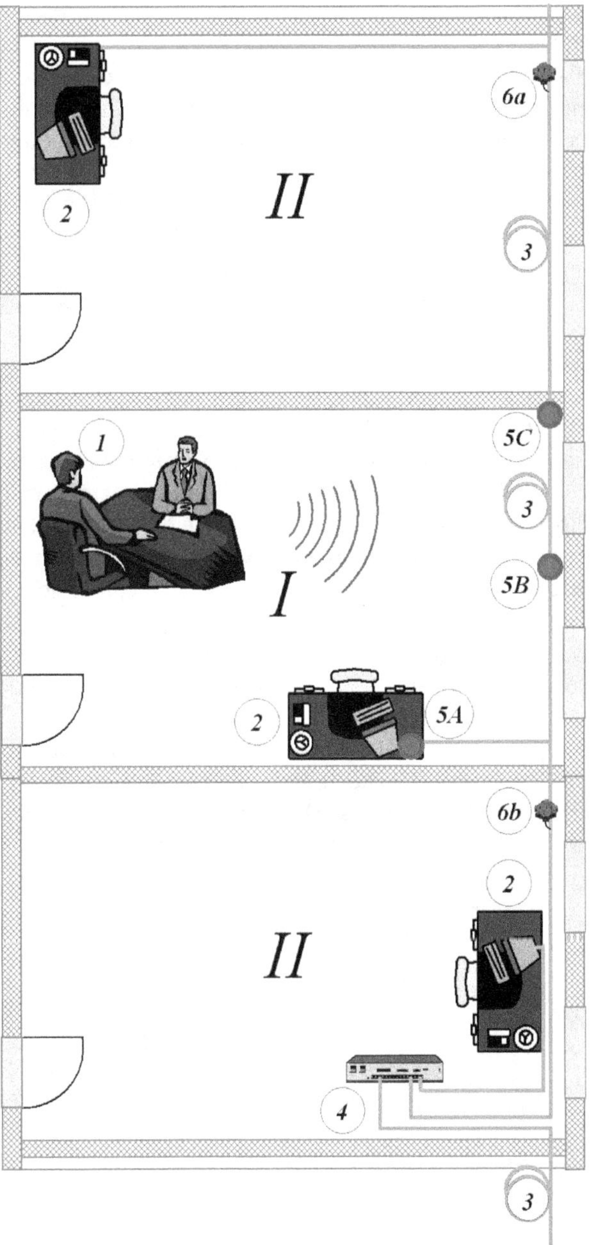

Figure 2. Generalized script of acoustic (speech) information leakage through fiber optic communications (the model of acousto-optic (fiber) leakage channel). *I*: allocated room; *II*: secondary rooms. 1: location of confidential negotiations; 2: workplace (workstation); 3: fiber optic communications; 4: regular active optical network equipment; 5: location of leakage channels such as *A*, *B*, *C*; 6: technical means of acoustic intelligence: *a* (source) and *b* (receiver) for leakage channel on passing of light; *a* or *b* (source and receiver in one location) for leakage channel in reflected light.

(fiber) information leakage channel is virtually impossible without physical access to optic cable that passes through selected rooms. Cabling must be free of active optical equipment on site between the infringer and the source of acoustical information, which is associated with recovery of regular shape signal and suppressing noise components of radiation in active equipment. Between the infringer and the source of acoustical information must be placed only passive optical elements, which do not change significantly modulation of light. To passive optical elements, except the optical cable relate sockets, adapters, splitters, couplers, attenuators. It should be noted that such a structure of the optical cable network is the most promising for subscriber access and rapidly developing as technology of passive optical networks.

Implementation of leakage channel requires applying technical facilities to connect to the cable and recording optical emission. Connection is implemented through regular plug connections, which are used to connect parts of network among themselves and to attach to optical line (OLT) and optical network (ONT) terminals. Connection is dropped and into gap is inserted insertion with input of probing radiation and outlet of part. Another method of connection is to apply coupler radiation on macrobends optic cable. All the proposed methods do not require special technical facilities, distribution of which is regulated by normative documents, such devices are used for installation the optical network. Another method is using cable break to insert the coupler by welding fibers.

Optical scheme of eavesdropping can be accomplished in several ways (**Figure 3**). First, it can be applied the special probe light sources which are not provided regular network. Probing by light can be produced by reflection or by passing from place of modulation. In this case it is possible to combine transmitting and receiving radiation. Second, for eavesdropping can be used regular radiation which applies for traffic within the network.

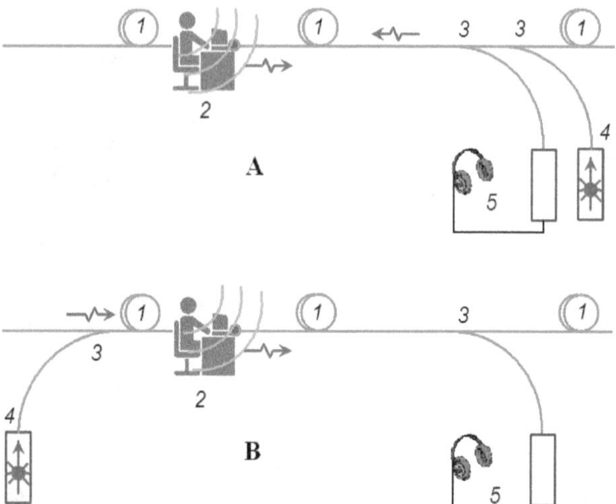

Figure 3. Structure of acousto-optic (fiber) leakage channel in scheme at reflection (A) and scheme for passage (B). 1: optical cable network; 2: confidential source (speech) information with sensitive to vibro-acoustic influence of optical cable; 3: optical coupler; 4: light source (laser); 5: analog optical detector with acoustic demodulator and headphones.

The danger leakage channel is determined by efficiency of acoustic modulation of light in location of sound source. Acoustic field causes various kinds of modulating light in optical fiber, by choosing parameters demodulation (amplitude, phase, polarization and frequency) is always possible to achieve very high efficiency of leakage channel acoustic (speech) information. Another danger associated with availability of installation equipment that can be used as special technical facilities of acoustic intelligence. For example, for voice communication between installers network uses fiber optic phone, which allows for direct connection to fiber carry voice communications over a distance of 200 km. Fiber optic phone can connect to fiber optic cable without it breaking through macrobend fiber. On the same principle joining works detection of optical signal in fiber, which allows establishing direction of optical signals in coated with 250 micron, 900 microns, as well as in standard optical cords up to 3 mm without gap. Level meters backscatter is designed for monitoring quality of polishing of single-mode fiber optic connectors and measure level of backscatter from other components of communication lines can be used for eavesdropping, also. Still has great potential optical time domain reflectometer (OTDR)—basic device condition monitoring optical. The above instruments are widely available commonly used for installation of optical cable systems, which increases their use in the channel leakage [10].

4. Preventing Eavesdropping Threats

All of the major ways to counter of speech information leakage through waveguide channels can be divided into the following types:

- Soundproofing channel environment, the passive method is to reduce influence of acoustic field on channel environment;
- Filtration of data carrier in transmission channel, the method consists in not passing through channel of irregular signals and modulations with confidential speech information;
- Masking data carrier in transmission channel, the method consists in concealment by addition of a special mask signal and modulations;
- Moisy channel environment, the active method consisting in creating synthetic interference and noise on acoustic frequencies [11,12].

Each method has its advantages and disadvantages, but the overall effectiveness of any security depends largely on the technical capabilities of detecting threats to information security [13]. Technical means to detect the fact of eavesdropping or preparing equipment to implement it will undoubtedly increase the reliability of the protection system. In the case of fiber optic communications should take into account physical characteristics of fiber optic communication channel, such as small size, direction of radiation and absence of side light beams that go beyond the channel.

Features fiber optic channel allows us to offer a simple and effective way to detect unauthorized output of information (eavesdropping) by monitoring the current in channel of light beams. Any attack on the security system via fiber optic channel for accessing acoustic (speech) information associated with light beams in fiber. Monitoring parameters of light beams in the channel allows identifying any possibility of unauthorized output. This will require registration of radiations pass through fiber optic elements, the allocation authorized by the data carriers (regular radiation), to identify unauthorized flows (irregular radiation) and modulation of acoustic frequencies in any of them. Irregular emission (from external sources) may have a spectral composition as the crossover with regular radiation and does not intersect with it, which is modulated by an external acoustic signal contains confidential information.

Preventing eavesdropping is achieved by performing the following rules. First, regular light beams should not be modulated on audio frequencies. Second, irregular flows that are not provided by the physical implementation of data transmission protocol of network must be absent, and when available, they should not be modulated sound. These simple rules make it possible to detect an attack on a security system and neutralize it. Thus, the degree of risk of acoustic (speech) information leakage is determined by the following features:

1) Irregular light beams is detected in the channel information transmission;

2) Regular light beams is modulated by one of the parameters of optical radiation (amplitude, phase, polarization, frequency) and/or simultaneously on several parameters by external acoustic signal;

3) Abnormal light beams which are separated from spectrum are modulated by one of the parameters of optical radiation (amplitude, phase, polarization, frequency) and/or simultaneously on several parameters by external acoustic signal on a given optical wavelength.

That at least one of these conditions is sufficient for the formation of acoustic (speech) information leakage and can be used to estimate threats to information security.

5. Practical Implementation Protection

The problem of detecting possibility of speech information leakage through regular fiber optic communication is solved by installing special equipment, registering light beams in transmission channel information. Implementation can be carried out based on standard or specially created items, which include photodetector, connected to the fiber optic link, also, optical, electronic and optoelectronic analytical element for allocation of acoustic oscillations parameters detected optical radiation. Protection device can be done in two structural decisions: as a separate unit, which has its own alarm system threats, or block the built-in active equipment, which has informational link with the main equipment. Let us discuss possible implementation of devices and their features function.

The external indicating device threat (**Figure 4**) includes in an optical channel with standard optical connectors and closes the communication link without a significant impact on passing traffic. The main risk associated with probing (illegal) radiation, which is separated from regular light by beamsplitters. Incident radiation at regular wavelength is reflected, and irregular radiation at otherwise wavelengths passes through it and is registered a photodetector. Part passing through beamsplitters of regular radiation is allocated and is recorded by another photodetector. Received at photodetector output signals are analyzed on existence of probing (illegal) radiation and on possible amplitude modulation. The decision about danger is taken from obtained data, which consists in answer to questions—what is the danger level? And on which side of indicator is a threat comes? The highest danger level corresponds to existence of irregular radiation or amplitude modulation of regular radiation. The average level corresponds to existence of amplitude modulation of regular radiation at the level noise in optical channel. Absence of irregular emissions and any irregular modulation corresponds to the safe mode.

Although the device registers only amplitude modulation of optical radiation and does not register other modulation types, but given that other types of modulation can be effectively observed only when using probing (illegal) radiation, we can assert control of all types of modulation by detecting irregular radiation. Another possibility inherent in this device is that it acts as a filter irregular optical radiation since the regular radiation passes indicator threats and irregular do not pass. Such property greatly limits the application optical design on the passage, which is more effective scheme for reflection. Reflected signal is always weaker than direct probing radiation. Scheme on reflection to the infringer demands more intense radiation to reach an acceptable echo. However for threat indicator any probe signal is a direct that goes either left or right of him so its check will be much safer than the infringer, recording only reflected signal.

The internal indicating device threat (**Figure 5**) can be integrated directly into the active optical network equipment. It can be integrated into equipment or join a removable modules—transceivers. In the last case, the physical changes to basic equipment may be required and

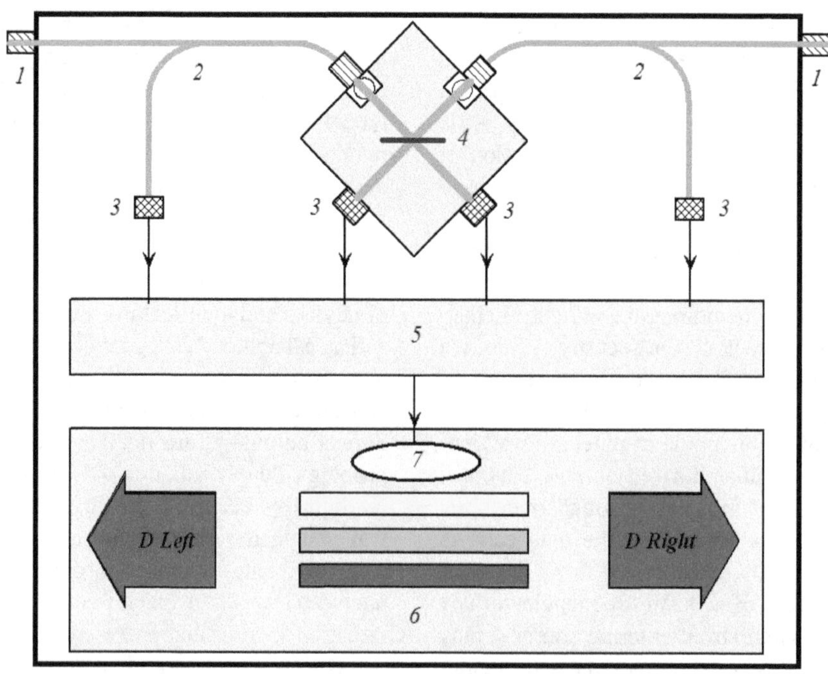

Figure 4. External indicator attacks. 1: optical inputs; 2: optic couplers; 3: photodetectors; 4: beamsplitters; 5: spectrum analyzer; 6: display unit; 7: sound indicator attacks. *D Left*—LED attack on the left, *D Right*—LED attack on the right, the color risk indicators.

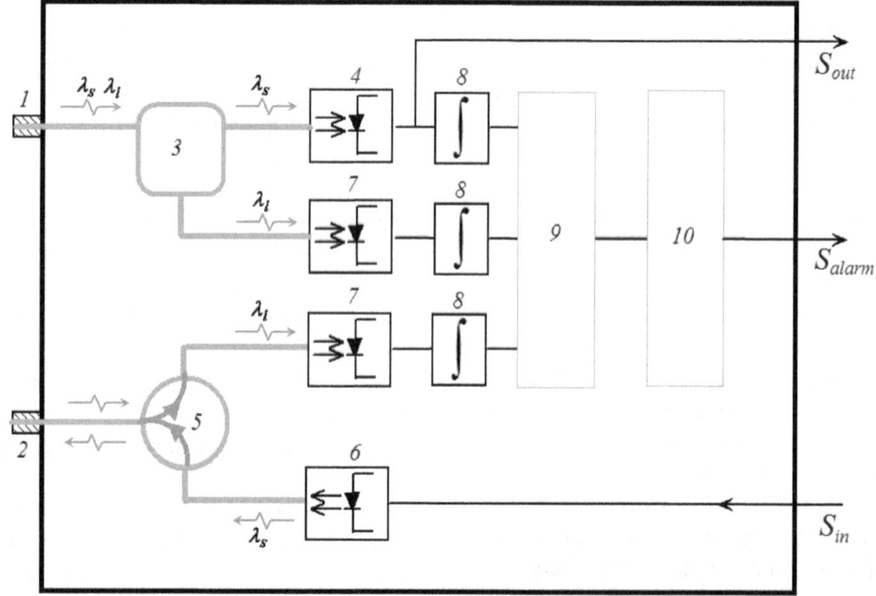

Figure 5. Integrated indicator attacks. 1: optical input; 2: optical output; 3: multiplexer which separates data signal at wavelength λ_s from probing light beam at wavelength λ_l; 4: regular photodetector with input information signal S_{out}, 5: coupler; 6: regular transmitter with output information signal S_{in}; 7: additional monitoring photodetectors; 8: integrating elements; 9: spectrum analyzer; 10: analog-digital converter, generating danger signal.

to change the driver itself transceiver. The main problem of this conversion is to place additional optical elements in required form factor of transceiver. Discuss the structure and operation of indicator threats in integrated dual-port active equipment with separate fiber optic input (the channel receiver) and output (the channel transmitter). Own monitoring system be put on each fiber in the form of additional sensor. In the port of receiver signal is divided into regular and irregular radiation through an optical circulator. Information signal from the regular receiver is processed by conventional means for transmission channel, and arrives at the integrator output which generates an analog signal from the regular radiation that can be modulated by an acoustic frequencies. Selection of irregular radiation is recorded and converted to its own receiver to an analog signal. In the port of transmitter there is no incoming radiation, thus the channel is required separation of radiation on regular and irregular, they are divided by propagation direction. Photodetector is connected to transmitter through coupler and the signal from it is also integrated. Thus, the control system has three receivers with integrated units that make up three analog signals, by which concludes that existence of a threat eavesdropping. Analysis is performed on the existence of irregular radiation and the presence typical components of speech in signal spectrum. On this basis is generated danger signal.

6. Advice on Protection

At present the implementation of methods described above to identify threats to speech information leakage does not exist. As can be seen from a general description of functioning principles of protection devices, to develop working models for detection of eavesdropping by fiber-optic communications is possible based on standard equipment. The main element of protection system is optical detector with an amplifier at sound frequencies, which is present in any analog fiber-optic phone. Standard analog fiber optic phone has high sensitivity which allows recording very small fluctuations in intensity and detect attempts at eavesdropping. However, it has significant disadvantages for the systems security one of them being sensitivity shift in the infrared spectrum, which does not register with highly reliable probing emission of visible spectrum. At distances of several hundred meters, total optical loss will amount to several dB at wavelengths in the visible range in a standard quartz fiber that cannot reliably detect weak optical radiation regular photodetectors.

Another disadvantage is need for additional fiber optic components to register modulation by polarization, frequency and phase. But in any case, a fiber optic phone is closest by principles of functioning for use in protection from eavesdropping through fiber optic communications.

Protection against eavesdropping of selected rooms through a fiber optic communications can be represented as follows (**Figure 6**). Optic cable passes by the selected room and connected to a computer at workplace. The whole cable with connecting elements inside the room appears as a system which is subject to acoustic effects, formed a speech of confidential information carriers. Light output is modulated a speech and exceeds the selected rooms and may be registered by an attacker. Dangerous for connecting technical reconnaissance attacker's are all parts of network in the selected room from one active equipment to another. Defining dangerous section, establish the device detecting attacks in the selected room, way optical insert.

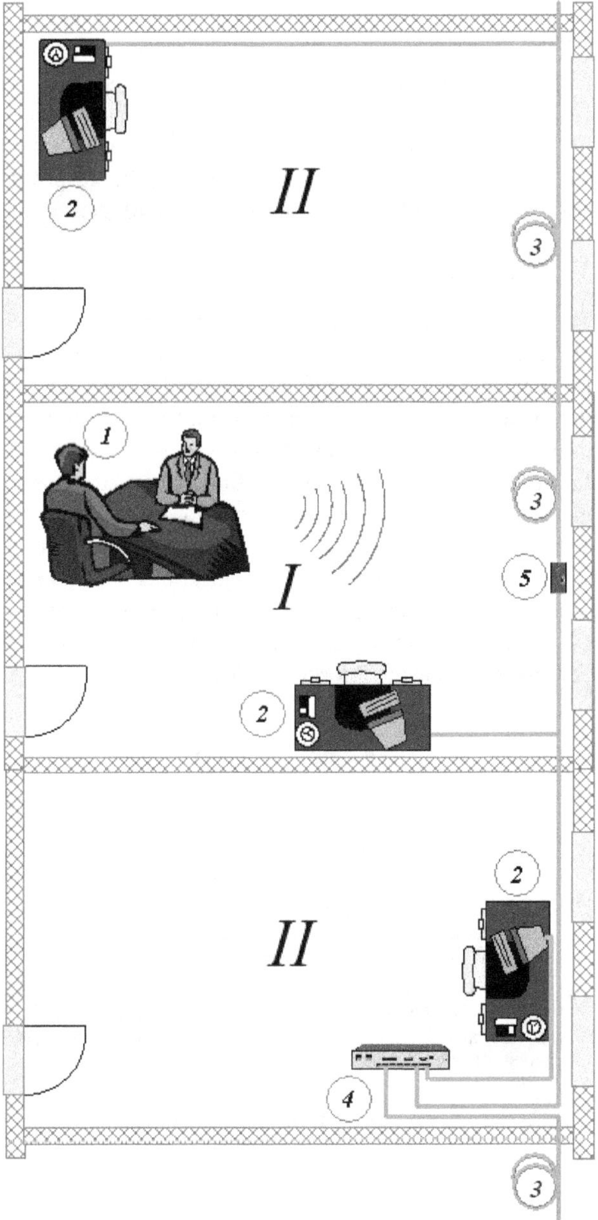

Figure 6. Schematic diagram of protection against leakage information through fiber optic communications, based on detector of attack. *I*: allocated room; *II*: secondary rooms. 1: location of confidential negotiations; 2: workplace (workstation); 3: fiber optic communications; 4: regular active optical network equipment; 5: inclusions detector attack.

We conducted a trial listening to fiber optic communication lines consisting of optical cable with dual fibers of length exceeding 25 m and a thickness of 3 mm each. Light output was formed an optical tester or a helium-neon laser and registered a fiber-optic phone with analog modulation. Acoustic effects produced locally using computer speakers, acting directly at cable and network elements. The acoustical signal was very noisy, but the words be recognized speech at the hearing.

The presented modeling studies confirmed possibility of implementing such schemes identify attacks even with the help not profile equipment. Production of specialized equipment can more reliably resolve the problem identification of eavesdropping and the security services to help protect speech information in modern rapid proliferation of fiber optic communications technologies.

7. Conclusion

This work is a development patent for invention [13], which proposes a solution to ensure information security talks in selected areas by identifying potential threats on formation leakage channels of acoustic (speech) information through fiber optic communication systems and proposed for use in systems to protect confidential voice communications. Detection of acoustic (speech) information leakage channel is carried out by monitoring optical emissions in regular fiber optic communications. Appearance of any irregular light emissions or modulation on acoustical frequencies of regular light streams creates a potential threat of acoustic information leakage.

REFERENCES

[1] F. L. Cedric, "Passive Optical Networks: Principles and Practice," Elsevier, San Diego, 2007.

[2] R. Hui and M. S. O'Sullivan, "Fiber Optic Measurement Techniques," Elsevier Academic Press, Waltham, 2009.

[3] E. Udd and W. B. Spillman Jr., "Fiber Optic Sensors: An Introduction for Engineers and Scientists," 2nd Edition, John Wiley & Sons, Hoboken, 2011.

[4] V. V. Grishachev, D. B. Khalyapin, N. A. Shevchenko and V. G. Merzlikin, "New Channels of Leakage of Confidential Information over the Voice of Fiber Optic Subsystems SCS," *Special'naya Tehnika*, No. 2, 2009, pp. 2-9.

[5] V. V. Grishachev and O. A. Kosenko, "The Practical Estimation of Convert Audio (Voice) Channel Efficiency from Fiber-Optic Communications," *Voprosy Zashity Informacii*, No. 2, 2010, pp. 18-25.

[6] J. A. Bucaro and T. R. Hickman, "Measurement of Sensitivity of Optical Fibers for Acoustic Detection," *Applied Optics*, Vol. 18, No. 6, 1979, pp. 938-940.

[7] B. Culshaw, D. E. N. Davies and S. A. Kingsley, "Acoustic Sensitivity of Optical Fiber Waveguides," *Electronics Letters*, Vol. 13, No. 25, 1977, pp. 760-761.

[8] J. C. Juarez and H. F. Taylor, "Field Test of a Distributed Fiber-Optic Intrusion Sensor System for Long Perimeters," *Applied Optics*, Vol. 46, No. 11. 2007, pp. 1968-1971.

[9] J. C. Juarez, E. W. Maier, K. N. Choi and H. F. Taylor, "Distributed Fiber-Optic Intrusion Sensor System," *Journal of Lightwave Technology*, Vol. 23, No. 6. 2005, pp. 2081-2087.

[10] Fiber Optic Devices Ltd. (FOD), "Products," http://www.fods.com

[11] V. V. Grishachev, D. B. Khalyapin and N. A. Shevchenko, "Method and Device for Actively Protecting Confidential Spoken Information from Leaking over an Acousto-Optic Fibre Channel by Using External Optical Noise Masking," 2010. http://www.wipo.int/patentscope/search/en/WO2010126400

[12] V. V. Grishachev, D. B. Khalyapin and N. A. Shevchenko, "Methods and Devices for Actively Protecting Spoken Information against Eavesdropping via an Acousto-Optic Fibre Leakage Channel," 2010. http://www.wipo.int/patentscope/search/en/WO2010126401

[13] V. V. Grishachev, "Fiber-Optic Detector for Detecting Threats of Verbal Information Leaks," 2011. http://www.wipo.int/patentscope/search/en/WO2011031186

8

Digital Image Watermarking Based on Mixed Error Correcting Code

Yonghong Chen, Jiancong Chen
College of Computer Science & Technology, Huaqiao University, Xiamen, China.

ABSTRACT

In this paper, we present a novel technique based on a mixed Error Correcting Code (ECC)—the convolutional code and the repetition code to enhance the robustness of the embedded watermark. Before embedding, the binary watermark is scanned to one-dimension sequence and later inputted into the (3, 1, 2) convolutional encoder and (3, 1) repetition encoder frame by frame, which will improve the error correcting capability of decoder. The output code sequence is scanned to some matrixes as the new watermark messages. The watermarking is selected in low frequency band of the Discrete Wavelet Transform (DWT) and therefore it can resist the destruction of image processing. Experimental results are presented to demonstrate that the robustness of a watermark with mixed ECC is much higher than the traditional one just with repetition coding while suffering JPEG lossy compression, salt and pepper noise and center cutting processing.

Keywords: Error Correcting Code; Discrete Wavelet Transform; Mixed ECC; Watermarking

1. Introduction

The rapid expansion of the Internet and overall development of digital technologies in the past years introduces a new set of challenging problems regarding security. One of the significant problems is to prevent unauthorized copying of digital production from distribution. Digital watermarking has provided a powerful way to claim intellectual protection. Watermark must have two most important properties: transparency and robustness. Transparency refers to the perceptual quality of the watermarked data. The watermark should be invisible over all types. Robustness is a most important property of watermark. It means that the watermark is still presented in the image and can be detected after distortion. Ideally, the amount of image distortion necessary to degrade the desired image quality should destruct and remove the watermark in the traditional watermarking without ECC. So it is need to enhance the robustness of the embedded watermark by introducing the ECC, which can control the mistake and improve the reliability of data transmission in digital communication. With ECC appending some redundancy bits in the original embedded watermark, the error part of the extracted watermark can be corrected [1-12].

In this paper a digital image watermarking method based on mixed Error Correcting Code is presented. The main work is to encode the watermark with mixed ECC before embedding. (3, 1, 2) convolutional encoder is selected to encode the binary watermark sequence inputted by frames into some code sequences, among which the hamming distances weight are heavy. Before being embedded in DWT domain as new watermark messages, the code sequences are encoded once more with repetition coding. This processing can add more redundancy among codes and increase the error correcting capability of decoder. In fact, the convolutional encoder is used to enlarge the hamming distance among message blocks. The error correcting capability is depended on the code distance. At the point of being free from the errors resulting from some destructions, the heavy code distance is always expected, because that the minimum distance means the worst situation in code blocks. The detection method of decoder is maximum likelihood method based on minimum distance principle. In our experiments, the results show that the proposed technique gives a larger error correcting extent and can recover the lost messages as more as possible against the JPEG lossy compression, salt and pepper noise and center cutting processing. When same degree of invisibility is maintained, the watermarking with mixed ECC offers a higher degree of robustness than the one just with repetition coding.

In the signal channel, watermark can be treated as a transmitted signal, while the destruction from attackers is regarded as a noisy distortion in channel. According to the viewpoint mentioned above, we provide an idea using ECC to detect and correct the error part of the extracted watermark. The organization of this paper is as follows. Section 2 presents the coding principle of Convolutional Code. Section 3 presents the characteristic of Convolutional Codes and the decoding principle. Section 4 describes the watermark insertion and extraction. Experimental results and discussions are given in Section 5 and conclusions are drawn in Section 6.

2. The Coding Principle of Convolutional Code

Convolutional encoder is a finite memory system. When it works, the input message sequence is divided into some k-length message blocks. The encoder, for every message block, will product (n-k) detecting elements and form an n-length code block, named subcode. At sometime, these (n-k) detecting elements have a relation not only with k message letters in its subcode, but also with m message letters prior to them. Convolutional code is written to be (n, k, m)-form as to emphasize three most important parameters, k represents the message bit, n the code length, k/n the code rate, m the coding storage or storage cycle of message blocks in encoder.

Here, convolutional coding is described with matrix, continuing the way of Linear Block Code. The (3, 1, 2) convolutional encoder is used as an example to perform the proposed technique. Let $M(=[m_0, m_1, m_2, \cdots, m_i, \cdots])$ and $c=([m_0, p_{01}, p_{02}, m_1, p_{11}, p_{12}, m_2, p_{21}, p_{22}, m_3, p_{31}, p_{32}, \cdots])$ denote the endless input message sequence and the output code sequence, respectively. (3, 1, 2) convolutional encoder is designed as follows:

$$c=[m_0\ m_1\ m_2,\cdots,\ m_i,\cdots]\times A = M\times G_\infty \tag{1}$$

$$\text{where } A=\begin{bmatrix} 1&1&1&0&1&0&0&0&1&0&0&0&0&0&0&\cdots \\ 0&0&0&1&1&1&0&1&0&0&0&1&0&0&0&\cdots \\ 0&0&0&0&0&0&1&1&1&0&1&0&0&0&1&\cdots \\ &&&&&&&&&1&1&1&0&1&0&\cdots \\ &&&&&&&&&0&0&0&1&1&1&\cdots \\ &&&&&&&&&0&0&0&0&0&0&\cdots \\ &&&&&&&&&&&\cdots&\cdots&\cdots&\cdots&\cdots \end{bmatrix}.$$

The generator matrix G_∞ of (3, 1, 2) convolutional encoder is a semi-unlimited matrix, in which rows and lines are countless. In G_∞, the later row is just a result from the former one's right moving for 3 steps. So G_∞ can be absolutely defined by the first row g_∞. And in g_∞, only 3 blocks are nonzero. The number 3(=m + 1) means the constraint degree in encoder. As k×n generator submatrixes, g_0, g_1, g_2 represent the nonzero blocks, $g_0 = [111]$, $g_1 = [010]$, $g_2 = [001]$. You will see that G_∞ can be obtained only all these generator submatrixes are known.

When the encoding is in process, the whole message sequence is not inputted into the encoder once a time. To increase the speed in decoding, it need introduce the time-delay. The message sequence M will be sent into encoder by frames and each frame contains L message blocks.

3. Characteristic and Decoding Principle of Convolutional Code

The performance of convolutional code lies on code distance and decoding method. The code distance is itself an attribute of convolutional code and determines the potential error correcting capability. And decoding method is a way that how to transform this potential error correcting capability into the practical one. Now, let C_1 and C_2 denote two different binary block sections which are randomly outputted from same G_∞. Code distance is actually the hamming distance weight after binary addition of corresponding code letters in C_1 and C_2. Owing to the closeness of linear convolutional code, if $C_1 + C_2 = C$, then C is also one of the output block sections. The rule can be generally described as:

$$d(C_1,C_2)=W(C_1+C_2)=W(C)=W(C+0)=d(C,0) \tag{2}$$

It had been shown that code distance of two random sequences is equivalent to hamming distance weight between some sequence and all-zero one. The error correcting capability of decoder lies on the minimum distance among the output sequences. As usual, maximum likelihood decoding is exactly the minimum distance decoding which becomes equivalent to finding the least-metric (shortest) path.

For any output coded frame, there is always an original unique one corresponding to it. But in decoder, once the error occurs in transmission or storage, the input received frame is a specious and intermittent sequence, just a reference for decoding, not the original one. The performance of maximum likelihood decoding is described as follows: Compute all the hamming distances between the received frame sequence and every original one. Choose an original sequence corresponding the minimum hamming distance as the output estimated value. In (3, 1, 2) convolutional encoder, k = 1, we let L = 8, and there are $2^{kL} = 256$ original sequences, named block sections, for detection. Generally speaking, maximum likelihood decoding does not mean to compare with the whole input code sequence. Instead, when receiving a frame, the decoder compares with all the block sections and chooses a most likelihood one, making the whole input code sequence corresponding to minimum distance in the end. It need point out that maximum likelihood decoding has a regular recursive structure in decoder. Its complexity is proportional to the 2^{km} shifting states in encoder, not L which only has a linear relation with the time used for decoding.

4. Watermark Insertion and Extraction

Except for the convolutional coding stated above, we also introduce repetition code as other error correcting encoding technique. The rule of repetition coding is repeating each original signal of a watermark N times in block section, named block section (N, 1). In the decoding process, we use the majority elements of the block section to reconstruct the original signal. For example, we set N = 5 in the binary signal and the (000) represents 0, the (111) represents 1. In the decoding process, the reconstructed signal is "0" if the number of "0" is more than 2 in a block section; otherwise it is "1". The mixed combination of convolutional code and repetition code once more enhances the error correcting capability of decoder and gives a larger error correcting extent.

We use a gray image F in our experiment of which size is $R_1 \times R_1$ in pixels as host image and the watermark W is a $R_2 \times R_2$ binary image. And $R_1 \times R_1/(2R_2 \times 2R_2 \times n \times N)$ is acquired to be a integer. The main steps of the watermark embedding procedure based on mixed ECC are presented here.

1) Divide F into $2R_1 \times 2R_1$ blocks and a subblock sequence $B(= B_1, B_2, \cdots, B_K)$ is obtained. According to the degree of texture complexity, B is arranged to $B'(=B_{a1}, B_{a2}, \cdots, B_{aK})$, $B_{a1} \leq B_{a2} \leq \cdots \leq B_{ak}$. In B′, the anterior (n × N) subblocks are chose for embedding with code message.

2) Scan W into a $R_2 \times R_2$-length message sequence M. Divided M into some k-length message blocks. Every L message blocks as a frame are sent into (n, k, m) convolutional encoder. c denotes the whole output code sequence, of which length is $n \times R_2 \times R_2$.

3) Scan c into n $R_2 \times R_2$ matrixes as the code message matrixes $(W_1, W_2, \ldots, W_n)$. Then repeat each matrix of code messages N times and orderly embed these coded matrixes into the chosen subblocks for an invisible watermarking. The way of pixel-to-pixel embedding is commonly used. The addition rule can be generally described as:

$$B_i' = \mathrm{IWDT}\left[\left(W_j + \beta \times B_{iLxy}\right) \oplus B_{iHxy}\right] \quad (3)$$

where β represents the set of parameter of the embedder, B_{iLxy} the low frequency subband, B_{iHxy} the high frequency subbands at scale 1. W_j and B_i' refer to one of coded matrixes and one watermarked subblock, respectively.

With an access to the original unwatermarked image F and generator matrix G_∞, the steps of watermark extraction are reverse processing of insertion. When extracting, the key step will be how to effectively decode. As to repetition decoding, the N multiple extracted messages are constructed to one multiple code message matrixes $(W_1, W_2, \cdots, W_n)$ according to principle of the fraction obeying the majority. The work of convolutional decoding is to search out the most likelihood block sections for each received frame in decoder. The n message matrixes are scanned to a one-dimension sequence which is constituted by some frames. According to maximum-likelihood-decoding principle, compare with block sections and choose the most likelihood one for each frame. At last, link all the most likelihood block sections back to the code sequence c which will be returned to the original message sequence M.

5. Experimental Results and Discussions

The 512 × 512 gray host image and the 64 × 64 binary watermark are shown in **Figure 1**. (3, 1, 2) convolutional code and (3, 1) repetition code are combined to be mixed ECC, L and β are set to 8 and 7, respectively. We have obtained PSNR of 44.0259 dB. Experimental result shows clearly that the watermarked image is not perceptually different from the original one.

5.1. Robustness in Image Distortion

In order to verify the capacity of the mixed ECC technique, we have watermarked image suffer some attacks and make sure our technique is able to detect and correct the error part of the extracted watermark. We find that the mixed ECC is robust to lower quality JPEG compression, salt-and pepper noise and center cutting processing (see **Figure 2**). So the result demonstrates an important aspect of mixed ECC is its adequate error correcting capability only if the attacked image becomes valueless. (a)

original host image

watermarked image

original watermark

extracted watermark

Figure 1. Experimental result.

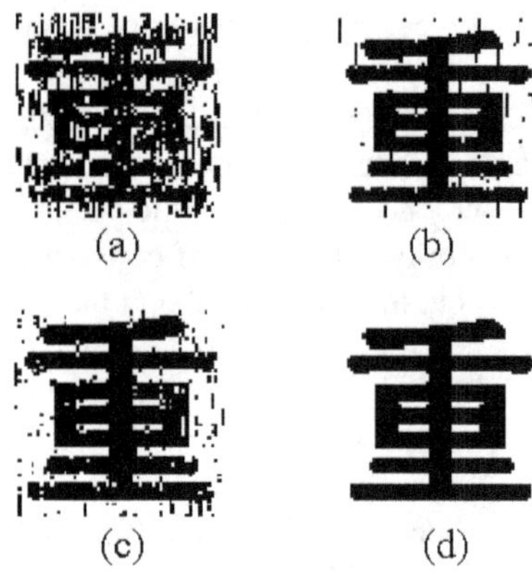

Figure 2. The extracted watermark.

multiplicative noise with density-0.01, NC = 0.7878; (b) salt-and-pepper noise with density-0.05, NC = 0.9722; (c) JPEG lossy compression with quality-50%, NC = 0.9419; (d) center cutting with size-200 × 200, some watermark messages are abandoned, NC = 1.

It can be also found from the experiment that the mixed ECC specially grants a higher degree of robustness to watermark therefore able to resist the JPEG lossy compression, salt-and pepper noise and center cutting processing while the watermarking with and without ECC have little difference in PSNR. Even if the watermarked image is tampered seriously, the mixed ECC technique can correct the error parts as more as possible and maintain the extracted watermark easy to be identified. **Figures 3**, **4** and **5** show the results graphically for easily distinguishing the differences between two techniques. So we are sure that the watermarking with mixed ECC is much better than the one only with repetition coding.

Figure 3 shows for us that even though when the JPEG qualities are smaller than 20, the quality of the extracted watermark can still provide a certification of the owner. However, when the JPEG quality downs to 40 or more below, the watermarked image is strictly destructed and commercially valueless. And **Figure 4** also reveals the prominent advantage of using mixed ECC technique. Considering that the different embedding positions for different host images, **Figure 5** just demonstrates that the mixed ECC can recover all the lost watermark messages at a certain correcting extent. In summary, the pretreatment done to watermark using mixed ECC actually exchanges robustness of watermark with increasing the message redundancy. In this paper, we obtain the expected effect when applying the Error Correcting Code to watermarking.

5.2. Transparency of the Embedded Watermark

To verify the stability of transparency, the test is performed on another 99 different images as original signals. The results shown in **Figure 6** verify that the proposed scheme has good and stable transparency.

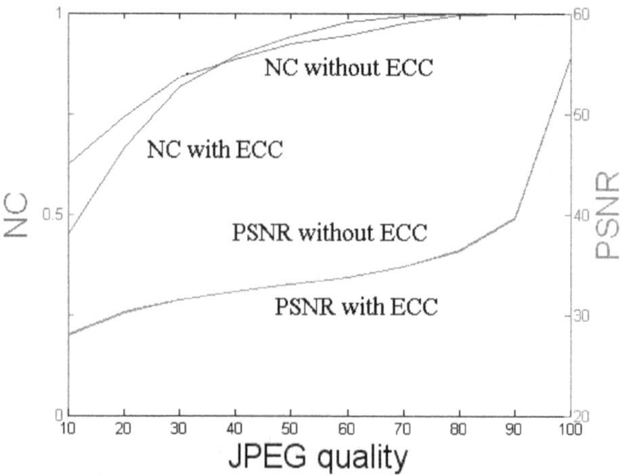

Figure 3. PSNR and NC of watermarking with two techniques under different JPEG qualities.

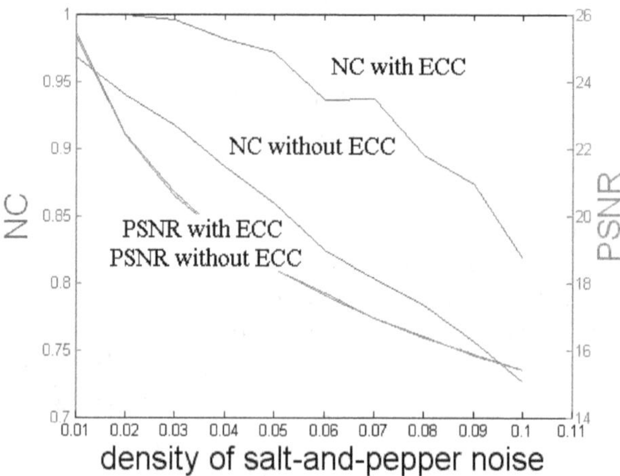

Figure 4. PSNR and NC of watermarking with two techniques under salt-and-pepper noise.

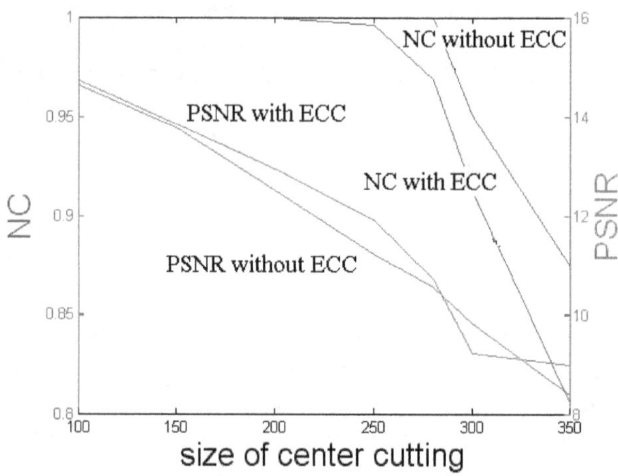

Figure 5. PSNR and NC of watermarking with two techniques under different center cutting sizes.

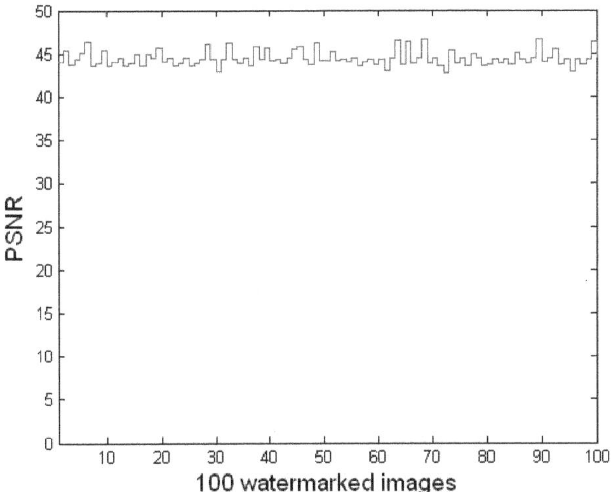

Figure 6. Transparency test results of 100 original images.

5.3. Security of the Embedded Watermark

The bit-error-rate (BER) is employed to measure the robustness of the proposed algorithm.

$$\mathrm{BER} = \left(\sum_{i=1}^{P} \sum_{j=1}^{Q} \left| W(i,j) - W^{*}(i,j) \right| \right) \Big/ (P \times Q) \tag{4}$$

where $P \times Q$ is the size of image.

Figure 7 shows the detection of the watermark to 100 random watermarks, among which there is only one matching the watermark we actually insert and detection BER is 0.

5.4. Comparing with Other ECC

We use two ECC algorithms and our mixed ECC algorithm in experiments:

1) Interlaced coding together with repetition 9 times coding: The encoded watermark is 9 multiple of the original watermark respectively (Mixed-Interlaced coding).

2) (7, 3) Cyclic redundancy check coding with repetition 4 times coding: The encoded watermark is probably 9 multiple of the original watermark respectively (Mixed-CRC coding).

We demonstrate the JPEG compression of the watermarked images with different JPEG qualities. **Figure 8** shows the results graphically for easily distinguishing the differences between various ECC algorithms. Even though when the JPEG qualities are smaller than 30, the NC of our algorithm are highest to other two ECC algorithms. So is the cutting attack. See **Figure** 9.

6. Conclusion

In this paper, we propose an idea to enhance the robustness of the watermark using the mixed ECC technique. The main work is to encode the watermark with (3, 1, 2) convolutional encoder and (3, 1) repetition encoder before embedding. The convolutional coding is introduced to automatically take maximum advantage of the interrelation

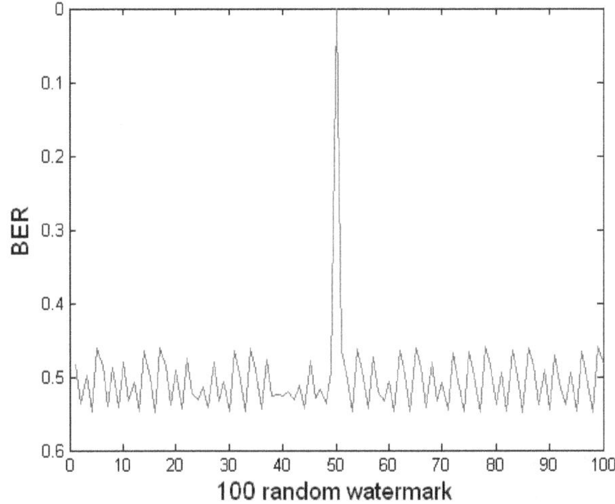

Figure 7. BER of watermark detection to 100 random watermarks.

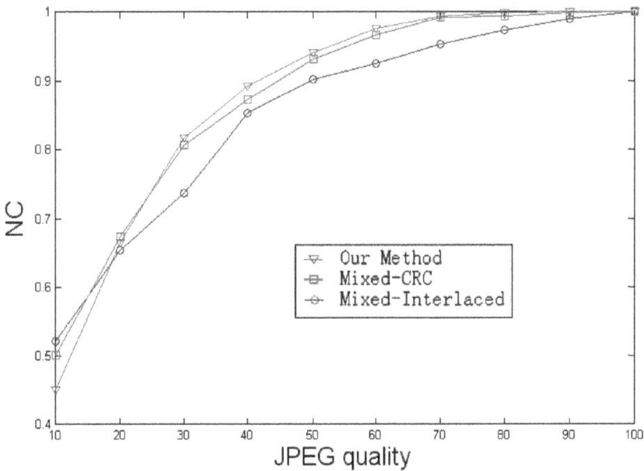

Figure 8. NC of watermarking with various ECC algorithms under different JPEG qualities.

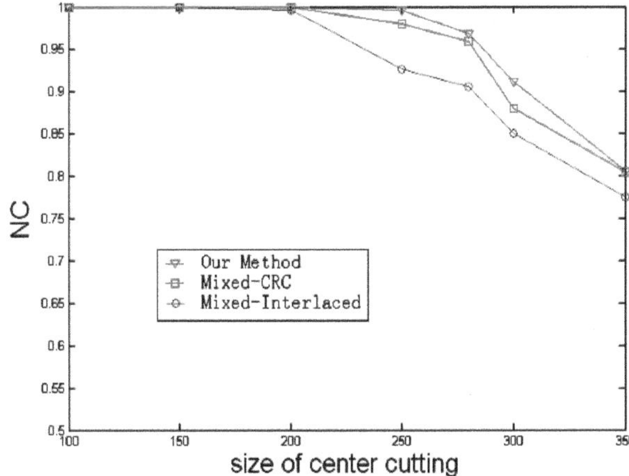

Figure 9. NC of watermarking with various ECC algorithms under different size of cutting attack.

of message blocks, among which the hamming distances will be enlarged therefore resulting convenient for decoding. Furthermore, the joining of the repetition coding can increase more message redundancy, once more enhancing the error correcting capability. After encoding, the output code sequence representing the watermark is invisibly embedded into low frequency bands of some subblocks in host image. Experimental results have confirmed that the mixed ECC based watermarking will have the property that corrects errors of the extracted watermark automatically. With the characteristic of mixed ECC, the robustness of a watermark with ECC is relatively higher than the traditional one just with repetition coding. The coded watermark can survive the lower quality JPEG compression, various salt-and-pepper noise and center cutting processing and maintain a better visual quality of the extracted watermark. Further research will focus on the development of robust watermarking methods with more powerful error correcting capability technique.

7. Acknowledgements

This work is supported by Huaqiao University Science and Technology Foundation (No. 10Y0199) and the Fundamental Research Funds for the Central Universities (No. JB-ZR1131), the Project-sponsored by SRF for ROCS, SEM. and the Natural Science Foundation of Fujian Province of China (No. 2011J05151), Natural Science Foundation Project of Chongqing (No. CSTC, 2008BB2070).

REFERENCES

[1] C.-H. Huang and J.-L. Wu, "Attacking Visible WaterMarking Schemes," *IEEE Transactions on Multimedia*, Vol. 6, No. 1, 2004, pp. 16-30.

[2] J. Tian, "Wavelet-Based Reversible Watermarking for Authentication," *Proceedings of SPIE Security and Watermarking of Multimedia Contents III*, San Jose, 21 January 2002, pp. 679-690.

[3] D. M. Thodi and J. J. Rodriquez, "Prediction-Error-Based Reversible Watermarking," *Proceedings of the International Conference on Image Processing of the IEEE ICIP*, 24-27 October 2004, pp. 1549-1552.

[4] I. J. Cox and M. L. Miller, "The First 50 Years of Electronic Watermarking," *Journal of Applied Signal Processing*, Vol. 56, No. 2, 2002, pp. 126-132.

[5] D. M. Thodi and J. J. Rodriquez, "Expansion Embedding Techniques for Reversible Watermarking," *IEEE Transactions on Image Processing*, Vol. 16, No. 3, 2007, pp. 721-730.

[6] Y. J. Hu, S. Kwong and J. W. Huang, "An Algorithm for Removable Visible Watermarking," *IEEE Transactions on Circuits Systems for Video Technology*, Vol. 16, No. 1, 2006, pp. 129-133.

[7] C. I. Podilchuk and E. J. Delp, "Digital Watermarking: Algorithms and Applications," *IEEE Signal Processing Magazine*, Vol. 18, No. 4, 2001, pp. 33-46.

[8] M. U. Celik, G. Sharma and A. M. Tekalp, "Lossless Watermarking for Image Authentication: A New Framework and an Implementation," *IEEE Transactions on Image Processing*, Vol. 15, No. 4, 2006, pp. 1042-1049.

[9] A. van Leest, M. van der Veen and F. Bruekers, "Reversible Image Watermarking," *Proceedings of the International Conference on Image Processing*, Barcelona, 14-17 September 2003, pp. 731-734.

[10] M. Barni, F. Bartolini and A. Piva, "Improved Wavelet-Based Watermarking through Pixel-Wise Masking," *IEEE Transactions on Image Processing*, Vol. 10, No. 5, 2001, pp.783-791.

[11] J. Yang, M. H. Lee, X. H. Chen, *et al*., "Mixing Chaotic Watermarks for Embedding in Wavelet Transform domain," *Proceedings of IEEE International Symposium on Circuits and Systems*, New York, 26-29 May 2002, pp. 668-671.

[12] K.-X. Yi, J.-Y. Shi and X. Sun, "Digital Watermarking Techniques: An Introductory Revive," *Journal of Image Graphics*, Vol. 6, No, 2, 2001, pp. 111-117.

A Fair Electronic Cash System with Identity-Based Group Signature Scheme

Khalid. O. Elaalim[1,2], Shoubao Yang[2]
[1]Department of Statistic and Computer Science, Faculty of Applied Sciences, Red Sea University, Port Sudan, Sudan
[2]School of Computer Science and Technology, University of Science and Technology of China, Hefei, China

ABSTRACT

A fair electronic cash system is a system that allows customers to make payments anonymously. Furthermore the trusted third party can revoke the anonymity when the customers did illegal transactions. In this paper, a new fair electronic cash system based on group signature scheme by using elliptic curve cryptography is proposed, which satisfies properties of secure group signature scheme (correctness, unforgeability, etc.). Moreover, our electronic cash contains group members (users, merchants and banks) and trusted third party which is acted by central bank as group manager.

Keywords: Elliptic Curve; Bilinear Pairings; Group Signature; Electronic Cash; Trusted Third Party; Tracing Protocol

1. Introduction

The first group signature scheme was proposed by David Chaum and van-Heyst in 1991 [1]. Group signature schemes allow a group member to sign messages on behalf of the group. Such signatures must be anonymous and unlinkable but, whenever needed, a designated group manager can reveal the identity of the signer [1-3]. Shamir proposed an identity based signature to simplify key management procedures of certificate-based public key infrastructures (PKI) [4]. A lot of identity based group signatures have been proposed after Shamir [5-8]. Many group signatures scheme have been proposed recently, but several of them were suggested application electronic cash. [9-11] introduced group signatures into electronic cash schemes which are anonymous and unlinkability.

Main Contribution

In this paper, identity based group signature scheme is proposed, which satisfies the electronic cash based on group signatures. Furthermore it provides to keep group member anonymous and unlinkability if he does not cheat. In this scheme we use trusted third party, which acts the group manager. The user is a group member who should register at TTP before start any interaction with the bank.

The rest of this paper is as follows: in the next section, we introduce some preliminaries work. Our identity based group signature is presented in Section 3. In Section 4, we propose a new electronic cash system. We explain security analysis of our scheme in Section 5. Final section concludes.

2. Preliminaries

In this section, we will describe the definition and properties of elliptic curve cryptography, bilinear pairings, Gap Diffie-Hellman Group and Group signature models.

2.1. Elliptic Curve Cryptography

2.1.1. Definition1: Addition Rules of Elliptic Curve [12]

It is possible to define an addition rule to add points on E. The addition rule is specified as follows:

Identity: $P+O=O+P=P \quad \forall P \in E(Z_q)$

Negation: if $P=(x,y)\in E(Z_q)$ then $P+Q=0$ where $Q=(x,-y)\in E(Z_q)$ and denoted by $-P$.

Note: $O=-O$

Add two points with different x-coordinates:

Let $P=(x_1,y_1)$ *and* $Q=(x_2,y_2)\in E(Z_q)$ be two points such that $x_1\neq x_2$ then $P+Q=R=(x_3,y_3)$ as shown in **Figure 1**, where

$$x_3=\left(\frac{y_2-y_1}{x_2-x_1}\right)^2-x_1-x_2$$

$$y_3=\left(\frac{y_2-y_1}{x_2-x_1}\right)(x_1-x_3)-y_1$$

Add a point to itself (double a point) with $x_1\neq 0$:

Let $P=(x_1,y_1)\in E(Z_q)$, then $P+P=2P=(x_3,y_3)$, where:

$$x_3=\left(\left(3x^2+a\right)/2y\right)^2-2x_1$$

$$y_3=\left(\left(3x^2+a\right)/2y\right)^2(x_1-x_3)-y_1$$

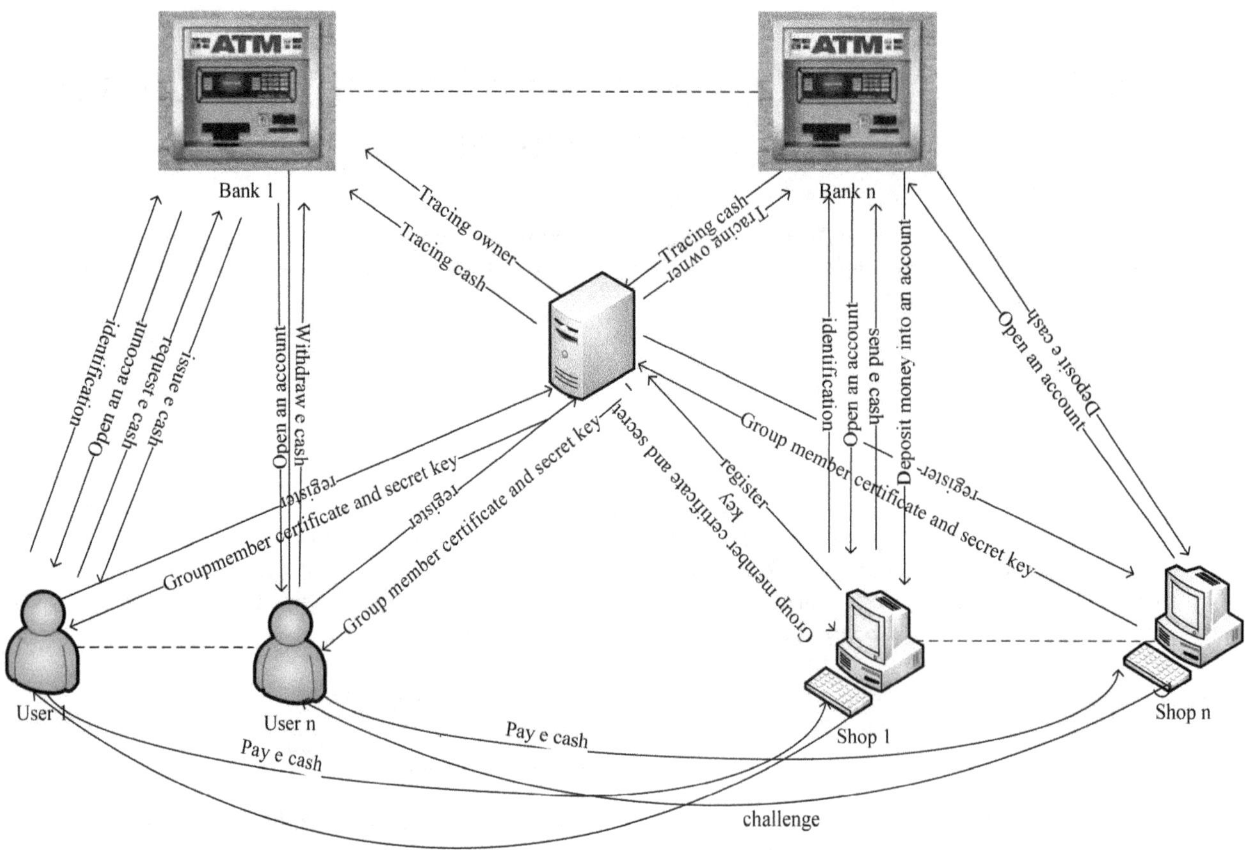

Figure 1. Architecture of our electronic cash scheme.

2.1.2. Definition 2 Elliptic Curve Discrete Logarithm Problem (ECDLP)

Given an elliptic curve E defined over a finite field Z_q, a point $P and Q \in E(Z_q)$ of order n, find the integer $x \in [0, n-1]$ such that $Q = xP$. The integer x is called the discrete logarithm of Q to the base P denoted as $x = \log_P Q$. If x is sufficient large, then it is infeasible to compute it [13].

2.2. Bilinear Pairings

Let G_1 and G_2 be two cyclic groups generates by P, whose order is a prime q, where G_1 is additive groups and G_2 is multiplicative group. A pairing is a function:

$e: G_1 \times G_1 \to G_2$

All pairing will satisfy the following properties:

1) Bilinear: For all $P, Q \in G_1$ and $a, b \in Z_q^*$ then $e(aP, bQ) = e(P, Q)^{ab}$

2) Non-degenerate: There exists $P, Q \in G_1$ such that $e(P, Q) \neq 1$

3) Computable: There is an efficient algorithm to compute $e(P, Q)$ for all $P, Q \in G_1$.

2.3. Gap Diffie-Hellman Group

We first introduce the following problems in G [14].

1) Discrete Logarithm Problem (DLP): if given P and Q, to find $n \in Z_q^*$ from $Q = nP$.

2) Computation Diffie-Hellman Problem (CDHP). Given (P, aP, bP) for $a, b \in Z_q^*/q$, to compute abP.

3) Decisional Diffie-Hellman Problem (DDHP).

Given (P, aP, bP, cP), or $a, b, c \in Z_q^*/q$, to decide whether $c = ab$.

We call G_1 a GDH group if DDHP can be solved in polynomial time but no polynomial times an algorithm can solve CDHP or DLP with non-negligible advantage within polynomial time.

2.4. Group Signature Model

A group signature scheme is comprised of the following procedures [5]:

1) Setup: An algorithm that generates the group public key and a group master key for the group manager.

2) Extract: A protocol between the group manager and a group member that generates the user's secret key and public key.

3) Sign: A probabilistic algorithm (with inputs as a group public key, a membership secret and a message m) outputs a group signature of m.

4) Verify: An algorithm for establishing the validity of an alleged group signature of a message with respect to the group public key.

5) Reveal: An algorithm that, given a message, a valid group signature on it, a group public key and a group manager's master key, determines the identity of the actual signer.

A secure group signature scheme should satisfy all or part of the properties:

1) Correctness: Group signatures produced by a group member must be valid.

2) Unforgeability: Only group members are able to sign messages on behalf of the group.

3) Anonymity: It is infeasible to find out the group member who signed a message without the group manager's secret key.

4) Unlinkability: Deciding whether two different valid signatures were computed by the same group member is computationally hard.

5) Exculpability: Neither a group member nor the group manager can sign on behalf of other group members.

6) Traceability: The group manager is always able to identify the actual signer for a valid signature in case of disputes.

7) Coalition-resistance: No coalition of members can prevent a group signature from being opened.

3. Our Identity Based Group Signature

In this section we consider ID-based group signature scheme from bilinear pairings, which can be implemented as follows:

3.1. Setup

Setup is a system generation. The group manager executes the following:

Choose p,q,G_1,G_2 as defined in 2.2 and choose $G_3 \in E(Z_q)$ .Select three hash function cryptography H_1, H_2 and H_3 which satisfy $H_1:\{0,1\}^* \times G_1 \to Z_q^*$ $H_2:\{0,1\}^* \times G_1 \to G_1$ and $H_3:\{0,1\}^* \to G_1$ Select $x_t \in Z_q^*$ as secret key.

Compute $P_t = x_t G, P_1 = x_t G_1, P_2 = x_t G_2$ *and* $P_3 = x_t G_{31}$ and publish $\left(E(Z_q), n, q, G, G_1, G_2, P, P_1, P_2, P_3, H_1\right)$ as public key.

3.2. Extract

Before the user joins the group, manager should execute this step:

1) Select random number $x_i \in Z_q^*$ as private key.

2) Compute $P_i = x_i G$ as public key.

When the user wants to become the member of group then the user i and the group manager can cooperates as follows:

1) The user sends his public key with ID (identification) to the group manager.

2) Group manager select random numbers $v_i \in Z_q^*$ for every member who want become group member.

3) Group manager calculate $sk_i = (v_i + x_t) Q_{ID_i}$ where $Q_{ID_i} = H_1(ID_i, P_i)$ and then sends (v_i, sk_i) to the user as the membership certificate.

3.3. Sign

When the user wants to sign message *m*, the user can do the followings:

The user selects random elements $k, x, d, \alpha, \beta, \gamma, r_1, r_2 \in Z_q^*$ and $M, W \in G_1$, and then calculates the followings:

$$A_1 = e(M, P_i),\ A_2 = e(S_{ID_i}, G)$$

$$A_4 = e(M, W),\ A_3 = e(W, G)$$

$$B_0 = x_i(v_i M + \alpha A_3),\ U = x_i^{-1} B_0 + kG - \alpha A_3$$

$$B = e(S_{ID_i}, U),\ B_1 = kP_i + vxx_i A_2$$

$$C = x_i^{-1} B_1 + \alpha A_3 - kP_i,\ B_2 = r_1 A_1 + dA_4$$

$$D = B_2 + r_2 B - dA_4,\ B_3 = r_2 B + \beta W$$

$$E = B_3 + dA_4 - r_2 B \quad U_1 = P_t + v_i G$$

$$F = H_2(ID \| U + C + D + W)$$

$$H = k\alpha dG \quad R = \gamma F + H$$

$$h = H_1(m \| U + C + D + W + R)$$

$$S = hk\alpha dP_i + x_i R \bmod p$$

The resulting signature on the message *m* is (*U*, *C*, *D*, *W*, *R*, *S*).

3.4. Verify

When the receiver wants to verify the group signature (*U*, *C*, *D*, *W*, *R*, *S*) of the message *m* which is signed by the signer, the receiver first computes $h = H_1(m \| U + C + D + W + R)$ and then verifies $e(S, G) = (hH + R, P_i)$.

3.5. Open

This algorithm is only executed by the group manager. Given valid group signatures the group manager can easily find the identity of the signer. The signer cannot deny his group signatures after group manager presents the followings:

$$e(S_{ID_i}, G) = e(Q_{ID_i}, U_1)$$

$$e(U + C, P_i)\, e(D + E, G) = e(B_0 + B_1 + B_2 + B_3, G)$$

4. Our Electronic Cash System

4.1. Electronic Cash Architecture

In this section, we describe our system architecture and how each protocol of e-cash works. **Figure 1** shows configuration of group signatures, which involves three protocols: withdraw protocol, payment protocol and deposit protocol. Thus group signatures architecture consists four main parties: Trust Third Party (TTP) acts the group manager; banks, users and shops acts the group member. Their relation between each part with other as follows:

1) Trusted Third Party (TTP) is acting as group manager and the users act group membership. The user should be registering at TTP before start any interaction with the bank. After registration, the user will get a valid membership certificate and a secret key from TTP.

2) The bank issues the valid electronic cash. The bank protects the privacy of the customers, and also uses the blind signature technique to sign the electronic cash.

3) The customer spends electronic cash in a payment protocol with a shop over an anonymous channel.

4) The shop deposits electronic cash that he gets from the user in the payment protocol into his bank account.

4.2. Setup

TTP (Central Bank (CB)) generates and publishes the same system parameters that proposed in Section 3.1.

When the bank i (B_i) registers in CB, they should perform the following steps:

1) B_i selects random number $x_{B_i} \in Z_q^*$ as private key and computes $P_{B_i} = x_{B_i} G$ as public key.

2) B_i sends public key with his identification ID_{B_i} to the CB.

3) The CB does the same in Section 3.2 and sends (sk_{B_i}, v_{B_i}) to B_i as membership certificate.

And also the user $i(u_i)$ and merchant i (M_i) should do the same steps that B_i does when they want to register in CB.

Then the central bank will send the group member ship (sk_{u_i}, v_{u_i}) and (sk_{M_i}, v_{M_i}) to u_i and M_i respectively.

4.3. Open an Account

Every group member should open an account in any bank he needs it. They need to do as follows:

1) The group member sends $\mathrm{ID_i}$ to the bank B_i.

2) B_i opens an account and sends it to the group member.

4.4. Withdraw Protocol

The withdrawal protocol involves u_i and B_i which the user opens an account in. When legal u_i wants to withdraw electronic cash from his account in the bank, the user must prove himself to the bank. The withdraw protocol request contains the amount of electronic cash, which is less than or equal the balance. If the amount is greater than balance then the withdraw protocol should be stopped, otherwise, the user and the bank execute the following steps:

1) the user chooses random number $s \in Z_q^*$ and computes $A_1 = s^{-1}(P_{u_i} + P_2) + P_1$ $A_2 = sG_1 + G$ sends A_1 and A_2 to the bank i.

2) the bank selects random number $a \in Z_q^*$ and $W_1, W_2 \in G_1$ and computes

$$a_1 = e(aA_1, W_1)$$
$$a_2 = e(x_{B_i} A_1, W_2)$$
$$a_3 = e(W_2, P_{B_i})$$
$$a_4 = e(W_1, aG)$$
$$a_5 = e(A_1, ax_{B_i} W)$$

sends a_1, a_2, a_3, a_4 and a_5 to u_i.

3) the u_i calculates $Z = P_{u_i} + P_2 + sP_1 = sA_1$ $Z_1 = x_{u_i} A_2 + P_{u_i}$ selects random numbers $s_1, r_1, r_2, x_1, x_2, u, v \in Z_q^*$ and computes
$A = s_1(P_{u_i} + G_1)$, $B = x_1G_1 + x_2G_2 + uv_{u_i}G_3$,
$C = r_2G + r_1x_1G_3$, $Y_1 = x_1a_1 + uG_2$
$Y_2 = r_1a_3 + x_2G_4$, $Y_3 = v_{u_i}sa_5 + x_1sk_{u_i}$
$Y_4 = r_2a_2 + s_1G_2$, $Y_5 = ur_1a_4 + x_2G_3$
$c = H(Z, Z_1, A, B, C, Y_1, Y_2, Y_3, Y_4, Y_5)$
$c' = c/u$ sends c' to B_i.

4) the B_i computes $S_1 = c'aW_1 + x_{B_i}W_2$ sends S to u_i.

5) the u_i checks

$$e(S_1, G) \stackrel{?}{=} a_4^{c'} a_3 \quad (1)$$

and

$$e(A_1, S_1) \stackrel{?}{=} a_1^{c'} a_2 \quad (2)$$

If (1) and (2) holds, then the user accepts and computes $S_2 = uS_1 + vQ_{ID_{u_i}}$

We can proof (1) and (2) as follows:

$$e(S_1, G) = e(c'aW_1 + x_{B_i}W_2, G)$$
$$= e(c'aW_1, G)e(x_{B_i}W_2, G)$$
$$= e(W_1, aG)^{c'} e(W_2, x_{B_i}G)$$
$$= a_4^{c'} a_3$$
$$e(A_1, S_1) = e(A_1, c'aW_1 + x_{B_i}W_2)$$
$$= e(A_1, c'aW_1)e(A_1, x_{B_i}W)$$
$$= e(aA_1, W_1)^{c'} e(x_{B_i}A_1, W_2)$$
$$= a_1^{c'} a_2$$

4.5. Payment Protocol

The payment protocol involves the customer and the merchant. If the customer wants to buy some goods from the merchant, they should execute the follows:

1) The customer chooses a random $w_1, w_2 \in Z_q^*$ and computes $D = w_1uG_1 + w_2vG_2$

User sends A, B, C, D, Z, Z_1, S_2 to merchant.

2) The merchant generates a transaction message of payment for the customer d as challenge and sends to user

$d = H_0(A, B, C, D, Z, Z_1, S_2, P_{M_i}, amount, amount\ type, date/time)$

3) User calculates responses

$$f_1 = w_1 uG_1 + ds_1 x_{u_i} P_t$$
$$f_2 = w_2 vG_2 + ds_1 P_1$$
$$f_3 = x_1(dP_1 + r_1 P_3)$$
$$f_4 = d(x_2 P_2 + ux_{u_i} S_1)$$
$$f_5 = d(uv_{u_i} P_3 + vx_{u_i} Q_{ID_{u_i}}) + r_2 P_t$$

User sends f_1, f_2, f_3, f_4 *and* f_5 to merchant.

4) The signature of electronic cash is $A, B, C, D, S_2, f_1, f_2, f_3, f_4$ *and* f_5.

5) Merchant accepts if and only if

$$e(f_1 + f_2, G) \stackrel{?}{=} e(D, G)e(A, P)^d \quad (3)$$

$$e(f_3 + f_4 + f_5, G) \stackrel{?}{=} e(B, P_t)^d e(C, P_t) e(dS_2, P_{u_i}) \quad (4)$$

Now we can proof (3) and (4) as followings:

$$\begin{aligned} e(f_1 + f_2, G) &= e(w_1 uG_1 + ds_1 x_{u_i} P_t + w_2 vG_2 + ds_1 P_1, G) \\ &= e(w_1 uG_1 + w_2 vG_2, G) e(ds_1 (x_{u_i} P_t + P)_1, G) \\ &= e(D, G) e(P_t ds_1 (x_{u_i} x_t G + x_t G_1), G) \\ &= e(D, G) e(ds_1 (P_{u_i} + G_1), P_t) \\ &= e(D, G) e(dA, P_t) \end{aligned}$$

$$\begin{aligned} &e(f_3 + f_4 + f_5, G) \\ &= e(x_1(dP_1 + r_1 P_3) + d(x_2 P_2 + ux_{u_i} S_1) + d(uv_{u_i} P_3 + vx_{u_i} Q_{ID_{u_i}}) + r_2 P_t, G) \\ &= e(d(x_1 P_1 + x_2 P_2 + uv_{u_i} P_3) + dx_{u_i}(uS_1 + vQ_{ID_{u_i}}) + x_1 r_1 P_3 + r_2 P_t, G) \\ &= e(x_t d(x_1 G_1 + x_2 G_2 + uv_i G_3), G) e(dx_{u_i}(uS_1 + vQ_{ID_{u_i}}), G) e(x_t(x_1 r_1 G_3 + r_2 G), G) \\ &= e(dB, P_t) e(dS_2, P_{u_i}) e(C, P_t) \end{aligned}$$

4.6. Deposit Protocol

In this protocol the merchant *i* sends electronic cash to his bank *i*. There are two cases we will discuss as follows:

First case: if the shop *i* and user *i* have accounts in the same bank. Since the deposit protocol involves merchant and bank, they will execute the following steps:

1) The merchant sends signatures of electronic cash $A, B, C, D, Z, Z_1, S_2, f_1, f_2, f_3, f_4$ *and* f_5 to the bank.

2) The bank verifies the validity of signature of e cash $A, B, C, D, Z, Z_1, S_2, f_1, f_2, f_3, f_4$ *and* f_5.

3) If the signature of e cash $A, B, C, D, Z, Z_1, S_2, f_1, f_2, f_3, f_4$ *and* f_5 is hold, then the bank searches the deposit database to find out the same electronic cash has been deposited before or not. If it has not been in its deposit database, the bank accepts the electronic cash and credits the amount to the shop account, otherwise the bank *i* rejects transaction.

Second case: if the user i and merchant i have accounts in different banks such as user i has an account in the bank i and shop i has an account in bank j.

Assume merchant i wants to deposit the received electronic cash from user i to his bank j, they will do the following steps:

1) The merchant sends signature of electronic cash $A, B, C, D, Z, Z_1, S_2, f_1, f_2, f_3, f_4$ *and* f_5 to bank j.

2) Bank j verifies the validity of signature of e cash $A, B, C, D, Z, Z_1, S_2, f_1, f_2, f_3, f_4$ *and* f_5 with bank i's public key.

3) If it succeeds then bank j sends the electronic cash to bank i.

4) Bank i searches the deposit database to find out whether electronic cash has been deposited before, if it is not has been stored in deposit database then bank i debits the amount from user i account and sends it to the merchant i account in his bank j, otherwise bank i can detect double depositing or double spending.

4.7. The Tracing Protocol

Customer Tracing Protocol

The customer tracing protocol involves the bank and the trusted third party. This protocol is used to determine the identity of the customer in a specific payment transaction. Money laundering is big problem of electronic cash; here it can be protected by detecting the identity of the illegal customers.

1) The customer tracing protocol is as follows:

The bank sends to the CB the signatures of electronic cash $A, B, C, D, Z, Z_1, S_2, f_1, f_2, f_3, f_4$ *and* f_5 that received from the merchant in the deposit protocol.

2) The CB verifies the validity of the signature of electronic cash as the merchant does in the deposit protocol.

3) The CB can calculate P_{u_i} from (Z, A_2) as follows:

$$\begin{aligned} Z &= P_{u_i} + P_2 + sP_1 \\ &= P_{u_i} + P_2 + s(x_t G_1) \\ &= P_{u_i} + P_2 + x_t(sG_1) \end{aligned} \quad (5)$$

From $sG_1 = A_2 - G$ then put it into (5)

$Z = P_{u_i} + P_2 + x_t A_2 - P_t$

Finally we get

$P_{u_i} = Z + P_t - (P_2 + x_t A_2)$

The CB sends P_{u_i} to the bank.

Then the bank can find the actual identity corresponding to P_{u_i} in his database.

5. Analysis of Security

Theorem 1

A group member and the group manager cannot sign electronic cash on behalf of the other group members with non-negligible probability.

Proof:

Assume there is a group member who has ID_j wants to sign electronic cash on behalf of the group member who has ID_i.

He chooses random number $s \in Z_q^*$, computes and sends A_1 *and* A_2 to bank *i*.

$$A_1 = s^{-1}\left(P_{u_j} + P_2\right) + P_1$$

$$A_2 = sG_1 + G$$

The bank calculates and sends a_1, a_2, a_3, a_4 *and* a_5 back to him as withdraw protocol.

He selects random numbers $s_1, r_1, r_2, x_1, x_2, u, v \in Z_q^*$ and computes Z, C, Y_1, Y_2, Y_4, Y_5 as withdraw protocol, computes Z_1, A, B, Y_3 as follows:

$A = s_1\left(P_{u_j} + G_1\right)$, $B = x_1G_1 + x_2G_2 + uv_jG_3$,

$Y_3 = v_j sa_5 + x_1 sk_j, Z_1 = x_{u_j} A_2 + P_{u_j}$

Finally he calculates *c* as

$$c = H\left(Z, Z_1, A, B, C, Y_1, Y_2, Y_3, Y_4, Y_5\right)$$

This equation can be equal to that equation in withdraw protocol, if and only if

$$s_1 P_{u_i} = s_1 P_{u_j}, uv_i G_3 = uv_j G_3, v_i sa_5 = v_j sa_5,$$

$$x_1 sk_i = x_1 sk_j \ and \ x_{u_i} A_2 = x_{u_j} A_2$$

The probability of $x_i = x_j$ is $1/(q-1)$, $x_i, x_j \in Z_q^*$. If he wants to choose exactly $x_j = x_i$, he needs to solve discrete logarithm problem $P_{u_i} = x_{u_i} G$ as $x_{u_i} = \log_G P_{u_i}$.

Theorem 2

The proposed fair electronic cash system can protect the customer's privacy and keep the system anonymous.

Proof:

Deciding whether a payment signature from a customer requires knowing ID_{u_i} of the user. However, to know ID_{u_i} of the user in our scheme requires solving discrete logarithm problem $P_{u_i} = x_{u_i} G$ to find out the user secret key. Since solving discrete logarithm problem is very difficult, then no one can know ID_{u_i} except CB.

Theorem 3

In the payment protocol, only users that register in the CB are able to sign a payment message with his membership key.

Proof:

It is difficult to find x_{u_i} from $P_{u_i} = xG$. The forger cannot find the same x_{u_i} then it is impossible to get certificate membership$\left(sk_i, v_i\right)$ to sign a payment message.

Theorem 4

Our proposed scheme keeps the system unlinkability.

Proof: To decide whether two signatures of electronic cash $A, B, C, D, Z, Z_1, S_2, f_1, f_2, f_3, f_4$ *and* f_5 and $A', B', C', D', Z', Z_1', S_2', f_1', f_2', f_3', f_4'$ *and* f_5' are from the same customer requires deciding whether

$$d' \log_{P_{u_i}} \left(e\left(f_1 + f_2, G\right)/e\left(D, G\right)\right)$$

$$= d \log_{P_{u_i}} \left(e\left(f_1' + f_2', G\right)/e\left(D', G\right)\right),$$

it is not easy to compute it.

From the four theorems and traceable protocol above, it is easy to deduce that our scheme satisfies the security properties of group signatures and provides electronic cash against double spending, blackmailing and money laundering.

6. Conclusion

We have presented new fair electronic cash system with identity based group signature scheme. It satisfies all basic requirements to protect electronic cash. Furthermore, we show how our group signature scheme could construct fair electronic cash, which satisfy properties of secure group signature scheme.

REFERENCES

[1] D. Chaum and E. van Heyst, "Group Signatures," In: J. Feigenbaum, Ed., *Advances in Cryptology: EUROCRYPT '91—Workshop on the Theory and Application of Cryptographic Techniques*, Springer-Verlag & GmbH & Co. K, Berlin and Heidelberg, 1991, pp. 257-265.

[2] S. Canard and M. Girault, "Implementing Group Signature Schemes with Smart Cards," *Proceedings of the 5th Conference on Smart Card Research and Advanced Application*, San Jose, 21-22 November 2002, pp. 1-10.

[3] L. Chen and T. Pedersen, "New Group Signatures Schemes," In: A. D. Santis, Ed., *Advances in Cryptology—EUROCRYPT* 94: *Workshop on the Theory and Application of Cryptographic Techniques*, Springer-Verlag, Berlin, 1995, pp. 171-181.

[4] A. Shamir, "Identity-Based Cryptosystems and Signature Schemes," *Proceedings of CRYPTO* 84 *on Advances in Cryptology*, Santa Barbara, 19-22 August 1984, pp. 47-53.

[5] X. Chen, F. Zhang and K. Kim, "A New ID-Based Group Signature Scheme from Bilinear Pairings," 2003. http://eprint.iacr.org/2003/116.2003

[6] S. Han, J. Wang and W. Liu1, "An Efficient Identity-Based Group Signature Scheme over Elliptic Curves," *Proceedings of the ECUMN* 2004, Porto, 25-27 October 2004, pp. 417-429.

[7] Z. Tan and Z. Liu, "A Novel Identity-Based Group Signature Scheme from Bilinear Maps," MM Research Pre-

prints, 2003, pp. 250-255.

[8] J. Cha and J. Cheon, "An Identity-Based Signature from Gap Diffie-Hellman Groups," *Proceedings of the PKC* 2003, Miami, 6-8 January 2003, pp. 18-30.

[9] A. Lysyanskaya and Z. Ramzan, "Group Blind Digital Signatures: A Scalable Solutionto Electronic Cash," *Proceedings of the Financial Cryptography: Second International Conference, FC*'98, Anguilla, 23-25 February 1998, pp. 184-197.

[10] T. Nakanishi, N. Haruna and Y. Sugiyama, "Unlinkable Electronic Couponprotocol with Anonymity Control," *Proceedings of the International Workshop on Information Security* (*ISW* 99), Kuala Lumpur, 6-7 November 1999, pp. 37-46.

[11] J. Traor´e, "Group Signatures and Their Relevance to Privacy-Protecting Off-Line Electronic Cash Systems," *Proceedings of the Australasian Conference on Information Security and Privacy* (*ACISP* 99), Wollongong, 7-9 April 1999, pp. 228-243.

[12] D. B. Johnson and A. J. Menezes, "Elliptic Curve DSA (ECDSA): An Enhanced DSA," 2000. http://www.certicom.com

[13] D. Hankerson, A. Menezes and S. Vanstone, "Guide to Elliptic Curve Cryptography," Springer-Verlag, New York, 2004.

[14] J. Cha and J. Cheon, "An Identity-Based Signature from Gap DiffieHellman Groups," *Proceedings of the PKC* 2003, Miami, 6-9 January 2003, pp. 18-30.

A Tree Model for Identification of Threats as the First Stage of Risk Assessment in HIS

Ahmad Bakhtiyari Shahri[1], Zuraini Ismail[2]
[1]Faculty of Computer Science and Information Systems, Universiti Teknologi Malaysia, Johor Bahru, Malaysia
[2]Advanced Informatics School, Universiti Teknologi Malaysia, Johor Bahru, Malaysia

ABSTRACT

Security remains to be a critical issue in the safe operation of Information Systems (IS). Identifying the threats to IS may lead to an effective method for measuring security as the initial stage for risk management. Despite many attempts to classify threats to IS, new threats to Health Information Systems (HIS) remains a continual concern for system developers. The main aim of this paper is to present a research agenda of threats to HIS. A cohesive completeness study on the identification of possible threats on HIS was conducted. This study reveals more than 70 threats for HIS. They are classified into 30 common criteria. The abstraction was carried out using secondary data from various research databases. This work-in-progress study will proceed to the next stage of ranking the security threats for assessing risk in HIS. This classification of threats may provide some insights to both researchers and professionals, who are interested in conducting research in risk management of HIS security.

Keywords: Health Information System; Threat; Security

1. Introduction

As the European Union has acknowledged, "innovation is important in today's society, but it should not go at the expense of people's fundamental right to privacy" [1]. An effective information security program includes a combination of human and technological controls to prevent loss of data, accidental or deliberate unauthorized activity, and illegal access to data [2].

However use of information and communication technology (ICT) in healthcare has created the electronic health environment and electronic health information is the core of an electronic health system that is managed by ICTs [3]. In addition because healthcare information technology has different potential to improve the quality of care and efficiency and it can also reduce medical costs and save lives so, it is currently one of the important factors for major innovations and is used in widespread around the world [4]. Therefore, if an E-health system guarantees privacy and security of patients it will succeed [5].

In recent years number of threats in health information systems (HIS) area has increased dramatically and lack of adequate security measures has caused in numerous data breaches, leaving patients vulnerable to economic threats, mental anguish and maybe social stigma. [6]. For example, between the years of 2006 to 2007 in hospitals alone, occurred exposing of more than 1.5 million names during data breaches [7]. In addition, result of 2010 Healthcare Information and Management Systems Society Security Survey suggests that the reports of more than 110 healthcare organizations have shown the loss of sensitive Protected Health Information or Personal Identifying Information affected over 5,306,000 individuals since January 2008. They were received as theft (stolen laptops, computers, or media), loss or negligence by employees or third parties, malicious insiders, system hacks, web exposure, and virus attacks [8]. So, storage information in electronic format increases the concerns about the security and privacy of patients [9]. Another study has shown that healthcare information systems of accidental events and deliberate action threats are two parameters that can severely damage HIS reliability and have negative effects on HIS [10]. However, poor organization of security measures, lack of an integrated security assessment architecture and framework and low awareness of risk analysis practices also need particular attention. As in developed countries standards of framework use in place. For example, using ISO/IEC 27002 (ISO 27799:2008) or the Health Insurance Portability and Accountability Act (HIPAA) in the healthcare environment in protecting computerized information assets [11].

By understanding the threats to health information security, the organization can better protect its information assets and strengthen the level of protection of information in health information system. Therefore management of E-Health information needs to identify the threats for an effective framework by considering the comprehensive incorporation of confidentiality, integrity and availability to be the core principles of information security. This raises major challenges that require new exhaustively attitudes such as a wide variety of policies, ethical, psychological, information and security procedures [5,12]. Hence the objective of this paper attempt to provide an up-to-date categorize of threats to healthcare assets.

2. Review and Role of Identification of Threats in Information Security Risk Management

Risk assessment requires an understanding of the threat sources, threat action and how that sources can be exploited vulnerability in a health information asset [4]. Although identifying of threats in information system is crucial stage in risk management [13] and discussion about privacy and security [12] has long been a major subject in the social science and business press, there has been controversy about lacking a systematic investigation to identify and categorize various sources of threats of information security and privacy in academic literature [6].

Figure 1 shows a conceptual framework for implementing of information security in HIS. This figure was adopted from works of Z. Ismail, *et al.* [14] and A. Yasinsac, *et al.* [15]. It was further adapted to include inputs, output, and also process of some steps. Based on ISO/IEC27002 [16] risk assessment is a critical strategy and identification

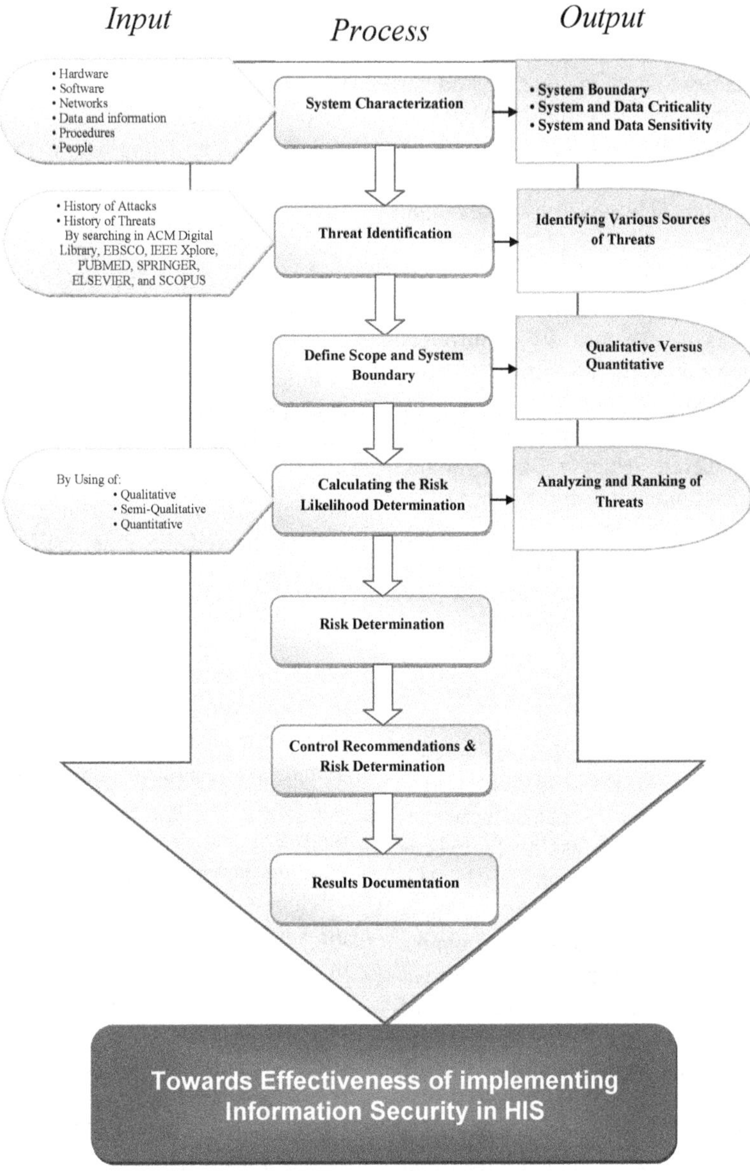

Figure 1. Conceptual Framework of Information Security.

of threats is one of the important stages in every Information Security framework [17,18]. Kotz recommended that the first step of HIS framework is to identify threats to patients' identity [19]. This is because it will help in conducting risk assessment and to assist in the development of health care security policy, guidelines and laws [4,15,20]. Hence, issues of security, identification and taxonomy of threats in the field of health care organizations are important and are mandatory parameters for health information systems [11,18].

Therefore, the research question for this paper is to categories the security threats to HIS. The next section will discuss the possible security threats to HIS.

3. State of Information Security Research in Healthcare

This section presents a comprehensive review of literature of threats to HIS. The results of CSI/FBI Annual Computer Crime and Security Survey in 2002, ranked the followings as significant threats: Virus, Insider Abuse of Net Access, Laptop, Denial of Service, Unauthorized Access by Insiders, System Penetration, Theft of Proprietary Info, Financial Fraud, Telecom Fraud, Sabotage, Telecom Eavesdropping, Active Wiretap [21].

According to Ref. [22] the most important threats about patients' confidentiality are: Accidental Disclosures, Insider Curiosity for infringers own curiosity or purposes, Insider Subornation done generally for profit, Uncontrolled Secondary Usage, and Unauthorized Access. The NIST 800-30 provides a categorization of threat sources in six items: Human Deliberate, Human Unintentional, Technical, Operational, Environmental, and Natural [23].

Recent policy-based studies broadly categorize privacy threats, or source of information security, into two areas: Organizational and Systemic threats. Organizational threats are categorized into five levels: Accidental Disclosure, Insider Curiosity, Data Breach by Insider, Data Breach by Outsider with physical intrusion and Unauthorized Intrusion of Network System [6].

A classification for the threats of IS like HIS were offered by Whitman to twelve items. [24]. He identified the priority of expenditures and to protect IS against these threats by provided an online survey by asking IT executives to rank the threats to information security [24]. The findings showed that the most critical threat for IS is "Deliberate Software Attacks" which was weighted almost twice more important in comparison to the second threat on the list. Technical Software Failures or Errors, Acts of Human Error, Failure and Deliberate Acts of Espionage or Trespass were also noted as high-risk threats for the HIS [25].

Each organization will need to prioritize the threats it faces, based on the particular security situation in which it operates, its organizational strategy regarding risk, and the exposure levels at which its assets operate [26]. Therefore, another categorization scheme has been done that consists of fourteen general categories that represents clear and present dangers to an organizations people, information, and systems. The results are generally similar to previous studies in which Espionage or Trespass and Software Attacks remain at the top of the list and Human Error or Failure in the third position. After them, there are new options, which are added in the last category namely: Missing Inadequate or Incomplete Organizational Policy or Planning and Missing Inadequate or Incomplete Controls [27]. Yeh and Chang [25] also identify fifty fundamental security countermeasures commonly adopted to evaluate the adequacy of IS security into seven categories.

According to [26], the following list, the significant threats have been classified and ranked by Annual Computer Crime and Security Survey in 2008: denial of Service, Laptop Theft, Telecom Fraud, Unauthorized Access, Virus, Financial Fraud, Insider Abuse, System Penetration, Sabotage, Theft/loss of Proprietary Info, Abuse of Wireless Network, Web Site Defacement, Misuse of Web Application, Bots, DNS, Attacks, Instant Messaging Abuse, Password Sniffing, Theft/Loss of Customer Data [28]. Additionally, ISO/IEC 27002 also addresses eleven standard areas related to information security management [16].

Study done by Narayana Samy, *et al.* [11] discovered that there are altogether 22 types of threats to Total Hospital Information system (THIS) and listed the critical threats to HIS. A year later in another study, they tested the categorization listed in a hospital in Malaysia. The results showed the most critical threats along with the ranking of threats [29].

Pardue and Patidar [20] on other hand, represent a preliminary effort at cataloging threats to electronic healthcare data associated with unauthorized access, data loss, and data corruption, which caused by vandalism, loss or corruption of data, due to faulty hardware and software, human error, malware, natural disaster and database attack.

Another model [4] of the threat tree was organized around the goal of an attacker or outcome of a threat, depending on whether the threat is intentional or not.

Then Kotz [19] provided a taxonomy consisting of 25 threats, organized around three main categories: identity threats, access threats, and disclosure threats. Threats are organized by different types such as misuse of patient identities, unauthorized access or modification of Personal Health Information (PHI), or disclosure of PHI. Each category considers three types of the adversary: Patient himself or herself, Insiders (authorized Personal Health Record (PHR) users, staff of the PHR organization, or staff of other mobile health support system), and

Outsiders (third parties acting without authorization).

Another study mentions that most people are familiar with common types of computer security breaches that are caused by Computer Viruses, The Internet, Hackers, Worms, and Malicious Software Designed to compromise or disrupt other computer systems, and the loss or theft of laptops containing sensitive data. Security of the computers embedded in sophisticated medical devices, and unauthorized communication may increase susceptibility to security breaches [18]. **Table 1** summarizes and reviewed previous work done in identifying threats to HIS. Outstanding works are itemized from the year 1992 till 2011. All in all, thirty (30) threats were classified. It is noted that "deliberate acts of theft of data", "misuse of system resources", "users errors", "deviations in quality of service" are among the common threats to HIS.

Table 1. Summary of related works on threat to HIS.

Threats to HIS	Samy (2011)	Pardue (2011)	Sharma (2011)	Kohno (2010)	Whitman (2009)	Summer (2009)	Caballero (2009)	Richardson (2008)	Ilias (2006)	Whitman (2003)	Power (2002)	Rindfleisch (1997)	Loch (1992)
Power Failure/loss	√						√		√				
Network Infrastructure Failures or Errors	√						√	√	√		√		
Technological Obsolescence	√				√					√			
Hardware Failures or Errors	√	√			√		√		√	√			
Software Failures or Errors	√	√			√	√	√		√	√			
Operational Issues	√								√				
Communications Interception	√										√		
Repudiation	√												
Espionage or Trespass	√						√						
Communications Infiltration	√							√	√		√		
Social Engineering Attacks	√												
Technical Failure	√												
Deliberate Acts of Theft of Data	√		√		√		√	√	√	√	√		
Misuse of System Resources	√		√		√		√		√	√	√	√	√
Unauthorized Communication				√				√			√		
Staff Shortage	√								√				
User Errors	√	√	√		√	√	√	√	√	√		√	√
Sabotage or Willful Damages	√				√	√	√		√	√			
Environmental Threats	√						√		√				√
Deviations in Quality of Service	√	√	√	√	√	√	√	√		√	√	√	√
Maintenance Error									√				
Misuse of Web Application	√							√	√				
Compromises to Intellectual Property					√					√			
Missing, Inadequate or Incomplete Organizational Policy or Planning			√		√								√
Missing, Inadequate or Incomplete Controls			√		√							√	√
Financial Fraud							√	√			√	√	
Terrorism	√												
Unauthorized Access to Information Database		√	√					√			√	√	√
Natural Disasters		√	√		√		√	√	√	√			√
Theft of Equipment	√		√	√	√		√	√		√	√		

4. Research Methodology

This paper proceeds in describing how the data were collected. Secondary data resources aided in providing the relevant data in identify the threats to HIS. A thorough on-line search was carried out. Among the various search databases were ACM Digital Library, AISeL, EBSCO, IEEE Xplore, PUBMED, SPRINGER, ELSEVIER, and SCOPUS. Keywords such as “threats of health information systems”, “threats to health technology”, “threats to information systems”, and “electronic health” are input for the search. From the initial 30 common criteria, it was further breakdown 70 threats. **Table 2** depicts the detailed two-level categorization of threats.

Table 2. Threat tree for HIS.

1. Power Failure/loss
    - 1.1. Power Failure of Server
    - 1.2. Power Failure of Workstation
2. Network Infrastructure Failures or Errors
    - 2.1. Technical Failure of Network Interface
    - 2.2. Technical Failure of Network Services
    - 2.3. Abuse of Wireless Network
3. Technological Obsolescence
4. Hardware Failures or Errors
    - 4.1. System’s Hardware Failures
        - 4.1.1. Switch
        - 4.1.2. Hub
        - 4.1.3. Router
        - 4.1.4. Server
        - 4.1.5. Firewall
        - 4.1.6. Others
    - 4.2. Network‘s Hardware Failures
5. Software Failures or Errors
    - 5.1. Introduction of Damaging or Disruptive Software
    - 5.2. System’s Software Failures
    - 5.3. Network‘s Software Failures
        - 5.3.1. Bugs
        - 5.3.2. Code Problems
        - 5.3.3. Unknown Loopholes
6. Operational Issues
7. Communications Interception
8. Repudiation
9. Espionage or Trespass
10. Communications Infiltration
    - 10.1. Device Reprogramming
    - 10.2. Unauthorized Data Extraction
11. Social Engineering Attacks
12. Technical Failure
13. Deliberate Acts of Theft Data
    - 13.1. Theft/loss of Customer Data or Proprietary Info
    - 13.2. Illegal Confiscation of Equipment or Information
    - 13.3. Dumping Physical Files with Critical Information in Public
14. Misuse of System Resources
    - 14.1. Third Party
    - 14.2. Information Extortion
15. Unauthorized Communication
16. Unauthorized Access to Information Database

Continued

17. Staff Shortage
18. User Errors
    - 18.1. User Errors in Using the Software Assets
    - 18.2. Masquerading the User Identity
    - 18.3. Unauthorized Use of a HIS Application
    - 18.4. Accidental Disclosure of Information
    - 18.5. Email Confidential Information to an Incorrect Address
    - 18.6. Accidental Entry Bad Data by Employees
19. Sabotage or Willful Damages
20. Natural Disasters (Acts of God)
    - 20.1. Flood
    - 20.2. Landslides
    - 20.3. Earthquake
    - 20.4. Electrical storms
    - 20.5. Lightning
    - 20.6. Tornadoes
    - 20.7. Avalanches
21. Environmental Threats
    - 21.1. Water Damage
    - 21.2. Fire
    - 21.3. Air-condition Failure
    - 21.4. Pollution
    - 21.5. Chemicals
    - 21.6. Liquid Leakage
22. Deviations in Quality of Service
    - 22.1. QoS Deviations from Service Providers
    - 22.2. Deliberate Software Attacks
        - 22.2.1. Nonetheless Purposeful, attempt to circumvent system security
        - 22.2.2. Malicious Attempt to gain unauthorized access
            - 22.2.2.1. Password Sniffing
            - 22.2.2.2. Telecom Eavesdropping
            - 22.2.2.3. Database Attack
            - 22.2.2.4. Denial of Service
            - 22.2.2.5. Web Site Defacement
            - 22.2.2.6. Bots
            - 22.2.2.7. DNS Attacks
            - 22.2.2.8. Malware Attack
                - 22.2.2.8.1. Worm
                - 22.2.2.8.2. Trojan Horses
                - 22.2.2.8.3. Spyware
                - 22.2.2.8.4. Virus
                - 22.2.2.8.5. Adware
                - 22.2.2.8.6. Macros
23. Maintenance Error
    - 23.1. Hardware
    - 23.2. Software
    - 23.3. Network
24. Misuse of Web Application
    - 24.1. Cross Site Scripts
    - 24.2. Information Leakage
    - 24.3. SQL Injection
    - 24.4. HTTP Response Splitting
25. Compromises to Intellectual Property
26. Missing, Inadequate or Incomplete Organizational Policy or Planning
27. Missing, Inadequate or Incomplete Controls
28. Financial Fraud
29. Terrorism
30. Theft of Equipment

5. Threat Tree for Risk Assessment

In order to protect the information in the organization, firstly, it is suggested to recognize the data protection and storage, transmission and processing systems. Secondly would be the category threats faced. So, information security personnel must be informed about the different threats to assets in information systems [27]. As for Health Information System there are six proposed components that include software, hardware, data, people, procedures, and networks. These six critical components enable information to be input, processed, output, and stored. Each of these IS components has some strengths and weaknesses, as well as characteristics and uses. Each component of the information system also has its own security requirements [27]. Therefore an organized classification of threats is required in order to discuss information security issues.

In this section authors propose a tree structure for cataloging threats to healthcare assets as a threat tree. The purpose of the threat tree presented here is to facilitate risk assessment and provision of the health care policy and legislation by using second data resources involves the use of different threat catalogs and literature to finding a comprehensive model which are shown in **Table 2**. The health information threat catalog has beneficial effects on risk assessment and needs categorization and documentation more than just what is shown in the **Table 2**. Risk assessment needs to provide the various sources of threats in HIS.

Each of the threats in the tree is used for providing a set of controls to decrease the risk of exploitation of vulnerability. It can also help analysts to assignment of threats as well as compare their assessment with the assessment of other analysts. From **Table 2**, we can represent the categorization in the pie format for better visualization and understanding. **Figure 2** also illustrates a simple view.

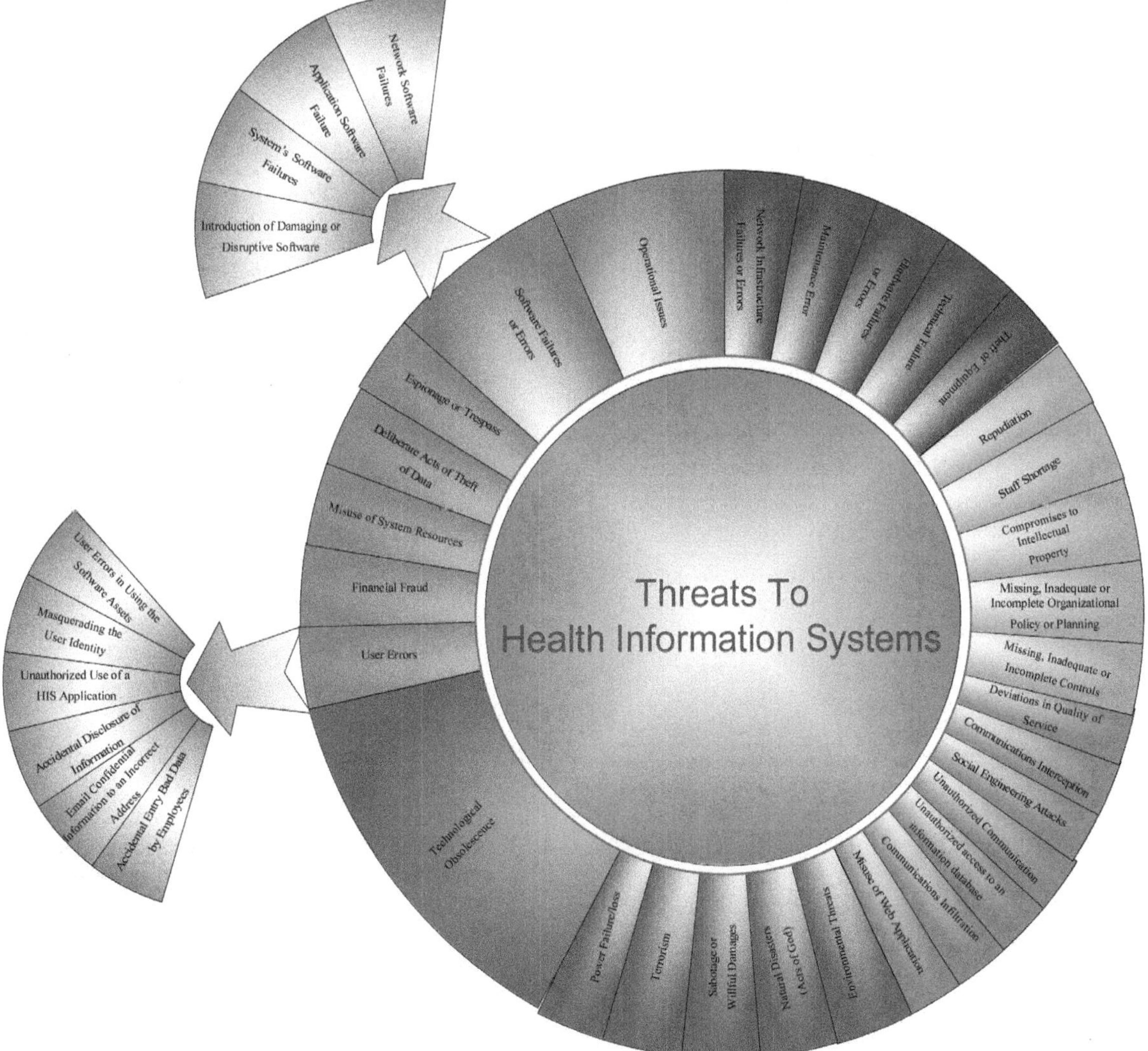

Figure 2. Simple model of threat tree for HIS.

6. Conclusion

This paper presents categorize different threats to healthcare information system. The identification of threat would play a role as an effective method in accessing security for risk management. The threat tree consolidated may provide initial step facilitating risk analysis process. Researchers and system developers may find this effort useful in the advancement of HIS security. Although this study attempts to provide a complete taxonomy for threats to HIS, it is still regarded as a work in progress as the research needs to proceed in ranking the potential security threats to HIS. Timely identification to threats is essential as technology improved and its assets progress.

7. Acknowledgements

This study was funded by the Research University Grant (RUG) from Universiti Teknologi Malaysia (UTM) and Ministry of Higher Education (MOHE) Malaysia with project number Q.K 130000.2138.01H98.

REFERENCES

[1] National Science Foundation, "Changing the Conduct of Science in the Information Age," 2011.

[2] H. Jahankhani, *et al.*, "Security Risk Management Strategy: Handbook of Electronic Security and Digital Forensics," World Scientific, New Jersey, London and Singapore, 2009, p. 237.

[3] K. M. Albert, "Integrating Knowledge-Based Resources into the Electronic Health Record: History, Current Status, and Role of Librarians," *Medical Reference Services Quarterly*, Vol. 26, No. 3, 2007, pp. 1-19.

[4] J. P. Landry, *et al.*, "A Threat Tree for Health Information Security and Privacy," *Proceedings of the 17th American Conference on Information Systems*, Detroit, 4-8 August 2011.

[5] C. A. Shoniregun, *et al.*, "Introduction to e-Healthcare Information Security," *Electronic Healthcare Information Security*, Vol. 53, 2010, pp. 1-27.

[6] A. Appari and M. E. Johnson, "Information Security and Privacy in Healthcare: Current State of Research," *International Journal of Internet and Enterprise Management*, Vol. 6, No. 4, 2010, pp. 279-314.

[7] HIMSS, "Kroll-HIMSS Analytics 2010 Report on Security of Patient Data," 2008.

[8] HIMSS, "Kroll-HIMSS Analytics 2010 Report on Security of Patient Data," 2010.

[9] G. N. Samy, *et al.*, "Threats to Health Information Security," *Proceedings of the 5th International Conference on Information Assurance and Security of the IEEE IAS*, Xi'an, 8-20 August 2009, pp. 540-543.

[10] S. Kahn and V. Sheshadri, "Medical Record Privacy and Security in a Digital Environment," *IT Professional*, Vol. 10, No. 2, 2008, pp. 46-52.

[11] G. N. Samy, *et al.*, "Security Threats Categories in Healthcare Information Systems," *Health Informatics Journal*, Vol. 16, No. 3, 2010, pp. 201-209.

[12] S. Samsuri, *et al.*, "User-Centered Evaluation of Privacy Models for Protecting Personal Medical Information," *Informatics Engineering and Information Science*, Vol. 251, 2010, pp. 301-309.

[13] A. Ekelhart, *et al.*, "AURUM: A Framework for Information Security Risk Management," *Proceedings of the 42nd Hawaii International Conference on System Sciences*, Hawaii, 5-8 January 2009, pp. 1-10.

[14] Z. Ismail, *et al.*, "Framework to Manage Information Security for Malaysian Academic Environment," *Information Assurance & Cybersecurity*, Vol. 2010, 2010, 16 p.

[15] A. Yasinsac and J. H. Pardue, "A Process for Assessing Voting System Risk Using Threat Trees," *Journal of Information Systems Applied Research*, Vol. 4, No. 1, 2010, pp. 4-16.

[16] R. Gomes and L. V. Lapão, "The Adoption of IT Security Standards in a Healthcare Environment," *Studies in Health Technology and Informatics*, Vol. 136, 2008, pp. 765-770.

[17] M. Sumner, "Information Security Threats: A Comparative Analysis of Impact, Probability, and Preparedness," *Information Systems Management*, Vol. 26, No. 1, 2009, pp. 2-12.

[18] W. H. Maisel and T. Kohno, "Improving the Security and Privacy of Implantable Medical Devices," *New England Journal of Medicine*, Vol. 362, 2010, pp. 1164-1166.

[19] D. Kotz, "A Threat Taxonomy for mHealth Privacy," *Proceedings of the 3rd International Conference on Communication Systems and Networks of the IEEE COMSNETS*, Bangalore, 4-8 January 2011, pp. 1-6.

[20] J. H. Pardue and P. Patidar, "Thrats to Healthcare Date: A Threat Tree for Risk Assessment," *Issues in Information Systems*, 5-8 October 2011.

[21] R. Power, "CSI/FBI Computer Crime and Security Survey: Computer Security Institute," SCI & FBI, 2002.

[22] T. C. Rindfleisch, "Privacy, Information Technology, and Health Care," *Communications of the ACM*, Vol. 40, No. 8, 1997, pp. 92-100.

[23] G. Stonebumer, *et al.*, "Risk Management Guide for Information Technology Systems," National Institute of Standards and Technology, 2002.

[24] M. E. Whitman, "Enemy at the Gate: Threats to Information Security," *Communications of the ACM*, Vol. 46, 2003, No. 8, pp. 91-95.

[25] M. E. Whitman, "In Defense of the Realm: Understanding the Threats to Information Security," *International Journal of Information Management*, Vol. 24, No. 1, 2004, pp. 43-

57.

[26] M. E. Whitman and H. J. Mattord, "The Enemy Is still at the Gates: Threats to Information Security Revisited," *Proceedings of the* 2010 *Information Security Curriculum Development Conference*, Kennesaw, 1-3 October 2010, pp. 95-96.

[27] M. E. Whitman and H. J. Mattord, "Principles of Information Security," Course Technology Ptr, Boston, 2011.

[28] R. Richardson, "CSI Computer Crime and Security Survey," Computer Security Institute, 2008, pp. 1-30.

[29] G. N. Samy, *et al.*, "Health Information Security Guidelines for Healthcare Information Systems," Zurich, 8-9 September 2011, p. 10.

11

Hardware Performance Evaluation of SHA-3 Candidate Algorithms

Yaser Jararweh[1], Lo'ai Tawalbeh[2], Hala Tawalbeh[1], Abidalrahman Moh'd[3]
[1]Computer Science Department, Jordan University of Science and Technology (CHiS), Irbid, Jordan
[2]Cryptographic Hardware and Information Security Lab (CHiS), Computer Engineering Department, Jordan University of Science and Technology, Irbid, Jordan
[3]Engineering Mathematics & Internetworking, Dalhousie University, Halifax, Canada

ABSTRACT

Secure Hashing Algorithms (SHA) showed a significant importance in today's information security applications. The National Institute of Standards and Technology (NIST), held a competition of three rounds to replace SHA1 and SHA2 with the new SHA-3, to ensure long term robustness of hash functions. In this paper, we present a comprehensive hardware evaluation for the final round SHA-3 candidates. The main goal of providing the hardware evaluation is to: find the best algorithm among them that will satisfy the new hashing algorithm standards defined by the NIST. This is based on a comparison made between each of the finalists in terms of security level, throughput, clock frequancey, area, power consumption, and the cost. We expect that the achived results of the comparisons will contribute in choosing the next hashing algorithm (SHA-3) that will support the security requirements of applications in todays ubiquitous and pervasive information infrastructure.

Keywords: Information Security; Secure Hash Algorithm (SHA); Hardware Performance; FPGA

1. Introduction

Cryptographic hash functions are very important for many security applications, especially for the authentication related applications, such as message authentication codes, password protection and digital signature. Data integrity verification is another field in which cryptographic hashing takes place. It is used to make sure that the data transmitted within a message is not being accessed or modified.

Secure hashing algorithms take a block of data (message), and return a fixed size bit string (hash value), such that any change on data leads to a change on the hash value (digest). This can be considered as a scenario that describes briefly the mechanism of the secure hashing algorithm. **Figure 1** shows this scenario. First, conversion of data and associated password into a digests, then it will be compared in order to make sure that the message is safe and well protected.

SHA robustness depends mainly on many factors. Among them is the ease of computing the hash value, the infeasibility of generating a message that has given a hash, the infeasibility of modifying a message without altering its hash. Adding to that, is the infeasibility of finding two different messages with the same hash value. Secure hashing algorithms not only protect data from theft or alteration, but also it can be used to ensure user authentication. SHA are used to provide digital fingerprint of file contents, and can be employed by many operating systems to encrypt and decrypt passwords. Current secure hashing algorithms e.g. SHA1 and SHA2 are very essential, and widely used for secure communications, even in wireless communications [1]. However, it shows many weakness and limitations that trigger the need to find an applicable replacement.

NIST held a competition of three rounds in order to find a new secure hash algorithm. The new algorithm must overcome the limitations of the previous secure hash algorithms. Now, we are in the final round with five candidates. The main goal of this paper is to find the best algorithm among the five candidates (Blake, Grostl, JH, Keccak and Skein) that reach the final round of the competition. The final selected algorithm will provide a higher level of security considering the cost and the complexity aspects. The selection of the best algorithm will be based on a hardware evaluation of the five candidates. The aspects of comparisons are: throughput in Mbps, frequency in MHz, and used area measured in Configurable Logic Blocks (CLBs).

2. Related Work

In recent years, many attacks have been reported against different cryptographic hash functions. In 2005, Xiaoyun

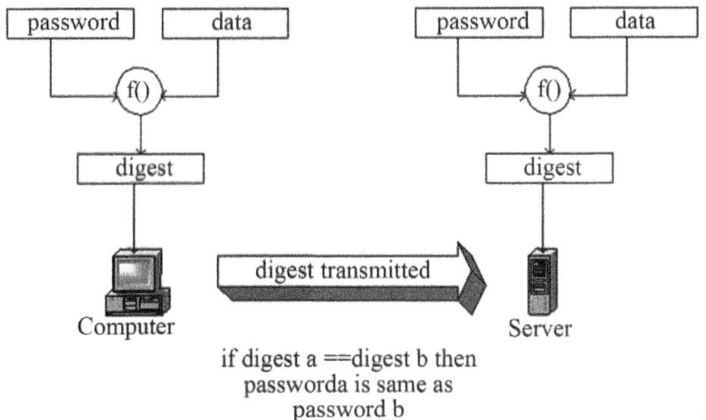

Figure 1. Digest authentication mechanism in hashing algorithms [2].

Wang announced a practical attack for SHA-1 [3]. As a quick response, NIST held a workshop for the purpose of studying the general status of cryptographic hash algorithms. Wang's attack affects some digital signature applications, time stamping and certificate signing operations [4]. A rapid transition to a new family of hash functions became very essential. SHA-2 was the new hash algorithm with a stronger family of hash functions that were suitable for many commercial applications.

At the same time, SHA-2 had a constraint that is the interoperability with many other systems [5]. In order to find a new cryptographic hash algorithm with a higher level of security and compatibility, NIST decided to hold a public competition to select a replacement algorithm. The main goal of finding new algorithm, is to stop using SHA-1 in digital signature, digital time stamping, and many other applications.

For SHA-2 many work in literature focused on how to optimize speed and throughput [6,7]. Many other works focused on finding a new implantations for SHA-2, or proposing techniques that improves SHA-2 implementations by many techniques, such as: operation rescheduling and area decreasing [7,8].

Another implementation in [9] which consumed 1373 slices for SHA-256 core, and 2726 slices for SHA-512 core with no power results provided. The implementation of [10] used ASIC core for 8-bit SHA-256 core. This is not practical because of the large number of clock cycles which led to a bad performance and more complex control logic. For the under development SHA-3 and its final round candidates (Blake, Grostl, JH, Keccak and Skein), there are many works that studied each one of them.

The work in [11] focused on the implementation of Skein as one of the finalists in order to investigate the performance characteristics resulted of using a different modern of FPGAs architectures.

A major criteria to compare the candidates is the chip area. The research in [12] shows that Skein consumed much less area than other candidates. Another important comparison criteria is the hardware overall performance in modern FPGAs families (Virtex5 and Virtex6 from Xilinx) [13,14]. Other researches evaluate the finalists according to their hardware implementation quality such as in [15].

In [16], candidate's hardware implementations, evaluations, definitions, and properties were discussed. In general, we can say that the research in [16] is a demonstration for the hardware evaluation process of SHA-3 final round candidates. Other works focused on comparing the algorithms that passed to second round of the competition (CubeHash, ECHO, Fugue, Hamsi, Luffa, Shabal, SHAvite-3, SIMD, Blake, Grostl, JH, Keccak and Skein). In [17], the authors describe, analyze, and rank a SHA3 hardware benchmark process for both FPGAs and ASICs. They come up with some insights about how designer can have different conclusions when working on the same most efficient SHA-3 candidates. Also, they investigated theSHA-3 hardware benchmarking results in different platforms.

Some other researches selected different algorithms of round two candidates, just like [18] that worked on Keccak, Luffa and BMW. They provided an efficient, fast, and high throuput hardware implementations for them. [19] shows the hardware implementations for another set of round two candidates reporting both ASIC and FPGA implantations. This paper provided a ranking for the 5 candidates based on their performance. ASIC evaluations presented in [20,21].

3. SHA 3 Candidate Algorithms

SHA is a group of hash functions approved and published by NIST. All of the current secure hash algorithms are published by the National Security Agency (NSA) [22]. SHA-0 is a 160 bit secure hash function published in 1993. Due to an undisclosed significant flaw, SHA-0 was withdrawn shortly after its publication and replaced directly by SHA-1. SHA-1 is also a 160-bit secure hash function. It is designed, developed, and published by NSA as a part of the digital signature algorithm. SHA1 is the most used algorithm among the hashing algorithms.

SHA2 is a family of two similar hash functions with different 4 block-sizes for the output, 224, 256, 384, and 512-bit. The SHA-224 and the SHA-256 are truncated versions of the SHA-384 and SHA-512. The same as SHA-1, all SHA-2 families were designed, developed, and published by NSA.

On the other hand, SHA-3 is the upcoming hash function which is still under development. It will be published in a public competition held by NIST to choose the best algorithm among all the candidates in March 2012.

3.1. The Need for New SHA

Due to many attacks reported on SHA1. One of these

attacks is the deferential attack applied to find a hash collision. It was 130,000 times faster than what was acceptable [23]. NIST decided to develop a new hashing stander that act as a new transition to more reliable and trustworthy hashing algorithm. To achieve this transition, NIST held a public competition started at the first quarter of 2007 [21].

Two years after the announcement, 64 competitors or candidates submitted their hashing algorithms to NIST for Evaluation (51) of them were qualified to compete within the first round. The NIST criteria's used to evaluate the first round candidates were: security, cost, performance, and algorithms software implementations. The performance of hardware implementations was not considered at this stage.

In the second quarter of 2009, a conference for announcing the 14 candidates who passed to the second round was hosted by NIST. Then, in the second quarter of 2010, the second conference for announcing the winners that passed to the third round was held by NIST. The third round is the final round for this competition with 5 candidates. The criteria's used to evaluate the candidates in all the rounds were the same. But, for round 3 it was extended to consider the hardware domain since the remaining 5 candidates were implemented in hardware. The winner of this competition will be announced in January 2012 and will be titled as SHA3 [21].

3.2. Common Hashing Algorithms Components

Two primitives are needed to build strong encryption algorithms: confusion and diffusion. Depending on Claude Shannon information theory confusion is the operation by which the relationship between the message and its digest will be kept obscure. On the other hand, diffusion is the operation of spreading the influence of each message bit in order to hide it is statistical property [10].

As it is so obvious, the confusion operation helps in maintain the one way property. While the diffusion helps in strengthen the collision resistance. All the candidates use almost the same components in order to carry out the two primitives of confusion and diffusion. Most of SHAs have common components that can be summarized as follow:

1) *Permutation*

It is the process of swapping data for the purpose of handling the diffusion operation. Depending on the algorithm itself, the size of data to be swapped will be determined. The data can be swapped in bits within swapping at smaller scales, and can swap multiple words at larger scales.

2) *Substitution*

It is the process of nonlinear transformation of the input for the purpose of handling the confusion operation, >Usually it is implemented using a substitution-boxes (S-box), which are carefully chosen to be resistant to cryptanalysis.

3) *Logical function*

Logical functions are performed using logical gates such as AND, OR and NOT. The most desired and commonly used logical function in cryptography is the XOR. And since it has the function of balancing it is impossible to know the input to an XOR with having a look only to its output.

4) *Modular arithmetic function*

Modular arithmetic functions are used for the purpose of handling the diffusion operation through generation and propagation of the carry. The most desired and commonly used arithmetic operations are the addition and multiplication. Performing this operation is slow due to the carry dependency.

3.3. SHA3 Candidate Algorithms Description

In this subsection, we present the description of each one of the five SHA-3 candidates.

1) *Blake*

This algorithm met all NIST criteria for SHA3 such as: message digest of 224, 256, 384 and 512 bits, same parameter size of SHA-2, one pass streaming mode, and maximum message length of at least 2^{64}-1 bits. Blake deserved to be one of the five finalists [24]. Blake's designers tried to keep it simple and familiar as possible to all cryptanalysis, since it is combined of well-known and trusted blocks.

Any superfluous features were avoided, and just provide what users really need. Blake can be considered as a family of 4 hash functions, Blake-224, Blake-256, Blake-384 and Blake-512. Also, Blake has a 32-bit version and a 64-bit version from which other instances are derived. Blake follows the Hash Iterative Framework construction for its iteration mode. Blake implementation requires low resources and its fast in both software and hardware environments [3]. **Figure 2** shows a detailed block diagram for BLAKE algorithm [15].

The internal structure of Blake is the local wide-pipe that makes the local collisions impossible for its hash functions. Regarding Blake's internal state, it is initialized by a set of initial values, counter values, and some constants. The state is updated using G function that contains modular addition, XOR, and rotates operation state [4]. The Blake's compression algorithm, it is a modified version of stream cipher ChaCha where the round function is based on it.

The message block goes through a permutation process and then enters into the round function. The round function has one layer of G functions with a stored internal state [11 silicon imp of sha3 finalists]. Two layers of G functions each of 4 functions will be used for one round which means that 8 G functions will be implemented.

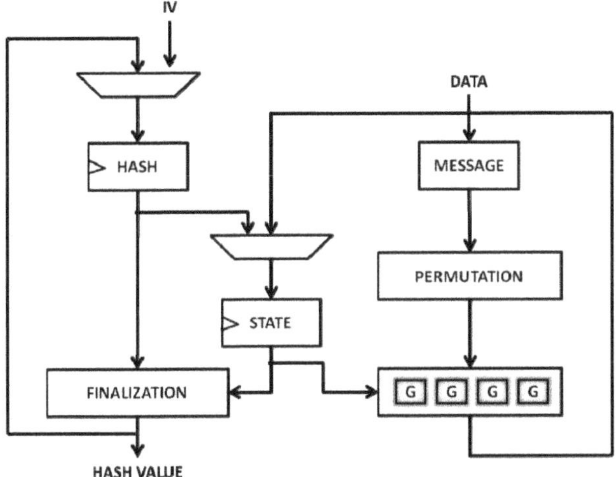

Figure 2. BLAKE algorithm block digram.

Only 4 G functions will be used during the first half of a round. The next 4 G functions along with the output of the first half which is stored in the internal state registers will be used in the other half processing. After each round for a current message block, the finalization process starts, and the chaining value for the next message block will be stored in the internal state registers. The used unrolling of G functions in two layers is important for reducing the latency, and raising the performance at the expense of maximum frequency and area state [13].

2) *Groestl*

It is an iterated hash function with a compression function. It's design is based on principles that are very different from those of SHA family [5]. Groestl is a byte-oriented SP-network that borrows components from the AES. The S-box used for Groestl and for AES is identical, and the diffusion layers of Groestl and AES are constructed in same manner. Since Groestl is based on a small number of permutations instead a block cipher with many permutations, it has some design specification as a result of this reduced number of permutations, such as the simplicity of analysis, the secure construction, the side channel resistance, allowing implementers to exploit parallelism within the compression function, and prevention of length extension attacks [22]. **Figure 3** shows a detailed block diagram for Groestl [15].

Groestl implements wide-pipe Merkel-Damgard construction which is similar to the plain Merkel-Damgard construction with the size of the internal state registers being different. Groestl has two functions: P and Q which are implemented in parallel. This parallelism leads to hardware resources sharing which results in low area of implementation. Both P and Q include four round functions performing XOR, permutation and substitution. The output of these functions will be the input for the XOR gate and its output will be stored as hash digest [21].

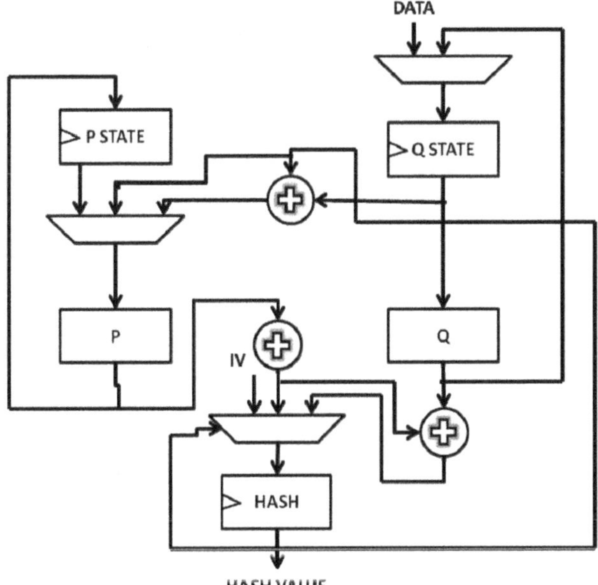

Figure 3. Groestl algorithm block digram.

3) *JH*

JH is a family of four hash functions, JH-224, JH-256, JH-384 and JH-512. The JH algorithm is efficient for hardware implementation since it is built using simple components, and in software with SIMD instructions and bit slice implementation. The JH compromised function is constructed from a large block cipher with constant key. The operation used are permutation, substitution, and logical XOR. Each input message is XORed twice, the first time before each round function with first half of chaining values. The second time at the end of each round function with second half of the chaining values [24].

JH has two similar modules for round operations: R6 and R8 that are used for the round constant generation and compression, respectively. For R6, the round constant generation can be achieved based on one of two ways, either the round constant from a previous cycle, or the initial constant value. On the other side, in R8, the chaining values are generated depending on the input message, the previous cycles, and the generated round constant. Three different layers are represented in R8, the layer of substitution, the layer of permutation, and the layer of linear transformation [24]. **Figure 4** shows a detailed block diagram for ***JH*** algorithm [15].

4) *Keccak*

It is based on the sponge construction [25], so Keccak can be considered as a family of sponge functions. The aims of using the sponge construction are to have a provable security against generic attacks and to make the use of compression function more simple, flexible, and functional. In sponge construction model, there are two portions for the internal stage registers. Also, there are two phases, absorbed and squeezed. The input message will

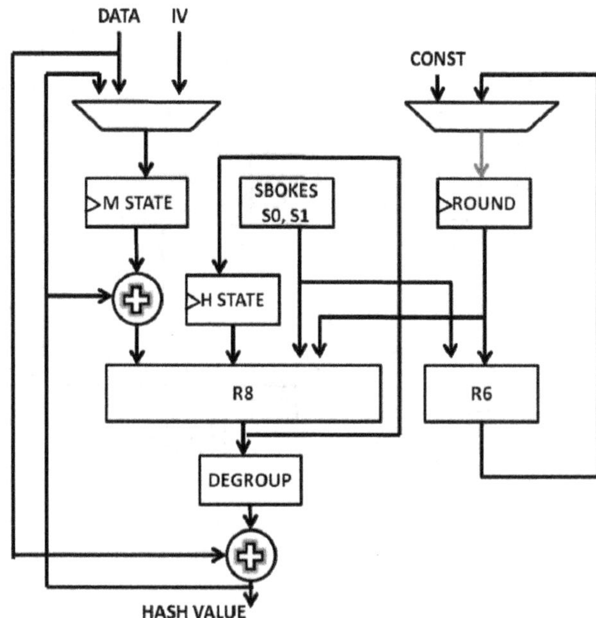

Figure 4. JH algorithm block digram.

be XORed with the data stored in the first portion of the internal stage registers during the absorption stage. And then the resulted value of the XORing process will be updated along with the data stored in the second portion of the internal stage register. During the squeezing phase, the data of the first portion will be used as a part of the output. It is worth mentioning that the sponge construction can accommodate the output of any size by updating the internal stage register. **Figure 5** shows a detailed block diagram for ***Keccak*** algorithm [15].

5) *Skein*

Skeins family has three different internal sizes for its functions 256, 512 and 1024 bits. The main idea of skein is to build a hash function that is out of tweak able block cipher. The skeins design is divided up into three components which are: Threefish, Unique Block Iteration (UBI), and Optional Argument System [4,26]. The Threefish block cipher is composed of subkey, mixing, and permutation, and is used to build the compression function using a modified Mateas-Meyer-Oseas configuration. **Figure 6** shows Skein 512-256 [15].

4. Results and Evaluation

The hardware design for SHA-3 candidate algorithms were coded in VHDL in [11]. Xilinx ISE 13.1 was used to synthesize the hardware designs using Virtex-5, Virtex-6 and Virtex-7 FPGA families. Virtex-7 is a new FPGA family based on 28 nm architecture designed for high performance, high throughput, and low power consumption. Virtex-7 power efficiency helps in mitigating the power requirements of the increased design area of the new SHA-3 algorithms compared to SHA-2 area.

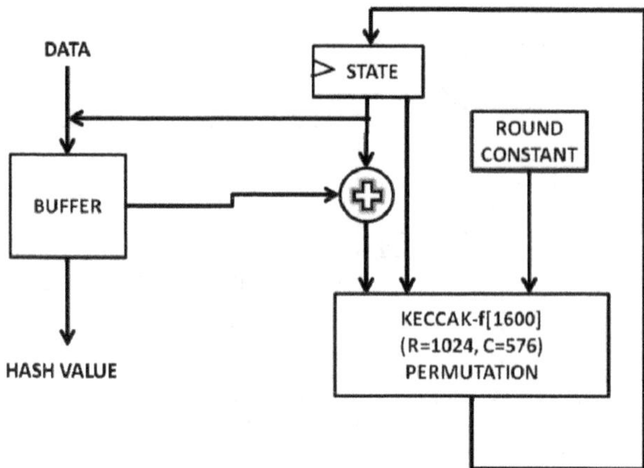

Figure 5. Keccak algorithm block digram.

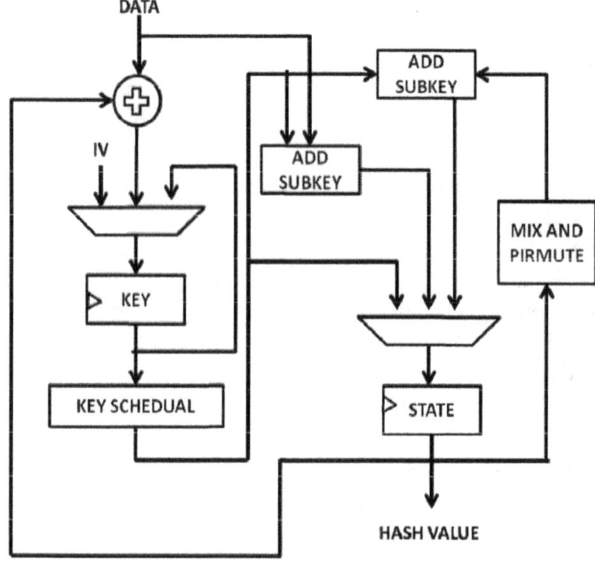

Figure 6. Skein algorithm block digram.

The synthesis results are shown in **Tables 1-3**. All the results are based on SHA-3 256-bit variants.

Table 1 shows the algorithms operating frequency results for different FPGA families. The results show that using Virtex-7 provides a higher operating frequency comparing with Virtex-5 and 6. JH and KECCAK algorithms show a higher frequency than other SHA-3 and SHA-2 algorithms. In contrast, BLAKE and SKEIN results show lower frequency when compared to SHA-2.

Table 2 shows the algorithms Area results (number of CLBs) for different FPGA families. The results show the use of Virtex-7 results in larger area comparing with Virtex-5 and 6. JH and SKEIN algorithms show a better area results than other SHA-3 candidates. On the other hand, BLAKE and GROESTL results show larger area requirements when compared to other SHA-3 algorithms.

Table 3 shows the algorithms throughput (Mbps) results for different FPGA families. The results show that the using of Virtex-7 has a little impact in on the throughput

Table 1. Clock frequencies of SHA-3 candidates and SHA 2 algorithm.

Algorithm	Xilinx Families		
	Virtex-5	Virtex-6	Virtex-7
BLAKE	131.576	146.709	151.253
GROESTL	212.648	242.242	233.111
JH	314.125	426.314	426.13
KECCAK	270.944	333.361	403.388
SKEIN	121.312	153.418	157.222
SHA2	179.509	225.739	232.631

Table 2. Area Results (CLBs) of SHA-3 candidates and SHA-2 algorithm.

Algorithm	Xilinx Families		
	Virtex-5		Virtex-5
BLAKE	1795	BLAKE	1795
GROESTL	2151	GROESTL	2151
JH	1272	JH	1272
KECCAK	1414	KECCAK	1414
SKEIN	1462	SKEIN	1462
SHA2	424	SHA2	424

Table 3. Throughput results (Mbps) of SHA-3 candidates and SHA-2 algorithm.

Algorithm	Xilinx Families		
	Virtex-5		Virtex-5
BLAKE	3207	BLAKE	3207
GROESTL	5284	GROESTL	5284
JH	4467	JH	4467
KECCAK	12282	KECCAK	12282
SKEIN	3269	SKEIN	3269
SHA2	1414	SHA2	1414

comparing with Virtex-5 and 6 except for KECCAK algorithm. JH and KECCAK algorithms show a higher throughput than other SHA-3 and SHA-2 algorithms. KECCAK algorithm shows the best results in term of throughput.

For the purpose of comparison, **Figures 7** and **8** show normalized SHA-3 algorithms results with respect to SHA-2 algorithm in terms of throughput and area. **Figure 7** shows that all SHA-3 candidates have better throughput compared to SHA-2. KECCAK algorithm outperforms all other SHA-3 algorithms in terms of throughput. **Figure 8** shows that all SHA-3 candidates' required larger area compared to SHA-2. BLAKE and GROESTL algorithms show the worst area results compared to other SHA-3 algorithms. **Figure 9** shows the "throughput to area ratio" of SHA-3 candidates normalized to the "throughput to area ratio" of SHA-2. Again, we can see that KECCAK algorithm outperform all other SHA-3 algorithms. **Figure 10** shows normalized power consumption estimation for the finalist algorithms with respect to SHA-2 for Virtex-6 and Virtex-7. Virtex-7 shows remarkable power efficiency up to 50% of power saving compared to Virtex-6.

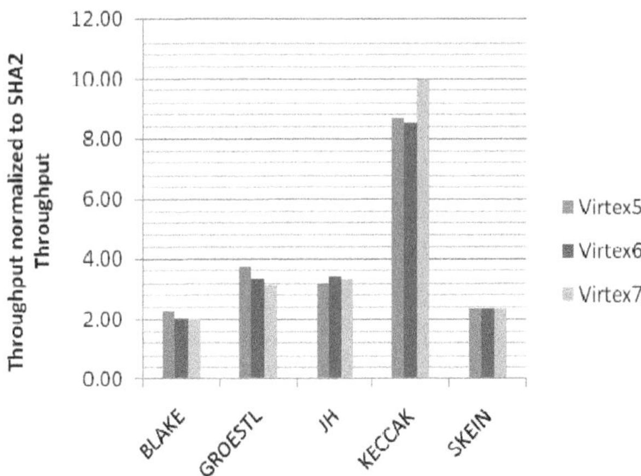

Figure 7. Throughput of SHA-3 candidates normalized to the throughput of SHA 2.

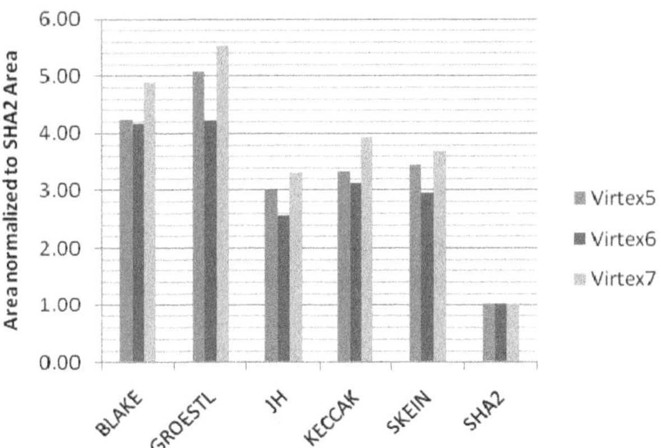

Figure 8. Area of SHA-3 candidates normalized to the area of SHA 2.

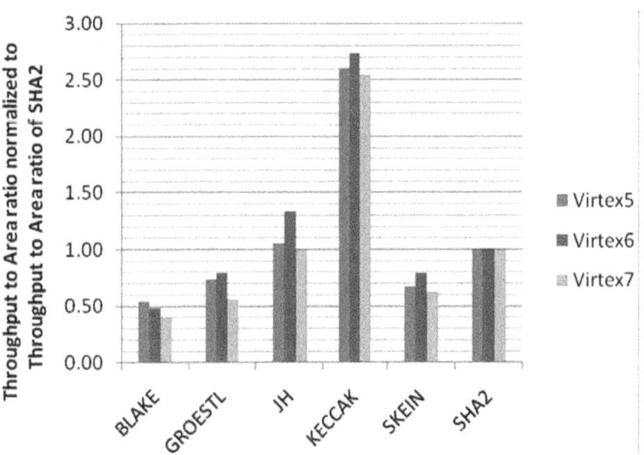

Figure 9. Throughput to Area ratio of SHA-3 candidates normalized to the throughput to area of SHA 2.

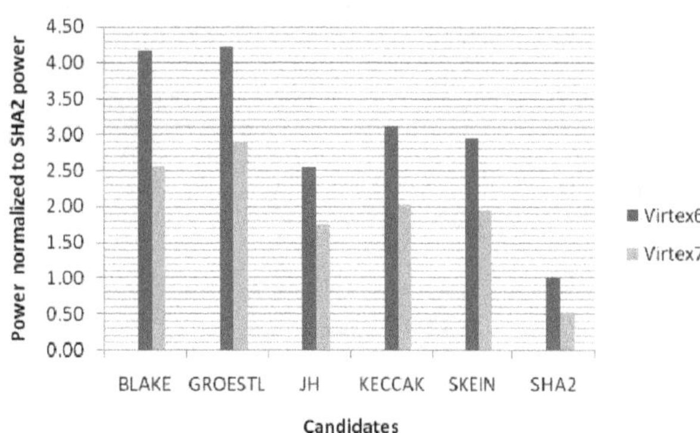

Figure 10. Power consumption of SHA-3 candidates normalized to the power consumption of SHA 2.

Based on the hardware synthesis results, the KECCAK algorithm outperforms all other SHA-3 algorithms. On the other hand, Virtex-7 shows promising results compared with older FPGA families from Xilinx like Virtex-5 and Virtex-6 especially in the power consumption side.

5. Conclusions

The demand on securing information and communication is increasing continuously. Secure Hashing Algorithms (SHA) are considered among the common and powerful cryptographic functions used today.

In this paper, we perform a detailed hardware performance evaluation of the final round SHA-3 candidates (JH, BLAKE, GROESTL, KECCAK and SKEIN). The hardware designs of the 5 algorithms were synthesized using Virtex-5, 6 an 7 FPGA chips to get area, frequency and Throughput results. The KECCAK algorithm outperforms all other SHA-3 algorithms in terms of clock frequency, area, and throughput. On the other side, BLAKE and GROESTL algorithms show the worst performance in terms in throughput, power and area. From obtained results, we conclude that KECCAK algorithm represent the best SHA-3 candidate from the hardware evaluation perspective.

6. Acknowledgements

The authors would like to thank their universities, and the Scientific Research Support Fund at the Ministry of High Education in Jordan for supporting this research. Also, we would to thank CERG team at George Mason University for their valuable supports and HDL resources.

REFERENCES

[1] A. Moh'd, N. Aslam, H. Marzi and L. A. Tawalbeh, "Hardware Implementations of Secure Hashing Functions on FPGAs for WSNs," *Proceedings of the 3rd International Conference on the Applications of Digital Information and Web Technologies* (*ICADIWT* 2010), Istanbul, 12-14 July 2010.

[2] "A Guide to Building Secure Web Applications," 2002. http://www.cgisecurity.com/owasp/html/guide.html

[3] J.-P. Aumasson, L. Henzen, W. Meier and R. C.-W. Phan, "SHA-3 Proposal BLAKE," NIST (Round 3), University of California Santa Barbara, Santa Barbara, 2010.

[4] X. Guo, M. Srivistav, S. Huang, D. Ganta, M. Henry, L. Nazhandali and P. Schaumont, "Silicon Implementation of SHA-3 Finalists: BLAKE, Grøstl, JH, Keccak and Skein," *ECRYPT II Hash Workshop* 2011, Tallinn, May 2011.

[5] P. Gauravaram, L. R. Knudsen, K. Matusiewicz, F. Mendel, C. Rechberger, M. Schläffer and S. S. Thomsen, "Grøstl—A SHA-3 Candidate," NIST, University of California Santa Barbara, Santa Barbara, 2011.

[6] R. Lien, T. Grembowski and K. Gaj, "A 1 Gbit/s Partially Unrolled Architecture of Hash Functions SHA-1 and SHA-512," *CT-RSA 2004*, Vol. 2964, 2004, pp. 324-338.

[7] R. Chaves, G. Kuzmanov, L. A. Sousa and S. Vassiliadis, "Improving SHA-2 Hardware Implementations," *Cryptographic Hardware and Embedded Systems—Ches*, Vol. 4249, 2006, pp. 298-310.

[8] NIST and FIBS-PUB 180-2, "Secure Hash Standard," 2002. http://csrc.nist.gov/publications/fips/fips180-2

[9] R. P. McEvoy, F. M. Crowe, C. C. Murphy and W. P. Marnane, "Optimisation of the SHA-2 Family of Hash Functions on FPGAs," *IEEE Computer Society Annual Symposium on VLSI*: *Emerging VLSI Technologies and Architectures* (*ISVLSI* 06), IEEE Computer Society, Washington DC, 2006, pp. 317-322.

[10] M. Feldhofer and C. Rechberger, "A Case against Currently Used Hash Functions in RFID Protocols," *Workshop on RFID Security* (*IS*'06), Graz, 13-14 July 2006, pp. 372-381.

[11] S. Tillich. "Hardware Implementation of the SHA-3 Candidate Skein," 2009. http://eprint.iacr.org

[12] S. Tillich, M. Feldhofer, W. Issovits, T. Kern, H. Kureck, M. Mühlberghuber, G. Neubauer, A. Reiter, A. Köfler and M. Mayrhofer, "Compact Hardware Implementations of the SHA-3 Candidates ARIRANG, BLAKE, Grøstl, and Skein," 2009. http://eprint.iacr.org/2009/349.pdf

[13] E. Homsirikamol, M. Rogawski and K. Gaj, "Comparing Hardware Performance of Round 3 SHA-3 Candidates Using Multiple Hardware Architectures in Xilinx and Altera FPGAs," *Encrypt II Hash Workshop—Tallinn*, Estonia, 19-20 May 2011.

[14] E. Homsirikamol, M. Rogawski and K. Gaj, "Comparing Hardware Performance of Round 3 SHA-3 Candidates Using Multiple Hardware Architecture in Xilinx and Altera FPGAs," *CRYPT II Hash Workshop* 2011, Tallinn, May 2011.

[15] X. Guo, M. Srivastav, S. Huang, D. Ganta, M. B. Henry, L. Nazhandali and P. Schaumont, "Silicon Implementation of SHA-3 Finalists: BLAKE, Grøstl, JH, Keccak and Skein," Center for Embedded Systems for Critical Applications (CESCA) Bradley Department of Electrical and Computer Engineering Virginia Tech, Blacksburg, 2010.

[16] S. Huang, "Hardware Evaluation of SHA-3 Candidates,"

Master's Thesis, Virginia Polytechnic Institute and State University, Blacksburg, 2011.

[17] X. Guo, S. Huang, L. Nazhandali and P. Schaumont, "On the Impact of Target Technology in SHA-3 Hardware Ben- chmark Rankings," *Report* 2010/536, IACR Cryptology ePrint Archive, 2010.

[18] B. Akin, A. Aysu, O. C. Ulusel and E. Savas, "Efficient Hardware Implementation of High Throughput SHA-3 Candidates Keccak, Luffa and Blue Midnight Wish for Single- and Multi-Message Hashing," *Proceedings of the Second SHA*-3 *Candidate Conference*, Santa Barbara, 23-24 August 2010.

[19] A. H. Namin and M. A. Hasan, "Implementation of the Compression Function for Selected SHA-3 Candidates on FPGA," University of Waterloo, Waterloo, 2010.

[20] X. Guo, S. Huang, L. Nazhandali and P. Schaumont, "Fair and Comprehensive Performance Evaluation of 14 Second Round SHA-3 ASIC Implementations," *Proceedings of the* 2*nd SHA*-3 *Candidate Conference*, Santa Barbara, 23-24 August 2010.

[21] NIST, "Cryptographic Hash Algorithm Competition," 2010. http://csrc.nist.gov

[22] NIST, "Secure Hashing," 2011. http://csrc.nist.gov

[23] X. Y. Wang, *et al*., "Finding Collisions in the Full SHA-1," *Proceedings of Crypto*, Santa Barbara, 14-18 August 2005, pp. 17-36.

[24] H. J. Wu, "The Hash Function JH," NIST (Round 3), 2011.

[25] G. Bertoni, J. Daemen, M. el Peeters and G. Van Assche, "Keccak Sponge Function Family Main Document," *NIST*, University of California Santa Barbara, Santa Barbara, 2009.

[26] N. Ferguson, S. Lucks, B. Schneier, D. Whiting, M. Bellare, T. Kohno, J. Callas and J. Walker, "The Skein Hash Function Family," *NIST Cryptographic Hash Algorithm Competition*, University of California Santa Barbara, Santa Barbara, 2008.

12

Reference Encryption for Access Right Segregation and Domain Representation

Lanfranco Lopriore
Dipartimento di Ingegneria dell'Informazione: Elettronica, Informatica, Telecomunicazioni, Università di Pisa, Pisa, Italy

ABSTRACT

With reference to a protection model featuring processes, objects and domains, we consider the salient aspects of the protection problem, domain representation and access right segregation in memory. We propose a solution based on protected references, each consisting of the identifier of an object and the specification of a collection of access rights for this object. The protection system associates an encryption key with each object and each domain. A protected reference for a given object is always part of a domain, and is stored in memory in the ciphertext form that results from application of a double encryption using both the object key and the domain key.

Keywords: Access Right; Domain; Protection; Symmetric-Key Cryptography

1. Introduction

We shall refer to a well-known protection model featuring active entities, the *processes*, that perform access attempts to passive entities, the *objects* [1,2]. Objects are typed; the type of a given object states the set of operations that can be carried out on this object and, for each operation, the *access rights* that a process must hold to accomplish this operation successfully. At any given time, a *protecttion domain* is associated with each process: this is a collection of access rights on the objects that the process can access at that time.

A salient aspect of the protection problem is the representation of access rights and protection domains in memory. A classical solution is based on the concept of a *capability* [3,4]. This is a pair <*B*, *AR*>, where *B* is the identifier of an object and *AR* is a set of access rights for this object. A protection domain takes the form of a collection of capabilities, which correspond to the access rights included in that domain.

Capabilities are sensitive objects that cannot be treated as ordinary data [5]: we must prevent processes from modifying the access right field and add new access rights, for instance. Capabilities can be segregated into *capability segments* [6,7]. In this case, a protection domain usually takes the form of a tree, where the root of the tree is a capability segment that includes the capabilities for other capability and data segments, and the data segments are the tree leaves. Alternatively, we can take advantage of a *tag* associated with each memory cell, which specifies whether this cell contains a capability or an ordinary data item [8,9]. In a third approach, a set of passwords is associated with each object, and each password corresponds to one or more access rights. A *password capability* is a pair <*B*, *PSW*> where *B* is an object identifier and *PSW* is a password [10,11]. If a match exists between *PSW* and one of the passwords associated with object *B*, then the password capability grants its holder the access rights corresponding to that password on *B*.

In the approaches to capability segregation in memory, outlined so far, a process that holds a capability can take full advantage of this capability, independently of the capability origin. This means that segregation does not prevent a process from taking advantage of a capability obtained illegitimately by means of a fraudulent action of capability copy, for instance.

In this paper, we propose an alternative approach to access right representation in memory, which solves the segregation problem by taking advantage of a form of *symmetric-key cryptography* [12,13]. In our approach, possession of an access privilege on a given object is certified by possession of a *protected reference* (*p-reference* from now on, for short) including the specification of a collection of access rights for this object. P-references are never stored in memory in plaintext. Instead, the protection system associates an encryption key, called the *object key*, with each object, and a further encryption key, the *domain key*, with each domain. A p-reference for a given object is always part of a protection domain and is stored in memory in the ciphertext form that results from application of a double encryption using both the object key and the domain key.

2. The Protection System

2.1. Protected References

Let T be an object type, let S_0, S_1, $\cdots$ be the operations that can be executed on an object of type T, and let AR_0, AR_1, $\cdots$ be the access rights defined by T. For each given operation S_m, the definition of type T states the subset of access rights AR_0, AR_1, $\cdots$ that is necessary to accomplish that operation successfully. P-reference R takes the form $R = <B, AR>$, where AR is a bit configuration that specifies a collection of access rights for object B: if the i-th bit of AR is asserted, R grants access right AR_i on B.

From now on, we shall use an underline to denote a ciphertext. Let k_B be the encryption key associated with object B, and k_D be the encryption key associated with the domain D of p-reference $R = <B, AR>$. **Figure 1** shows the transformation of R into ciphertext quantity $\underline{R}$. The transformation proceeds as follows. Let $\underline{B}$ be the result of encrypting quantity $\underline{B}$ by using a symmetric-key cipher with key k_D, and let $\underline{AR}$ be the result of encrypting pair $<\underline{B}, AR>$ by using a symmetric-key cipher with key k_B. Quantity $\underline{R}$ is given by relation $\underline{R} = <\underline{B}, \underline{AR}>$.

Figure 2 shows the reverse transformation of ciphertext quantity $\underline{R} = <\underline{B}, \underline{AR}>$ into the corresponding plaintext p-reference R. The transformation proceeds as follows. Domain encryption key k_D is used to decrypt quantity $\underline{B}$ into object name B. Then, the object key k_B associated with object B is used to decrypt quantity $\underline{AR}$. Let $<\underline{B}^*, AR>$ be the result of the decryption. Quantity $\underline{B}^*$ is compared with $\underline{B}$ to validate AR; if a match is found, validation is successful and p-reference R is given by pair $<B, AR>$.

2.2. Processes, Domains and Objects

When a new process is generated that has no parent (*i.e.* a process directly generated by the kernel), a new domain is created and is associated with this process. When a process generates a child process, the new process is assigned the same domain as the parent process. Thus, the tree structure originated by recursive actions of child process generation is entirely confined within the boundaries of the same domain, which is the domain of the root process. All the processes in the tree are *tightly coupled, i.e.* they share the same domain and consequently, the same domain key.

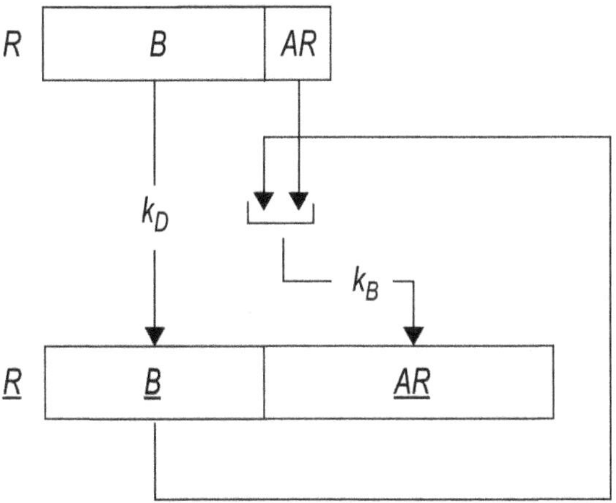

Figure 1. Transformation of plaintext p-reference $R = <B, AR>$ into ciphertext quantity $\underline{R} = <\underline{B}, \underline{AR}>$.

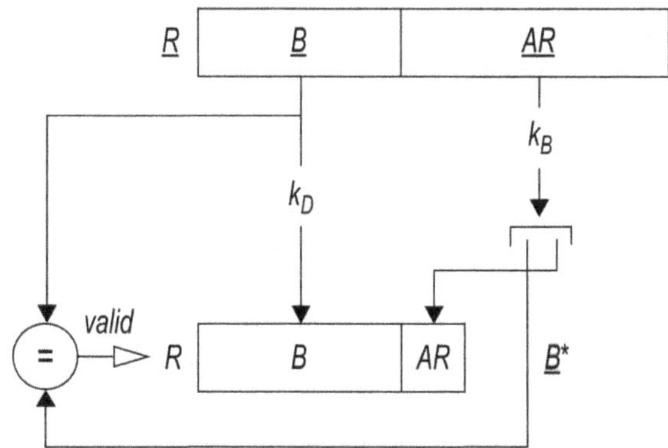

Figure 2. Transformation of ciphertext quantity $\underline{R} = <\underline{B}, \underline{AR}>$ into the corresponding plaintext p-reference $R = <B, AR>$, and validation of the result.

When a process creates a new object, it receives a p-reference for this object with full access rights. If the identifier of every given object is equal to the address of this object in the virtual space, a simple approach to generation of new object identifiers is a sequential generation, according to which objects are allocated at increasing virtual addresses, and the address of a given object is equal to the address of the previous object incremented by the length of the previous object.

2.3. Accessing Objects

Let P be a process, let D be its domain, and let $\underline{R}$ be a p-reference stored in ciphertext form in the memory area reserved for P. In order to take advantage of $\underline{R}$, process P must preventively translate it into the corresponding plaintext $R = <B, AR>$ so that both the name B of the object referenced by $\underline{R}$ and the access rights AR granted by $\underline{R}$ on this object become visible. Of course, after translation into plaintext, p-reference R is a sensitive information item that must be stored in a protected memory region. To this aim, the protection system reserves a *protection table* for each given process; each entry of the protection table can contain a p-reference in plaintext.

Process P can load a p-reference into an entry of its own protection table by executing the *LoadRef*(*addr*, *i*) protection system primitive. Execution of this primitive causes the actions necessary to translate ciphertext p-reference $\underline{R}$ stored in memory at address *addr* into a plaintext by using the key k_D of the domain D of P (see **Figure 2**); the result $R = <B, AR>$ of the translation is stored into the i-th protection table entry.

Let T be the type of object B and $S_0, S_1, \cdots$ be the operations defined by this type. The operation call primitive *Call*(m, i) starts up execution of operation S_m on B. Argument i is the index of the protection table entry containing a p-reference for B. The value AR of the access right field of this p-reference is transmitted to S_m as an input parameter. The actions involved in the execution of S_m will include the access right checks necessary to ascertain whether AR contains the access rights required to accomplish S_m successfully. If this is not the case, execution of S_m fails and generates an exception of violated protection.

2.4. Transferring P-References

Let P_1 and P_2 be tightly coupled processes, and let D be their common domain. Suppose that P_1 holds p-reference $\underline{R}$. In order to grant P_2 the access permissions included in $\underline{R}$, P_1 transfers $\underline{R}$ to P_2 by a simple action of a memory copy. In fact, the two processes share the same domain key k_D. By issuing the *LoadRef*() primitive, P_2 will decrypt $\underline{R}$ into the corresponding plaintext p-reference R. Then, by issuing the *Call*() primitive, P_2 will be in the position to use R for object access.

Let us now suppose that P_1 and P_2 belong to different domains, D_1 and D_2, and let k_1 and k_2 be the keys of these domains. If P_1 transfers a copy of $\underline{R}$ to P_2, no access privilege is actually granted to P_2. In fact, if P_2 issues *LoadRef*() to decrypt $\underline{R}$, the $\underline{B}$ component of $\underline{R}$ will be decrypted by using the key k_2 associated with domain D_2 instead of the key k_1 that was originally used to encrypt $\underline{B}$. The result of this translation will be the identifier of an arbitrary object whose key will be used to translate the $\underline{AR}$ component of $\underline{R}$ into plaintext. Of course, validation of the result of this translation is destined to fail.

Instead, the copy of a p-reference between two processes of different domains must be preceded by a conversion of the p-reference, from the domain of the granting process to the domain of the process that receives the p-reference (the *target domain*). To this aim, an object called the *encryption channel* is associated with each domain. The protection system maintains the association between each encryption channel and the key of the corresponding domain. P-reference conversion will be actually obtained by taking advantage of the *StoreRef*(i, j, *addr*) primitive. Arguments i and j of this primitive are the indexes of two entries in the protection table of the process issuing the primitive; these entries contain a p-reference for the encryption channel of the target domain and the p-reference to be converted. Execution of this primitive converts this p-reference into a ciphertext using the key associated with the encryption channel, and stores the result of the conversion into memory at address *addr*.

In our previous example, let $\underline{EC}$ be the ciphertext form of a p-reference for the encryption channel of the target domain D_2. In order to grant the access privileges in $\underline{R}$ to P_2, process P_1 will issue the *LoadRef*() primitive twice, to translate $\underline{EC}$ and $\underline{R}$ into plaintext and load the results EC and R of these translations into free protection table entries. Then, P_1 will issue the *StoreRef*() primitive to convert R into a ciphertext using the domain key k_2 associated with EC. Finally, P_1 will copy this ciphertext to process P_2, which will be able to take advantage of it, as it is now part of its own domain, D_2.

3. Discussion

P-references are stored in memory as ordinary information items, albeit in ciphertext form. Consequently, a process may well try to modify an existing p-reference and amplify the access rights it contains, or attempt to generate a p-reference for an existing object from scratch. A process may even perform fraudulent actions of p-reference copy. Storage of p-references in the stack and heap memory areas results in occasions for application of well-known techniques for data stealing [14,15], for instance. As a matter of fact, these attempts to p-reference manipulation are destined to fail.

3.1. Forging P-References

Let us refer to p-reference $R = <B, AR>$, and let $\underline{R} = <\underline{B}, \underline{AR}>$ be the corresponding ciphertext in memory. The $\underline{AR}$ field of $\underline{R}$ is the result of application of an encryption involving both quantity $\underline{B}$ and the access right specification AR (see **Figure 1**). We shall hypothesize that the cipher guarantees a careful mixing of the bits of $\underline{B}$ and AR. In a situation of this type, it is impossible to modify the resulting ciphertext $\underline{AR}$ for the sole portion corresponding to the access rights without corrupting quantity $\underline{B}$. In order to use the modified $\underline{R}$ to access B, the process holding $\underline{R}$ must preventively issue the *LoadRef*() primitive to translate $\underline{R}$ into plaintext and load the result R into the protection table. The actions involved in the translation from $\underline{R}$ to R include a validation of AR that involves quantity $\underline{B}$ (see **Figure 2**). If $\underline{AR}$ has been modified, the probability of a casual match leading to successful validation depends on the size of object identifiers; for large identifiers, e.g. 64 bits, this probability is vanishingly low [16]. When *LoadRef*() fails, an exception of violated protection is generated.

Of course, similar considerations can be made for a process attempting to forge a new p-reference for an existing object. The process will have to issue *LoadRef*() to translate the forged p-reference into plaintext and load it into the protection table; in this case, too, validation of the result of this translation is destined to fail.

3.2. Stealing P-References

Let D_1 be the domain of process P_1, and let k_1 be the key associated with this domain. Suppose that P_1 holds a p-reference in the ciphertext form $\underline{R}$ = <$\underline{B}$, $\underline{AR}$> obtained by using key k_1. Suppose also that a different process P_2, which is part of domain D_2, steals a copy of $\underline{R}$ from P_1. In order to take advantage of $\underline{R}$ and access the object it references, P_2 has to issue the *LoadRef*() primitive to translate $\underline{R}$ into plaintext and load the result of this translation into its own protection table. In the execution of *LoadRef*(), quantity $\underline{B}$ will be decrypted using the key k_2 associated with domain D_2 instead of the key k_1 that was originally used to encrypt $\underline{B}$. The result of this action will be an object identifier *BB*. In the hypothesis of large object names, the probability that *BB* be the identifier of an existing object will be low, and the search for the decryption key k_{BB} associated with *BB* is likely to fail. Even in the improbable situation that *BB* is a valid identifier, the corresponding key k_{BB} will not match the key that was used to generate $\underline{AR}$, and consequently, validation of the result of the translation of $\underline{AR}$ into plaintext is destined to fail. In both cases, *LoadRef*() terminates with an exception of violated protection.

4. Concluding Remarks

With reference to a protection environment featuring processes, objects and domains, we have approached the salient aspects of the protection problem, domain representation and access right segregation in memory. We have proposed a solution based on protected references, each consisting of the identifier of an object and the specification of a collection of access rights for this object. The protection system associates an encryption key with each object and each domain. A p-reference for a given object is always part of a domain, and is stored in memory in the ciphertext form that results from application of a double encryption using both the domain key and the object key.

Double encryption enhances security only marginally [17]; in our protection system, we take advantage of a double encryption and the duality between object keys and domain keys to guarantees the practical impossibility to acquire access permissions for an existing object by forging a new p-reference for this object or modifying an existing p-reference to amplify the access rights it contains. Furthermore, a process running in a given domain cannot take advantage of a p-reference encrypted as part of a different domain. In sharp contrast with capability and password-capability systems, this aspect of p-reference segregation in memory prevents the stealing of access permissions between processes of different domains. On the other hand, two processes that share the same father process belong to the same domain; these processes are considered mutually trustworthy, and the transfer of a p-reference between them can be obtained by a simple action of memory copy, at low processing time cost.

REFERENCES

[1] L. Lopriore, "Access Control Mechanisms in a Distributed, Persistent Memory System," *IEEE Transactions on Parallel and Distributed Systems*, Vol. 13, No. 10, 2002, pp. 1066-1083.

[2] R. S. Sandhu and P. Samarati, "Access Control: Principle and Practice," *IEEE Communications Magazine*, Vol. 32, No. 9, 1994, pp. 40-48.

[3] H. M. Levy, "Capability-Based Computer Systems," Butterworth-Heinemann, Oxford, 1984.

[4] I. Kuz, G. Klein, C. Lewis and A. Walker, "CapDL: A Language for Describing Capability-Based Systems," *Proceedings of the* 1*st ACM Asia-Pacific Workshop on Systems*, New Delhi, 30 August-3 September August 2010, pp. 31-36.

[5] M. de Vivo, G. O. de Vivo and L. Gonzalez, "A Brief Essay on Capabilities," *SIGPLAN Notices*, Vol. 30, No. 7, 1995, pp. 29-36.

[6] G. Klein, *et al*., "seL4: Formal Verification of an OS Kernel," *Proceedings of the* 22*nd ACM Symposium on Operating Systems Principles*, Big Sky, 11-14 October 2009, pp. 207-220.

[7] E. I. Organick, "A Programmer's View of the Intel 432 System," McGraw-Hill, New York, 1983.

[8] P. G. Neumann and R. J. Feiertag, "PSOS Revisited," *Proceedings of the* 19*th Annual Computer Security Applications Conference*, Las Vegas, 8-12 December 2003, pp. 208-216.

[9] L. Lopriore, "Capability Based Tagged Architectures," *IEEE Transactions on Computers*, Vol. C-33, No. 9, 1984, pp. 786-803.

[10] M. D. Castro, R. D. Pose and C. Kopp, "Password-Capabilities and the Walnut Kernel," *The Computer Journal*, Vol. 51, No. 5, 2008, pp. 595-607.

[11] G. Heiser, K. Elphinstone, J. Vochteloo, S. Russell and J. Liedtke, "The Mungi Single-Address-Space Operating System," *Software*: *Practice and Experience*, Vol. 28, No. 9, 1998, pp. 901-928.

[12] M. Stamp, "Information Security: Principles and Practice," 2nd Edition, Wiley, Hoboken, 2011.

[13] J. Burke, J. McDonald and T. Austin, "Architectural Support for Fast Symmetric-Key Cryptography," *Proceedings of the* 9*th International Conference on Architectural Support for Programming Languages and Operating Systems*, Cambridge, 12-15 November 2000, pp. 178-189.

[14] N. Tuck, B. Calder and G. Varghese, "Hardware and Binary Modification Support for Code Pointer Protection

from Buffer Overflow," *Proceedings of the 37th Annual IEEE/ACM International Symposium on Microarchitecture*, Portland, 4-8 December 2004, pp. 209-220.

[15] Y. Younan, F. Piessens and W. Joosen, "Protecting Global and Static Variables from Buffer Overflow Attacks," *Proceedings of the 4th International Conference on Availability, Reliability and Security*, Fukuoka, 16-19 March 2009, pp. 798-803.

[16] M. Anderson, R. D. Pose and C. S. Wallace, "A Password-Capability System," *The Computer Journal*, Vol. 29, No. 1, 1986, pp. 1-8.

[17] P. Gaži and U. Maurer, "Cascade Encryption Revisited," *Proceedings of the 15th International Conference on the Theory and Application of Cryptology and Information Security*, Tokyo, 6-10 December 2009, pp. 37-51.

13

Comparative Evaluation of Semifragile Watermarking Algorithms for Image Authentication

Archana Tiwari[1], **Manisha Sharma**[2]
[1]Chhatrapati Shivaji Institute of Technology, Durg, India
[2]Bhilai Institute of Technology, Durg, India

ABSTRACT

Technology has no limits today; we have lots of software available in the market by which we can alter any image. People usually copies image from the internet and after some changes they claim that these are their own properties. Insuring digital image integrity has therefore become a major issue. Over the past few years, watermarking has emerged as the leading candidate to solve problems of ownership and content authentications for digital multimedia documents. To protect authenticity of images semifragile watermarking is very concerned by researchers because of its important function in multimedia content authentication. The aim of this paper is to present a survey and a comparison of emerging techniques for image authentication using semifragile watermarking. In present paper comprehensive overview of insertion and extraction methods used in different semifragile water marking algorithm are studied using image parameters, potential application, different algorithms are described and focus is on their comparison according to the properties cited above and future directions for developing a better image authentication algorithm are suggested.

Keywords: Image Authentication; Selective Authentication; Content Recovery; Robustness; Semifragile Watermarking; Tamper Detection; PSNR

1. Introduction

Many multimedia authentication systems have been proposed in the last few years for ensuring the integrity and origin of multimedia data such as images. Image authentication is used for verifying the integrity and authenticity of digital images [1]. An image authentication can 1) detect the tampering activities, 2) locate the positions of alternations, and 3) repair the corrupted regions automatically. In general, an image authentication scheme consists of a stamping stage and a verification stage. The stamping stage derives and embeds the authentication code to serve as the attestations for the integrity of the image; the verification stage evaluates the consistence between the authentication code evaluated from a query image and the one calculated in the stamping stage to decide whether the image is altered or not. According to the processing of the generated authentication code, image authentication techniques can be divided into two categories: 1) label based systems, 2) watermarking-based approach. In label based systems, an authenticator is appended to the original signal for integrity verification of the protected signal. The authenticator can be a sensitive function of the signal (e.g. hash) or a set of coarser content features such as block histogram or edge maps. In watermark-based systems, the authenticator is imperceptibly embedded in the signal rather than appended to it, reducing the extra storage requirements of label based methods. Another advantage of watermark based systems is that lossless format conversion of the secured multimedia does not necessarily change its authenticity results.

The method by embedding authentication codes in an image itself has the advantage that no extra storage is needed, that benefits the transmission of the image [2].

The authentication watermark can be classified to fragile watermark and semifragile watermark according to its fragility and sensitivity. The fragile watermark is very sensitive and designed to detect every possible change in marked image; so it fits to verify the integrity of data, and is viewed as an alternative verification solution to a standard digital signature scheme. But in most multimedia applications, minor data modifications are acceptable as long as the content is authentic, so the semifragile watermark is developed and widely used in content verifying. Semifragile watermark fragile to malicious modifications while robust to incidental manipulations is drawing many attentions in image authentication. However, watermark security has not received enough attention yet. The primary advantage of employing semifragile watermarking over digital signature and fragile watermarking technology is that there is greater potential in characterizing the tamper distortion, and in designing a method which is robust to certain kinds of processing [3]. Lossless and lossy compression, smoothing, format conversion and light additive noise, are typically acceptable modifications since image content interpretation is not affected but the exact representation during exchange and storage need not be guaranteed. The alterations on the documents can occur unintentionally or can be implanted intentionally. The so-called unintentional or innocent alterations typically arise from such diverse facts as bit errors during transmission and storage, or signal processing operations such as filtering, contrast enhancement, sharpening, and compression. Intentional or malicious alterations, on the other hand, are assumed to be due to an explicit forgery attempt by a pirate with the explicit purpose of changing the contents of a document [4]. The main distinction then, is whether the content is altered as in malicious and intentional attacks or whether only the representation, but not the content, of the document is altered, as occurs in unintentional, nonmalicious cases. The line of demarcation between these two attacks categories is, however, not always clear-cut, as it depends very much on the application domain.

In present paper existing semifragile watermarking schemes are discussed for image authentication application. In Section 2 challenges in front of image authentication watermarking are discussed, Section 3 discusses what requirements of semifragile watermarking schemes to combat these challenges are discussed, Section 4 discusses methods and domain used by different watermarking schemes, Section 5 presents discussion of semifragile algorithms, Section 6 gives analysis and future directions, finally Section 7 presents brief conclusion of paper.

2. Challenges for Selective Image Authentication Techniques

Image authentication can be divided in two groups: strict and selective authentication. Strict authentication is used for applications where no modifications in the image are allowed, whereas selective authentication is used especially when some image processing operations must be tolerated which are image protecting operations uses Selective authentication based on semifragile watermarking to provide some kind of robustness against specific and desired manipulations.

- It is desirable in many applications to design a multipurpose watermarking scheme. There are three extra technical challenges in designing such a system. First, the embedding order of multiple watermarks should be analyzed in detail. Second, how to reduce the effect of the latter embedded watermarks on the former watermarks is a hard problem to solve. Third, the detection of such watermarks should be independent.
- In applications, such as in law enforcement, medical image systems, it is desired to be able to reverse the stego-media back to the original cover media for legal consideration. Semi-fragility which allows lossy compression or noise disturbing to some extent is required for an integrated and powerful authentication system. It is a real tough task to design an effective reversible semifragile authentication watermark (RSAW) scheme with features as tamper localization, good perceptual invisibility, detection without requiring explicit knowledge of the original image.
- One design challenge for authentication watermarks is to achieve a good balance between robustness against mild incidental image distortions and fragility to tampering attacks. A authentication watermark should protect the integrity of the image content rather than its exact representation.
- One difficulty these algorithm face is the original host is not available at the receiver side for authentication verification. In practical applications, the original host generally has a much larger magnitude than the allowed legitimate channel distortions. The unavailability of the original host makes it hard to differentiate legitimate distortions from illegitimate ones. This challenge motivates to investigate the semifragile nature of multimedia authentication [5].

3. Prerequisites for Semifragile Watermark-Based Image Authentication Systems

There are certain requirements which are essential for any authentication system; these requirements are discussed here for semifragile watermarking techniques.

- Overemphasis on robustness, questions security issues for authentication applications. A well-designed semifragile system should, therefore, simultaneously address the robustness and fragility objective [5].
- The semifragile authentication system must be secure to intentional tampering. For security, it must be computationally infeasible for the opponent to devise a fraudulent message.
- Given the watermark is an authenticator, embedding must be imperceptible.
- The authentication embedding and verification algorithms must be computationally efficient, especially for real time applications.
- The Peak Signal to Noise Ratio (PSNR) metric is widely used to measure the amount of difference between two images based on pixel differences. High value of PSNR shows the watermarked image has a

better quality, the difference between the original image and the watermarked image is imperceptible.

- Reconstruction of altered regions: The system may need the ability to restore, even partially, altered or destroyed regions in order to allow the user to know what the original content of the manipulated areas was.
- Asymmetrical algorithm: Contrary to classical security services, an authentication service requires an asymmetrical algorithm.
- Tolerance: The system must tolerate some loss of information and more generally nonmalicious manipulations.

4. Semifragile Authentication Techniques and Domains

In semifragile watermarking to provide image authentication it should tolerate image manipulations while detecting content changes. The authentication watermark used can be fragile to against content changing manipulations while robust to content preserving operations. In this section various techniques available are discussed in brief.

4.1. Integer Wavelet Transform (IWT) Domain

Digital watermarking in wavelet transform is one of study-intensive activities. IWT can be computed starting from any real valued wavelet filter by means of a straightforward modification of the lifting scheme.

It can reconstruct the original image without distortion, has strong robustness and good invisibility [6-8].

4.2. Principal Component Analysis (PCA)

Principal component analysis (Principal Component Analysis (PCA)), is a commonly used method based on the variable covariance matrix of information processing, compression and extraction [9].

4.3. Discrete Cosine Transform (DCT) Coefficient in High Frequency Domain

The characteristics of this algorithm are robust, well hidden and resistant to a variety of signal deformation resistance. The digital watermark of DCT transform domain has inherent ability of lossy compression resistance. The disadvantage is its large amount of calculation [10-13].

4.4. Slant Transform

Slant Transform that has the performance of gradually changing the image signal intensity has been successfully used for image coding in recent years. The basic idea according to the relevance of image signal, the brightness of a line has performance of unchanged or linear gradient [14].

4.5. Contourlet Transform

The contourlet transform is a directional multiscale decomposition scheme. It is constructed by combining: a multiscale decomposition followed by a directional decomposition, thus capturing geometric and directional information. Finally, the image is represented as a set of directional subbands at multiple scales [15].

4.6. Quantization Technique

In quantization-based schemes, a watermark is embedded by quantizing the host. The structure of the quantizer should provide a compromise among semi fragility, embedding distortion, and security. The basic idea of multistage VQ is to divide the encoding task into successive stages, where the first stage performs a relatively crude quantization of the input vector using a small codebook. Then, a second-stage quantizer operates on the error vector between the original and quantized first-stage output. The quantized error vector then provides a second approximation to the original input vector thereby leading to a refined or more accurate representation of the input. A third-stage quantizer may then be used to quantize the second-stage error to provide a further refinement and so on [16,17].

4.7. Pinned Sine Transform

In PST (Pinned Sine Transform), the image is divided into overlapped blocks which introduce an inter-block relationship to the pinned sine transformed images. Therefore the watermarking of any particular block also depends on its location in the image instead of depending only on its own content [18].

4.8. Discrete Wavelet Transform

Discrete wavelet transforms (DWT), which transforms a discrete time signal to a discrete wavelet representation. It converts an input series x_0, x_1, x_m, into one high-pass wavelet coefficient series and one low-pass wavelet coefficient series [3,19,20].

4.9. Arnold Transform

Arnold transform has much to do with the size of image. The amount of calculation will be too much if we recover the original image [21].

Summary representing algorithms used by different authors, PSNR values, applications suggested by authors and verification methods is given in **Table 1**. Here value of PSNR is average PSNR of different images used in paper.

5. Discussion of Different Semifragile Watermarking Methods

According to this summary **Table 1**, algorithms performances are similar. The properties of each group of methods are provided with references to algorithms. In fact, most of algorithms offer acceptable detection and localization of image manipulations while restoration performances still need to be improved. Semifragile algorithms show good results for detecting and locating malevolent manipulations while providing acceptable reconstruction performances. Unfortunately, their tolerance against desired manipulations includes mainly compression, noise addition and rotation by small angles, whereas, many of the desired manipulations need to be tolerated in practice.

Tellate watermarks are semifragile watermarks that can survive small distortions and minor transformations

Table 1. Semifragile watermarking algorithms.

S. N.	Author	Insertion Domain	Control Area	Verification Method	PSNR	Applications
1	Bassen Abdul Aziz (2003)	DWT using Tellate watermarking	-	Benchmarking	44 dB	Real work applications
2	A Piva (2004)	DWT using scrambling	128 × 128 bits	Inverse scrambling	36 dB	Video surveillance and remote sensing images
3	Yuan liang Tang (2004)	DWT domain	8 × 8 block	Coefficient quantization	33 dB	No specific application suggested
4	Guo rui Feng (2005)	DCT quantization technique	64 × 64 bits	Chaotic permutation	37.04 dB	Still images for multimedia
5	Anthony T. S. (2005)	Pinned sine transform	8 × 8 block	Normalized cross relation using threshold	40 dB	Satellite remote sensing images.
7	Zhe-Ming Lu(2005)	DWT and DCT	128 × 128 bits	Vector quantization(VQ)	30:553 dB	No specific application suggested
6	Nadia Baziz (2006)	Contourlet transform	5128 × 128 bits	Error Control Coding	36.6 dB	No specific application suggested
8	Kurato maeno (2006)	Wavelet domain	5 × 31 integer	Threshold criteria used	65 dB	All natural, printed and real time images
9	Xiaoping liang (2007)	I W T using reversible semifragile watermark	-	3rd level I I W T	43.4 dB	Law, commerce, defense journalism
10	Xiaoyun Wu (2007)	IWT domain	128 × 128 bits	Inverse I W T, histogram shifting	43.4 dB	No specific application suggested
11	Li Bo (2008)	D C T domain	8 × 8 block	Normalized correlation	39 .1 dB	No specific application suggested
12	Zhu Xian (2008)	Arnold Transform	-	Human visual system	33.61 dB	No specific application suggested
13	Jean-Philippe Boyer (2008)	DCT transform	8 × 8 block	Scalar DC-QIM scheme	43 dB	
14	Ching Yu Yang (2009)	IWT coefficient bias algorithm	4× 4 block	Semifragile reversible data hiding	33.91 dB	No specific application suggested
15	Chuhong Fei (2009)	DCT	8 × 8 block	IDCT	42.9 dB	No specific application suggested
16	Wen Hsin Chang (2010)	Tchebichef moment		Human visual system	36.98 dB	No specific application suggested
17	Rafiazullan Chamlawi (2010)	DCT and wavelet transform	-	Correlation method	42 dB	Video surveillance and remote sensing
18	Li Yaquin (2010)	Principal Component analysis using Wavelet transform	-	Correlation coefficient	26. 9 dB	Copyright and authentication
19	Jordi Serrwa Ruiz (2010)	DWT and vector quantization	8 × 8 block	IDWT	61.37 dB	Remote sensing images
20	Hongwen Lin (2011)	LSB using quantization	2 × 2 block	Correlation	38.58 dB	Color image authentication
21	Rui Bao (2011)	Slant transform and channel coding	30 × 30 integer	Inverse slant transform	37.31 dB	No specific application suggested

such as lossy compression, but are destroyed when an image is heavily modified [3].

As suggested by Bassem Abdel-Aziz high sensitivity to de-synchronization is inherent in the wavelet transform. Rotation-invariant transforms such as Fourier-Mellin can be used to overcome that weakness.

Frequency-domain watermarking techniques usually insert the watermark into the mid-frequency subband because they are relative robust and have little impact on the image quality. Watermark embedding by quantizing the distance between coefficients is more robust than that by quantizing the coefficient itself watermark is protected by a private key but also building relations between coefficients significantly discourages an adversary from performing the collage attack [3].

DCT has many important properties that help significantly in image processing, especially in image compression. But does not perform efficiently for binary images characterized by large periods of constant amplitude (low spatial frequencies), followed by brief periods of sharp transitions [10,11,22]. Discrete wavelet transform is having higher flexibility in comparison to DCT. Wavelet domain is used with semifragile watermarks for achieving better robustness [20]. The wavelet transform has a number of advantages over other transforms as it provides a multiresolution description, it allows superior modeling of the human visual system (HVS), the high-resolution sub bands allow easy detection of features such as edges or textured areas in transform domain [9].

The VQ-based watermarking algorithm can reduce the amount of the data transmitted [17].

In PST the watermark is embedded into the pinned field, which contains the texture information of the original image. This important property of the pinned field provides the scheme with special sensitivity to any texture alteration to the watermarked image [5]. It is thus suitable in applications where texture information is needed. Arnold transform has much to do with the size of image [12].

PCA is a widely used in many areas like pattern recognition, quantitative analysis of chemical composition, multi-component determines the number of components, the dynamics of the reaction mechanism, etc. [9].

Slant Transformation has the property that intermediate frequency coefficients unchanged when host image suffered non-malicious tempered. So it is often used in image processing [14].

The amount of calculation will be too much if we recover the original image depending on this periodicity, so the application of Arnold transform is limited. When compared to the discrete wavelet transform, the contourlet with their extra feature of directionality yield some improvements and new potentials in image analysis applications [9].

The quantization based embedding method outperforms spread spectrum in the tradeoff between algorithm robustness and fragility [23].

6. Analysis and Future Directions

It can be inferred from **Table 1**, almost all algorithm do well on detecting and substitution and have low rate of prone to attacks and they offer acceptable detection and localization of image manipulation while restoration performances still need to be improved, All algorithms can detect manipulation to certain content preserving operation is application specific. To study their relative performance one should consider following points.

1) The tamper indication must be statistically sound.

2) It should be possible to integrate the tamper over arbitrary region on images It should be robust to significant subset of signal processing attacks [4].

Some observation are made based on these algorithms are

- A flexible algorithm that allows user to specify list of desirable and malevolent manipulation algorithm be implemented. As existing algorithms offer tolerance against some specific content preserving manipulations.
- A combination of DCT and DWT can be used to improve performance tradeoff between alterations and can improve PSNR in comparison to DCT.
- An image with many edges and texture could decrease algorithm's performance since it is based on differences between adjacent fixed in special domain. So for images having more texture and edges strength should have lager value of watermark.
- Frequency domain watermarking is preferred over spatial domain as it is more robust against image processing such as image compression.
- Some methods use threshold to decide about image authenticity. The threshold is supposed to be adapted to a specific image within a specific region so fixed value of threshold may create problem.
- Discrete moment functions are preferred over continuous moment function because they do not numerical approximation capability.
- If there are multiple watermarks used in the application hiding order must be taken into consideration as different watermarks will influence each other. How to analyze the embedding order in general sense is a problem to solve.
- In applications such as space explorations, military investigation and medical diagnosis, where data authentication and original content recovery required at same time reversible technique can be used [24].
- For each authentication algorithm legitimate and illegitimate transition region is application dependent

and that the semifragile methodology should employ this information during the design phase.

- To enhance the watermark invisibility, one can also introduce some additional local distortion constraint provided by a human visual system (HVS).
- In a number of sensitive medical and military applications where perceptual integrity of even fine spatial detail has utmost importance, aggressive lossy compression can be considered as a malicious attack that causes loss of vital information. In such a scenario, it is desirable that watermarks: 1) are robust against mild compression; 2) distinguish manipulated regions from other areas; and 3) vanish under aggressive compression to indicate the loss of significant visual content [25].

7. Conclusion

In present paper various semifragile watermarking algorithm are studied to verify image authenticity. In addition to comparison based on image quality matrix, some observation is also suggested to efficiently develop an efficient semifragile watermarking algorithm for image authentication. As content preserving operations are specific to application, a practical algorithm that allows users to specify list of desirable and malicious manipulation can be developed. Moreover, restoration capabilities need additional improvements.

REFERENCES

[1] I. J. Cox and M. I. Miller, "The First 50 Years of Electronic Watermarking," *Journal of Applied Signal Processing*, Vol. 2, 2002, pp. 126-132.

[2] A. Tiwari and M. Sharma, "Evaluation and Comparison of Semifragile Watermarking Methods for Image Authentication," *International Journal of Computational Intelligence and Information Security*, Vol. 2, No. 8, 2011, pp. 36-42.

[3] B. A. Aziz, "Performance Analysis of a Content Authentication Semifragile Watermark," *Proceedings of IEEE International Conference*, Vol. 3, 2003, pp. 2055-2058.

[4] O. Ekici, "Comparative Evaluation of Semi Fragile Watermarking Algorithms," *Journal of Electronic Imaging*, Vol. 13, No. 1, 2004, pp. 209-216.

[5] C. H. Fei and H. Kwong, "A Hypothesis Testing Approach to Semifragile Watermark-Based Authentication," *IEEE Transactions on Information Forensics and Security*, Vol. 4, No. 2, 2009, pp. 479-492.

[6] X. P. Liang, W. Z. Liang and W. Zhang, "Reversible SemiFragile Authentication Watermark," *Proceedings of IEEE International Conference on Multimedia and Expo*, 2-5 July 2007, pp. 2122-2125.

[7] X. Y. Wu, "Reversible Semi fragile Watermarking Based on Histogram Shifting of Integer Wavelet Coefficients," *Proceedings of IEEE International Conference on Signal Processing*, 21-23 February 2007, pp. 501-505.

[8] C. M. Hwang, C. Y. Yang, P. Y. Chang and W.-C. Hu, "A Semifragile Reversible Data Hiding by Coefficient Bias Algorithm," *Proceedings of IEEE International Conference on Intelligent Information Hiding and Multimedia Signal Processing*, Vol. 1, 2009, pp. 132-139.

[9] Y. Q. Li, "Semifragile Watermarking Algorithm Based on Bi Watermarking Technology," *Proceeding of IEEE International Conference on Computer Applications and System Modelling*, Vol. 15, 2010, pp. 138-142.

[10] G. R. Feng, L. G. Jiang and C. He, "Permutation Based Semi-Fragile Watermark Scheme," *IEICE Transaction Fundamentals*, Vol. E88-A, 2005, pp. 375-378.

[11] B. Li, "A New Semifragile Watermarking Algorithm for Image Authentication," *Proceedings of International Conference of World Congress on Intelligent Control and Automation*, 25-27 June 2008, pp. 5928-5932.

[12] R. Chamlawi and C. T. Li, "Authentication and Recovery of Digital Images Potential Application in Video Surveillance and Remote Sensing," *Proceeding of IEEE International Conference*, 10-14 January 2009, pp. 26-27.

[13] J. S. Ruiz and D. Magias, "DWT and TSVQ Based Semi Fragile Watermarking Scheme for Tampering Detection in Remote Sensing Images," *Proceeding of IEEE International Symposium on Image and Video Technology*, 14-17 November 2010, pp. 331-336.

[14] R. Bao, T. Q. Zhang, *et al.*, "Semi-Fragile Watermarking Algorithm of Color Image Based on Slant Transform and Channel Coding," *Proceeding of IEEE International Conference on Image and Signal Processing*, Vol. 2, 2011, pp. 1039-1043.

[15] N. Baziz, "A Novel Image Authentication Scheme Based on Contoured and Error Control Coding," *Proceedings of IEEE International Symposium on Signal Processing and Information System*, 2006, pp. 34-39.

[16] K. Maeno, "New Semifragile Image Authentication Techniques Using Random Bias and Nonuniform Quantization," *IEEE Transactions on Multimedia*, Vol. 8, No. 1, 2006, pp. 32-45.

[17] Z.-M. Lu and D.-G. Xu, "Multipurpose Image Watermarking Algorithm Based on Multistage Vector Quantization," *IEEE Transactions on Image Processing*, Vol. 14, No. 6, 2005, pp. 822-832.

[18] T. S. Authony, "A Semifragile Pined Sine Transform Watermarking System for Content Authentication of Satellite Image," *Proceedings of IEEE International Conference*, 2005, pp. 737-740.

[19] A. Piva and R. Caldelli, "Semifragile Watermarking for Still Images Authentication and Content Recovery," *International Workshop on Image Analysis for Multimedia Interactive Services*, 21-23 April 2004, pp. 511-515.

[20] Y. L. Tang and C. T. Chen, "Image Authentication Using Relation Measures of Wavelet Coefficients," *Proceedings of IEEE International Conference on Signal Processing*, 2004, pp. 156-159.

[21] X. A. Zhu, "A Semi-Fragile Digital Watermarking Algo-

rithm in Wavelet Transform Domain Based on Arnold Transform," *Proceedings of IEEE International Conference on Signal Processing*, 26-29 October 2008, pp. 2217-2220.

[22] H. W. Lin and S. Q. Yang, "Watermark Algorithm for Color Image Authentication and Restoration," *Proceedings of IEEE International Conference on Electronic and Mechanical Engineering and Information Technology*, 2011, pp. 2773-2776.

[23] J.-P. Boyer, P. Duhamel and J. Blanc-Talon, "Scalar DC-QIM for Semifragile Authentication," *IEEE Transactions on Information Forensics and Security*, Vol. 3, No. 4, 2008, pp. 776-782.

[24] Z. Ni, Y. Q. Shi, N. Ansari and W. Su, "Reversible Data Hiding," *IEEE Transaction of Circuits and Systems for Video Technology*, Vol. 16, 2006, pp. 354-361.

[25] O. Altun, G. Sharma and M. Bocko, "A Set Theoretic Framework for Watermarking and Its Applications to Semifragile Tamper Detection," *IEEE Transactions on Information Forensics and Security*, Vol. 1, No. 4, 2006, pp. 479-492.

14

Digital Forensics and Cyber Crime Datamining

K. K. Sindhu[1], B. B. Meshram[2]
[1]Computer Engineering Department, Shah and Anchor Kutchhi Engineering College, Mumbai, India
[2]Computer Engineering Department, Veermata Jijabai Technological Institute, Mumbai, India

ABSTRACT

Digital forensics is the science of identifying, extracting, analyzing and presenting the digital evidence that has been stored in the digital devices. Various digital tools and techniques are being used to achieve this. Our paper explains forensic analysis steps in the storage media, hidden data analysis in the file system, network forensic methods and cyber crime data mining. This paper proposes a new tool which is the combination of digital forensic investigation and crime data mining. The proposed system is designed for finding motive, pattern of cyber attacks and counts of attacks types happened during a period. Hence the proposed tool enables the system administrators to minimize the system vulnerability.

Keywords: Cyber Forensic; Digital Forensic Tool; Network Forensic Tool; Crime Data Mining

1. Introduction

Computer forensics is the process that applies computer science and technology to collect and analyze evidence which is crucial and admissible to cyber investigations. Network forensics is used to find out attackers' behaviours and trace them by collecting and analyzing log and status information.

A digital forensic investigation is an inquiry into the unfamiliar or questionable activities in the Cyber space or digital world. The investigation process is as follows (As per National Institute of Standards and Technology) [1]. **Figure 1** shows the complete phases of Digital Forensic investigation processes.

Collection phase: The first step in the forensic process is to identify potential sources of data and acquire forensic data from them. Major sources of data are desktops, storage media, Routers, Cell Phones, Digital Camera etc. A plan is developed to acquire data according to their importance, volatility and amount of effort to collect [2].

Examination: Once data has been collected, the next phase is to examine it, which involves assessing and extracting the relevant pieces of information from the collected data [2].

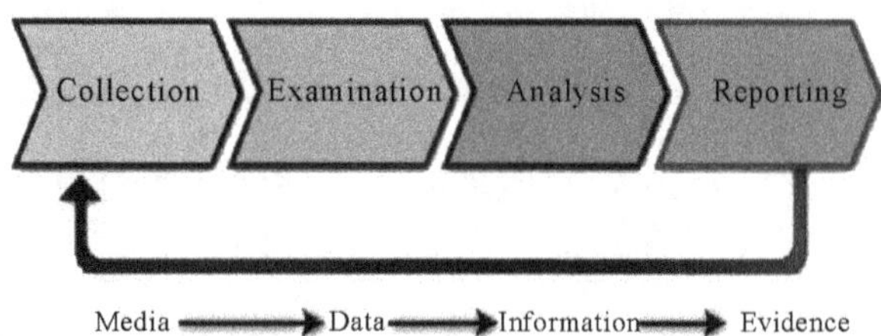

Figure 1. The digital forensic investigation processes [1].

Analysis: Extracted and relevant data has been analysed to draw conclusions. If additional data is sought for detail investigation will call for in depth data collection.

Reporting: This is the process of preparing and presenting the outcome of the Analysis phase.

Digital Forensic Science covers Computer forensics, Disk forensics, Network forensics, Firewall forensics, Device forensics, Database forensics, Mobile device forensics, Software forensics, live systems forensics etc.

2. File System Forensics

The File system investigation is the identification, collection and analysis of the evidence from the storage media. File systems or file management systems is a part of operating system which organize and locate sectors for file storage [3,4].

2.1. Basic Steps in Storage Media Investigation

1) Replication of forensic image: Nonintrusive acquisition of a replicated image of data extracted from the questioned device.

2) For integrity perform Hash value calculation.

3) Conducting a file-fragment recovery procedure to recover files and folders to a new location.

4) Examine all files especially deleted files.

5) Reviewing typical evidentiary objects such as:

a) Analyse free spaces, slack spaces and bad sectors.

b) Application software file.

c) Digital camera, printer and ancillary devices.
d) E-mails, Games & Graphics images.
e) Internet chat logs & Network activity logs.
f) Recycle folders.
g) System and file date/time objects.
h) User-created directories, folders, and files.
i) Latent data extraction from page, temp, and registry space.

6) Copy the content of the evidentiary object into text files.

7) Searching for key-term strings.

8) Reviewing file notations.

9) Scrutinize applications or indications of as file eradications, file encryption, file compressors or file hiding utilities.

10) Preparing evidence summaries, exhibits, reports, and expert findings based on evidentiary extracts and investigative analysis.

2.2. Hidden Evidence Analysis in the File System

Suspects can hide their sensitive data in various areas of the file system such as Volume slack; file slack, bad clusters, deleted file spaces [5].

1) *Hard Disk*: The maintenance track/Protected Area on ATA disks are used to hide information. The evidence collection tools can copy the above contents.

2) *File System Tables*: A file allocation table in FAT and Master File Table (MFT) in NTFS are used to keep track of files. **Figure 2** shows MFT structure. MFT entries are manipulated to hide vital and sensitive information [5].

3) *File Deletion*: When a file is deleted, the record of the file is removed from the table, thereby making it appear that it does not exist anymore. The clusters used by the deleted file are marked as being free and can now be used to store other data. However, although the record is gone, the data may still reside in the clusters of the hard disk. That data we can recover by calculate starting and end of the file in Hex format and copy it into a text file and save with corresponding extension.

Recover a JPEG file

a) Open file in the hex format.

b) Check the file signature.

c) Copy From starting signature upto ending signature.

d) For example (JPEG/JPG/JPE/JFIF file starting signature is FF D8 FF E1 XX XX 45 78 69 66 00 (EXIF in ascii Exchangeable image file format trailer is FF D9).

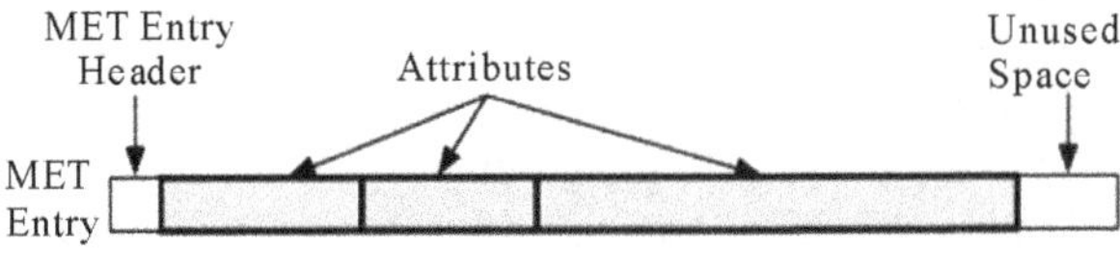

Figure 2. MFT structure [5].

e) Open the file with corresponding application.

4) *Partition Tables*: Information about how partitions are set up on a machine is stored in a partition table, which is a part of the Master Boot Record (MBR). When the computer is booted, the partition table allows the computer to understand how the hard disk is organized and then passes this information to the operating system. When a partition is deleted, the entry in the partition table is removed, making the data inaccessible. However, even though the partition entry has been removed, the data still resides on the hard disk.

5) *Slack Space*: A file system may not use an entire partition. The space after the end of the volume called *volume slack* that can be used to hide data. The space between Partitions is also vulnerable for hiding data, *file slack* space is another hidden storage. **Figure 3** shows slack spaces in a Disk.

When a file does not end on a sector boundary, operating systems prior to Windows 95 a fill the rest of the sector with data from RAM, giving it the name *RAM slack*. When a file is deleted, its entry in the file system is updated to indicate its deleted status and the clusters that were previously allocated to storing are *unallocated* and can be reused to store a new file. However, the data are left on the disk and it is often possible to retrieve a file immediately after it has been deleted. The data will remain on the disk until a new file overwrites them however, if the new file does not take up the entire cluster, a portion of the old file might remain in the slack space. In this case, a portion of a file can be retrieved long after it has been deleted and partially overwritten.

6) *Free Space*: However, when a file is moved from one hard disk or partition to another, it is actually a multistep process of copying and deleting the file. First, a new copy of the file is created on the target partition. After the file has been copied, the original file is then deleted. This process also requires some housekeeping in the FAT or MFT tables. A new entry is created in the table on the partition where it has been copied, whereas the record for the deleted file is removed from the table on its partition. When a file get deleted, that space considered as free space, there also criminal can hide sensitive information [6].

7) *Faked Bad Clusters*: Clusters marked as bad may be used to hide data. In NFTS, bad clusters are marked in metadata file called $BadClus, which is in MFT entry 8.

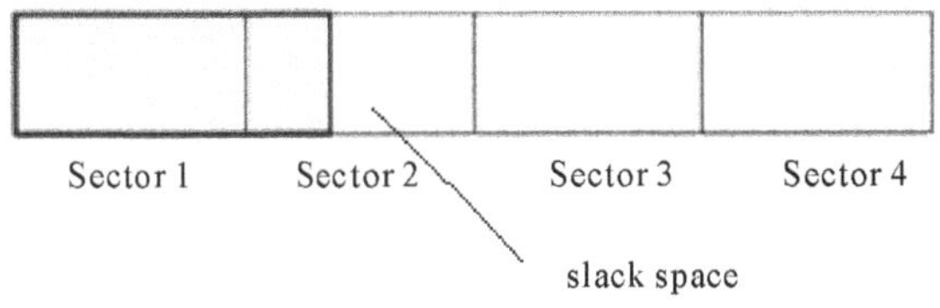

Figure 3. File slack [5].

Originally, $BadClus is a sparse file which file size is set to the size of entire file system. When bad clusters are detected, they will be allocated to this file. The size of data that can be hidden with this technique is unlimited. Suspects can simply allocate more clusters [6].

3. Network Forensic Analysis

Network forensics is capturing, recording and analysis of network events in order to discover the source of cyber attacks. In network forensics there are two major types of investigation [7,8] *i.e.* Network Traffic Analysis & Log Files Analysis.

3.1. Network Traffic Analysis

Network traffic analysis can be used to reconstruct and analyse network-based attacks, inappropriate network usage. The content of communications carried over networks, such as e-mail, chat etc can also support of an investigation. A Packet Sniffer tool is used for capturing network traffic. The header information encapsulated in the captured packet can be analysed by the forensic analyst [8,9].

This is very important when an investigation conducting on active network intrusions or attacks. Some cases evidences are available only in running processes or RAM.

Procedure for Network Live Acquisition

1) Create a bootable forensic CD.

2) Perform Remote access to the suspected machine or insert bootable CD in suspects machine directly.

3) Record or keep a log of all the actions of forensic investigator.

4) If need to take out away the evidence then use USB.

5) Next, Take a copy of the physical memory using a forensic tool example memfetch.

6) Create an image of the drive.

7) For Intrusion first check Root kit is installed or not, for that root kit revealers are available.

8) Perform hash value of the created image for integrity checking.

3.2. Network Investigation Tools

There is a powerful windows tools available at Sysinternals:

- Filemon shows file system activity.
- RegMon shows all Registry data in real time.
- Process Explorer shows what files, registry keys and dynamic link libraries (DLLs) are loaded at a specific time.
- Pstools is a suite created by SysInternals that includes the following tools.
- PsExec—Run processes remotely.
- PsGetSid—Displays the security identifier of a computer.
- PsKill—Kills processes by name or processes ID.
- PsList—Lists detailed information about processes.
- PsLoggedOn—Displays who's logged on locally.
- PsPassword—Allows user to change account passwords.
- PsService—Enables to view and control services.
- PsShutDown—Shut down and optionally restarts a computer.
- PsSuspend—Allows to suspend processes.
- Tcpdump and Ethereal—Packet sniffers.

3.3. Log Files Analysis

During investigation to recognize malicious activities by mining user log files. Access logs can contain vast amount of data regarding each user activities [10].
Analysis steps:

1) Input a server log file;

2) Identify each sessions;

3) Log file parser converts dump file into formatted order;

4) Using a Search function find the required data. Or Data mining algorithms give relations or sequential patterns.

4. Data Mining for Digital Forensics

Cyber Crime Data mining is the extraction of Computer crime related data to determine crime patterns. With the growing sizes of databases, law enforcement and intelligence agencies face the challenge of analysing large volumes of data involved in criminal and terrorist activities. Thus, a suitable scientific method for digital forensics is data mining. Crime data mining is classified as follows [11,12].

1) *Entity extraction* has been used to automatically identify person, login ID, Password, ID no, IP of the system, and personal properties from reports or logs.

2) *Clustering techniques* such as "concept space" have been used to automatically associate different objects (such as persons, organizations, hardware systems) in crime records [12].

3) *Deviation detection* has been applied in fraud detection, network intrusion detection, and other crime analyses that involve tracing abnormal activities [12].

4) *Association* rule has been applied to finding aassociations and sequential patterns between web transactions are based on the Apriori Algorithm.

Mining results shows motive, pattern and counts of similar types of attacks happened during a period.

4.1. Crime Data Mining Algorithm

1) Identify variables/itemsets from a case report (our proposed system stores these variables as attributes of tables, filesystem table, network table).

2) Item sets I = {I1, I2, I3 ⋯ Im}.

3) Set of actions D = {t1, t2, t3 ⋯ tn}.

4) Find frequent item sets by using Apriori algorithm.

Employs an iterative level to find set of frequent item sets.

E.g. if an attacker attacked database, login attempt results a data loss/Data tampering and case report show actions like Data deleted, Login attempt, attack type = SQL injection, If these item sets are frequent then we can set a rule " motive of attack is Data theft".

5) Make Association Rules

i.e. It is a rule in the form X → Y showing an association between X and Y that if X occurs then Y will occur.

If the attacker accessed operating system files then we can say motive of attack is system Crash.

If the attacker attacked Database login and Password steel then we can say criminal motive for data theft/data change.

This maximum frequent item sets also shows attack patterns.

Finding other signs of evidence Correlation, contingences (Consider these values while making rule sets).

6) Set SQL queries according to the rules.

7) Retrieve data.

4.2. Proposed Digital Forensic Tool

Our proposed model is the combination of digital forensics and data mining. Our proposed system helps to increase the security of the organization. When an incident reported, it investigates and report is saved in the database. Using crime data mining tool the nature of the attack is identified and alert administrator about similar attacks in future. Proactive measures can be initiated to prevent future cyber attacks. **Figure 4** shows the Block diagram of our proposed tool.

4.2.1. Block Diagram of the Proposed System

Graphical User Interface: It is used by the forensic investigator to enter case details and apply tools (File system, Network) to collect evidences. Investigators can input their queries in the system. This also displays the result of the query in the form of Bar chart or report. It is the presentation layer of our three tier architecture.

File System Analyser: This tool Collects evidence from the file system, it recovers all files, searches data in the free space, slack spaces and deleted spaces.

Network Analyser: This tool collects data from the network traffics and server log files.

Database: Database loader collects evidences from the above tools and loader loads into the database as attributes of the tables. OLTP (Online Transaction Processing): Set relations between the tables of the detected crime attributes. This applies data mining and extracts of required data. OLAP (Online Analytical processing) apply analytical queries and retrieves the output/decisions. Database server helps to store and retrieve crime attributes and results.

Decision Making System: This module applies data mining algorithm and also SQL queries into the database and generates reports.

Log file analyser module parses the web server logs,

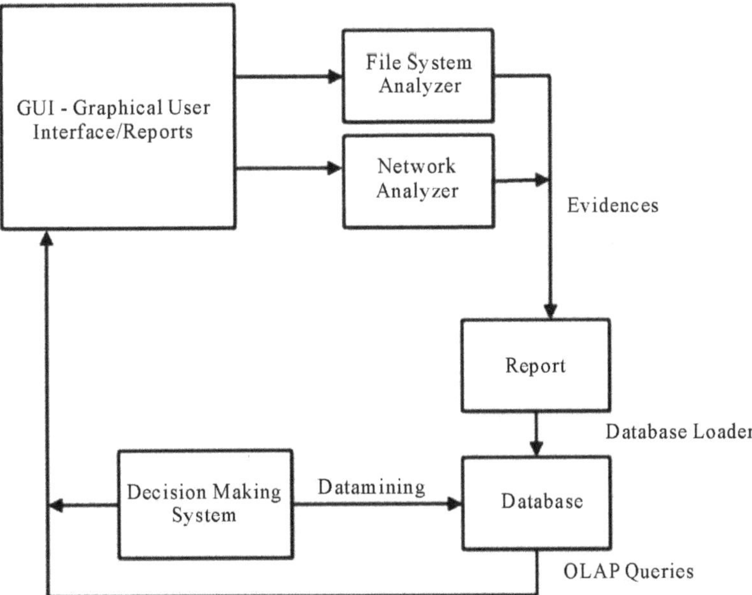

Figure 4. Block diagram of proposed system.

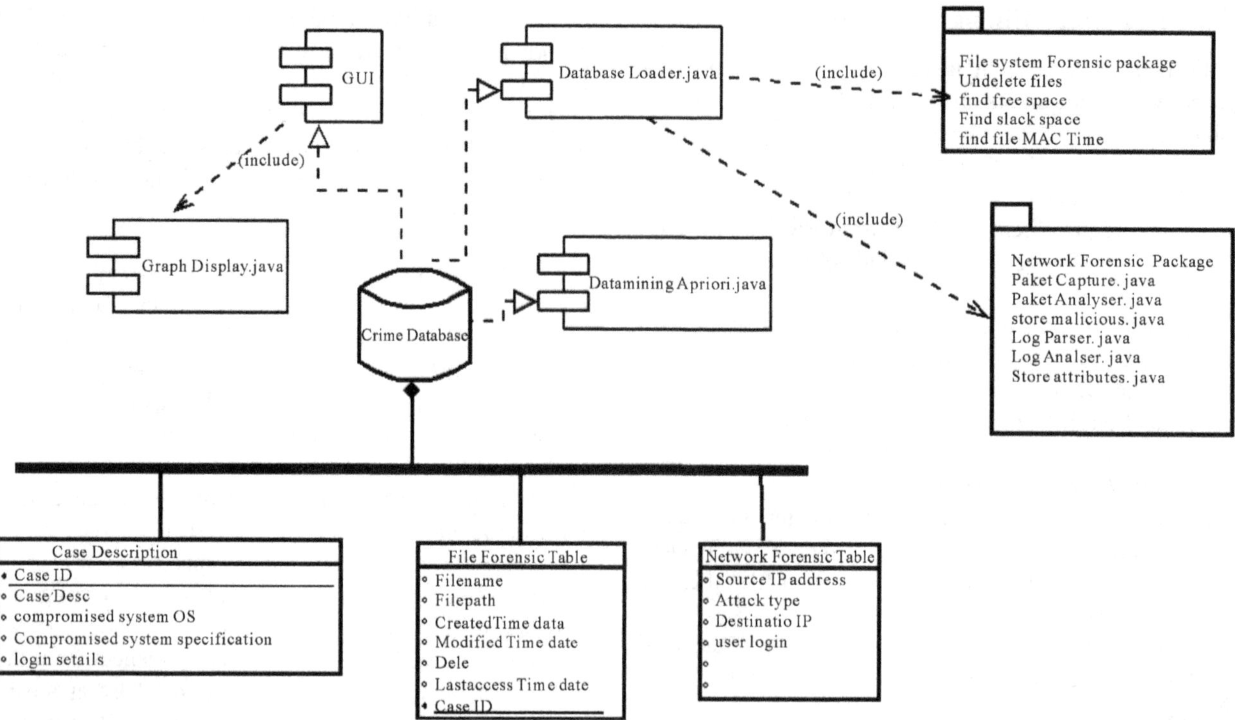

Figure 5. Software architecture of proposed tool.

syslogs and searches required keywords and patterns, which helps investigator to detect attacks like SQL injection, Brute Force attack for the login attempt.

4.2.2. Software Design of the System

Network forensic module is equipped with a traffic monitoring tool for data/evidence collection. A packet analyzer provides live forensic information about an attack. Java has API Jpcap captures information from the live network. The Network Analysis module analyse different types of packets ICMP, TCP, UDP.

File system analyzer module finding the evidence from the deleted files, free spaces (File slack, Volume slack).

The above modules give the output to flat file or CSV file.

A Java program module (File converter/Database Loader) converts as Table format and loads into the database.

Apply an Association mining (Apriori Algorithm) finding relation between these item sets of Crime Data and generate a prediction.

Graphical visualization module generates the required results in the form of Bar Charts or Graphs. **Figure 5** shows the Software Architecture of the proposed System.

5. Conclusion

This paper explains the hidden evidence acquisition from file system. Second section explains investigation on the Network. There are two types of investigation in network, live data acquisition (Packet capturing and analysis) and log file analysis. Third section explains crime data mining. On the basis we propose a new system with Digital forensic tool for decision making in the computer security domain.

REFERENCES

[1] K. Kent, S. Chevaller, T. Grance and H. Dang, "Guide to Integrating Forensic Techniques into Incident Response," NIST SP800-86 Notes, 2006.

[2] S. K. Brannon and T. Song, "Computer Forensics: Digital Forensic Analysis Methodology," *Computer Forensics Journal*, Vol. 56, No. 1, 2008, pp. 1-8.

[3] D. Klieiman, K. Timothy and M. Cross, "The Official CHFI Study Guide for Forensic Investigators," 2007.

[4] B. Carrier, "File System Forensic Analysis," Addison Wesley Professional, 2005.

[5] C. Kaiwee, "Analysis of Hidden Data in NTFS File System," Whitepaper.

[6] M. Alazab, S. Venktraman and P. Watters, "Effective Digital Forensic Analysis of the NTFS Disk Image," *Ubiquitous Computing and Communication Journal*, Vol. 4, No. 3, 2009, pp. 551-558.

[7] N. Meghanathan, S. R. Allam and L. A. Moore, "Tools and Techniques for Network Forensics," *International Journal of Network Security & Its Applications*, Vol. 1, No. 1, 2009, pp. 14-25.

[8] E. Casey, "Network Traffic as a Source of Evidence: Tool Strengths, Weaknesses, and Future Needs," *Journal of Digital Investigation*, Vol. 1, No. 1, 2004, pp. 28-43.

[9] H. Achi, A. Hellany and M. Nagrial, "Network Security Approach for Digital Forensics Analysis," *International Conference on Computer Engineering & Systems*, 25-27 November 2008, pp. 263-267.

[10] A. R. Arasteh, M. Debbabi, A. Sakha and M. Saleh, "Analyzing Multiple Logs for Forensic Evidence," *Digital Investigation*, Vol. 4S, 2007, pp. S82-S91.

[11] H. Chen, W. Chung, Y. Qin, M. Chau, J. J. Xu, G. Wang, R. Zheng and H. Atabakhsh, "Crime Data Mining: An Overview and Case Studies," *Proceeding of ACM International Conference*, Vol. 130, 2003, pp. 1-5.

[12] V. Justickis, "Criminal Datamining," Security Handbook of Electronic Security and Digital Forensics, 2010.

A New Steganography Method Based on the Complex Pixels

Amin Hashemi Pour[1], **Ali Payandeh**[2]
[1]Department of Information Technology, Tehran University, Kish, Iran
[2]Department of Information and Communication Technology, Malekeashtar University, Tehran, Iran

ABSTRACT

Today steganography has attracted the attention of many researchers. In this paper, we propose a new steganography method for secure Data communication on half tone pictures. Using the halftone pictures improve the security and capacity. In this method, the complexity of every pixel in picture is computed, then a neibourhood is defined to compute the complexity of every pixel, and then the complexity of every pixel is computed in the neibourhood. Placing data in the monotonous areas of halftone can explain the presence of hidden data. A method has been represented that surveys the position of every pixel neibouring others and prevents including in monotonous areas. If that was a complicated one, steganography bit after stonehalf will be hidden after scrolling the whole, the process of spreading error will be done. Performing the suggested method improves the quality of placing picture and increases its security.

Keywords: Steganography; Halftone; Fluyd Steinberg; Attacker; Steganalysis

1. Introduction

Steganography has enjoyed a lot of importance since last decade. The Art of steganogeraphy has attracted human attention for many years. It is very important because disclosing a message even as encoded is dangerous many times. Steganography is a branch of hiding information. It contains a few branches as cryptography, Watermarking, Fingerprinting [1]. The stego medium that a hidden message is inserted in it is called cover medium. It may be a picture, a sound, and a film. After inserting a message by Algorithm containing, it is called placed medium span. The data that we insert in cover medium is secret message. The key which is used to insert message and take out secret message is called placing key. The techniques that help us to recognize cover medium and span are called disclosing [2]. When we disclose a secret, target is just to understand the hidden message, and we don't observe the obligation to discover the contents of message. A method has been given to disclose halftone. They are vastly used in printing a book, magazine newspaper and computer printers. The pictures that have been saved by fax or pictures taken form pdf of some documents have the scanner format of printed texts include halftone. Changing the grey colour pictures into a two surface picture which its pixels range 0 - 255 (black and white) is called the process of making halftone. Generally, they are 3 groups [3] in the traditional method of halftone that is the oldest one, there are alternative arrays of threshold surfaces. The extent of light surface each of the pixels less than they should level is 0, and if it is more, it is changed to 255 [4]. In two surface process with blue noise, It is tried to insert the resulting noise of halftone in high frequencies [5]. The usage of the method is because the vision system of human is less sensitive to higher frequency noise in a picture. In binary direct search, it is tried some amount to be chosen for every pixel in halftone that will optimize the quality norm. The best quality among halftone methods is binary based search. There is different Algorithm for making halftone. One of the most important is fluyd Steinberg Algorithm that have been used here [6]. This Algorithm was published by Robert W. Fluyd and Luis Steinberg which is used for making changes [7]. For example, it changes a picture with GIF format with maximum 255 colours. In the mentioned method the light surface of every pixel is compared with threshold amount of $\frac{255}{2}$ and if greater than threshold it is changed to 255 if smaller it is changed to 0 and so we can show every pixel with a bit. This change creates a little error in the new picture. This Algorithm for one pixel to its neibouring acts mutually with considering expansion distribution error. If it be the first pixel amount and its new value be 255, the error value equals e = 255 – F. In Fluyd Steinberg's method the error value in neibouring pixels is like what is shown in **Figure 1**, Will spread the value of error with different weights between neibouring pixels spreads that are at the right side or under pixel. For example if the right side pixel value mentioned be A, the new value will be A + $\frac{7e}{16}$. In the method, we begin from the left corner and upper part of picture, and measure them as row and perform the error spread halftone.

We divide the pictures into blocks with proper dimension, and then survey them to be simple or complicated [8]. If the total or most of pixels of a block are black or white, That block is simple. **Figure 2** shows a simple 8 × 8 block.

Blocks which are not very monotonous are complicated blocks. **Figure 3** shows an 8 × 8 complicated block.

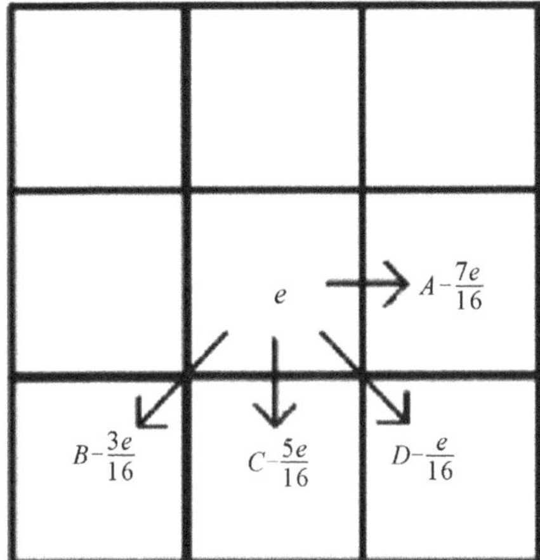

Figure 1. The error based on fluyd steinberg.

Figure 2. Simple block.

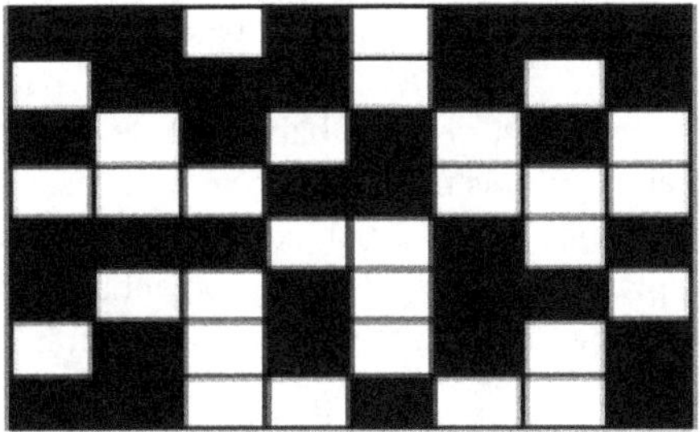

Figure 3. Complicated block.

The norm we have used for being complicated is the norm of complication between black and white that have explained in the reference. We divide the picture into block with proper dimensions of 16 × 16, then insert information in it. Suppose there is a border block between every two pixels. Generally, the number of border blocks are shown with measurement of N × M equals M(N – 1) + N(M – 1). M and N are the number of a picture blocks. These observations let us define a norm for complication based on the total of common borders between black and white pixels. Suppose T to pixel border is placed in a block and ∂ number of then are between black and white pixels. Then we can define the complication norm as a = $\frac{\partial}{T}$ This norm exists in the extension of [0 - 1]. With the amount of threshold a_0, we can differentiate the simple and complicated blocks. If $a(B) \geq a_0$, it is a complex B block and if not it is a simple B block the amount of a_0 is usually chosen experimentally 0.3 [9]. The paper is organized as follow:

1) Proposed method;

2) Performance and security analysis of proposed method;

3) Simulation results;

4) Conclusion.

2. Proposed Method

Suppose q bit data is to place in a picture. The row of bits will be considered as the following set d = $\{d_0, d_1, d_2, \cdots, d_{n-1}\}$ [10]. Simple method function in **Figure 4** shows data embedded algorithm in pictures based on a block classification image.

First, we divide the image into blocks, we accommodate The block scheduling pseudo-random numbers with uniform distribution with a key value. Embedded in a uniform image areas make attack visual in uniform areas. To prevent these attacks should be do embedded in non-uniform regions. Then we examine the complexity of each block, if there is complexity Block, placing for halftone Otherwise the blocks are going to next. The Floyd Steinberg method to generate an error, this reduces image quality. You can optimize the above method. So instead we calculate the complexity in the block, we review of this complexity in the pixels. The compete placing trend for halftone with complex areas is shown in **Figure 5**.

Based on shown Algorithm in **Figure 5** at first a PRNG is given value with a key. Then the picture is measured for left side and upper part, and the number of complex pixel of picture is obtained. In order to place the data monotonously in complex pixels, it is necessary to compute the number of complex pixels before begin the inserting. In this research a method has been represented

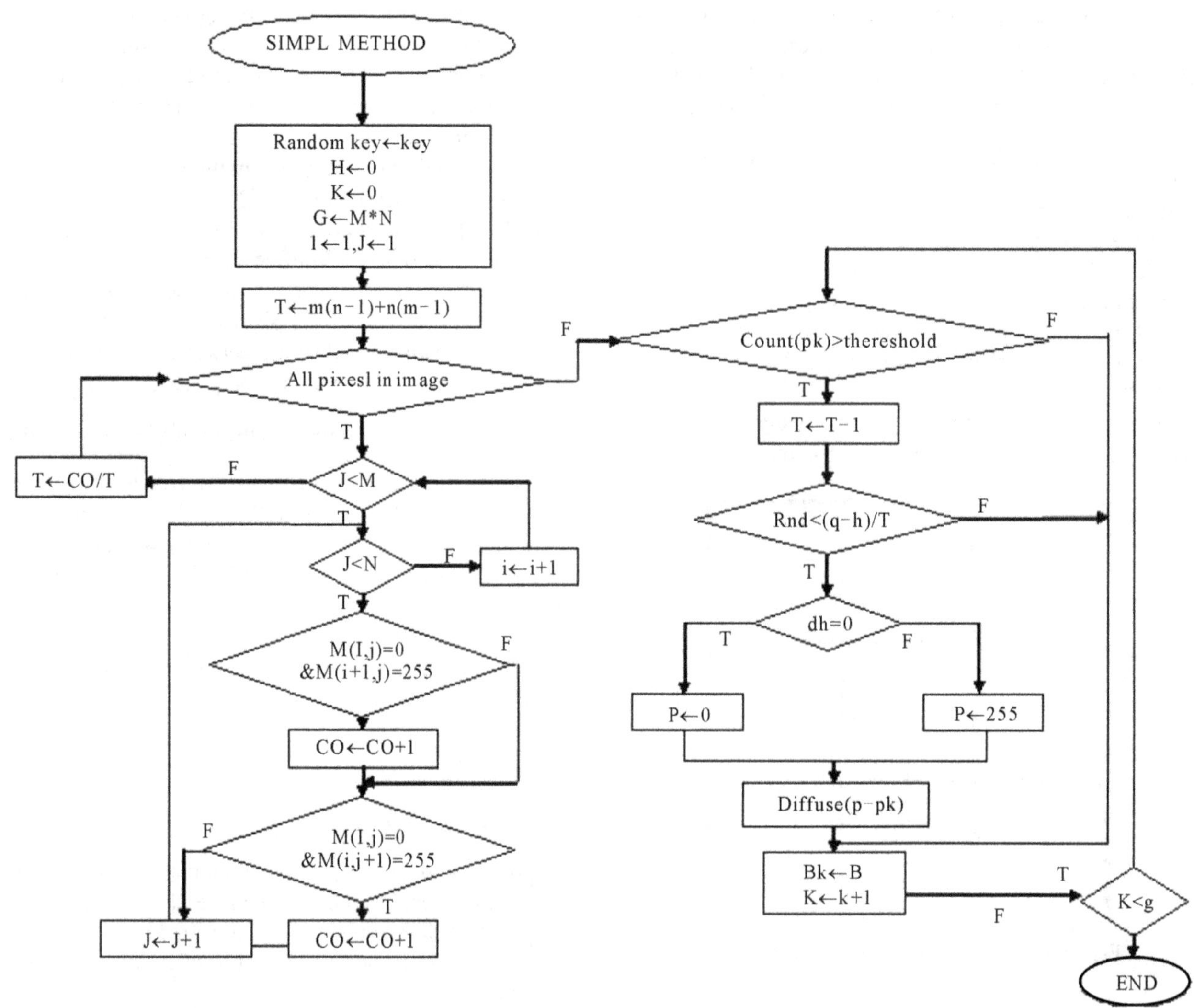

Figure 4. Simple method algorithm.

that complexity for every pixel is computed. A neibourhood is defined to compute the complexity of every pixel, and then the complexity of every pixel is computed in the neibourhood. After computing the number of complicated pixel on the grey surface all pixels on the grey surface are scrolled in this method. When there is complexity pixel, one complicated pixel is reduced, and a semi-random number is produced in the other case. For every pixel the semi-random no with monotonous distribution Rnd between 0 and 1 will be produced, and If it is less than $\frac{q-h}{NC}$, One bit will be placed or embedded. So if the considered bit dh equals zero, the new value of pixel p is zero, and if the new pixel value be one, the new pixel value will be 255. If we compare semi-random NO produced with $\frac{q-h}{NC}$, in the end of placing exactly q bit data, and a monotonous will be inserted in picture surface. It is possible to miss the complexity of pixel because of inserting, and changes into a simple one, and it may disorder the process of taking out. For this reason, the pixel is tested after placing for complexity, and if it is still complex, one extra pixel is added to the index of data. If it has lost its complexity, the semi-random produced NO which is used to decide for inserting, it will be used for the next complex pixel in order to take out a row of random correctly. After getting new value pixel, the error taken place *i.e.* (p − pk) will be expanded that function Diffuse (p − pk) is carried out. It is natural that changing grey picture into halftone one creates some errors. Here, SNR[1] is used as a norm to measure the created error. SNR norm is usual method to clarify error rate which explains the ratio of power potential of signal to noise. For a picture as large as M × N pixel, SNR is defined in Formula 1:

[1]Signal to Noise Ratio.

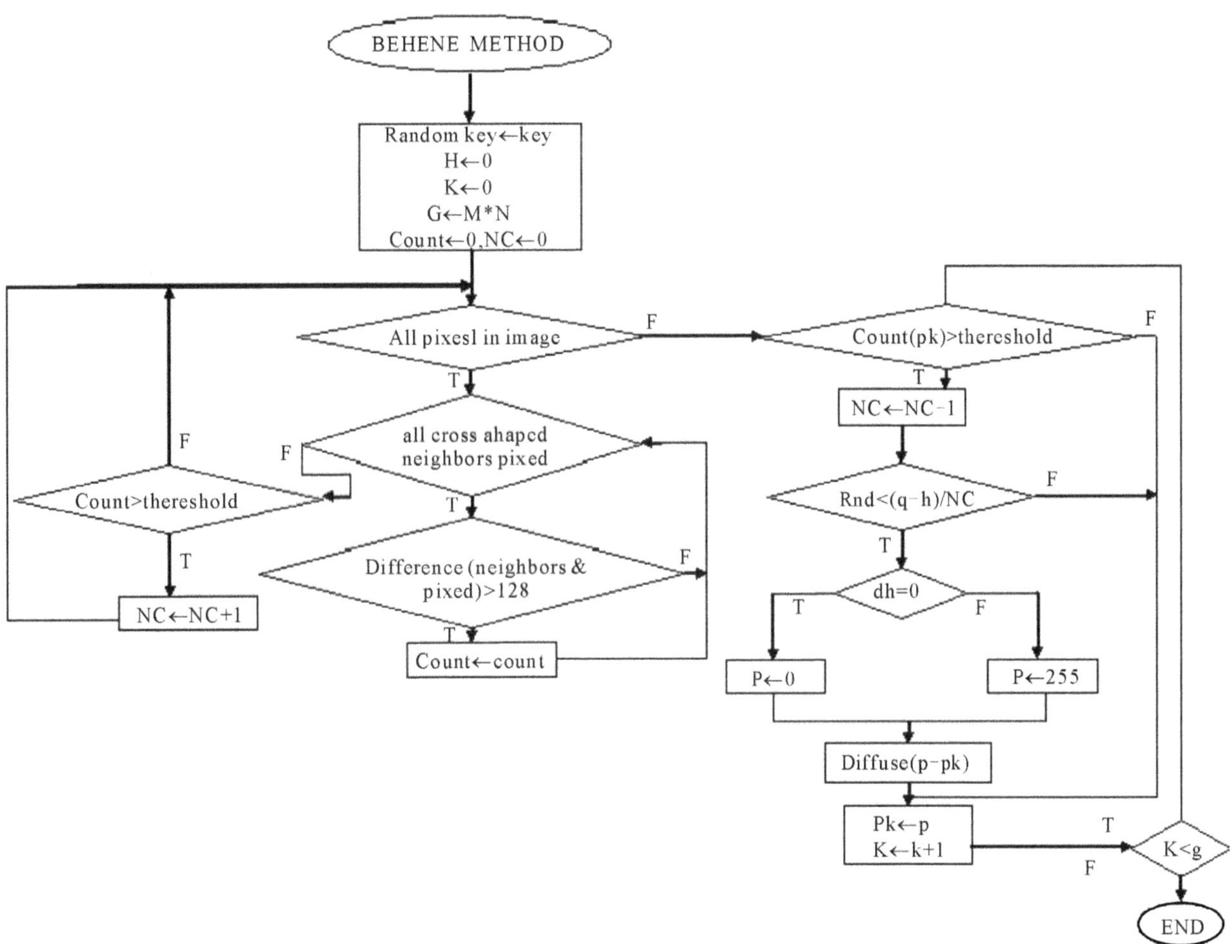

Figure 5. Behine method algorithm.

$$\text{SNR}(d_b) = 10\lim_{10}\left(\frac{\sum_{i,j} x(i,j)^2}{\sum_{i,j}(x(i,j)-y(i,j))^2}\right) \quad (1)$$

$$0 < i \le m-1$$

$$0 < j \le n-1$$

In it x(i, j) the value of pixel in line i and column j in real picture, and y(i, j) is the corresponding pixel value in changed picture. The important point is that because of inserting a block, it is possible for a block not to be complicated any more. This possibility creates problems for taking out the data. Because the procedure of exploiting is so that at first the picture is made as a block, and then examine if it is complex or not. If it was not a complex block, we go to the next one, if it was complex the data bits will be got out from semi-random place with the same key that has been used for placing. If the block was complex before inserting but the next one is not complex, when taking out we suppose NO data has been embedded. Of course this problem happens rarely. In this case, to solve this problem in placing process, after inserting every block, its complicated situation should be computed. If the block is not complicated any more, the placed data in it should be inserted or embedded in the next one again (h → hp). To exploit the inserted data in the stage medium picture when have the key and length of inserted data PRNG[2] used for the first value, At first based on the above method we should compute the number of complex pixels [11]. Then from the left corner and the upper part of the picture begin to calculate the complexity of every pixel and if so a semi random number is produced and we recognize the PRNG pixels containing data. **Figure 6** shows the Algorithm extract.

3. Performance and Security Analysis of Proposed Method

Photos are sensitive to visual attacks it means the visual system of human is able to recognize the existence of data in the picture [12]. Data placement in photos in white areas causes the picture be attacked by vision. So then in this case it maybe possible that human be able to recognize

[2]Pesudo Random Number Generator.

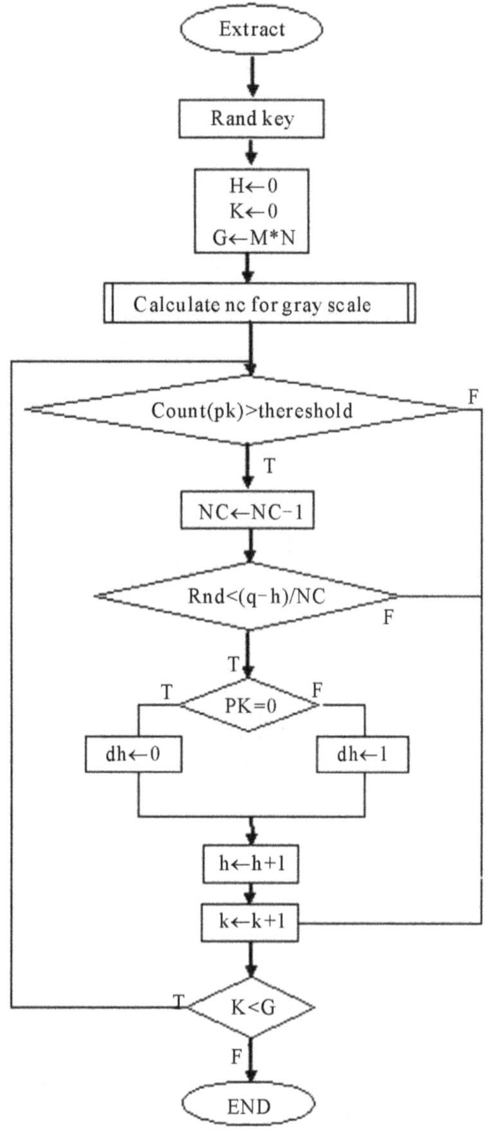

Figure 6. Extract algorithm.

the hidden data in the picture. Placement in white area creates some black points that it shows placement of zero bits message has been performed in that areas, it is the major fault of data placement in the picture [13]. Now inorder to prevent these attacks we should divide the photo in blocks as M × N. Then place information in the blocks which are not monotonous. Blocks which are not monotonous are all called complicated ones. So we should compute the complexity for every block and then place the information. To do this, we begin the review from the left side of the first block. Performing the suggested method improves the quality of placing picture and increases its security.

4. Simulation Results

The placement is carried out after making halftone in the presented methods in refrences [4-6]. Placement of data in photos after creating halftone causes some noise be performed around the area of filter which has a medium grey color. In the suggested method, placement of information in the picture takes place simultanously with creating halftone so that created error because of plaçement of information like halftone of performing error is distributed in neibouring pixels. Placement in the process of making halftone in relation to placement in halftone increase the quality of picture that inturn causes the increase of security or capacity. In this method, the embedded data in image Halftone such that the error resulting from the spread to adjacent pixels. The proposed method of error resulting from data embedded in the adjacent pixels Maintain image quality and higher capacity utilization has been. This method of uniform or non-uniform criteria for the pixels in images which has significantly reduced errors and improved quality. The proposed method has been implemented by matlab software The implementation for the second image has been reviewed and the results in **Table 1** are shown.

Figure 7 has been shown Main Picture, **Figure 8** has been shown after making Halftone action will not be

Table 1. Show the simulation result.

Error	Capacity	Method	Picture
0.695	4500 bit	Simplemethod	1
0.998	4500 bit	Behinemethod	1
0.792	2500 bit	Simplemethod	2
0.925	2500 bit	Behinemethod	2

Figure 7. Main picture.

Figure 8. Halftone picture.

Figure 9. Simple method.

embedded and **Figure 9** has been shown placing with Simple method and **Figure 10** has been shown placing with Behine method.

5. Conclusion

A method for steganography was presented. The action of inserting and halftone is performed at the same time, and the resulted error from placing diffused to neibouring pixels, placing in simple picture can discover steganography by eyes. A norm was used to distinguish simple blocks, and suggested a method to prevent inserting in simple picture blocks. In some steganographies the step of inserting comes after making halftone that reduces the capacity a lot. In the suggested method the diffusion of error resulted by inserting in the neibouring pixels improves the picture quality and usage compared with former methods. The suggested method has used the norm of complexity that reduces error clearly and improves quality. Disassembling operations show the precision and correctness of the method.

Figure 10. Behine method.

REFERENCES

[1] C.-S. Shich, H.-C. Huang, F.-H. Wang and J.-S. Pan, "Genetic Watermarking Based on Transform-Domain Techniques," *Pattern Recognition*, Vol. 37, No. 3, 2004, pp. 555-565.

[2] P. Wayner, "Disappearing Cryptography: Information Hiding: Steganography and Watermarking," 2nd Edition, Morgan Kaufmann Publishers Inc., San Francisco, 2002.

[3] M. Y. Wu and J. H. Lee, "A Novel Data Embedding Method for Two-Color Facsimile Images," *Proceeding of International Symposium on Multimedia Information Processing* (*ICASSP*), Vol. 2, 1998, pp. 1161-1164.

[4] Y. C. Tseng, Y. Y. Chen and H.-K. Pan, "A Secure Data Hidding Scheme for Binary Images," *IEEE Transaction on Communications*, Vol. 50, No. 8, 2002, pp. 1227-1231.

[5] T. Mitsa and K. Parker, "Digital Halftoning Using a Blue Noise Mask," *Journal of Optical Society of America A*, Vol. 9, No. 11, 1992, pp. 1920-1929.

[6] M. Wu, E. Tang and B. Liu, "Data Hiding in Digital Bi-

nary Image," *Proceeding of IEEE International Conference on Multimedia & Expo*, New York, 2000, pp. 393-396.

[7] R. W. Floyd and L. Steinberg, "Adaptive Algorithm for Spatial Grayscale," *Proceedings of SID*, Vol. 17, No. 2, 1976, pp. 75-77.

[8] T. N. Pappas, J. P. Allebach and D. L. Neuhoff, "Model-Based Digital Halftoning," *IEEE Signal Processing Magazine*, Vol. 20, No. 4, 2003, pp. 14-27.

[9] E. Kawaguchi and R. O. Eason, "Principle and Applications of BPCS Steganography," *Proceedings of SPIE's International Symposium on Voice, Video, and Data Communications*, 1998, pp. 464-473.

[10] M. S. Fu and O. C. Au, "Data Hiding Watermarking for Halftone Images," *IEEE Transactions on Image Processing*, Vol. 11, No. 4, 2008, pp. 477-484.

[11] M. Jiang, E. K. Wong, N. Memon and X. Wu, "Steganalysis of Halftone Images," *Proceedings of ICASSP*, Vol. 2, 2009, pp. ii/793-ii/796.

[12] S. H. Kim and J. P. Allebach, "Impact of Human Visual System Models on Model Based Halftoning," *IEEE Transaction on Image Processing*, Vol. 11, 2004, pp. 258-269.

[13] H. K. Verma and A. N. Singh, "Robustness of the Digital Image Watermarking Techniques against Brightness and Rotation Attack," *International Journal of Computer Science and Information Security*, Vol. 5, No. 1, 2010.

16

The Application of Mixed Method in Developing a Cyber Terrorism Framework

Rabiah Ahmad, Zahri Yunos
Center for Advanced Computing Technology, Faculty of Information and Communication Technology,
Universiti Teknikal Malaysia Melaka (UTeM), Melaka, Malaysia

ABSTRACT

Mixed method research has becoming an increasingly popular approach in the discipline of sociology, psychology, education, health science and social science. The purpose of this paper is to describe the application of mixed method in developing a cyber terrorism framework. This project has two primary goals: firstly is to discover the theory and then develop a conceptual framework that describes the phenomena, and secondly is to verify the conceptual framework that describes the phenomena. In order to achieve conclusive findings of the study, a mixed method research is recommended: qualitative data and quantitative data are collected and analyzed respectively in a separate phase. The mixed method approach improves the rigor and explanation of the research results, thus bring conclusive findings to the study outcome. By utilizing qualitative and quantitative techniques within the same study, we are able to incorporate the strength of both methodologies and fit together the insights into a workable solution.

Keywords: Mixed Method Research; Methodology; Data Analysis; Data Collection; Cyber Terrorism

1. Introduction

Methodology can be simplified as a plan of action where the method used brings to the desired outcome. The context of methodology as described by Crotty [1] cited in Levy [2], defines methodology as "the strategy, plan of action, process or design lying behind choice of particular methods and linking the choice and use of methods to the desired outcome". Methodology refers to the theoretical arguments that researchers use in order to justify their research methods and design [3].

The purpose of this paper is to describe the application of mixed method in developing a cyber terrorism framework. This project has two primary goals, firstly is to discover a theory and then develop a conceptual framework that describes the phenomena by using qualitative method. Secondly is to verify the conceptual framework that describes the phenomena by quantitative method. By utilizing both techniques within the same study, the researcher is able to incorporate the strength of both methodologies and fit together the insights into a workable solution.

2. Literature Review

2.1. Cyber Terrorism

In this digital age, the concept of cyber terrorism or the use of cyberspace to carry out terrorist activities has emerged. The convergence of physical terrorism and new advancement of ICT have spawned a new term called cyber terrorism [4]. It can be summarized that cyber terrorism is the perpetration of attack through the cyberspace and the virtual world. However, there is no universally accepted definition of cyber terrorism, which seems to be a fundamental issue and challenge in countering threats from cyber terrorism.

At the international front and among the researchers, there is no common agreement on the concept of cyber terrorism [5-10]. While there are many definitions of cyber terrorism, these suggest a trend that in-depth analysis of this concept can be conducted. This can also be evidence that the study of this concept has been the focus of policy makers and scholarly studies, but their standpoints and views vary. Due to multidimensional structure (or components) of cyber terrorism, we can say that the concept of cyber terrorism is a contested concept whereby various parties interpret it differently.

The concept of cyber terrorism has several attributes (or components) such as motivation, impact and target [11]. Due to complexity of various interacting variables in the concept of cyber terrorism, to formulate a framework in describing its influential components would be beneficial. Therefore, accurate knowledge of the context of cyber terrorism enhances clarity and helps to avoid obscuring intent. Thus, there is a need for a more structured approach in understanding the various components of cyber terrorism. The outcome of this study serves the basis for various strategic decisions for policy and decision makers as well as useful foundation for academic research in understanding the context of cyber terrorism.

2.2. Mixed Method Research

One important way to strengthen a study design is through triangulation, or the combination of qualitative and quantitative approaches in the study of a situation or a certain phenomenon [12]. Usually, the researchers triangulate the two methods in order to check on the accuracy of the data gathered by each method, to make the choices available more concrete, to amplify strengths and lessen weaknesses in a study, and to answer broader and more complete range of research problems [13].

Currall *et al.* [14] study the use of qualitative and quantitative methods and conclude that the mixed methods promoted both theory development and theory evaluation (or verification). Srnka and Koeszegi [15] conclude that qualitative studies are accepted in the social sciences as exploratory or triangulation efforts that complement quantitative studies, which provide quality checks for each of these stages for result's validity and reliability. A detailed study that examine the ways in which quantitative and qualitative research were integrated and combined in practice was conducted by Bryman [16]. He defines triangulation as traditional view where quantitative and qualitative researches are combined to triangulate findings in order to be mutually corroborated.

3. Knowledge Management Architecture in Developing Cyber Terrorism Framework

Knowledge management is a matter of managing analytical process to transform data into information, and information into knowledge, and knowledge into wisdom [17]. Recent research suggests that architectural knowledge, such as design decisions, is important and should be recorded alongside the architecture description [18]. In this research, the conceptual framework describing cyber terrorism is developed by using the grounded theory method. In grounded theory, the main source of data collection are interviews conducted with participants and observed by the researcher, whereby the researcher looks for common patterns among the sets of data [19]. Grounded theory is a rigorous process that involves generating a conceptual model (or theory) that is grounded in the data [20].

Egan [21] recommended five steps in the process of grounded theory research; initiating research, data selection, initiation and ongoing data collection, data analysis and concluding the research (**Figure 1**). Jones and Alony [22] suggest five steps in grounded theory approach: acknowledgement of researchers' bias, data selection, data collection, data coding & analysis and compilation of results. Likewise, the grounded theory method employed by Esteves *et al.* [23] composed of the following phases: research design phase, data collection phase, data analysis phase and comparison phase. Overall, the steps of grounded theory approach discussed above are more or less similar with each other. For this research, we adopted Egan's recommendation.

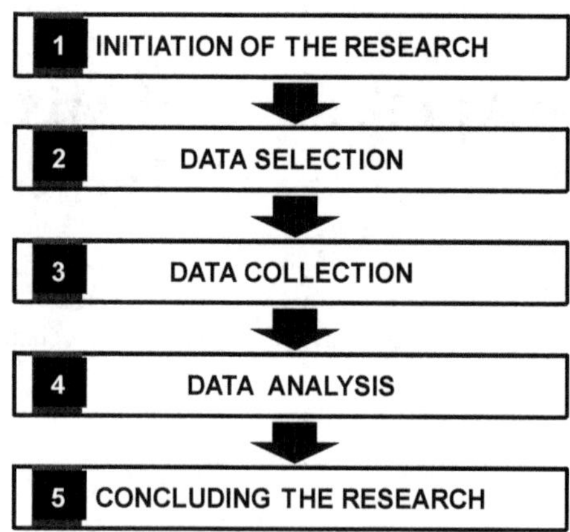

Figure 1. Grounded theory process (adapted from Egan [21]).

The first level, initiation of the research involves the selection of an area of inquiry. The research begins with an awareness of the context of the research by reviewing literatures relevant to the area of inquiry. In the second level, data selection, involves the identification of potential data sources (individuals and organizations they represent) associated with the research questions. The respondents are chosen from various expert positions to reflect variety of expertise.

The third level is initiation of data collection from targeted respondents. Data collection is an ongoing process, whereby the researcher can return to the interviewees for clarification and elaboration besides comparing related documents or records with data collected during initiation of the research.

In the fourth level, data analysis, involves a constant comparison method for generating and analyzing data. Data analysis is defined as a process of systematically searching and arranging the interview transcripts, field notes and other materials with the objectives to increase the understanding and to enable researcher to present what have been discovered. Lastly, concluding the research, involves documenting the grounded theory based on researcher observation of the data saturation and sufficient theory which has emerged from the data. Data saturation is the evident when data collection no longer contributes to elaboration of the phenomenon being investigated.

4. Conceptual Framework of This Study

Two research methods that are commonly used are qualitative research and quantitative research. It is suggested that when the goal of a research is to develop a conceptual model for the purpose of building theory around a particular phenomenon or process, an interpretive approach utilizing a qualitative methodology may be more appropriate [2]. On the other hand, if the primary goal of a research problem is to test the validity of a model where all the variables of influence a phenomenon or process is already known, then quantitative methodology may be appropriate [2]. In summary, qualitative research approaches seek to explore phenomena while quantitative research approaches seek to confirm hypothesis about phenomena.

This research is about exploring the context of cyber terrorism, focusing on the attributes or components of cyber terrorism. Since this project is exploratory in nature, a qualitative research by using a grounded theory method is adopted for this study. The phrase grounded theory refers to theory that is developed from a corpus of data through literatures, interviews and observations [24]. In this method, the objectives are to investigate the phenomena under study, to identify and construct attributes of the phenomena, and to develop a conceptual framework that describe the phenomena.

Once the theory discovery and conceptual framework have been developed, the next stage is to test or verify the conceptual framework. The outcome can be achieved by using quantitative method to quantify them and then applied statistical test to conduct the hypothesis test. In this method, the objectives are to evaluate the framework and to test the dynamic relationship of attributes (or components) of the framework.

In short, we believe that a mixed method approach is appropriate to be used in this study in order to accomplish both theory discovery and verification within a single research project. Theory discovery is achieved by using qualitative data to sharpen our theoretical ideas about the phenomena under investigation, while verification is achieved by using quantitative data to quantify them and then applied statistical test to conduct hypothesis test. The combination of qualitative and quantitative techniques within one research study able to incorporate the strength of both methodologies. The framework of research methodology is described below (**Figure 2**).

The approach discussed in this paper is well described by Srnka and Koeszegi [15] where they state that the combination of two separate studies, one collects and analyzed qualitative and quantitative data sequentially, has been acceptable to researchers in the social science. By conducting qualitative method in a preliminary stage, the objective is for the researchers to develop a conceptual framework (or to generate hypothesis) for the quantitative study. Thus, when qualitative data collection precedes the quantitative data collection, the intent is to first explore the problem under study then follow up on this study with quantitative data that are amenable to studying a large sample so that results might be inferred to a population [25]. We believe that by merging the results provides an overall picture of the research problem.

5. Framework of Data Collection and Data Analysis

In this study, mixed method research involves both collecting and analyzing quantitative and qualitative data in sequential order. The first stage in the analysis cycle is to frame a theory or hypothesis from the literatures which can be used as initial guidance for data collection and data analysis. Once the theory or hypothesis has been generated, the researchers develop questionnaires to get in-depth understanding on the phenomena under investigation. Data collection is a semi-structured method by using in-depth interviews. Interviews are part of most

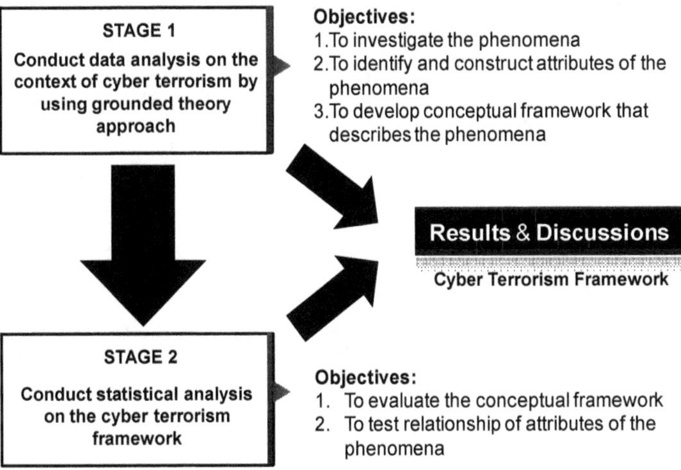

Figure 2. The framework of research methodology.

interpretive studies and as a key way of accessing the interpretations of informants in the field [26]. Since the first stage is explanatory in nature, data analyses are done by using grounded theory approach. Qualitative research includes a variety of methodological approaches and one example is grounded theory [27]. As have been mentioned earlier, the phrase grounded theory refers to theory that is developed from a corpus of data through literatures, interviews and observations.

In the next stage, quantitative approach is applied to corroborate the researcher's initial discovery. A survey with close-ended questions format are used for data collection to determine the views and opinions of the population that represents various groups in the society. In this phase, the researcher's goal is to test the theory or hypothesis, which finding is generalized from a larger representative sampling. Statistical analysis is performed to test the validity of the theory or hypothesis. The numerical findings help to interpret the results, where clearer interpretations of the statistical results are obtained. **Figure 3** shows the summary on how the data are collected and analyzed.

6. Suitability of Mixed Method in This Research

All the relevant methodological issues discussed in this paper provide justification and practical approach on how the research is conducted. The methodology explained in this paper provides the researchers with the right direction and understanding in conducting the research by choosing the right research design. Research design as defined by Cooper and Schindler [27] is a plan and structure of investigation so conceived as to obtain answers to research questions. It includes an outline on what the researcher will do from initiation of the research to the final analysis of the data.

In this study, we suggest that a mixed method research approach is appropriate to be applied. The motivation factors in applying the mixed method (as opposed to a single method) are due to the following reasons. Firstly, the nature of the research is exploratory and explanatory in nature, and is grounded in theory. The goals are to discover theory and to develop a conceptual framework that describes the phenomena (qualitative method); and to test or verify the conceptual framework that describes the phenomena (quantitative method). As noted by Yauch and Steudel [13], the mixed method research complements each other, which explains the results of analyses. The qualitative research is interpretive, which allow for the discovery of new ideas and unanticipated occurrences. Qualitative research aims to achieve an in-depth understanding of a situation or a certain phenomenon [27]. Focus of the research is to explore (understand and interpret) of a situation or a certain phenomenon. On another hand, quantitative research aims to achieve precise measurement of something such as participants behavior, knowledge or opinion [27]. Focus of the research is to confirm (describe and explain) hypothesis about a situation or a certain phenomenon. Therefore, by utilizing a mixed method research, we believed it would bring conclusive findings on outcome of this study.

Secondly, mixed method approach helps to answer questions that cannot be answered by qualitative or quantitative approaches alone, thus, provide breadth and depth to the study [28]. Researchers who conduct mixed methods research are more likely to select methods and approaches with respect to their underlying research questions in ways that offer the best opportunity for answering important research questions [28]. In this research, a survey questionnaire using qualitative in-depth interviews is conducted as a way to tap into participants' perspectives and insights. During analysis, the qualitative researcher uses content analysis of written or recorded materials drawn from participants' expressions and observations [27] or documents review [2]. Qualitative research study via questionnaires interview, and supplement with close-ended survey systematically provide

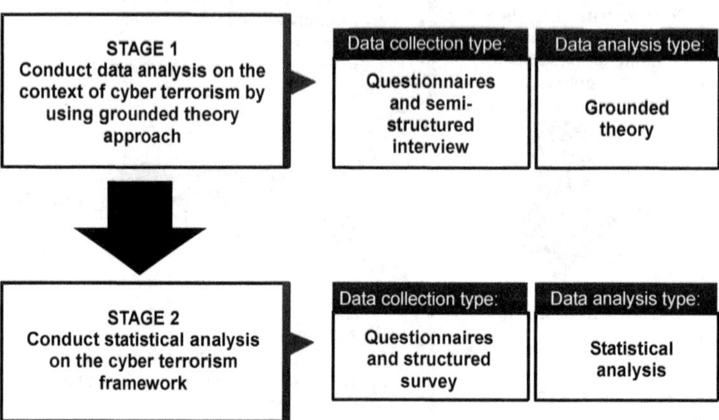

Figure 3. Framework for data collection and data analysis.

breadth and depth to the research [12]. Quantitative research looks at the frequency [27] or any kind of research that produces findings arrived at by means of statistical procedures [2]. Through this approach, it is believed that the findings are corroborated across different approaches, thus provide greater confidence in the conclusion.

Lastly, the research framework of mixed method is chosen to apply the concept of triangulation. As noted by Paton [12], one important way to strengthen a study design is through triangulation, or the combination of methodologies in the study of a situation or a certain phenomenon. Paton [12] also argues that triangulation provides accuracy of the data gathered while Olsen [29] argues that triangulation provides validation besides deepening and widening one's understanding. Triangulation is a term derived from navigation and surveying where different bearings are taken in order to arrive at a precise location. In this study, triangulation involves locating a true position by referring to two or more other coordinates [12]. As noted by Yauch and Steudel [13], triangulation corroborates data and obtains convergent validity. Moreover, triangulation reduces biasness besides be able to heighten the validity of the data collection and analysis.

7. Conclusions

The study on the context of cyber terrorism is quite complex as it is about threat perception which makes the concept differ from one to another. Understanding similarities and differences in perception of what constitutes cyber terrorism can provide insight on the concept of cyber terrorism. The outcome of this study serves the basis for various strategic decisions for policy and decision makers as well as useful foundation for academic research in understanding the context of cyber terrorism. Detail focus analysis can be conducted to investigate and analyze the context of cyber terrorism.

This paper provides information on how this research is conducted. It also describes the framework of research methodology, where we have recommended that the study to be conducted by using a mixed method research: qualitative data and quantitative data are collected and analyzed respectively in a separate phase. This paper also established the conceptual framework that guides the data collection and data analysis techniques. Finally, the research methodology explained in this paper provides the researchers with the right direction by choosing the right research design. The mixed method improves the rigor and explanation of the results, thus bring conclusive findings to the research outcome. By utilizing qualitative and quantitative techniques within the same study, a mixed method research should be able to incorporate the strength of both methodologies and fit together the insights into a workable solution.

8. Acknowledgements

The authors would like to thank the following individuals who provided valuable input to this paper: Dr. Solahuddin Shamsuddin and Zaleha Abd Rahim of CyberSecurity Malaysia. We also would like to thank the Center for Advanced Computing Technology, Faculty of Information and Communication Technology, Universiti Teknikal Malaysia Melaka (UTeM) that provided research grant for this project.

REFERENCES

[1] M. Crotty, "The Foundation of Social Research: Meaning and Perspective in the Research Process," Allen and Unwin, St Leonards, 1998.

[2] D. Levy, "Qualitative Methodology and Grounded Theory in Property Research," *Pacific Rim Property Research Journal*, Vol. 12, No. 4, 2006, pp. 369-388.

[3] J. M. Case and G. Light, "Emerging Methodologies in Engineering Education Research," *Journal of Engineering Education*, Vol. 100, No. 1, 2011, pp. 186-210.

[4] D. A. Simanjuntak, H. P. Ipung and C. Lim, "Text Classification Techniques Used to Facilitate Cyber Terrorism Investigation," *Proceeding of Second International Conference on Advances in Computing, Control, and Telecommunication Technologies* (*ACT* 2010), Jakarta, 2-3 December 2010, pp. 198-200.

[5] M. Dogrul, A. Aslan and E. Celik, "Developing an International Cooperation on Cyber Defense and Deterrence against Cyber Terrorism," *3rd International Conference on Cyber Conflict*, Tallinn, 7-10 June 2011, pp. 1-15.

[6] M. Conway, "Against Cyberterrorism," *Communications of the ACM*, Vol. 54, No. 2, 2011, p. 26.

[7] Z. Yunos, S. H. Suid, R. Ahmad and Z. Ismail, "Safeguarding Malaysia's Critical National Information Infrastructure (CNII) against Cyber Terrorism: Towards Development of a Policy Framework," *IEEE Sixth International Conference on Information Assurance & Security, Atlanta*, 23-25 August 2010, pp. 21-27.

[8] P. A. H. Williams, "Information Warfare: Time for a Redefinition," *Proceedings of the 11th Australian Information Warfare & Security Conference*, Perth Western, 30 November-2 December 2010, pp. 37-44.

[9] C. Czosseck, R. Ottis and A. M. Taliharm, "Estonia after the 2007 Cyber Attacks: Legal, Strategic and Organisational Changes in Cyber Security," *International Journal of Cyber Warfare and Terrorism*, Vol. 1, No. 1, 2011, pp. 24-34.

[10] J. Matusitz, "Social Network Theory: A Comparative Analysis of the Jewish Revolt in Antiquity and the Cyber Terrorism Incident over Kosovo," *Information Security Journal: A Global Perspective*, Vol. 20, No. 1, 2011, pp.

34-44.

[11] R. Ahmad and Z. Yunos, "A Dynamic Cyber Terrorism Framework," *International Journal of Computer Science and Information Security*, Vol. 10, No. 2, 2012, pp. 149-158.

[12] M. Q. Paton, "*Qualitative Evaluation and Research Methods*," 2nd Edition, SAGE Publications, Thousand Oaks, 1991.

[13] C. Yauch and H. Steudel, "Complementary Use of Qualitative and Quantitative Cultural Assessment Methods," *Organizational Research Methods*, Vol. 6, No. 4, 2003, pp. 465-481.

[14] S. C. Currall, T. H. Hammer, L. S. Baggett and G. M. Doniger, "Combining Qualitative and Quantitative Methodologies to Study Group Processes: An Illustrative Study of a Corporate Board of Directors," *Organizational Research Methods*, Vol. 2, No. 1, 1999, pp. 5-36.

[15] K. J. Srnka and S. T. Koeszegi, "From Words to Numbers: How to Transform Qualitative Data into Meaningful Quantitative Results," *Schmalenbach Business Review*, Vol. 59, No. 1, 2007, pp. 29-57.

[16] A. Bryman, "Integrating Quantitative and Qualitative Research: How Is It Done?" *Qualitative Research*, Vol. 6, No. 1, 2006, pp. 97-113.

[17] R. J. Chenail, "Conducting Qualitative Data Analysis: Qualitative Data Analysis as a Metaphoric Process," *The Qualitative Report*, Vol. 17, No. 1, 2012, pp. 248-253.

[18] A. Tang, P. Avgeriou, A. Jansen, R. Capilla and M. Ali Babar, "A Comparative Study of Architecture Knowledge Management Tools," *Journal of Systems and Software*, Vol. 83, No. 3, 2010, pp. 352-370.

[19] R. Hoda, J. Noble and S. Marshall, "Using Grounded Theory to Study the Human Aspects of Software Engineering," *Proceeding of HAoSE* 10 *Human Aspects of Software Engineering*, Nevada, 17-21 October 2010.

[20] A. A. Singh, A. Urbano, M. Haston and E. Mcmahan, "School Counselors' Strategies for Social Justice Change: A Grounded Theory of What Works in the Real World," *American School Counselor Association*, Vol. 13, No. 3, 2010, pp. 135-145.

[21] T. M. Egan, "Grounded Theory Research and Theory Building," *Advances in Developing Human Resources*, Vol. 4, No. 3, 2002, pp. 277-295.

[22] M. Jones and I. Alony, "Guiding the Use of Grounded Theory in Doctoral Studies—An Example from the Australian Film Industry," *International Journal of Doctoral Studies*, Vol. 6, 2011, pp. 95-114.

[23] J. Esteves, U. Politécnica and J. Carvalho, "Use of Grounded Theory in Information Systems Area: An Exploratory Analysis," *European Conference on Research Methodology for Business and Management*, 2000, pp. 129-136.

[24] J. W. Creswell, "Qualitative Inquiry and Research Design: Choose among Five Traditions," Sage Publications, London, 1998.

[25] J. M. Azorin and R. Cameron, "The Application of Mixed Methods in Organisational Research: A Literature Review," *Electronic Journal of Business Research Methods*, Vol. 8, No. 2, 2010, pp. 95-105.

[26] G. Walsham, "Doing Interpretive Research," *European Journal of Information Systems*, Vol. 15, No. 3, 2006, pp. 320-330.

[27] D. R. Cooper and P. S. Schindler, "Business Research Method," McGraw-Hill Companies, Inc., New York, 2008.

[28] R. B. Johnson and A. J. Onwuegbuzie, "Mixed Methods Research: A Research Paradigm Whose Time Has Come," *Educational Research*, Vol. 33, No. 7, 2004, pp. 14-26.

[29] W. Olsen, "Triangulation in Social Research: Qualitative and Quantitative Methods Can Really Be Mixed," In: M. Holborn, Ed., *Development in Sociology*, Causeway Press, Ormskirk, 2004, pp. 1-30.

17

Data Stream Subspace Clustering for Anomalous Network Packet Detection

Zachary Miller, Wei Hu
Department of Computer Science, Houghton College, Houghton, USA

ABSTRACT

As the Internet offers increased connectivity between human beings, it has fallen prey to malicious users who exploit its resources to gain illegal access to critical information. In an effort to protect computer networks from external attacks, two common types of Intrusion Detection Systems (IDSs) are often deployed. The first type is signature-based IDSs which can detect intrusions efficiently by scanning network packets and comparing them with human-generated signatures describing previously-observed attacks. The second type is anomaly-based IDSs able to detect new attacks through modeling normal network traffic without the need for a human expert. Despite this advantage, anomaly-based IDSs are limited by a high false-alarm rate and difficulty detecting network attacks attempting to blend in with normal traffic. In this study, we propose a StreamPreDeCon anomaly-based IDS. StreamPreDeCon is an extension of the preference subspace clustering algorithm PreDeCon designed to resolve some of the challenges associated with anomalous packet detection. Using network packets extracted from the first week of the DARPA '99 intrusion detection evaluation dataset combined with Generic Http, Shellcode and CLET attacks, our IDS achieved 94.4% sensitivity and 0.726% false positives in a best case scenario. To measure the overall effectiveness of the IDS, the average sensitivity and false positive rates were calculated for both the maximum sensitivity and the minimum false positive rate. With the maximum sensitivity, the IDS had 80% sensitivity and 9% false positives on average. The IDS also averaged 63% sensitivity with a 0.4% false positive rate when the minimal number of false positives is needed. These rates are an improvement on results found in a previous study as the sensitivity rate in general increased while the false positive rate decreased.

Keywords: Anomaly Detection; Intrusion Detection System; Network Security; Preference Subspace Clustering; Stream Data Mining

1. Introduction

Since the explosion of internet usage in thc carly 1990s, people are now able to communicate over larger distances at a faster rate than previously possible. As the number of Internet-capable devices available to consumers increases, new forms of communication are created. This new level of connectivity is often exploited as computer attackers are now able to share and distribute malicious programs and ideas effectively allowing inexperienced attackers to create sophisticated viruses and malware. Because of the increased need for network security, Intrusion Detection Systems (IDSs) are an integral part of any network [1].

Intrusion Detection Systems focus on preventing modern-day attacks directed towards a network through two techniques. The first type use signatures created by a human expert to represent and detect previous attacks. The signature-based IDSs provide a simple and effective security tool through signature matching, but are unable to detect new attacks [2]. The second type, anomaly-based IDSs, take a different approach by modeling normal traffic and comparing each incoming packet to this model [1]. Although anomaly-based IDSs can automatically detect new attacks, they generally suffer from a high false positive rate (normal packets being classified as abnormal) and are vulnerable to polymorphic attacks. These attacks try to fool anomaly-based IDSs by making malicious packets appear normal. Because anomaly-based IDSs can detect new attacks, several anomaly-based IDSs have addressed the high false positive rate while improving detection.

Numerous anomaly-based IDSs have been proposed and developed. NIDES [3], one of the first anomaly-based IDSs, models network behavior using source and destination IP addresses as well as the TCP/UDP port numbers to detect statistically deviant packets as abnormal attacks. Another early system, NETAD [4], analyzes the first 48 bytes of IP packets and constructs models for the most common types of network protocols to detect anomalies specific to the packets' protocol. Mahoney *et al.* [5] developed a two tiered IDS formed by the parts PHAD and ALAD [5]. PHAD creates a model using the packet headers from each packet, and ALAD analyzes the TCP connections to detect anomalies. Using the two system approach, Mahoney *et al.* [5] developed a two-fold Intrusion Detection System able to detect individual and sets of anomalous packets. Two recently proposed IDSs, PAYL and McPAD employ *n*-gram features to represent network packets.

PAYL [6,7] creates a histogram model based on 1-gram features from the ASCII characters in the packet's payload. As new packets come in, PAYL generates a histogram based on the each packet's payload and compares the incoming histogram with the model using the Mahalanobis distance. Although PAYL achieves a high level of accuracy detecting abnormal packets, it suffers from a high false positive rate and low detection rate of polymorphic attacks. To improve these results, Roberto Perdisci *et al.* [8] developed McPAD, an IDS which utilizes multiple one-class support vector machines to accurately classify packets. In the McPAD [1,8] study, Perdisci represented network packets through 2-gram features as well as 2_v-gram where v is the space between two characters in the packet used to capture structural information within the payload. With 2_v-gram features, McPAD detects the polymorphic attacks while keeping the false positive rate minimal. Despite the high detection rates of PAYL and McPAD, they cannot treat the dynamic nature of network packets.

A changing flow of network traffic can be viewed as a stream of packets. Therefore, stream mining algorithms can naturally be applied to anomaly-based intrusion detection [9]. Because data streams are very different from traditional batch data, data stream mining algorithms must resolve numerous challenges. These algorithms must process a large (sometimes infinite) number of data points in an online fashion with one pass. As a result of the restrictions on processing time, memory usage and the need for making use of the most recent data points, stream mining algorithms tend to perform worse than batch algorithms [9].

In 2011 we created two anomaly-based IDSs based on stream mining algorithms, and tested the IDSs on network packets represented by 2-gram features [10]. The first IDS used a modification of the density-based stream clustering algorithm DenStream [11]. This IDS preformed moderately well given its simple concept and small number of parameters. The second was a streaming histogram IDS based on the approach of PAYL. The histogram IDS performed better than the DenStream IDS but required more parameters to tune. After testing the IDSs with network packets represented by 2-gram features, we tested 1-gram features as a comparison. Even though the IDSs using the 1-grams did not achieve the detection rates of the 2-gram tested IDSs, they took much less time to process the data. This study planned to extend and improve the detection and false positive rates of the previous stream IDSs with StreamPreDeCon, a modified subspace clustering algorithm for an evolving data stream.

2. Materials and Methods

2.1. Data

Two publically available datasets were combined to provide testing data for our proposed IDS. The first was the DARPA '99 intrusion detection evaluation dataset (http://www.ll.mit.edu/mission/communications/ist/corpora/ideval/data/1999data.html) and the second was provided by the creators of McPAD [1]. The DARPA data was used in this study as an example of normal traffic and was extracted from the HTTP requests in the first week of the dataset. The payload information was retrieved using Jpcap (http://netresearch.ics.uci.edu/kfujii/Jpcap/doc/) and the payload characters were converted to their corresponding ACSII numbers if the packet length was above 1400 characters. This preprocessing resulted in 5594 packets of normal traffic grouped by day. The number of times each ASCII character occurs was counted to generate 256 1-gram features. These features were selected instead of the 2-gram features as they provide a compact representation of network packets.

The anomaly detection algorithm proposed in this study was tested with packets of three attack types. To simulate attacks to a network, 66 different types of Generic HTTP attacks were included in our study. These HTTP attacks included threats caused by standard attacks like buffer overflow, URL decoding error and input validation error. Shellcode attacks were also included as they are a special type of packet where the payload contains executable code. CLET attacks attempt to hide from the detection algorithm by polymorphically enciphering the payload of the packet to appear normal. These attacks were also extracted from the packet's payload using Jpcap and inserted into the normal packet stream. On each day of the DARPA dataset, the first 20% of the packets were set aside for a parameter-tuning phase, and the remaining 80% for a full-scale anomaly detection testing phase.

2.2. Methods

PAYL and McPAD perform well in a static network environment, but are not designed to consider the dynamic nature of real network traffic. To remedy this, we explore the use of the modified density based clustering algorithm PreDeCon [12]. PreDeCon is inspired by a well-known algorithm DBSCAN [13] and its generalization

OPTICS [14]. DBSCAN stands for Density Based Spatial Clustering of Applications with Noise and uses two simple parameters to cluster dense points together [13]. The first of these is ϵ, which defines the radius of a neighborhood of a point, termed ϵ-neighborhood. When the ϵ-neighborhood of a point is calculated, DBSCAN clusters the points together if the number of points in the ϵ-neighborhood is larger than the second user-specified parameter minPts. Because DBSCAN is a fairly simple and effective algorithm, it is the basis for several density based clustering algorithms such as OPTICS [14]. Instead of assigning points to particular clusters, OPTICS orders the points in the way that the DBSCAN algorithm would cluster the points if an infinite number of epsilon values exist.

DBSCAN and OPTICS are proven to efficiently cluster dense points together; however, the accuracy of the clustering models decreases with high-dimensional data. To extend the effectiveness of DBSCAN and OPTICS to high dimensional datasets, the notion of a preference subspace is introduced in the clustering algorithm PreDeCon [12]. The preference subspace is formally defined as the subset of features for a point in Euclidean space that exhibit a low user-specified variance when compared with its other features.

2.2.1. PreDeCon

PreDeCon uses the preference subspace concept to compute the ϵ-neighborhood of a point to cluster points together. The preference subspace is defined as a vector computed using the variance along a feature of a point to a given ϵ-neighborhood. The variance of an ϵ-neighborhood is calculated using the following formula:

$$VAR_{A_i}(N_\epsilon(p)) = \frac{\sum_{q \in N_\epsilon(p)} \left(dist\left(\pi_{A_i}(p), \pi_{A_i}(q)\right)\right)^2}{|N_\epsilon(p)|}, \quad (1)$$

where p and q are points, $\pi_{A_i}(p)$ is the ith feature of p, and $N_\epsilon(p)$ is the ϵ-neighborhood of p or all points r where $dist(p,r) \le \epsilon$. The preference vector is then calculated by defining the subspace preference vector as

$$\bar{w}_p = (w_1, w_2, \cdots w_d), \quad (2)$$

$$w_i = \begin{cases} 1 \text{ if } VAR_{A_i}(N_\epsilon(p)) > \delta \\ k \text{ if } VAR_{A_i}(N_\epsilon(p)) \le \delta \end{cases} \quad (3)$$

where $k \gg 1$. Using the subspace preference vector, a preference weighted similarity measure associated with a point p is defined as

$$dist_p(p,q) = \sqrt{\sum_{i=1}^{d} w_i * \left(\pi_{A_i}(p) - \pi_{A_i}(q)\right)^2} \quad (4)$$

A preference weighted ϵ-neighborhood $\left(N_\epsilon^{\bar{w}_o}(o)\right)$ can then be formed using this weighted distance function. The ϵ-neighborhood is formally defined as:

$$N_\epsilon^{\bar{w}_o}(o) = \left\{x \in D \middle| dist_p(o,x) \le \epsilon\right\} \quad (5)$$

Using $N_\epsilon^{\bar{w}_o}(o)$, a preference weighted core point is defined as a point whose preference dimensionality of its ϵ-neighborhood is at most a user defined parameter λ and the ϵ-neighborhood contains at least μ minimum points. If a point is a preference weighted core point, the ϵ-neighborhood of the point is inserted into a queue. PreDeCon then iterates through the queue and checks to see if the points in the ϵ-neighborhood can reach different points in the data set using the preference weighted subspace. A point q is reachable by a point p if q is a core point and is within the preference weighted ϵ-neighborhood of p. If a point is reachable but unclassified, the point is added to the queue. Using these definitions, PreDeCon then creates the clusters using the ExpandCluster method described in **Figure 1**.

2.2.2. PreDeConInc

The incremental version of PreDeCon attempts to update the clustering model built by the original algorithm as new data comes in through an added update step [15]. This update step simply checks to see if the new point causes a core point to change its preference vector or to become a non-core point and vice versa. Once an affected point (one of the points that has changed) from the insert is found, all reachable points are found using the new preference weighted subspace and updated with the new subspace preference vector. This approach minimizes the number of distance queries between two points because the extra steps to find the reachable neighbors of a point x are not executed unless the new point affects x. Although the incremental version of PreDeCon allows

```
ExpandCluster():
For each unclassified o ∈ D do
  if o is a core point then:
    generate new clusterID;
    insert all x ∈ N_ε^{w_o}(o) into queue Φ;
    while Φ ≠ φ do
      q = first point in Φ;
      Compute R = {x ∈ D | DirReach_den^pref(q,x)};
      for each x ∈ R do
        if x is unclassified then:
          insert x into Φ;
        if x is unclassified or noise then:
          assign current clusterID to x
      remove q from Φ;
  else
    mark o as noise;
end;
```

Figure 1. Expand cluster method to create preference weighted subspace clusters.

the clustering model to update itself as new points arrive into the system, this algorithm needs to be modified to handle streaming data.

2.2.3. StreamPreDeCon

Here we propose a new algorithm StreamPreDeCon, which applies the preference weighted subspace clustering techniques of PreDeConInc to the stream setting. To accomplish this, we apply a decay factor to the Euclidean Distance and the Preference Weighted Similarity Measure so that the algorithm can capture the concept shifting and drifting nature of a data stream. Due to the potentially large volume of data in a data stream, a weighted distance deletion method of noise points is implemented to maintain an effective model of constant size.

The large amount of data that needs to be processed as well as the possibility for data evolution warrants a decay factor be applied to the distances between points. This allows for recently arrived points to have greater influence on the clustering. The decay factor was generated using the function:

$$f(t) = 2^{\theta t}, \tag{6}$$

where θ is a predefined constant greater than 0 and t is the difference in the timestamp between the current point and the point already in the model. After the decay factor is determined, the distance between the points is calculated with the weighted distance function multiplied by the decay factor through the formula:

$$dist_p(p,q) = \sqrt{\sum_{i=1}^{d} f(p_t - q_t) * w_i * (\pi_{A_i}(p) - \pi_{A_i}(q))^2} \tag{7}$$

where p_t is the timestamp of a point p. This multiplication causes older points to seem further away from newer points. The decay factor is also applied to the preference vector calculation by modulating the variance depending on the timestamp.

In order to process the large amount of stream data while keeping only the recent information in our model, PreDeConInc needs to be modified further to allow deletion of old points in the model. This is done by adding a new step immediately after the new point arrives. During this step, StreamPreDeCon checks the decayed distance between the new point and the model of core points. If this distance is above a certain threshold parameter γ and the point is currently a noise point, it is deleted. This step not only reduces the size and maintains recent information stored in the model, but also improves clustering efficiency and accuracy by removing old points that are very far from the clusters in the data stream. Core points are also eligible for future deletion because they are not guaranteed to remain core points in the future. By implementing the deletion step in **Figure 2**, the model remains current within the stream of data.

```
For each incoming point p do
    Place p into the database
    Compute the subspace preference vector w̄_p .
    //Check preferred dimensionality with database:
    //Check changes in core member property of N_ε^{w̄_o}(p) .
    Calculate Weighted Distance for Deletion of Model:
    Delete any noise points where distance is greater than γ.
    For each q ∈ N_ε^{w̄_o}(o) do
        Update w̄_p
        Check changes in core member property of N_ε^{w̄_o}(q)
        If change exists, update core members.
            Expand cluster using Decayed Euclidean Distance.
end;
```

Figure 2. StreamPreDeCon algorithm for anomalous packet detection.

The clustering models generated by StreamPreDeCon can be used to classify data points in the stream. When a new point arrives, StreamPreDeCon calculates the preference vector for the new point and checks where the new point is clustered. After the point has been clustered or marked as noise, StreamPreDeCon classifies the point as a core or non-core point. Since a point can either be classified as a core or non-core point, this approach lends itself well to binary classification problems such as the detection of abnormal packet within a network stream. To apply StreamPreDeCon, we consider packets classified as core points normal and noise points as abnormal.

The classification of network packets is evaluated through the performance metrics of sensitivity and false positive rate. Sensitivity measures the detection rate of abnormal packets and the false positive rate measures the number of false-alarms. These are defined as:

$$\text{sensitivity} = \frac{TP}{TP + FN}, \tag{8}$$

$$\text{false positive rate} = \frac{FP}{TN + FP}, \tag{9}$$

where *TP* is the number of correctly classified abnormal packets, *FP* is the number of incorrectly classified normal packets, *TN* is the correctly classified normal packets, and *FN* is the number of incorrectly classified abnormal packets.

3. Results and Discussion

In this section, we describe the setup of our evaluation tests for the StreamPreDeCon IDS. After the appropriate values of parameters were determined through a parameter-tuning phase, the performance of the StreamPreDeCon IDS was tested with the remaining 80% data. This new IDS performed well in all but one day. To gain understanding of this anomaly, we analyzed both the packets themselves and the algorithm's output at each step.

An initial setup of the StreamPreDeCon algorithm was required due to the number of parameters used. To find which parameters have the highest influence on the clustering, each virus type for a particular day was run. Because ϵ was found to have the greatest effect on the outcome of the algorithm, we fixed the remaining parameters to values that gave us a good initial clustering model. The values of the parameters used for both the tuning and the testing phases are displayed in **Table 1**.

Once the initial values of the parameters were identified, we tuned the ϵ parameter to get a basic idea of ϵ values we should try in the full-scale test. Using the 20% data set, we began with $\epsilon = 500$ and increased this value if we desired a lower false positive rate, and lowered it if we wanted a better detection rate. By using the small 20% data set, we quickly found a range of parameter values ideal to start the full scale tests on the 80% of data.

Keeping the same parameter values from the parameter-tuning phase, we began testing different values for ϵ. The effect ϵ has on the classification is demonstrated in **Figure 3**. As ϵ is increases, the detection rate and the false positive rate both decrease. In other words, to maintain a low false positive rate at the expense of a lower detection rate, a higher ϵ must be selected. For the Monday data, when ϵ is less than 480, the sensitivity is greater than 94% for all attack types, but the false positive rate is above 40%. Then when ϵ is greater than 680, the false positive rates and the sensitivity decrease to less than 10% and 54% respectively. This trend is further observed for greater ϵ values, the false positive and detection rates both continue to decrease. We also noticed slight differences in the detection rates of the different virus types in this preliminary tuning phase. The CLET attacks generally had lower detection rates but higher false positive rates in comparison with the other two attack types. This means that the overall range of ϵ values would most likely be much smaller than those for

Table 1. Parameter values used for streamPreDeCon parameter-tuning and testing phases.

	Tuning (20% data)	Testing (80% data)
ϵ	400 - 1100	490 - 1610
min_pts	5	5
λ	200	200
δ	0.5	0.5
θ	0.06	0.06
γ	5	20

Generic Http and Shellcode attacks. Also, the Shellcode attacks exhibited a near perfect detection rate while the false positive rate was below 10%. This gave us some room to work as we could get the false positive rate below 1% with a higher ϵ value. Because of the larger number of packets, the ϵ ranges needed to be altered slightly as the amount of variation between packets increases with the number of packets. Also to keep the algorithm running efficiently, we multiplied the gamma parameter by a factor of four to reflect the number of packets in the 80% test data.

After performing multiple experiments on a set of ϵ values, we displayed three test runs for each virus type and day. We selected the test that demonstrated the highest detection rate while keeping the false positive rate below 10%, a run where the lowest false positive rate occurred while keeping the detection rate above 60% and a ϵ in between the highest and lowest. The sensitivity and false positive rates are displayed in **Table 2**.

As demonstrated by **Table 2**, the StreamPreDeCon based IDS is an improvement over previous stream anomaly-based IDSs. For all days except for Thursday, the StreamPreDeCon clustering algorithm achieved the highest detection rates with the least false positive rates for the Shell-code attacks averaging 94 percent with the

Sensitivity Rate as a Function of Epsilon Values on Monday Data

Sensitivity

1
0.9
0.8
0.7
0.6
0.5
0.4
0.3
0.2
0.1
0

60 300 500 580 660 740 820 900 980 1060 1140

Epsilon

CLET
Generic
Shellcode

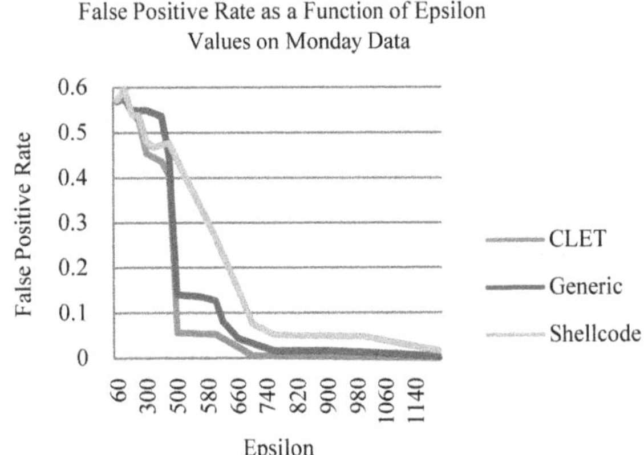

Figure 3. Anomalous packet detection sensitivity and false positive rates of the StreamPreDeCon IDS.

Table 2. StreamPreDeCon ID detection results of anomalous packets within the 80 testing data.

Day	CLET			Generic HTTP			Shell-code		
	ϵ	FP	Sens	ϵ	FP	Sens	ϵ	FP	Sens
Mon	489 (30)	5.6 (20)	61.8 (78)	550 (30)	13.6 (20)	76 (95)	650 (30)	9 (20)	94.5 (100)
	500 (45)	5.6 (9)	60 (67)	625 (45)	8 (10)	74.5 (76)	800 (45)	5 (10)	94.5 (95)
	750 (60)	0.5 (6)	52.7 (49)	1200 (60)	0.3 (7)	74.5 (73)	1290 (60)	0.2 (7)	63.6 (93)
Tue	625 (65)	10 (35)	71.8 (62)	630 (65)	8 (35)	82.1 (74)	625 (65)	10.2 (35)	94.8 (86)
	650 (80)	5 (33)	71.8 (56)	950 (80)	5.5 (34)	82.1 (72)	700 (80)	1.8 (34)	94.8 (81)
	1610 (100)	0.5 (33)	53.8 (50)	1180 (100)	0.13 (33)	56.4 (69)	1250 (100)	0.8 (33)	94.8 (79)
Wed	615 (95)	11 (11)	72 (37)	650 (95)	3 (11)	79 (62)	615 (95)	10.5 (11)	94.4 (81)
	625 (110)	2 (10)	70 (29)	1200 (110)	1 (10)	81.1 (60)	700 (110)	0.7 (10)	94.4 (78)
	1000 (125)	0.7 (8)	64.7 (25)	1250 (125)	0.3 (8)	65.2 (56)	1280 (125)	0.4 (8)	72.2 (72)
Thu	1300 (5)	42.5 (4)	73 (98)	1300 (5)	68.3 (3)	96.9 (100)	1300 (5)	69.3 (3)	94.8 (100)
	1400 (30)	38.7 (2)	61 (84)	1350 (30)	38.1 (1)	52 (90)	1350 (30)	46.7 (1)	65.5 (93)
	1420 (55)	24.5 (2)	40 (76)	1400 (55)	38 (1)	51.6 (81)	1400 (55)	31 (1)	48.3 (82)
Fri	610 (55)	8 (9)	62.9 (58)	800 (55)	11 (9)	77 (77)	625 (55)	7.9 (9)	94 (94)
	1000 (65)	5 (9)	58.1 (53)	110 (65)	5.4 (9)	77 (74)	1100 (65)	4.8 (9)	94 (92)
	1040 (75)	0.3 (8)	46.8 (49)	1260 (75)	0.3 (9)	51.6 (71)	1280 (75)	0.2 (8)	60 (88)
Best Sens Avg		15.4 (15.8)	68.3 (66.6)		20.8 (15.6)	82.3 (81.6)		21.4 (15.6)	94.5 (92)
Best FP Avg		5.3 (11.4)	51.6 (49.9)		7.8 (11.6)	59.9 (70)		6.5 (11.4)	67.8 (85.2)
Best Sens Avg*		8.7 (18.8)	67.1 (58.8)		8.9 (18.8)	78.6 (77)		9.4 (18.5)	94.4 (90.3)
Best FP Avg*		0.5 (14.3)	54.5 (43.3)		0.3 (14.3)	61.9 (67.3)		0.4 (14)	72.7 (83)

In this table, we displayed the sensitivity and false positive rates of the StreamPreDeCon-based IDS. The values within the parenthesis are taken from the 1-gram tests of [10] to show the improvement. To show the overall rates, we took the averages of the ϵ values that gave the best sensitivity and false positive rates for each day and virus type. The averages with the asterisks are the average rates with Thursday tests omitted.

smallest ϵ values. StreamPreDeCon also achieved moderate results for the Generic HTTP and CLET attacks.

Because the CLET attacks are meant to fool the anomaly-based IDS through polymorphic techniques, these attacks cause the lowest acceptable detection rates. Despite the slightly poor detection of CLET attacks, the StreamPreDeCon IDS on average had mostly higher sensitivity values with substantially lower false positive rates than the results of [10].

The poor results for the Thursday data are attributed to the data itself. Within the initial 200 normal packets, there is a large amount of variation between packets in the same ϵ -neighborhood. This causes StreamPreDeCon to create an inaccurate initial clustering model as its preferred subspace dimensionality is larger than 200. In fact, for StreamPreDeCon to initially cluster the packets, all 265 features are needed compared to the other days needing fewer than 200. Also, after a certain packets, every single normal packet is the same. This causes normal packets to be classified as abnormal once an abnormal packet is classified as normal. Because of this, both the sensitivity and false positive rates for Thursday data are very close for all parameter values tested.

To further analyze the data, we counted the occurrence of each ASCII character in each normal and abnormal packet and then normalized frequency counts and grouped them by day and attack type. In **Figure 4**, we display the histogram generated for Monday since all the days except Thursday shared a similar distribution pattern. We also generated separate histograms for each attack type to view their differences.

There is a clear difference between the typical normal packets and the Thursday normal packets (**Figure 4**). In general, the normal packets have a high normalized occurrence of the ACSII code 0 and low normalized counts for the rest. In particular the normal packets for Thursday

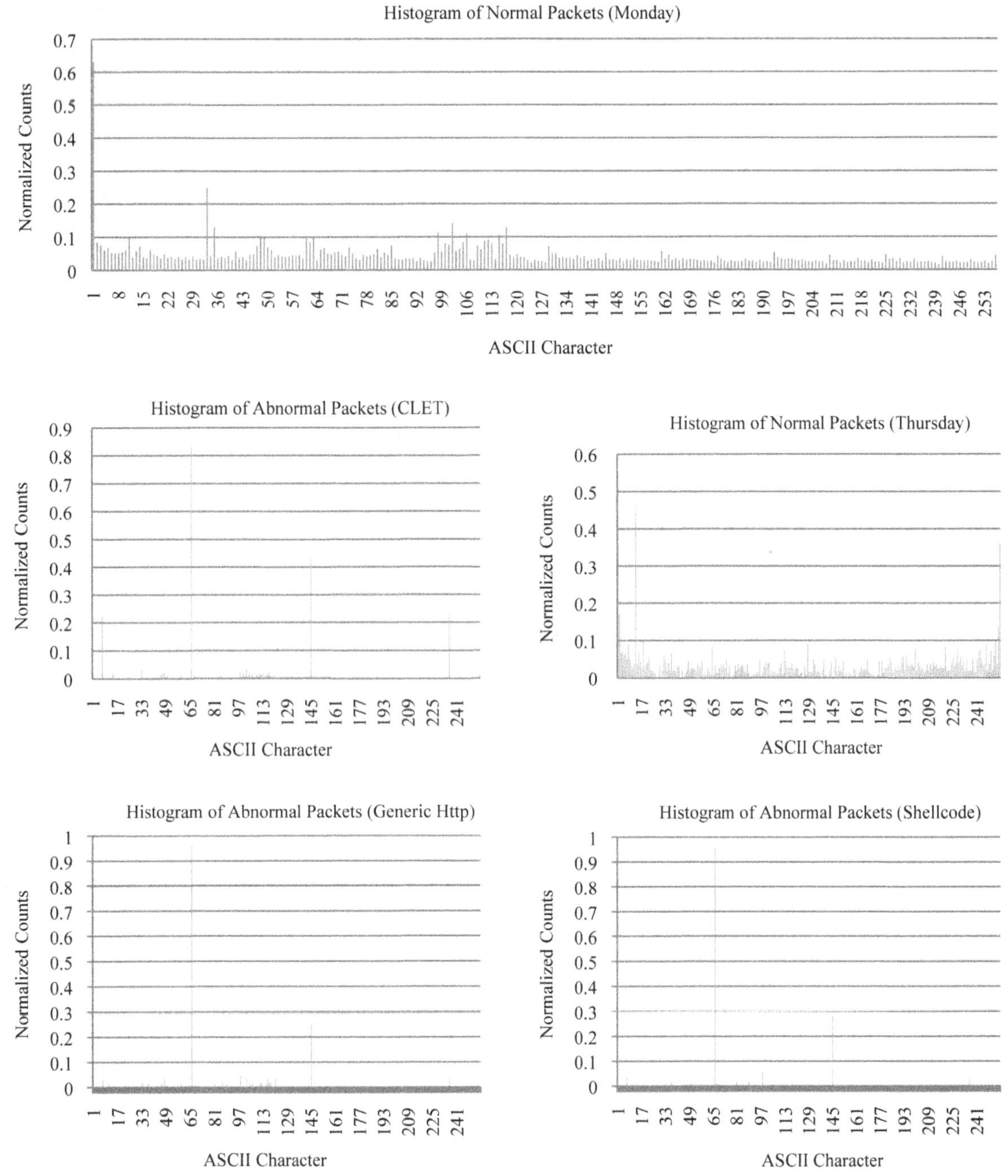

Figure 4. Assorted histograms generated using byte frequency distribution.

do not have the high occurrence of ASCII code 0 which might have caused the poor performance rates on those tests. The abnormal packets each have unique signatures in comparison to normal packets which offer the basis for anomaly detection. Each of the three attack types has peaks at positions 66 and 145. CLET has two more peaks at position 7 and 236 which might help these attacks blend in with normal traffic. Because StreamPreDeCon monitors the stream one packet at a time, there could be packets appear to be normal. This would explain the high detection rates in certain attack types on particular days. The histograms illustrate the different distribution patterns of the average packet payload.

4. Conclusions

This study aimed to create an anomaly-based IDS based on StreamPreDeCon. In general, anomaly-based IDSs are characterized by being able to detect new attacks but suffer from a high false-positive rate and difficulty detecting polymorphic attacks. The preference subspace clustering algorithm offers a unique method to analyze how particular subspaces interact which could maximize the detection of polymorphic attacks while maintaining a low false positive rate. In order for the PreDeCon algorithm to handle data changes within the network packet stream, we modified PreDeCon by adding a decayed distance measurement along with a deletion scheme and binary classification technique, which allow the IDS to detect anomalous packets. The addition of a decay factor give the most recent points in the model a greater influence on the clustering of the incoming points. The deletion step keeps the model current and manageable by deleting old noise points that have no effect on the clustering.

Tested on a dataset comprised of normal packets from the first week of the DARPA '99 intrusion detection evaluation dataset and various types of malicious traffic from [1], the IDS based on StreamPreDeCon out-performed previous stream-based IDS [10] using the same dataset in all days except for one day. For these days, the anomalous packet detection of the StreamPreDeCon IDS improved the sensitivity rate of the DenStream based IDS from 30% - 90% to 60% - 94% and reduced the false positive rates from a high of 20% to between 1% and 10%.

Although our proposed IDS achieved better results when compared with other IDSs of the same type, there is still room for improvement. First StreamPreDeCon needs to be more efficient. This could be implemented with the help of micro-clusters utilized by other stream clustering algorithms such as DenStream [11]. Micro-clusters will allow the Intrusion Detection System to store a compact representation of a set of points and thus reduce the number of distance calculations. Second, a smarter classification technique could be developed to better differentiate the normal core points from abnormal core points to increase the detection rate and decrease the number of false positives. These two adjustments will potentially help both the efficiency and effectiveness of the StreamPreDeCon IDS.

5. Acknowledgements

We thank Houghton College for its financial support and William Deitrick for his help with data preprocessing and editing of this manuscript. We also thank Dr. Ntoutsi for sharing the code of PreDeConInc.

REFERENCES

[1] R. Perdisci, G. Gu and W. Lee, "Using an Ensemble of One-Class SVM Classifiers to Harden Payload-Based Anomaly Detection Systems," *Proceedings of the Sixth International Conference on Data Mining*, Hong Kong, 18-22 December 2006, pp. 488-498.

[2] R. Perdisci, "Statistical Pattern Recognition Techniques for Intrusion Detection in Computer Networks, Challenges and Solutions," Ph.D. Thesis, University of Cagliari, Italy, 2006.

[3] D. Anderson, T. Lunt, H. Javits and A. Tamaru, "Nides: Detecting Unusual Program Behavior Using the Statistical Component of the Next Generation Intrusion Detection Expert System," Technical Report SRI-CSL-95-06, Computer Science Laboratory, SRI International, Menlo Park, 1995.

[4] M. Mahoney, "Network Traffic Anomaly Detection Based on Packet Bytes," ACM-SAC, Melbourne, 2003, pp. 346-350.

[5] M. Mahoney and P. Chan, "Learning Non Stationary Models of Normal Network Traffic for Detecting Novel Attacks," *ACM SIGKDD International Conference on Knowledge Discovery and Data Mining*, Edmonton, July 2002, pp. 376-385.

[6] K. Wang and S. Stolfo, "Anomalous Payload-Based Network Intrusion Detection," *Recent Advances in Intrusion Detection*, Vol. 3224, 2004, pp. 203-222.

[7] K. Wang, "Network Payload-Based Anomaly Detection and Content-Based Alert Correlation," Ph.D. Thesis, Columbia University, New York, 2006.

[8] R. Perdisci, D. Ariu, P. Fogla, G. Giacinto and W. Lee, "McPAD: A Multiple Classifier System for Accurate Payload-Based Anomaly Detection," *Computer Networks, Special Issue on Traffic Classification and Its Applications to Modern Networks*, Vol. 5, No. 6, 2009, pp. 864-881.

[9] J. Gama, "Knowledge Discovery from Data Streams," CRC Press, Boca Raton, pp. 7-9.

[10] Z. Miller, W. Dietrick and W. Hu, "Anomalous Network Packet Detection Using Data Stream Mining," *Journal of Information Security*, Vol. 2, No. 4, 2011, pp. 158-168.

[11] F. Cao, M. Ester, W. Quan and A. Zhou, "Density-Based Clustering over an Evolving Data Stream with Noise," 2006 *SIAM Conference on Data Mining*, Bethesda, 20-22 April 2006.

[12] C. Bohm, K. Kailing, H. Kriegel and P. Kroger, "Density Connected Clustering with Local Subspace Preferences," *Proceedings of the Fourth IEEE International Conference on Data Mining*, Brighton, 1-4 November 2004, pp. 27-34.

[13] M. Ester, H. Kriegel, J. Sander and X. Xu, "A Density-Based Algorithm for Discovering Clusters in Large Spatial Databases with Noise," *International Conference on Knowledge Discovery in Databases and Data Mining* (*KDD*-96), Portland, August 1996, pp. 226-231.

[14] M. Ankerst, M. Breunig, H. Kriegel and J. Sander, "OPTICS: Ordering Points to Identify the Clustering Structure," SIGMOD, Philadelphia, 1999, pp. 49-60.

[15] H. Kriegel, P. Kroger, I. Ntoutsi and A. Zimek, "Towards Subspace Clustering on Dynamic Data: An Incremental

Version of PreDeCon," *Proceedings of First International Workshop on Novel Data Stream Pattern Mining Techniques*, Washington DC, 2010, pp. 31-38.

18

Enhanced Timestamp Discrepancy to Limit Impact of Replay Attacks in MANETs

Aziz Baayer[1], Nourddine Enneya[2], Mohammed Elkoutbi[1]
[1]Laboratory SI2M, ENSIAS, University of Mohammed-V-Souissi, Rabat, Morocco
[2]Laboratory LaRIT, Faculty of Sciences, University of Ibn Tofail, Kenitra, Morocco

ABSTRACT

Mobile Ad hoc NETworks (MANETs), characterized by the free move of mobile nodes are more vulnerable to the trivial Denial-of-Service (DoS) attacks such as replay attacks. A replay attacker performs this attack at anytime and anywhere in the network by interception and retransmission of the valid signed messages. Consequently, the MANET performance is severally degraded by the overhead produced by the redundant valid messages. In this paper, we propose an enhancement of timestamp discrepancy used to validate a signed message and consequently limiting the impact of a replay attack. Our proposed timestamp concept estimates approximately the time where the message is received and validated by the received node. This estimation is based on the existing parameters defined at the 802.11 MAC layer.

Keywords: MANET; Replay Attack; Denial-of-Service (DoS); 802.11 MAC Layer; Network Allocation Vector (NAV); Security Countermeasure

1. Introduction

Mobile Ad hoc NETwork (MANET) [1] is consisted of mobile nodes MNs which can be either router or normal nodes, are able to communicate by using wireless network interfaces without the aid of any fixed infrastructure or centralized administration. A MANET is considered as an infrastructure less network because their MNs can dynamically establish routes among themselves to transmit messages temporarily. In a MANET, two given MNs can communicate directly when each one is in the transmission communication range of the other one. Otherwise, those MNs communicate throw intermediate MNs that relay their messages [2]. So, the success of a given communication between the sender and receiver MNs is strongly dependent on the cooperation of the intermediate MNs.

Denial-of-Service (DoS) attacks in MANET can seriously affect the network connectivity and disrupt further the networking functions, such as control and data message delivery. In other words, we can say that DoS attacks are capable to harshly degrade the overall MANET performance [3,4]. Indeed, at the physical layer, the attacker can launch a DoS attack with a wireless Jammer by sending a high power signal to cause an extremely low signal-to-interference ratio at a legitimate receiver MN [5]. At the 802.11 MAC layer [6], a replay attack [2,7,8] can be done by intercepting a valid signed messages of MN (the validation is assured by the timestamp concept) and by retransmitting them later in order to produce a DoS attack. At the network layer, a DoS attacker makes the use of the existing protocols vulnerabilities, that can be classified further into three types: routing disruption, forwarding disruption and resource consumption attacks [4,9,10]. At the application layer, a random DoS attack [11] is to flood a network with a large number of service requests. Since the MNs have a limited transmission range, they expect that their neighbors relay messages to remote receiving MNs. The relayed messages are supposed to be performed by intermediate MNs with a good cooperation as a fundamental assumption of MANETs. This assumption becomes invalid when MNs have tangential or contradicting objectives. To overcome their security problems, MANETs adopt new secure solutions [2]. When the most known attacks can be avoided, replay attacks are still subject of various research works due to their easy technique based on recording and re-sending a valid signed messages in the network. So, to avoid those replay attacks in MANET, a timestamp concept is developed [12-15]. Indeed, the timestamp concept permits to a receiving MN to validate the received signed messages. Consequently, a signed message, injected by a replay attacker, arriving with invalid timestamp discrepancy MUST be dropped.

In a MANET, the fixed value of the timestamp discrepancy Δt is pre-negotiated between two communicating MNs [13,14]. In reality, the choice of the threshold Δt is large enough and consequent MANET becomes more exposed to a wide range of DoS attacks including replay attacks. In this attack, the objective of the attacker is to resend the intercepted signed messages without exceeding the threshold defined by the timestamp discrepancy in the beginning of a communication. So, to avoid this problem a new timestamp discrepancy is required.

In this paper, we present a new timestamp discrepancy to limit the impact of replay attacks. Our proposed timestamp approach is based on the 802.11 MAC layer parameters and on MN capabilities in term of buffering and CPU processing. Moreover, our proposition of timestamp discrepancy enables MNs to limit and reduce the redundant messages injected by a replay attacker.

The rest of this paper is organized as follows. Section 2 presents a related work that gives an overview on DoS attacks related to the 802.11 MAC Layer. Section 3 presents the 802.11 MAC Layer functions. Section 4 presents our improvement. Section 5 presents simulations and results. The conclusion is given in the last Section 6.

2. Related Works

In a MANET, communications between MNs are articulated on the 802.11 MAC layer protocol that is vulnerable to DoS attacks [4,16-20]. In papers [17,20], it was discussed that a DoS attacker can exploit the binary exponential back-off scheme to access the channel. Moreover, in the RTS/CTS attack [21], a malicious MN can send the RTS/CTS frames to spuriously reserve the channel without real data transmissions. In the NAV attack [3], an attacker sets large duration values in RTS or CTS frames to reserve channel for maximum time duration. In paper [16], a misbehaving MN can get better throughput by modifying unilaterally the binary exponential back-off algorithm parameters.

Other DoS attack is replay attack [2,4] where the malicious MN can perform attack by recording old valid messages and by re-sending them. This makes other MNs update their internal data structure with stale information (for example updating routing table with a wrong route). The replay attack is achieved when control messages bear a digest or a digital signature without including a timestamp [3,13]. Indeed, while existing mechanisms provide the guarantee to the receiving MN that the message was received as sent, there is no absolute guarantee that a message is being used as intended. The originated MN and the sent message are authenticated, but nothing else. A message that has been captured or intercepted by a malicious MN and is replayed later. It will still be authenticated properly as long as the encryption keys were not changed and the timestamp discrepancy was still valid. Also, it's relatively hard to avoid replay attacks at the 802.11 MAC layer due to the stochastic nature of the DCF and to the similarities between the effects of DoS attacks and congested traffic conditions. Indeed, paper [16] describes that if legitimate MNs can link sequential transmissions from a malicious MN, statistical models can be used to detect MNs that cheat the DCF by choosing low back-off values in order to gain an advantage in terms of throughput. Also, a malicious MN can be readily identified by a detection technique, in which neighbor MNs calculate the actual transmission time by sensing DATA/ACK frames [21]. Assuming the random back-off values are observable, a receiving MN can carry out a sequential test to analyze the distribution of this random variable [16].

3. 802.11 MAC Layer Overview

The 802.11 MAC protocols support two models of operation called Distributed Coordination Function (DCF) and Point Coordination Function (PCF). Whereas DCF does not use a centralized control, PCF needs an access point (AP) to coordinate the activity of nodes in its area and to operate only in infrastructure-based networks. When PCF is an optional feature at different 802.11 implementations, DCF is obligatory.

The DCF is based on the CSMA/CA protocol. Before a node starts to transmit a packet, it senses the channel idle for a duration DIFS plus an additional backoff time. The backoff time is an integer multiple of a basic slot duration δ, where the back-off number is drawn randomly in the range $[0, CW-1]$, where CW is called a contention window. Once the channel becomes idle, the node waits for another DIFS period before it starts to decrement its counter after each idle slot. When the backoff number reaches to zero, the node transmits its packet. When the receiver finishes its receiving, it waits for a shorter period SIFS and then sends back to the sender an ACK packet to inform the sender that the transmission is successful. If the sender hasn't received the ACK for a specified timeout or if it finds out some other node is transmitting a packet on the channel, the sender doubles its contention window CW and chooses a random number in the range $[0, CW-1]$. **Figure 1** shows that the IEEE 802.11 adds two more signaling packets: the request to send (RTS) and the clear to send (CTS). When sending (RTS) to the destination node, the length of the transmission is attached; hence every node receiving this packet stores this information in a local variable named network allocation vector (NAV). After waiting a SIFS, the destination node replies with a CTS packet. This CTS packet also contains the duration of the transmission, therefore any node hearing this packet will set its NAV. All nodes within the range of the source node and the destination node are informed that the medium is allocated. The sender node, after waiting for SIFS, starts the data transmission. Then, the receiver node, after another SIFS, sends back the acknowledgement (ACK) packet. Afterwards, when the transmission is over, the NAV in each node marks the medium as free, and the process can start.

4. Our Improvement

The replay attack is an easy DoS attack which can be produced by a malicious MN through two basic operations. The first operation is the record of listened valid messages. The second is the resend of the recorded valid messages. Indeed, for a given communication between two MNs in the network, the replay attacker intercepts messages sent to destination MN and re-sends them later within a valid timestamp discrepancy Δt, independently, to any encryption mechanisms used by the sender MN. So the standard timestamp concept is not enough to limit impact of this type of DoS attacks on network performance.

The **Figure 2** illustrates a typical replay attack scenario where malicious MN, in the first step, intercepts and records signed messages listened from sender MN *S*. In second step and after a waiting time, within the timestamp discrepancy interval Δt, the attacker MN re-sends the stored signed messages, towards the receive MN *D*. As a result, all re-send messages by the replay attacker that verify the timestamp discrepancy present an overhead of messages which impact directly the network performance.

Recent works [22-24] are still using, in the process of message signature, a *prefixed timestamp discrepancy* Δt negotiated in the step of encryption key exchange [25]. This choice of static timestamp gives a greatest weakness due to its independence on MN characteristics and duration of communication. Indeed, as shown in **Figure 3**, the replay attacker intercepts and stores the valid signed message before the end of time interval $\Delta t - \tau$. Thereafter, he achieves its attack by re-sending the previous stored messages in the dead time denoted τ.

In this section, we present an enhanced timestamp discrepancy aiming to limit the impact of duplicated valid messages injected by a replay attacker intercalated between a pair of communicated MNs. Our approach has the advantage not to require any additional functions because it only based on the existing parameters defined in the MAC layer of the IEEE 802.11 standard. Our timestamp approach estimates approximately the date when the signed message is received and processed by a destination MN. Moreover, this estimation is a lightweight calculation and it is based on the standard parameters of 802.11 MAC layer. Referring to the **Figure 1**, the sender MN begins communication after receiving the CTS message sent by the receiver MN. In the same time, the neighbors MNs update their NAV parameter to defer

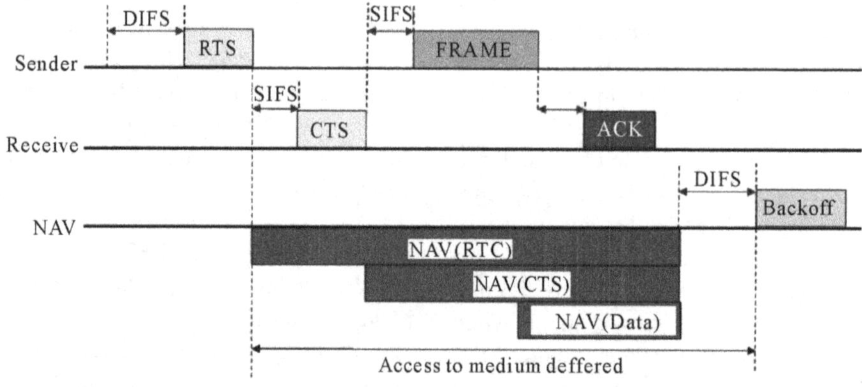

Figure 1. RTS/CTS mechanism in IEEE 802.11.

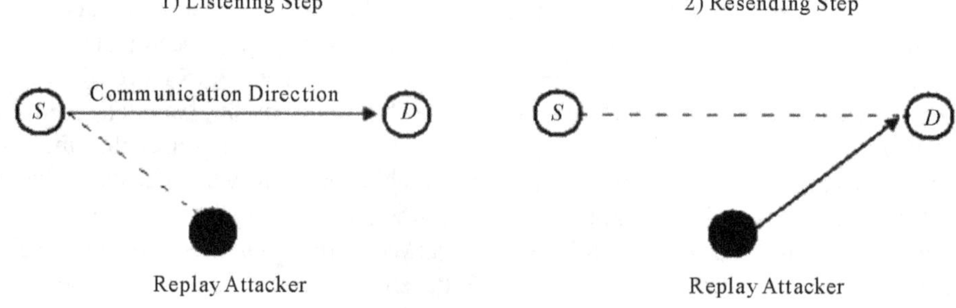

Figure 2. Typical scenario of replay attack.

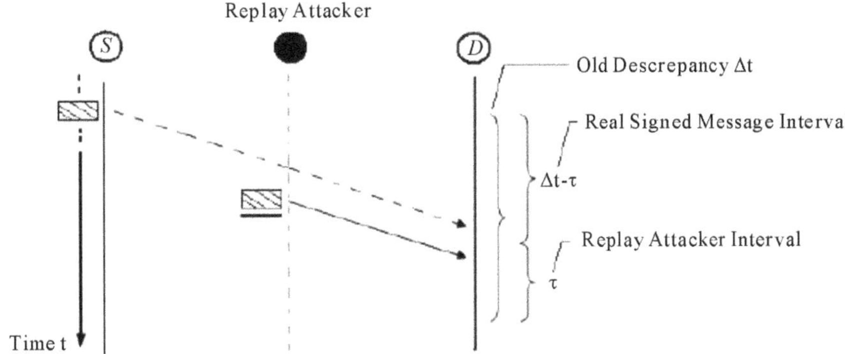

Figure 3. Vulnerability with the classical timestamp discrepancy.

access (DA) to the communication medium to avoid collisions. So, a sent signed message from a sender MN should arrive, to the receiver MN, and be processed before the NAV time expiration. The NAV expiration is delimited by the two messages: RTS (sent by the sender MN) and CTS (sent by the receiver MN). This means that the maximum time for a signed message to reach destination is the total time including NAV time plus processing times at the sender and receiver MNs.

Based on this observation, we can define the enhanced timestamp discrepancy between two given communicating MNs, *S* and *D* (See **Figure 4**) as follow [26]:

$$\Delta t_{\text{dynamic}}(S,D) = T_S + NAV(CTS) + T_D \qquad (1)$$

where:

- T_S is the time to process message at MN *S*.
- T_D is the time to process message at MN *D*.
- $NAV(CTS)$ is the time duration of communication between sender (*S*) and receiver (*D*) MNs.

In the following part of this work, in order to show the importance of our proposed improvement, we suppose that the communicating MN clocks are synchronized. This is a necessary condition for a replay attacker to re-send valid signed messages [22]. The times T_S and T_D represent respectively the total time at two MNs *S* and *D* including times of buffering and CPU processing. In the literature, buffering and CPU processes are respectively represented by the queuing and service systems. Precisely, the model that represents these two systems is an M/M/1 model [27], characterized by the following assumptions:

1) The messages arrive according to a Poisson process with a total *average arrival rate* λ (*i.e.* arrival messages/sec).

2) The receiver MN (that plays the role of a single server characterized by an exponential service times, by an unlimited FIFO (or not specified queue) and by an unlimited messages population. We denote *the average service rate* at the receiver MN by μ.

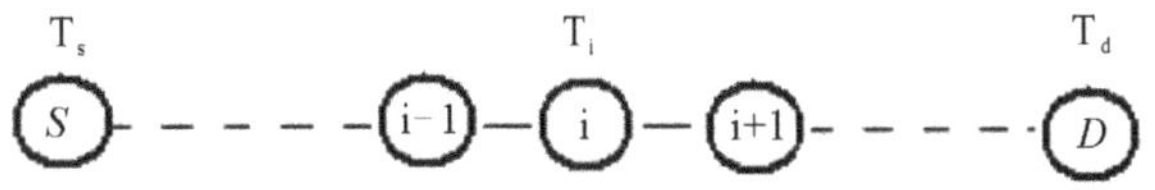

Figure 4. Typical path between sender and receiver MNs.

By supposing that MNs in MANET having the same characteristics, we can consider that $T_i = T_j = T$. So, the total time including queering and service times according to the M/M/1 model, at each MN, is given by the following formula:

$$T = \frac{1}{\mu - \lambda} \qquad (2)$$

Consequently, the Equation (1) becomes as follow:

$$\Delta t_{\text{dynamic}}(S,D) = \frac{2}{\mu - \lambda} + NAV(CTS) \qquad (3)$$

Based on the Equation (3), we can define a *local discrepancy timestamp* between two closed MNs (or neighbor MNs) in MANET as the average of *total discrepancy timestamp* $\Delta t_{\text{dynamic}}(S,D)$ divided by the number of hop count, that we denoted *N*, between S and D nodes. So, the local discrepancy timestamp $\delta t_{\text{local}}(i,i+1)$ between nodes i and $i+1$ (see **Figure 4**) is defined as follow:

$$\delta t_{\text{local}}(i,i+1) = \frac{\Delta t_{\text{dynamic}}(S,D)}{N} \qquad (4)$$

In the next section, we proceed to apply our proposed approach on a two given communicating MNs in MANET, using 802.11 MAC layer to allow medium to exchange their messages. Our approach is integrated in the standard 802.11 MAC Layer without any additional parameters or extra processing costs at MNs in the network.

5. Simulation and Result

5.1. Simulation Environment

To improve the impact of our proposed timestamp concept, we simulated a local replay attack when a replay attacker is intercalated between two closed MNs in a MANET (each MN is in the transmission range of the other MN). Moreover, to have the same conditions of simulation, we assumed that all MNs in the network have the same characteristics of buffering (λ) and processing (μ) with a stable M/M/1 system, *i.e.* the rate service is greater than the arrival rate. That's why we choose the values 30 and 33 for λ and μ respectively for all MNs in the MANET.

In the next sub-section we proceeded to a comparison between two scenarios of communication with the *same replay attack behavior*. The first scenario is called a *classic scenario* where the communicated MNs use the classical timestamp discrepancy. The second scenario is called an *enhanced scenario* that uses our enhanced timestamp discrepancy. This comparison study is carried out in the Network Simulator (NS2) platform [28]. The communicating MNs, in a network, uses an UDP traffic to exchange data during a total time of simulation equal to 150 seconds. Moreover, we suppose that the MNs are homogenous in terms of transmission range (*i.e.* all MNs have a same transmission range equal to 250 m), and in order to show the effect of our approach, we have neglected the mobility produced by the free move of MNs. Finally, the considered replay attack interval when the attacker performs the attack is defined, in seconds, by the interval (100, 150).

5.2. Result and Discussion

To achieve a replay attack, the MN of the attacker requires a high performance, in terms of buffering λ_r and processing μ_r, compared to the ordinary MNs in the network. For this end, we have taken in our simulation the malicious behavior of the replay attacker when it's varying their proper parameters λ_r and μ_r. Precisely, to study the impact of each parameter on our enhanced timestamp discrepancy, we fixed, in first time, the parameter μ_r and we varied λ_r. In second time, we fixed the parameter λ_r and we varied μ_r.

By fixing μ_r at 33 and varying λ_r, **Figure 5** provides a light enhancement of our proposed timestamp (*red line*) discrepancy comparing to the old timestamp discrepancy (*black line*). Indeed, for all values of λ_r (5, 10, 15, 20, 25, 30, 40, 45 and 49), the enhanced scenario that implements the dynamic timestamp discrepancy have the same behavior compared to the classic scenario with a limit of 2% approximately of the messages retransmitted and injected by the replay attacker. According to this result, it can be seen that our solution limits the number of the injected messages by the replay attacker even it changes the λ_r parameter.

According to **Figure 6**, it can be seen that our enhanced scenario gives good result when the replay attacker changes its processing parameter. Indeed, for all values of μ_r (50, 55, 60, 65, 70, 75, 80, 85, 90, 95 and 100), the enhanced scenario (*red line*) that implement the dynamic timestamp discrepancy keeps the same behavior as the classic scenario (*black line*) with more rigorous limitation of injected messages. In particular, our approach

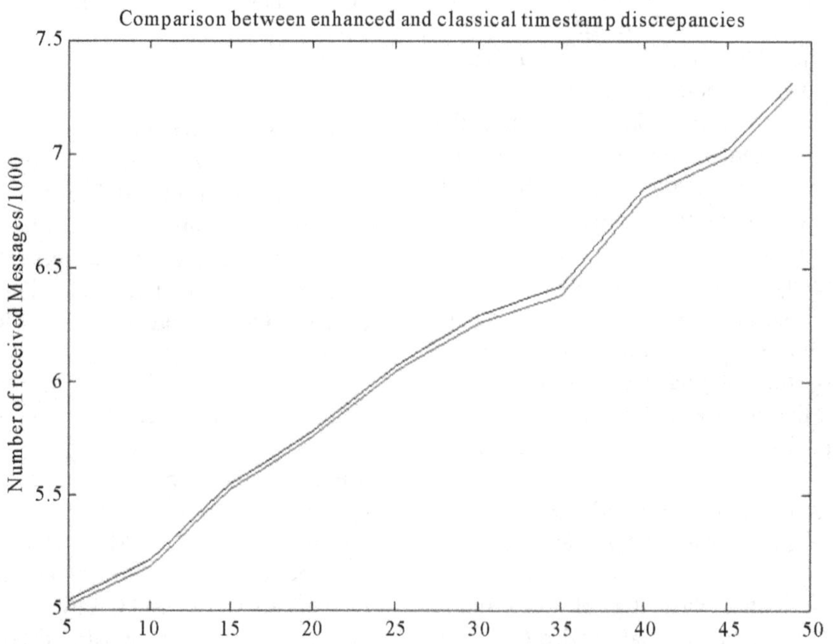

Figure 5. Enhanced timestamp discrepancy when replay attacker varies λ_r.

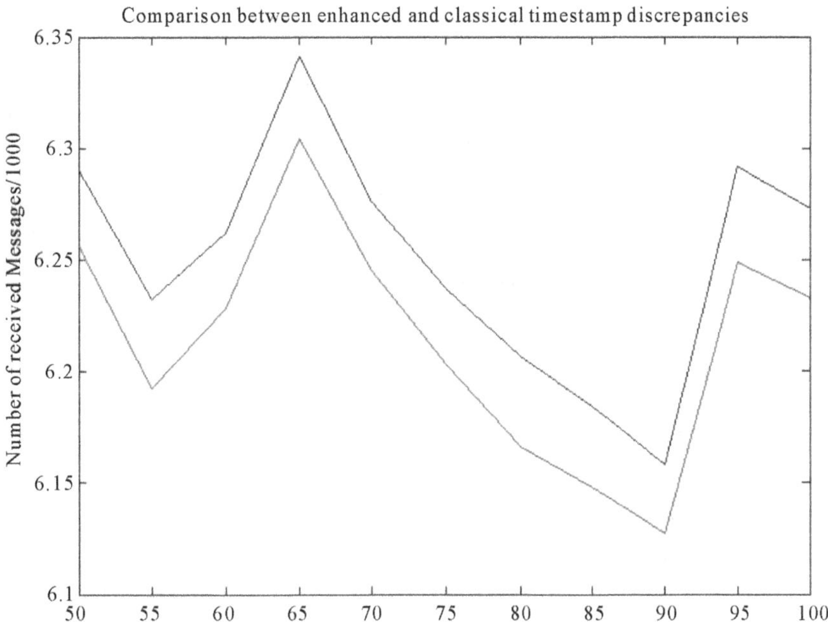

Figure 6. Enhanced timestamp discrepancy when replay attacker varies μ_r.

gives a better reduction of replay attacker messages at points where μ_r takes the following values: 55, 80 and 95.

According to this result, we can say that our solution is reactive and watchful when the replay attacker changes its processing parameter μ_r.

Based on the above results, we conclude that our proposed timestamp discrepancy presents two big advantages: The first, it reduces the unwanted messages injected by a replay attacker. The second it takes into consideration the replay attacker behavior even when changing its proper parameters of buffering and processing.

6. Conclusions and Perspectives

In this paper, we propose a dynamic timestamp discrepancy to limit the impact of replay attacks in MANETs. Our approach reduces the number of unwanted messages injected by the replay attacker comparing to the classic timestamp discrepancy based on a fixed threshold defined at the beginning of a communication.

Therefore, the overhead produced by those types of attacks is reduced which increase the MANET performance. As a future work, we plan to study the MANET performance in the case where we combine our timestamp approach, at 802.11 MAC Layer, with the existing routing protocols. The routing protocols that we consider are AODV (*with reactive nature*) [29] and OLSR [30] (*with proactive nature*).

REFERENCES

[1] J. Macker, "Mobile Ad Hoc Networking (MANET): Routing Protocol Performance Issues and Evaluation Considerations," Internet Engineering Task Force (IETF), Network Working Group (RFC 2501), January 1999.

[2] B. Wu, J. Chen, J. Wu and M. Cardei, "A Survey of Attacks and Countermeasures in Mobile Ad Hoc Networks, in Wireless Network Security," In: Y. Xiao, X. Shen and D.-Z. Du, Eds., *Signals and Communication Technology*, Springer, 2007.

[3] J. Bellardo, S. Savage and D. Medina, "802.11 Denial-of-Service Attacks: Real Vulnerabilities and Practical Solutions," *Proceedings of the USENIX Security Symposium*, Washington DC, August 2003, pp. 15-27.

[4] I. Aad, J. Hubaux and E. W. Knightly, "Impact of Denial of Service Attacks on Ad Hoc Networks," *IEEE/ACM Transactions on Networking*, Vol. 16, No. 4, 2008, pp. 791-802.

[5] K. Pelechrinis, M. Iliofotou and S. V. Krishnamurthy, "Denial of Service Attacks in Wireless Networks: The Case of Jammers," *IEEE Communication Surveys and Tutorials*, Vol. 13, No. 2, 2011, pp. 245-257.

[6] Wireless LAN Medium Access Control (MAC) and Physical Layer (PHY) Specifications, IEEE Standards 802.11, 1997.

[7] P. Syverson, "A Taxonomy of Replay Attacks," *Proceedings of the Computer Security Foundations Workshop* (*CSFW*97), 1994, pp. 187-191.

[8] S. Malladi, J. A. Foss and R. B. Heckendorn, "On Preventing Replay Attacks on Security Protocols," *International Conference on Security and Management*, June 2002, pp. 77-83.

[9] J. V. E. Molsa, "Increasing the DoS Attack Resiliency in Military Ad Hoc Networks," *Proceedings of IEEE MILCOM*, Atlantic City, 2005, pp. 1-7.

[10] Q. Gu, P. Liu, S. Zhu and C.-H. Chu, "Defending Against

Packet Injection in Unreliable Ad Hoc Networks," Proceedings of the IEEE Global Telecommunications Conference (GLOBECOM 05), 28 November-2 December 2005.

[11] Y. Xie and S. Yu, "Monitoring the Application-Layer DDoS Attacks for Popular Websites," *IEEE/ACM Transactions on Networking*, Vol. 17, No. 1, 2009, pp. 15-25.

[12] R. M. Needham and M. D. Schroeder, "Using Encryption for Authentication in Large Networks of Computers," *Communications of the ACM*, Vol. 21, No. 12, 1978, pp. 993-999.

[13] D. E. Denning and G. M. Sacco, "Timestamps in Key Distribution Protocols," *Communications of the ACM*, Vol. 24, No. 8, 1981, pp. 533-536.

[14] T. H. Clausen, C. Adjih, P. Jacquet, A. Laouiti, P. Muhltahler and D. Raffo, "Securing the OLRS Protocol," *Proceedings of IFIP Med-Hoc-Net*, June 2003.

[15] A. Hafslund, A. Tnnesen, R. B. Rotvik, J. Andersson and O. Kure, "Secure Extension to the OLSR Protocol," *Proceedings of the OLSR Interop and Workshop*, San Diego, 2004.

[16] J. Suet and H. N. Liu, "Protecting Flow Design for DoS Attack and Defense at the MAC Layer in Mobile Ad Hoc Network," International Conference, ICAIC, Xi'an, Vol. 224, Part 1, 2011.

[17] S. Xu and T. Saadawi, "Revealing the Problems with 802.11 Medium Access Control Protocol in Multi-Hop Wireless Ad Hoc Networks," *Computer Networks*, Vol. 38, No. 4, 2002, pp. 531-548.

[18] V. Gupta, S. Krishnamurthy and M. Faloutsos, "Denial of Service Attacks at the MAC Layer in Wireless Ad Hoc Networks," *MILCOM Proceedings*, Anaheim, Vol. 2, pp. 1118-1123.

[19] T. Farooq, D. L. Jones and M. Merabti, "MAC Layer DoS Attacks in IEEE 802.11 Networks," *The 11th Annual Conference on the Convergence of Telecommunications, Networking and Broadcasting* (*PGNet* 2010), Liverpool, 2010. http://www.cms.livjm.ac.uk/pgnet2010/MakeCD/Papers/2010063.pdf

[20] F. Xing and W. Wang, "Understanding Dynamic Denial of Service Attacks in Mobile Ad Hoc Networks," *Proceedings of the* 2006 *IEEE Conference on Military Communications* (*MILCOM*'06), Washington DC, 25-28 September 2006.

[21] J. Sobrinho, R. Haan and J. Brazio, "Why RTS-CTS Is Not your Ideal Wireless LAN Multiple Access Protocol," *Proceedings of IEEE Wireless Communications and Networking Conference*, New Orleans, 2005.

[22] D. Raffo, "Security Schemes for the OLSR Protocol for Ad Hoc Networks," Ph.D. Thesis, University Paris 6—INRIA Rocquencourt, 2005.

[23] E. Winjum, A. M. Hegland, Ø. Kure and P. Spilling, "Replay Attacks in Mobile Wireless Ad Hoc Networks: Protecting the OLSR Protocol," *Proceedings of International Conference on Networking* (*ICN* 2005), Springer-Verlag, Volume 3421/2005, 2005, pp. 741-479.

[24] B. Vaidya, M. Denko and J. R. Rodrigues, "Security Mechanism for Voice over Multipath Mobile Ad Hoc Networks," *Journal of Wireless Communications and Mobile Computing*, Vol. 11, No. 2, 2011, pp. 196-210.

[25] D. E. Denning and G. M. Sacco, "Timestamps in Key Distribution Protocols," *Magazine Communications of the ACM*, Vol. 24, No. 8, 1981.

[26] N. Enneya, A. Baayer and M. El koutbi, "A Dynamic Timestamp Discrepancy against Replay Attacks in MANET," *Communications in Computer and Information Science* (*CCIS* 254), Springer-Verlag, 2011, pp. 479-489.

[27] D. Gross, J. F. Shortle, J. M. Thompson and C. M. Harris, "Fundamentals of Queueing Theory Book," 4th Edition, Wiley Series in Probability and Statistics, 2008.

[28] The Network Simulator (NS-2), 2012. http://www. isi.edu/nsnam/

[29] T. Clausen and P. Jacquet, "Ad Hoc On-Demand Distance Vector (AODV) Routing," RFC 3561, July 2003. http://www.ietf.org/rfc/rfc3561.txt

[30] T. Clausen and P. Jacquet, "RFC 3626: The Optimized Link-State Routing Protocol," Internet Engineering Task Force (IETF) Request for Comments, 2003.

19

Feedback Reliability Ratio of an Intrusion Detection System

Usha Banerjee[1*], Gaurav Batra[1], K. V. Arya[2]
[1]Department of Computer Science and Engineering, College of Engineering Roorkee (COER), Roorkee, India
[2]Department of ICT, Atal Bihari Vajpayee Indian Institute of Information Technology and Management, Gwalior, India

ABSTRACT

The behavior and nature of attacks and threats to computer network systems have been evolving rapidly with the advances in computer security technology. At the same time however, computer criminals and other malicious elements find ways and methods to thwart such protective measures and find techniques of penetrating such secure systems. Therefore adaptability, or the ability to learn and react to a consistently changing threat environment, is a key requirement for modern intrusion detection systems. In this paper we try to develop a novel metric to assess the performance of such intrusion detection systems under the influence of attacks. We propose a new metric called feedback reliability ratio for an intrusion detection system. We further try to modify and use the already available statistical Canberra distance metric and apply it to intrusion detection to quantify the dissimilarity between malicious elements and normal nodes in a network.

Keywords: Attacks; Canberra Metric; Feedback; Intrusion Detection; Performance; Reliability

1. Introduction

Nowadays the risk of attacks in data networks is exponentially rising. Thus, the area of network security is gaining importance for researchers and practioners. Attack could be either from outside or from the inside of a network. Further compared to wired networks, mobile ad-hoc networks have several disadvantages with respect to security the most important being the dynamic nature of such networks. In such networks node act as routers and participate in the routing process following some routing protocol. Till date several routing protocols have been formulated for such networks. However, attackers have been always successful to penetrate and harm such networks. Attacks have been classified by several researchers [1] based on the behavior of attacks. Attacks might be internal or external [2]. External attackers try to hamper network performance using any one of the technique like eavesdropping, message intercepting, replay etc. However, the problem is more severe in case of an internal attacker [3] and thus in such a situation the task to detect the misbehaving node becomes daunting. A single intruder can manage to create havoc in a network. This is referred as an intrusion in the system, where a node or malicious element from within a network tries to hamper the normal functioning of the network. To resolve this cumbersome task various Intrusion Detection Systems (IDS) have been developed, which uses different techniques to identify threats in a network. All the available algorithms are based on some assumptions and consider some measure which determine the misbehaving nature of a node. Different approaches are used to determine an intruder in a system, with every approach having its own merits and demerits [4]. One of the approaches used in intrusion detection system maintains a pre-defined knowledge of intrusion with it. Every time an abnormal activity is encountered, this predefined list of intrusions is checked for a match. But this type of technique can determine only a specified number of intrusions. While this list for intrusions can be updated from time to time, but this static approach known as signature-based intrusion detection [5], is not considered an efficient approach for real time network systems. Another approach used for the detection of misbehavior of an insider node considers a measure in which a threshold value is set on the basis of normal activities. Then value of the measure is determined for the node considering all of its parameters. If this calculated value shows some deviation from the threshold value, then the node is declared as an intrusion for the system. This kind of approach known as anomaly based detection helps in detecting new threats introduced in the network. Similarly, various other intrusion detection systems are available,

*Corresponding author.

but there is no particular measure available which can successfully rank these presently available IDS on the basis of their capability and performance.

In this paper, a novel approach has been proposed which can predict the performance level of an Intrusion Detection System on the basis of its activities recorded for a particular interval. For this purpose, real time data packets information are captured on a network of both types: pure network data, and data containing various attacks. A statistical approach is adopted in this proposal, known as Canberra metric. Canberra Metric is used to determine dissimilarity between different groups of elements based on various parameters.

Prior Work

Various attempts have been made in the past to define a reasonable measure which can measure the level of trust for an IDS such that the reliability of an IDS can be calculated and a confidence level can be defined for a particular network. The biggest problem that is yet to be resolved is to decide the key factors to be taken into account for describing and analyzing the performance of an IDS. Various options like false positive, false negative, number of packets observed, number of detections, cost of the maintenance, confidence value etc. have been proposed by researchers. Numerous techniques and methodologies have been adopted by researchers to illustrate and benchmark an IDS.

In [6] a survey of IDS technologies available have been analyzed and the authors have proposed an evaluation scheme which considered false positive rate, false negative rate, vulnerability etc. as the key dimensions of an intrusion detection system. And showed that these parameters are to be taken into account to analyze and improve the quality of Network IDS. [7] proposed a new measure metric called Intrusion Detection Capability, which considered ratio of the mutual information between the IDS input and output to the entropy of the input and proved it to be a better measuring tool to determine the capability of an IDS. The authors in [7] showed an analysis comparing previously available cost-based approaches and the proposed metric results in a scenario.

The authors in [8] summarize and present a few test cases to demonstrate various evaluation environment methodologies. A new technology has also been proposed with open source environment which is based on both Artificial Intelligence and real network traffic data. The approach included injecting artificial attacks in the isolated test environment to realize the capability of a system. A similar approach has been adopted by the authors in [9] in which a TCL script is executed in a set environment a TELNET environment and can reveal important information about an IDS and capabilities.

Benchmarking an IDS is not a fully evaluative task and cannot be accomplished by applying some logical technique. Hence, no perfect evaluation methodology has been developed so far to analyze an IDS to be installed on a system [10]. Approaches adopted so far lack depth in one or in another aspect and need some modification looking at the challenges present in real environment at present scenario [11]. Some of those challenges faced in the real-time network are: 1) ever increasing network traffic; 2) the use of encrypted messages to transport malicious information; 3) use of more complex, subtle, and new attack scenarios and many more.

[12] presented a brief description comparing different avail able approaches to evaluate the performance of an Intrusion Detection System. This article concluded on a note that there is lot of scope for further research in this field, as the best suitable approach is yet to be discovered. In this paper, a statistical approach has been proposed to untie the node of the problem explained above. This paper aims at presenting a metric based solution for the evaluation and analysis of the performance and reliability of an IDS. And provide a tool to network intrusion detection system analyst with a tool, which can be used to judge an IDS before installing it on a system. And predictions can be made for IDS regarding its reliability and trust level of its detections and security of data. [13] has previously shown that Canberrra and Chi Square are metrics which could be used in intrusion detection.

The rest of the paper is organized as follows. Section 2 discusses various statistical techniques available to evaluate similarities and dissimilarities and goes on to discuss how these statistical techniques could be applied to the field of intrusion detection. Section 3 presents the approach that we have followed. In Section 4 we present the mathematical and programmatical implementation of the problem. Section 5 deals with results and discussions.

2. Statistical Techniques

Statistics deals with huge volumes of data and has several established techniques to analyze the data based on their similarity or dissimilarity. In huge volumes of data a small anomaly can be easily identified from historical data. This phenomenon can be adapted to network intrusion detection. Since warnings are based on actual usage patterns, statistical systems can adapt to behaviors and therefore create their own rule usage-patterns. The usage-patterns are what dictate how anomalous a packet may be to the network.

Anomalous activity is measured by a number of variables sampled over time and stored in a profile. Based on the anomaly score of a packet, the reporting process will deem it an alert if it is sufficiently anomalous; otherwise, the IDS will simply ignore the trace. The IDS will report the intrusion if the anomalous activity exceeds a threshold value.

Statistical techniques of intrusion detection usually measure similarities or dissimilarities between network variables like users logged in, time of login, time of logout, number of files accessed in a period of time, usage of disk space, memory, CPU, IP addresses, number of packets transferred etc. The frequency of updating can vary from a few minutes to, for example, one month. The system stores mean values for each variable used for detecting exceeds that of a predefined threshold.

Similarity is defined as a quantity that reflects the strength of relationship between two objects or two features. This quantity is usually having range of either –1 to +1 or normalized into 0 to 1. If the similarity between feature and feature is denoted by δ, we can measure this quantity in several ways depending on the scale of measurement (or data type) that we have. On the other hand, dissimilarity measures the discrepancy between the two objects based on several features. Dissimilarity may also be viewed as measure of disorder between two objects. These features can be rep resented as coordinate of the object in the features space. There are many types of distance and similarity. Each similarity or dissimilarity has its own characteristics. Let the dissimilarity between object i and object j is denoted by δ_{ij}. The relationship between dissimilarity and similarity is given by

$$S_{ij} = 1 - \delta_{ij} \tag{1}$$

for similarity bounded by 0 and 1. When the objects are similar, the similarity is 1 and dissimilarity is 0 and vice versa. If similarity has a range of –1 to +1 and the dissimilarity is measured with range of 0 and 1, then

$$S_{ij} = 1 - 2\delta_{ij} \tag{2}$$

There are several distance metrics available for measuring the similarity or dissimilarity between quantitative variables. The simplest distance variable is the Euclidean Distance [14]. Euclidean distance or simply “distance” examines the root of square differences between coordinates of a pair of objects and is given by

$$d_{ij} = \sqrt{\sum_{k=1}^{n} \left(x_{ik} - x_{jk}\right)^2} \tag{3}$$

Manhanttan distance metric is another such metric. It represents distance between points in a city road grid. It examines the absolute differences between coordinates of a pair of objects and is given by

$$d_{ij} = \sqrt{\sum_{k=1}^{n} \left|x_{ik} - x_{jk}\right|} \tag{4}$$

Chebyshev distance [15] is another such statistical distance metric and is also called maximum value distance. It examines the absolute magnitude of the differences between coordinates of a pair of objects and is given by

$$d_{ij} = \max_k \left|\left(x_{ik} - x_{jk}\right)\right| \tag{5}$$

Chebyshev metric is actually a special case of the Minowski metric with $\lambda = \infty$ and has been used to calculate the dissimilarities between normal events and malicious events in networks. In this paper we use the Canberra metric. Canberra distance was proposed by Lance and Williams in 1967. It examines the sum of series of a fraction differences between coordinates of a pair of objects. Each term of fraction difference has value between 0 and 1. The Canberra distance itself is not between zero and one. If one of coordinate is zero, the term become unity regardless the other value, thus the distance will not be affected. Note that if both coordinate are zeros, we need to be defined as $\frac{0}{0} = 0$. This distance is very sensitive to a small change when both coordinates are near to zero.

$$d_{ij} = \sum_{k=1}^{n} \frac{\left|x_{ik} - x_{jk}\right|}{\left|x_{ik}\right| + \left|x_{jk}\right|} \tag{6}$$

3. Our Approach

We start with selection of the key factors which can best describe a system in words of capability and vulnerability.

Using these key factors, a formula based approach is used to calculate a reliability value, which shows the level to which a user can rely on IDS. A Threshold value is defined in accordance with the normal functioning of an Intrusion detection system in a real time environment. A distance measuring metric known as Canberra metric is applied to determine the similarity or dissimilarity between the predefined threshold value and the observation value. Comparison results are provided by the Canberra metric, which depict the trust level of the IDS. If the observed value is less than the defined threshold value, it shows that IDS under consideration is not a reliable one.

Now these similarity based values generated by Canberra metric are passed to an evaluation tool which generates the receiver operating characteristics (ROC) graph showing the comparison between the observed value and the predefined value.

3.1. Feedback Reliability Ratio (FRR)

The primary task of our approach is the selection of the attribute on which the evaluation of IDS is to be classified.

For this purpose four parameters are taken into consideration namely: True Positive (TP), False Positive (FP), True Negative (TN), and False Negative (FN). True

Positive depicts the number of detections caught by IDS when the detections are actually a threat to the system. False Positive value shows the incorrect decision made by IDS about a threat, while they were not actually involved in any threatening event. True Negative is the condition when IDS correctly determine an activity about its harmless nature. False Negative is the situation when IDS declares an activity as harmless, while the activity was a threat and was capable of causing harm to a system.

The fundamental property of a good Intrusion Detection System is not only to detect a threat but is also to provide a correct and reliable decision about an activity. Performance of a system degrades if the IDS installed on the system provide an improper feedback about an activity. So, the reliability factor converges to the False Positive (FP) and False Negative (FN) values of IDS, and these two attribute can describe the capability of an IDS to a reasonable extent. Lower the FP and FN values indicate better reliability on feedback provided by IDS. Mathematically, Reliability on a feedback provided by an IDS can be shown as:

$$\text{Feedback Reliability Value} = \alpha * \frac{1}{\text{FP}+\text{FN}} \quad (7)$$

Total value of both the factors (FP and FN) represents the number of incorrect decisions declared by the IDS. So, a feedback ratio can be determined on the basis of these two factors which can describe the reliability value of IDS on the basis of its past judgments. Hence,

$$\text{Feedback Reliability Value} = \frac{(\alpha * \text{FP}) + (\beta * \text{FN})}{\text{Total No. of Activities Observed}} \quad (8)$$

where α = Coefficient of false positives and β = Coefficient of false negatives.

Depending upon the environment in which the IDS is installed, expectations from an IDS varies in terms of performance. In some situations a very low value of FN is desired, as a high value of FN can harm a system if a strong attack passes through the IDS filter. However, in some cases a high value of FP can drastically degrade the system performance, as the user will not be able to execute any task if the IDS blocks most of the activities by marking them as a threat. Hence, the coefficients (α and β) used in the above equations can take values between 0 and 1 depending upon the expectation of the environment on which IDS is to be applied on. **Figure 1** shows a flowchart of our approach.

3.2. Canberra Metric to Predict the Performance of an IDS

Canberra metric is a measure used for determining the distance between groups in terms of similarity between the elements. Canberra metric operates as a rectangular metric having numerical values, with different cases as its rows and variations observed in a case as its column values. A square symmetric matrix is generated as the output of the metric algorithm with zero's as its diagonal elements. The values of the output matrix represent the distance between the variations of cases. The distance between any two elements is determined using the formula shown below:

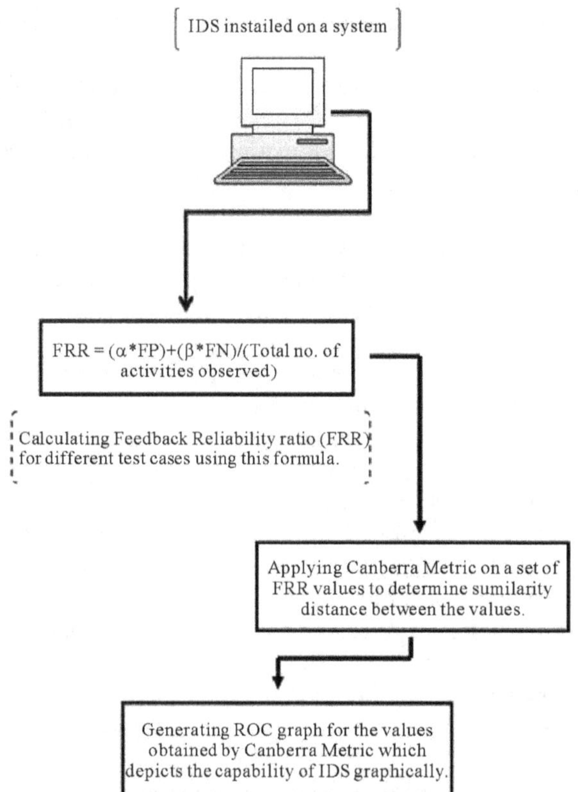

Figure 1. Flowchart.

$$d_{ij} = \sum_{k=1}^{n} \frac{|x_{ik} - x_{jk}|}{|x_{ik}| + |x_{jk}|} \quad (9)$$

where, i and j are the cases for which distance is to be determined, and k is the variation index for the cases. For the evaluation of an Intrusion Detection System using the Canberra distance metric various test cases are taken under consideration which provide us with the numerical values to be passed as the input to Canberra metric. To generate different test cases for evaluation of computer network intrusion detection systems, the Dataset made available by MIT Lincoln Laboratory, under Defense Advanced Research Projects Agency (DARPA ITO) and Air Force Research Laboratory (AFRL/SNHS) sponsorship in 1998 and 1999 [16] and [17] evaluation is used. These data sets contain examples of both attacks and background traffic. Canberra metric determine the distance between the FRR values using the above equation and finally output the distance values in a square symmetric matrix form. These output values shows the distance or dissimilarity in our case for different test cases. Canberra metric provides a mathematical representation of the similarity/dissimilarity between various cases available, the values of different columns can be compared to see the different trust levels of IDS. This observation helps an analyst to decide upon the IDS to be used on a system for securing data and to protect it from any external threat.

3.3. Weka

To demonstrate the results obtained by Canberra metric graphically, any graphical tool can be used. In our case a famous tool named Weka [18] is used. Waikato Environment for Knowledge Analysis (Weka) is an evaluation Tool used for Data Mining for data analysis and predictive modeling purposes. Present version of Weka is built on Java programming language, so provides better flexibility and can be deployed on any platform [19]. The values generated by Canberra Metric are passed as an input to Weka through a file in Comma separated values (CSV) format. Weka use these values in CSV file to output a Receiver operating characteristics (ROC) graph which shows a deviation between different curves, more the deviation observed shows less capability of the IDS.

4. Implementation of Canberra Metric

A slightly modified form of Canberra Metric is implemented for the evaluation of distance measure. Pseudocode for modified Canberra Metric algorithm is given below: Consider "C" is the number test cases generated and "v" is the number of variation observed in a test case. And "X" is a temporary variable. Let "M" (of order C*v) is the input matrix containing all the data required to be processed by the algorithm. And "O" (of order C*C) is the output matrix, which is a square symmetric matrix.

```
CANBERRA-DETERMINE (C, v)
1) For i = 0 to C
2) Begin
3) For j = 0 to C
4) Begin
5) Val = 0
6) For k = 0 to v
7) Begin
8) Yik = M[i][k];
9) Yjk = M[j][k];
10) X = (Yik – Yjk)/(Yik + Yjk)//Standard formula for Canberra metric
11) End
12) O[i][j] = Val; //Save this value in the output matrix
13) End
14) End
15) Output 'Matrix O'
```

This output matrix "O" provides us with the values depicting the deviation between performances of the IDS in different cases, which helps us in determining overall capability of the IDS. The values passed to the Canberra algorithm are obtained by applying Feedback Reliability Ratio (FRR) formula on various test cases (By taking moderate value for both the constants a and SS as 0.5 in Equation (2)). After applying Canberra algorithm on these values of the test cases, a square matrix is obtained that clearly depicts the effective value for every case. **Figure 2** shows the structure of the matrices, input values and the output matrix generated.

Finally, a graphical representation of the observed values is generated. The sum of the effective value for every case from the output matrix is used to locate points in the graph on y-axis, along with the intervals given on the x-axis. Joining these points in the graph generates a polyline graph, which shows the capability of an Intrusion Detection System for various test cases.

5. Results and Discussion

The peak point of the ROC graph shown in **Figure 3** shows the poor performance of IDS in real time environment. While a point at lower level shows better feedback results provided by the IDS. Thus, from the ROC graph for an IDS it can easily be predicted that in what scenario an IDS can perform efficiently. The ROC can also predict at what situation IDS does not provide a reliable detections and the trust level of the IDS.

The approach followed in this paper makes use of easily available attributes like False Positive (FP), False Negative (FN) and Total number of activities that helps in determining the Feedback Reliability Ratio (FRR). Further a distance based metric is used to determine the

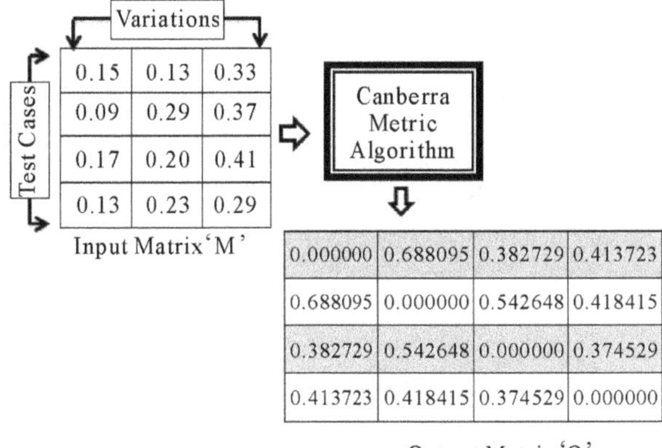

Figure 2. Structure of matrices.

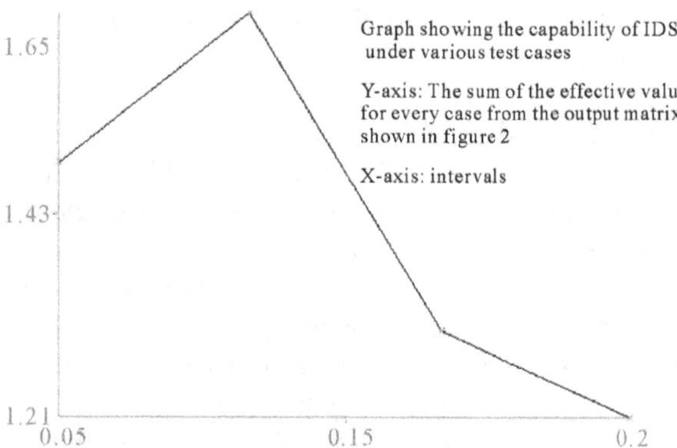

Figure 3. ROC curve.

similarity or dissimilarity in the behavior of an IDS. In our case, Canberra Metric is implemented for this purpose on the data set provided by DARPA analysis in 1999 for the evaluation of Intrusion Detection Systems. Finally the results produced by Canberra Metric are shown graphically using a Java based data mining tool by drawing a ROC graph.

The approach shown in this paper proved its importance in the field of network security as data security is a crucial factor in networks, where many sites interact with each other for data sharing and transaction of information. In such areas, a single threat can hamper the whole system due to its malicious nature. And hence need of a reliable Intrusion Detection System rises, which can secure both data and transactions on a system. But for this purpose, there should be a proper evaluation methodology which can predict the nature and performance of an IDS before installing it on a real time scenario. Our approach accomplishes that purpose by defining an evaluation technique for IDS using information of its behavior in the past.

6. Future Work

Unlike the norm that an IDS should be executed as often as possible to minimize the effects of intrusions we have shown that the IDS should be operated at optimum times with a view to maximize reliability o the IDS. The optimal position at which reliability is a maximum depends n several factors like attacker types, network characteristics etc. Thus, our aim should be to optimize performance and hence reliability of IDS in such varying circumstances. In future we hope to devise methods to increase performance and predict more accurate reliability of intrusion detection systems.

7. Acknowledgements

The first author wishes to acknowledge the support of a WOS-A project (ref. no. : SR/WOS-A/ET-20/2008) funded by the Department of Science and Technology, Government of India.

REFERENCES

[1] M. Mahoney, "Computer Security: A Survey of Attacks and Defenses," 2000. http://docshow.net/ids.htm

[2] U. Banerjee and A. Swaminathan, "A Taxonomy of Attacks and Attackers in MANETs," International Journal of Research and Reviews in Computer Science, Academy Publishers, Vol. 2, 2011, pp. 437-441.

[3] P. Ning and K. Sun, "How to Misuse AODV: A Case Study of Insider Attacks against Mobile Ad-Hoc Routing Protocols," *Journal Ad Hoc Networks*, Vol. 3, No. 6, 2005, pp. 60-67.

[4] S. E. H. Smaha, "An Intrusion Detection System," *Proceedings of the IEEE Fourth Aerospace Computer Security Applications Conference*, Orlando, December 1988, pp. 37-44.

[5] H. Debar, M. Dacier and A. Wespi, "Towards a Taxonomy of Intrusion Detection Systems," *Computer Networks*, Vol. 31, No. 8, 1999, pp. 805-822.

[6] J. Allen, A. Christie, W. Fithen, *et al.*, "State of the Practice of Intrusion Detection Technologies," Carnegie Mellon University, Software Engineering Institute, CMU/SEI-99-TR-028 ESC-TR-99-028, 2000. http://citeseerx.ist.psu.edu/viewdoc/summary?doi=10.1.1.155.4719

[7] G. F. Gu, P. Fogla, D. Dagon, W. Lee and B. Skori, "Measuring Intrusion Detection Capability: An Information-Theoretic Approach," *Proceedings of the* 2006 *ACM Symposium on Information, Computer and Communications Security*, New York, 2006, pp. 90-101.

[8] A. Nicholas, A. Randal, L. John, O. Henry and R. George, "Intrusion Detection Testing and Benchmarking Methodologies," *Proceedings of the First IEEE International Workshop on Information Assurance*, Washington DC, 2003.

[9] N. J. Puketza, K. Zhang, M. Chung, B. Mukherjee and R. A. Olsson, "A Methodology for Testing Intrusion Detection Systems," *IEEE Transactions on Software Engineering*, Vol. 22, No. 10, 1996, pp. 719-729.

[10] M. Ranum, "Experiences Benchmarking Intrusion Detection Systems," 2001. http://www.nfr.com/

[11] Anonym, "Testing Intrusion Detection Systems: A Critique of the 1998 and 1999 DARPA Intrusion Detection System Evaluations as Performed by Lincoln Laboratory," *ACM Transactions on Information and System Security*, Vol. 3, No. 4, 2000, pp. 262-294.

[12] Wilkison, "Intrusion Detection FAQ: How to Evaluate Network Intrusion Detection Systems?" http://www.sans.org/security-resources/idfaq/eval ids.php

[13] S. M. Emran, and N. Ye, "Robustness of Chi-Square and Canberra Distance Metrics for Computer Intrusion Detection," *Quality and Reliability Engineering International*, Vol. 18, No. 1, 2002, pp. 18-28.

[14] R. A. Johnson and D. W. Wichern, "Applied Multivariate

Statistical Analysis," Prentice Hall, New Jersey, 1998, pp. 226-235.

[15] T. P. Ryan, "Statistical Methods for Quality Improvement," John Wiley & Sons, New York, 1989.

[16] R. Lippmann, D. J. Fried, I. Graf, J. W. Haines, K. R. Kendall, D. McClung, D. Weber, S. H. Webster, D. Wyschograd, R. K. Cunningham and M. A. Zissman, "Evaluating Intrusion Detection Systems: The 1998 DARPA Off-Line Intrusion Detection Evaluation," IEEE Computer Society Press, Vol. 2, 2000, pp. 12-26.

[17] R. Lippmann, J. W. Haines, D. J. Fried, J. Korba and K. Das, "The 1999 DARPA Off-Line Intrusion Detection Evaluation," Springer, Berlin Heidelberg, New York, 2000, pp. 162-182.

[18] Weka. http://www.cs.waikato.ac.nz/ml/weka/

[19] Z. Markov and I. Russell, "An Introduction to the WEKA Data Mining System," *Proceedings of the* 11*th Annual SIGCSE Conference on Innovation and Technology in Computer Science Education*, 2006, pp. 367-368.

Perception on Cyber Terrorism: A Focus Group Discussion Approach

Rabiah Ahmad[1], Zahri Yunos[1], Shahrin Sahib[1], Mariana Yusoff[2]
[1]Center for Advanced Computing Technology, Faculty of Information and Communication Technology, Universiti Teknikal Malaysia Melaka (UTeM), Melaka, Malaysia
[2]Centre for Languages and Human Development, Universiti Teknikal Malaysia Melaka (UTeM), Melaka, Malaysia

ABSTRACT

Focus group discussion is an exploratory research technique used to collect data through group interaction. This technique provides the opportunity to observe interaction among participants on a topic under this study. This paper contributes to an understanding on the cyber terrorism conceptual framework through the analysis of focus group discussion. The proposed cyber terrorism conceptual framework which was obtained during the qualitative study by the authors has been used as a basis for discussion in the focus group discussion. Thirty (30) participants took part in the focus group discussion. The overall results suggest that the proposed cyber terrorism framework is acceptable by the participants. The present study supports our initial research that the cyber terrorism conceptual framework constitutes the following components: target, motivation, tools of attack, domain, methods of attack and impact.

Keywords: Cyber Terrorism Components; Framework; Focus Group

1. Introduction

A more holistic way in describing cyber terrorism is useful in understanding the concept of cyber terrorism. Based on literatures review, it is noted that there is no consensus agreement on the concept of cyber terrorism [1-5]. However, to have a common understanding on this term is important in order to get a better apprehension on what constitutes cyber terrorism. While there are many definitions of cyber terrorism, these suggest a trend that further analysis of the phenomena could be further conducted. This is evidence as the study of this concept has been the focus of many policy makers and scholarly studies, but their standpoints and views vary.

Cyber terrorism is about threat perception that makes the concept differ from one to another. This is due to multidimensional structures (or components) of cyber terrorism that made people interprets it differently at different levels. Therefore, understanding similarities and differences in perception of what constitutes cyber terrorism can provide insight to the policy makers and researchers to countering such threats.

2. Method

2.1. Background of This Study

The focus group discussion on cyber terrorism conceptual framework was held in conjunction with the 3-days cyber terrorism workshop organized by the South East Asia Regional Center for Counter Terrorism (SEARCCT), an agency under the Malaysia's Ministry of Foreign Affairs, in collaboration with the CyberSecurity Malaysia (an agency under the Malaysia's Ministry of Science, Technology and Innovation) and the Universiti Teknikal Malaysia Melaka, Malaysia.

The focus group discussion was held on the last day of the 3-days workshop. The discussion was designed as a platform to address the cyber terrorism framework in a holistic approach. The workshop gave an insight and a basic understanding of terrorism and cyber terrorism, issues and challenges revolving around them and complexity in coming up with one single universal definition before finally embarking to focus group discussion. Speakers from various agencies who are responsible in the area of counter terrorism and counter cyber crimes were invited to provide their thoughts and perspectives on these topics on the first 2-days of the workshop. In addition, detail explanation about the cyber terrorism conceptual framework was presented by the moderator on day 3 of the workshop. The sessions were designed in such a way to trigger the minds of the participants and to channel all relevant issues to the focus group discussion.

2.2. Participants

Focus group discussion is often used as an exploratory

technique and is one source of data collection method [6]. Normally, it consists of a group of people, typically between 5 to 10 participants and is led by a moderator.

In this study, 30 participants took part in the focus group discussion. However, they were divided into smaller groups consists of 6 participants for each group. This approach is similar to the focus group discussion conducted by Bray, Johns and Kilburn [7]. The background of the participants varies: management, policy, laws enforcement and prosecution, research and technical and the range of working experiences of the participants is between 10 years to 34 years. All participants were from the government agencies whereby all of them were nominated by the SEARCCT.

2.3. Procedures

The participants were divided into 5 groups and each group consists of 6 participants who are differed in term of age, organizations and working experiences. The rationale to have small number in a group is to give everyone the opportunity to express their views and opinions.

First, a briefing session was conducted in order to ensure that each focus group followed the same structure and had the same understanding on the key objectives as well as the discussion guidelines. Each group was given a flip chart to write their discussion points during the group brainstorming session. Before the group discussion, the proposed cyber terrorism conceptual framework was explained to the participants: target, motivation, tools of attack, domain, methods of attack and impact. Overall, the discussion and presentation sessions took about 3 hours.

Focus group discussion was identified as the appropriate and accessible technique, given the exploratory nature of the research [7]. The objectives of focus group discussion were as follows. Firstly, to discuss factors that make-up the components (or elements) of cyber terrorism and secondly, to evaluate the proposed conceptual framework that describes the components of cyber terrorism. In a nutshell, the focus group discussion was conducted to get consensus on people perception towards the proposed concept of cyber terrorism that was derived from the qualitative study. The proposed cyber terrorism conceptual framework is based on the author's initial study as described in **Figure 1**.

The primary output of this focus group was to gauge the participants view on the proposed cyber terrorism framework. The focus group discussion was facilitated by a moderator to provide guidance to the group and allowing respondents to talk freely and spontaneously in expressing ideas, views and experiences on the given topic. Although the moderator initiated the topic for discussion and thus exercises a certain control over what was to be discussed, he did not offer any viewpoints during the talk-in-process session [6]. As recommended by Bray, Johns and Kilburn [7], a relaxed and conversational method was used during the focus group discussion in order to produce a free flowing discussion with minimum intervention from the moderator.

Kamarulzaman [8] explained that in a focus group, people interacting with each other with the help of a moderator to get more information and to share their own experience. It is noted that the usefulness of focus group data are affected to the extent that the participants are openly communicating their ideas, views, or opinions during the focus group discussions. This is ascertained by Ho [6] whereby the author explained that, people are

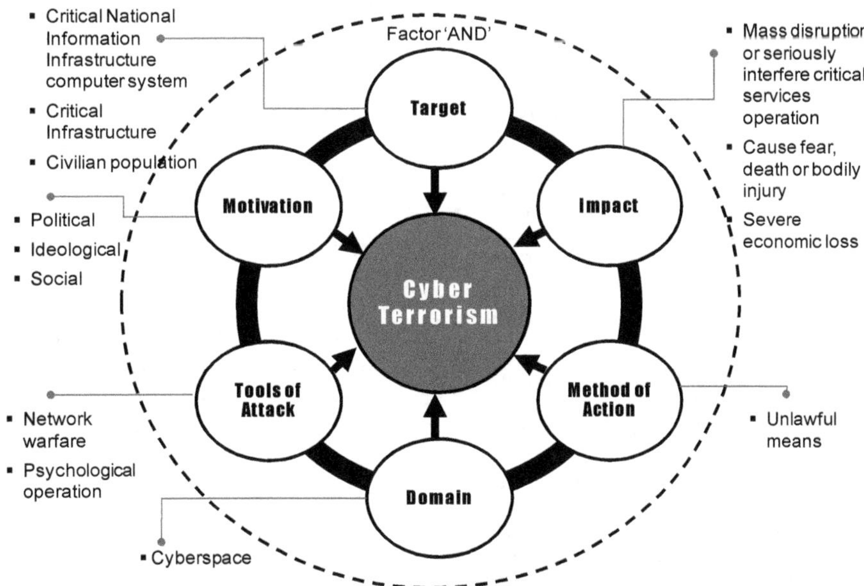

Figure 1. Proposed cyber terrorism conceptual framework.

gathered together to voice their opinions and perceptions about a study topic in a comfortable environment. During the discussion, participants are encouraged to talk to one another, asked questions and exchanged comment on the group's presentation. The focus group study allows a flexible and in-depth exploration of participants' attitudes and experiences as well as reveals differences in perspective between groups of individuals [9].

For context setting, the participants were asked several questions (**Table 1**). The questions did not run in any sequential order, rather to provide guidelines and overviews on the topic under discussion. In order to ensure that the objectives of the focus group discussions were met, the questions were focused on the components of cyber terrorism. The questions were selected from the questionnaires which had been used for the in-depth interviews, which were done prior to the focus group discussion.

2.4. Data Collection

In exploratory research, the hypotheses that obtained during the in-depth interview (qualitative data) is useful for enriching and comparing the effectiveness of the initial findings [10]. Besides, the ideas and observations are often used for later quantitative testing [10]. Prior to the focus group discussion, separate in-depth interviews were conducted to explore on the concept of cyber terrorism. Meaning to say, the focus group discussion was conducted on top of the in-depth interview to explore the concept of cyber terrorism. The group discussions were tape-recorded and the discussion points that were noted down on the flip chart were collected at the end of the session.

3. Results

3.1. Similarity in Views on the Proposed Conceptual Framework

The overall result of the focus group discussion is presented in **Table 2**. We included several recommendations from the groups in the findings table. Out of the 5 groups, 3 groups are fully agreed with the proposed framework. The other 2 groups partially agreed with the proposed framework with some recommendations.

Table 1. Questions for the focus group discussion.

Q1. What are the factors that make up the components (or elements) of cyber terrorism?
Q2. What are the factors that should not be considered as component (or element) of cyber terrorism?
Q3. From the various literatures, a conceptual framework describeing the core components of cyber terrorism can be described as follows (but not limited to): Target, Motivation, Tools of Attack, Domain, Method of Action and Impact. What is your view?
Q4. The components of cyber terrorism are bound or linked to each other to form the concept of cyber terrorism. We need to combine the components with the conjunction "AND", which means that, each of those components is necessary to constitute cyber terrorism. If one or more components are not provided, the statement would not constitute cyber terrorism. What do you think?

Group 1 explained, "Overall, our group found that the proposed cyber terrorism framework is sufficient enough. There are a few things we would like to simplify further just in the terms only, not the content. The content is still important." Group 1 further clarified, "Regarding to the impact, I think the examples of 3 elements: mass disruption or seriously interfere critical services operation; caused fear, death or bodily injury; and severe economic loss, I think that are covered."

Group 3 indicated that, "First of all, I would to extend our appreciation to our speaker today for his very comprehensive presentation. In fact, I think that, the presentation today should be brought back to our first day, to give us a basic understanding on the components of cyber terrorism itself." However, Group 3 stressed that "Domain" and "Motivation" should not be too rigid, as they viewed that the components keep changing and have a wide interpretation.

Group 4 pointed out that, "My group agrees on the proposed framework. However, as for the motivation component, we would like to add an economical factor". One of the respondents from Group 4 stated that, "We agree on the term cyber terrorism. We feel we should stick to that. For a simple reason, it looks like international term now where all countries are using this kind of term. If we deviate, we will be different. And secondly, even if it is cyber terrorism, we only looking at the terrorism, the terrorism act itself. Just because the mean of doing is through cyber, it is known as cyber terrorism. Likewise, why we call human trafficking? Drug trafficking? The offence is trafficking but it involves another way. Likewise, I think cyber terrorism is a better word, stick to it."

With regards to statement that the components of cyber terrorism are bound or linked to each other to form the concept of cyber terrorism, all groups agreed with the statement. For example, Group 4 indicated that, "In our discussion, all of the components must be there. In the absence of any of the components, there will be no cyber terrorism. The inner components must be "AND". If you take out target, that is it, no cyber terrorism."

Further question was posed to Group 1. Question: "In order to consider cyber terrorism, we need to combine all factors such as motivation, target and impact. Do you agree with that?" Answer: "Yes, we agree."

3.2. Difference in Views on the Proposed Conceptual Framework

Group 5 agreed with most of the proposed cyber terrorism

Table 2. Results of the focus group discussion.

Proposed Components	Group 1		Group 2		Group 3		Group 4		Group 5	
Target	Target	Critical National Information Infrastructure computer system Critical Infrastructure	Target	CNII Civil population Critical Infrastructure	Target	Critical National Information Infrastructure computer system Critical Infrastructure Civil population	Target	Critical National Information Infrastructure computer system Critical Infrastructure Civil population	Target	Government Country Corporation CNII
Motivation	Motivation	Political Ideological Social Economic	Initiator 100% personal or group with motiva-tion	The person or group must have the intention to commit the act of cyber terrorism (Refer to Note 3)	Motivation	Political Ideological Social Economic	Motivation	Political Ideological Social Economic	Motivation	Political Ideological Social Economic
Tools of Attack	Tools & Methods of Action	Network warfare Psychological operation The method of action is through unlawful means	Medium	Computer network	Tools of Attack	Network warfare Psychological operation	Tools of Attack	Network warfare Psychological operation	Medium (Tools & Methods) (Refer to Note 5)	Techniques (e.g. recruitment) Domain (e.g. cyberspace)
Domain	Refer to Note 1		Domain	Cyberspace Physical world	Domain	Cyberspace	Domain	Cyberspace		
Methods of Attack	Refer to Note 2		Method	Unlawful means	Methods of Attack	Unlawful means	Methods of Attack	Unlawful means		
Impact	Impact	The target must be impactful	Impact	Mass disruption lead to • destruction • cause-fear, death, instability of country • Severe economic loss • Doc-trinazation	Impact	• Mass disruption or seriously interfere critical services operation • Cause fear, death or bodily injury • Severe economic loss	Impact	• Mass disruption or seriously interfere critical services operation • Cause fear, death or bodily injury • Severe economic loss	Impact	Physical Non Physical National • Security • Economic • Image • Govern-ment to function • Health and safety
							Attempt	(Refer to Note 4)	Perpetrator	Group/ Individual Country

Note: 1) Group 1 excludes "Domain" as the factor which is by default is part of cyber terrorism. 2) Group 1 combines "Tools of Attack" and "Methods of Action" as one component, "Tools & Methods of Action". 3) Group 2 starts the concept of cyber terrorism with initiator, where the person or group has the intention to commit the act of cyber terrorism. The person or group also must have the motivation to do the act of cyber terrorism. 4) Group 4 suggests "Attempt" should be considered as part of cyber terrorism. 5) Group 5 combines "Tools of Attack", "Domain" and "Methods of Action" as one component, "Medium".

framework (Motivation, Target and Impact). However, they suggested that "Tools of Attacks", "Domain" and "Methods of Attack" should be combined as one component, "Medium". Similarly, Group 1 also suggested combining "Tools of Attack" and "Methods of Action" as one component, "Tools & Methods of Action".

Domain here refers to cyberspace, which is defined as an "interactive domain that made up of digital networks that is used to store, modify and communicate information. It includes the internet, but also the other information systems that support our businesses, infrastructure and services" [11]. In this particular study, "Domain" is similar to "Medium", but not "Tools of Attacks" or "Methods of Attack".

"Tools of Attacks" means computers and networks that are used as the weapons through which computers are attacked and exploited (via worms, denial-of-service, bots) [12]. While "Methods of Attack" refers to way and mean the attack was conducted, and in this particular case is referred to *unlawful* means. As mentioned by Denning [13], cyber terrorism is generally understood to mean *unlawful attack* against computers, networks and the information stored therein when done to intimidate or coerce a government or its people in furtherance of political or social objectives.

Group 5 also added one new component, "Perpetrator" which consists of group/individual and country. This is more or less similar with Group 2 where the group identified "Initiator" as one component of cyber terrorism. However, this can be further argued whether "Perpetrator" or "Initiator" is the right component of cyber terrorism. Rollins and Wilson [14] argue that, there are two views in defining cyber terrorism, one of it is the impact (effect-based). They clarify that, effect-based cyber terrorism exists when computer attacks result in effects that are disruptive enough to generate fear comparable to a traditional act of terrorism, even if done by criminals. This implies that, cyber terrorism should focus on the act rather than the doer. Likewise, Tun Dr Mahathir Mohamad [15], a former Malaysia's Prime Minister said, "If we have to determine who a terrorist is and who is not then we have to base it on the act, not on the person, the group, the race or the religion. Once we agree on what constitutes an act of terror, then it would be easy to identify a terrorist."

Although Group 4 agreed with all components of the proposed cyber terrorism framework, they suggested "Attempt" as part of cyber terrorism. One of the participants stated that, "Under the criminal laws, attempt is considered as an offence. What if the terrorist does all this, preparation is done but is unsuccessful in hitting the target? Everything is well prepared but the mission is not achieved. The possibility of causing harm should also be considered as offence in cyber terrorism. Example is murder or manslaughter. The action can cause death, likewise the person conduct whatever action under terrorism, it is possible of causing massive destruction, causing some kind of injury or fear, but the perpetrator did not achieve it. Does is it mean that there is no offence? Does is it mean that he/she is not a terrorist?" One of the objectives of this study is to identify factors that make up the components (or elements) of cyber terrorism. The components then describe the concept and the meaning of cyber terrorism. In this particular case, the authors suggest that an "attempt" should not be considered as factor that make-up the components of cyber terrorism as it is already an offence under the criminal laws. Under the Malaysian law, terrorist means any person who commits, or *attempts* to commit any terrorist act [16]. It means that, if the components are met with supporting evidence, action by the perpetrator can be classified as cyber terrorism and subsequently the person may be charged under the court of laws. In fact, attempt should be part of any criminal action, including cyber terrorism.

3.3. Proposed Future Works in Related to This Study

For future works, the groups have recommended several action plans which can be considered for implementation. The first proposal is amendment to the law. Their argument is that, effective legislation on cyber terrorism is regarded high priority as the countermeasure in counter-cyber terrorism plans. Group 1 recommended that, "We would like to propose amendment to our laws (to counter threats on cyber terrorism)". This is supported by Group 2, "After this, we need to develop further on the counter action of cyber terrorism. If enforcement is not effective enough, cyber terrorism can easily happen". Group 2 further stated that, "From time to time, we need to revise the laws. If such crimes are becoming more violent and cyber terrorism becoming so developed in times to come, perhaps there is a need specific definition on cyber terrorism."

The second proposal is the preventive measure. One of the participants said, "My views, all of these (the framework) are responsive action. What happen if we want to take preventive measure when it comes to mass disruption or national casualty? We cannot wait the attack to happen and then react. So, we need to think on preventive measure as we don't want to wait until the thing happen, we need to have measure on how to prevent this from happening."

Another participant responded that, "For response, a lot of things need to be considered. For root causes, there is mention the origin of attack. Then, there is non-state issue that gets involve. Also, there are ways and means toward cyber terrorism." In response to this issue, the moderator stated that, "That discussion will be in a different forum. The objective of this research is to provide baseline in understanding the components that make cyber terrorism. After this, we need to come out with response and action plan on how we are going to handle this issue."

The third proposal is the need to have a proper definition on the concept of cyber terrorism. Group 3 stated that, "I think it is crucial for us to have an understanding on the overall definition on the concept of cyber terrorism first before we can approach to the component. There are a few factors that we have to consider in approaching the questions: the perpetrator, the policy of various ministries, the enforcement, and the judicial authority. We think that cyber terrorism is quite similar with other crime. There are starting points and there are ending points. The starting point could be the action itself and the ending points could be the prosecution in court."

Group 3 further explained that, "We would like to admit that there is a need to have a mutual understanding between countries because cyber terrorism is a trans-boundary issue. It is very crucial for each country to have basic understanding or common understanding on what constitute cyber terrorism." Group 3 continued that, "I would like to take example on Convention on Cyber Crimes. In fact in this convention, we do not have any specific definition or understanding what cyber crimes is, but it provides what constitute cyber crimes. Perhaps in one day, we could have convention on cyber terrorism that would provide understanding to each country or at least common understanding on how or what constitute cyber terrorism."

3.4. Research Limitation

This study has several limitations. Therefore, some of the imperfections may lead to the unreliability of the data collected [10]. First, the constraint of this study is that majority of the participants were representatives from the defense & security and the government sectors of the Critical National Information Infrastructure (CNII). In Malaysia, there are 10 CNII sectors: water, banking & finance, defense & security, transportation, information & communication, government, emergency services, food & agriculture, energy and health. Therefore, the participants of the focus group discussion did not represent the CNII sectors as a whole. The second constraint is that from observation, not all participants were participating in the discussion. As a result, not all the participants' viewpoints were heard and well noted.

4. Conclusions

Cyber terrorism is a serious matter at the national and international level, and this is demonstrated through the conduct of this workshop. The present study supports our initial research [17] that the cyber terrorism conceptual framework constitutes the following components: target, motivation, tools of attack, domain, methods of attack and impact. This is evident from the overall result whereby 3 out of 5 groups are fully agreed with the proposed framework, while the other 2 groups agreed with the proposed framework with some recommendations. Although there are differences in opinions on some of the components, but their views are not that critical and can be further justified. These results suggest that the proposed cyber terrorism framework is acceptable.

Further research can be conducted to test or verify the conceptual framework. The outcome can be achieved by using quantitative method to quantify them and then applied statistical method to test the dynamic relationship of components of the cyber terrorism framework. Additionally, future research from this study could be used to help better in defining and adopting the concept of cyber terrorism in a holistic manner.

5. Acknowledgements

The authors would like to thank Sazali Sukardi and Zaleha Abd Rahim of CyberSecurity Malaysia who provided valuable input to this paper. The authors also would like to thank the Center for Advanced Computing Technology, Faculty of Information Technology and Communication, Universiti Teknikal Malaysia Melaka (UTeM) that provided research grant for this project.

REFERENCES

[1] J. Matusitz, "Social Network Theory: A Comparative Analysis of the Jewish Revolt in Antiquity and the Cyber Terrorism Incident over Kosovo," *Information Security Journal: A Global Perspective*, Vol. 20, No. 1, 2011, pp. 34-44.

[2] M. Dogrul, A. Aslan and E. Celik, "Developing an International Cooperation on Cyber Defense and Deterrence against Cyber Terrorism," 2011 *3rd International Conference on Cyber Conflict*, Tallinn, 7-10 June 2011, pp. 1-15.

[3] M. Conway, "Against Cyberterrorism," *Communications of the ACM*, Vol. 54, No. 2, 2011, pp. 26-28.

[4] Z. Yunos, S. H. Suid, R. Ahmad and Z. Ismail, "Safeguarding Malaysia's Critical National Information Infrastructure (CNII) Against Cyber Terrorism: Towards Development of a Policy Framework," *IEEE Sixth International Conference on Information Assurance & Security*, Atlanta, 23-25 August 2010, pp. 21-27.

[5] P. A. H. Williams, "Information Warfare: Time for a Redefinition," *Proceedings of the 11th Australian Information Warfare & Security Conference*, Perth Western, 30 November-2 December, 2010, pp. 37-44.

[6] D. Ho, "The Focus Group Interview: Rising to the Challenge in Qualitative Research," *Australian Review of Applied Linguistics*, Vol. 29, No. 1, 2006, pp. 1-19.

[7] J. Bray, N. Johns and D. Kilburn, "An Exploratory Study into the Factors Impeding Ethical Consumption," *Journal of Business Ethics*, Vol. 98, No. 4, 2011, pp. 597-608.

[8] Y. Kamarulzaman, "A Focus Group Study of Consumer Motivations for e-Shopping: UK versus Malaysia," *African Journal of Business Management*, Vol. 5, No. 16, 2011, pp. 6778-6784.

[9] F. Saleem, M. Hassali, A. Shafie, S. Bashir and M. Atif, "Perceptions of Disease State Management among Pakistani Hypertensive Patients: Findings from a Focus Group Discussion," *Tropical Journal of Pharmaceutical Research*, Vol. 10, No. 6, 2011, pp. 833-840.

[10] D. R. Cooper and P. S. Schindler, "Business Research

Method," McGraw-Hill Companies, Inc., New York, 2008.

[11] UK Cabinet Office, "The UK Cyber Security Strategy—Protecting and Promoting the UK in a Digital World," 2011. http://www.cabinetoffice.gov.uk/sites/default/files/resources/The UK Cyber Security Strategy-web ver.pdf

[12] N. Veerasamy and J. H. P. Eloff, "Application of Non-Quantitative Modelling in the Analysis of a Network Warfare Environment," *World Academy of Science, Engineering and Technology Conference*, Paris, 2008.

[13] D. E. Denning, "Cyberterrorism," Testimony given to the House Armed Services Committee Special Oversight Panel on Terrorism, 23 May 2000.

[14] J. Rollins and C. Wilson, "Terrorist Capabilities for Cyberattack: Overview and Policy Issues," CRS Report for Congress, 2007.

[15] M. Mohammad, "The Need to Identify Terrorists and Remove the Causes of Terrorism," In: H. Makaruddin, Ed., *Terrorism and the Real Issues*, Pelanduk Publications (M) Sdn Bhd, Subang Jaya, 2003, pp. 29-40.

[16] ACT 574 Penal Code, "Chapter VIA—Offences Relating to Terrorism. Section 130B (1)-(5)," Zul Rafique & Partner Report, 1997.

[17] R. Ahmad and Z. Yunos, "A Dynamic Cyber Terrorism Framework," *International Journal of Computer Science and Information Security*, Vol. 10, No. 2, 2012, pp. 149-158.

The Extended Tanh Method for Compactons and Solitons Solutions for the CH(n,2n – 1,2n,–n) Equations

Xinqian Lin*, **Shengqiang Tang, Wentao Huang**
School of Mathematics and Computing Science, Guilin University of Electronic Technology, Guilin, China

ABSTRACT

In this paper, by using the sine-cosine method, the extended tanh-method, and the rational hyperbolic functions method, we study a class of nonlinear equations which derived from a fourth order analogue of generalized Camassa-Holm equation. It is shown that this class gives compactons, solitary wave solutions, solitons, and periodic wave solutions. The change of the physical structure of the solutions is caused by variation of the exponents and the coefficients of the derivatives.

Keywords: The CH(n,2n – 1,2n,–n) Equation; Compactons; Sine-Cosine Method and the Extended Tanh Method; Rational Hyperbolic Functions Method

1. Introduction

Recently, S. Tang [1] studied the nonlinear dispersive variants the CH(n,n,m) of the generalized Camassa-Holm equation in (1 + 1), (2 + 1) and (3 + 1) dimensions respectively by using sine-cosine method, it is shown that this class gives compactons, conventional solitons, solitary patterns and periodic solutions.

It is the objective of this work to further complement our studies in [1] on the CH(n,n,m) equation. Our first interest in the present work being in implementing the tanh method [2,3] to stress its power in handling nonlinear equations so that one can apply it to models of various types of nonlinearity. The next interest is the determination of exact travelling wave solutions with distinct physical structures to the CH(n,2n – 1,2n,–n) given by

$$\begin{aligned} u_{tt} &= \left(a_0u+b_0u^n+d_0u^{2n-1}\right)_{xx}+\left(a_1u+b_1u^n+d_1u^{2n-1}\right)_{yy} \\ &+\left(a_2u+b_2u^n+d_2u^{2n-1}\right)_{zz} \\ &+\left[k_0u^{2n}\left(u^{-n}\right)_{xx}+k_1u^{2n}\left(u^{-n}\right)_{yy}+k_2u^{2n}\left(u^{-n}\right)_{zz}\right]_{tt}, \end{aligned} \tag{1.1}$$

$a_i, k_i > 0\ (i = 0,1,2),\ n \geq 2,$

in (3 + 1) dimensions. Our approach depends mainly on the sine-cosine method [4], the tanh method [2,3], and the rational hyperbolic functions method [5] that have the advantage of reducing the nonlinear problem to a system of algebraic equations that can be solved by using Maple or Mathematica. As stated before, our approach depends mainly on the sine-cosine method, the extended tanh method, and the rational hyperbolic functions method. In what follows, we highlight the main steps of the proposed methods.

2. Analysis of the Methods

For the three methods, we first use the wave variable $\xi = x - ct$ to carry a PDE in two independent variables

$$P\left(u,u_t,u_x,u_{xx},u_{xxx},\cdots\right)=0, \tag{2.1}$$

into an ODE

$$Q\left(u',u'',u''',\cdots\right)=0, \tag{2.2}$$

Equation (2.2) is then integrated as long as all terms contain derivatives where integration constants are considered zeros.

2.1. The Sine-Cosine Method

The sine-cosine algorithm admits the use of the ansätz

$$u(x,t)=\lambda\cos^{\beta}(\mu\xi), |\xi|\leq\frac{\pi}{2\mu}, \tag{2.3}$$

or the ansätz

$$u(x,t)=\lambda\sin^{\beta}(\mu\xi), |\xi|\leq\frac{\pi}{\mu}, \tag{2.4}$$

where λ, μ, β are parameters that will be determined.

2.2. The Tanh Method

The standard tanh method introduced in [2,3] where the tanh is used as a new variable, since all derivatives of a

*Corresponding author.

tanh are represented by a tanh itself. We use a new independent variable

$$Y=\tanh(\mu\xi), \tag{2.5}$$

that leads to the change of derivatives:

$$\begin{aligned}\frac{\mathrm{d}}{\mathrm{d}\xi}&=\mu\left(1-Y^2\right)\frac{\mathrm{d}}{\mathrm{d}Y},\\ \frac{\mathrm{d}^2}{\mathrm{d}\xi^2}&=-2\mu^2Y\left(1-Y^2\right)\frac{\mathrm{d}}{\mathrm{d}Y}+\mu^2\left(1-Y^2\right)^2\frac{\mathrm{d}^2}{\mathrm{d}Y^2}.\end{aligned} \tag{2.6}$$

We then apply the following finite expansion:

$$u(\mu\xi)=S(Y)=\sum_{k=0}^{M}a_kY^k \tag{2.7}$$

and

$$u(\mu\xi)=S(Y)=\sum_{k=0}^{M}a_kY^k+\sum_{k=0}^{M}b_kY^{-k}, \tag{2.8}$$

where M is a positive integer that will be determined to derive a closed form analytic solution.

2.3. The Rational Sinh Functions Method

It is appropriate to introduce rational hyperbolic functions methods where we set

$$u(x,t)=\frac{Af(x,t)}{1+Bf(x,t)}, \tag{2.9}$$

where A and B are parameters that will be determined, and

$$f(x,t)=\begin{cases}\cosh\left[\mu(x-ct)\right]\\ \sinh\left[\mu(x-ct)\right]\end{cases}, \tag{2.10}$$

The rational hyperbolic functions methods can be applied directly in a straightforward manner. We then collect the coefficients of the resulting hyperbolic functions and setting it equal to zero, and solving the resulting equations to determine A, B, μ and c. This assumption will be used for the determination of solitons structures the CH(n, $2n-1$, $2n$, $-n$) equations.

3. Using the Sine-Cosine Method

For the CH(n, $2n-1$, $2n$, $-n$) equation given by (1.1), using the wave variable $\xi=x+y+z-ct$ carries (1.1) into the ODE, respectively

$$c^2u''=\left(a_j^*u+b_j^*u^n+d_j^*u^{2n-1}\right)''+c^2k_j^*\left(u^{2n}\left(u^{-n}\right)''\right)'', \tag{3.1}$$

where

$$a_j^*=\sum_{i=0}^{i=j}a_i,\ b_j^*=\sum_{i=0}^{i=j}b_i,\ d_j^*=\sum_{i=0}^{i=j}d_i,\ k_j^*=\sum_{i=0}^{i=j}k_i,\ j=0,1,2. \tag{3.2}$$

Integrating (3.1) twice, respectively, using the constants of integration to be zero we find

$$\left(a_j^*-c^2\right)u+b_j^*u^n+d_j^*u^{2n-1}+c^2k_j^*u^{2n}\left(u^{-n}\right)''=0, \tag{3.3}$$

Substituting (2.3) into (3.3) gives

$$\begin{aligned}&\left(a_j^*-c^2\right)\lambda\cos^{\beta}(\mu\xi)+b_j^*\lambda^n\cos^{n\beta}(\mu\xi)\\ &+d_j^*\lambda^{2n-1}\cos^{(2n-1)\beta}(\mu\xi)\\ &+c^2k_j^*\left(-n^2\mu^2\beta^2\lambda^n\cos^{n\beta}(\mu\xi)\right.\\ &\left.+n\mu^2\lambda^n\beta(n\beta-1)\cos^{n\beta-2}(\mu\xi)\right)=0,\end{aligned} \tag{3.4}$$

Equation (3.4) is satisfied only if the following system of algebraic equations holds:

$$\begin{aligned}&n\beta+1\neq 0,\ a_j^*-c^2=0,\\ &b_j^*\lambda^n=c^2k_j^*n^2\mu^2\beta^2\lambda^n,\\ &n\beta-2=(2n-1)\beta,\\ &d_j^*\lambda^{2n-1}=-c^2k_j^*n\mu^2\lambda^n\beta(n\beta+1),\end{aligned} \tag{3.5}$$

Solving the system (3.5) gives

$$\begin{aligned}&c=\pm\sqrt{a_j^*},\ \beta=\frac{-2}{n-1},\ \mu^2=\pm\frac{(n-1)^2}{4n^2}\cdot\frac{b_j^*}{a_j^*k_j^*},\\ &\lambda=(\theta)^{\frac{1}{n-1}},\ \theta=\frac{-b_j^*(n+1)}{2nd_j^*}\end{aligned} \tag{3.6}$$

The results (3.6) can be easily obtained if we also use the sine method (2.4). Combining (3.6) with (2.3) and (2.4), the following compactons solutions

$$u(X_j,t)=\begin{cases}\left\{\theta\sec^2\left[\frac{n-1}{2n}\sqrt{\frac{b_j^*}{a_j^*k_j^*}}\left(x_j\pm\sqrt{a_j^*}t\right)\right]\right\}^{\frac{1}{n-1}}, & 0<\left|x_j\pm\sqrt{a_j^*}t\right|<\frac{\pi}{2\mu},\ a_j^*,b_j^*,k_j^*>0,\ d_j^*<0,\ j=0,1,2,\\ 0, & \text{otherwise.}\end{cases} \tag{3.7}$$

and

$$u(X_j,t)=\begin{cases}\left\{\theta\csc^2\left[\frac{n-1}{2n}\sqrt{\frac{b_j^*}{a_j^*k_j^*}}\left(x_j\pm\sqrt{a_j^*}t\right)\right]\right\}^{\frac{1}{n-1}}, & 0<\left|x_j\pm\sqrt{a_j^*}t\right|<\frac{\pi}{\mu},\ a_j^*,b_j^*,k_j^*>0,\ d_j^*<0,\ j=0,1,2,\\ 0, & \text{otherwise}\end{cases} \tag{3.8}$$

are readily obtained, where

$$X_1 = x, X_2 = (x,y), X_3 = (x,y,z),\quad x_1 = x, x_2 = x+y, x_3 = x+y+z, \tag{3.9}$$

However, for $b_j^* < 0, a_j^*, d_j^*, k_j^* > 0,$ we obtain the following solitary wave solutions

$$u(X_j,t) = \left\{\theta \sec h^2\left[\frac{n-1}{2n}\sqrt{\frac{-b_j^*}{a_j^* k_j^*}}\left(x_j \pm \sqrt{a_j^*}t\right)\right]\right\}^{\frac{1}{n-1}}, \tag{3.10}$$

and

$$u(X_j,t) = \left\{\theta \csc h^2\left[\frac{n-1}{2n}\sqrt{\frac{-b_j^*}{a_j^* k_j^*}}\left(x_j \pm \sqrt{a_j^*}t\right)\right]\right\}^{\frac{1}{n-1}}. \tag{3.11}$$

4. Using the Extended Tanh Method

Using the assumptions of the tanh method (2.5)-(2.7) gives

$$\begin{aligned}&\left(a_j^* - c^2\right)S + b_j^* S^n + d_j^* S^{2n-1}\\&+c^2 k_j^*\left[n(n+1)S^{n-2}\mu^2\left(1-Y^2\right)^2\left(\frac{\mathrm{d}S}{\mathrm{d}Y}\right)^2\right]\\&-\left[nS^{n-1}\mu^2\left(1-Y^2\right)\left(-2Y\frac{\mathrm{d}S}{\mathrm{d}Y}+\left(1-Y^2\right)\frac{\mathrm{d}^2 S}{\mathrm{d}Y^2}\right)^2\right]=0.\end{aligned} \tag{4.1}$$

To determine the parameter M we usually balance the linear terms of highest order in the resulting Equation (4.1) with the highest order nonlinear terms. This in turn gives

$$M = M(n-1) + 4 + M - 2, \tag{4.2}$$

so that

$$M = -\frac{2}{n-1}. \tag{4.3}$$

To get a closed form analytic solution, the parameter M should be an integer. A transformation formula

$$u = v^{-\frac{1}{n-1}}, \tag{4.4}$$

should be used to achieve our goal. This in turn transforms (3.6) to

$$\begin{aligned}&\left(a_j^* - c^2\right)(n-1)^2 v^3 + b_j^*(n-1)^2 v^2 + d_j^*(n-1)^2 v\\&+c^2 k_j^* n\left[\left(v'\right)^2 + (n-1)vv''\right] = 0.\end{aligned} \tag{4.5}$$

Balancing vv'' and v^3 gives $M = 2$. The extended tanh method allows us to use the substitution

$$v(x,t) = S(Y) = A_0 + A_1 Y + A_2 Y^2 + B_1 Y^{-1} + B_2 Y^{-2}. \tag{4.6}$$

Substituting (4.6) into (4.5), collecting the coefficients of each power of Y and using Mapple to solve the resulting system of algebraic equations we obtain the following three sets:

$$\begin{aligned}&A_2 = \frac{-4d_j^* n}{b_j^*(n+1)}, \mu = \Delta,\\&\Delta=(n-1)\sqrt{\frac{2b_j^* d_j^*}{k_j^*\left[16a_j^* d_j^* n^2 + \left(b_j^*\right)^2(1-3n)(n+1)\right]}}\\&\Omega = \pm\frac{1}{4n}\sqrt{\frac{16a_j^* d_j^* n^2 + \left(b_j^*\right)^2(1-3n)(n+1)}{d_j^*}},\\&A_0 = A_1 = B_1 = B_2 = 0, c = \Omega,\end{aligned} \tag{4.7}$$

$$\begin{aligned}&B_2 = \frac{-4d_j^* n}{b_j^*(n+1)}, \mu = \Delta,\\&A_0 = A_1 = B_1 = A_2 = 0, c = \Omega,\end{aligned} \tag{4.8}$$

and

$$\begin{aligned}&\frac{1}{2}A_0 = A_2 = B_2 = \frac{-d_j^* n}{b_j^*(n+1)}, \mu = \frac{\Delta}{2},\\&A_1 = B_1 = 0, c = \Omega.\end{aligned} \tag{4.9}$$

Noting that

$$u = v^{-\frac{1}{n-1}},$$

for

$$b_j^* > 0, d_j^* > \frac{\left(b_j^*\right)^2(3n-1)(n+1)}{16a_j^* n^2}$$

or

$$b_j^* > 0, d_j^* < 0,$$

we obtain the solitary wave solutions

$$u(X_j,t) = \left\{\frac{-b_j^*(n+1)}{4d_j^* n}\cot h^2\left[\mu_1\left(x_j - ct\right)\right]\right\}^{\frac{1}{n-1}}, \tag{4.10}$$

$$u(X_j,t) = \left\{\frac{-b_j^*(n+1)}{4d_j^* n}\tan h^2\left[\mu_1\left(x_j - ct\right)\right]\right\}^{\frac{1}{n-1}}, \tag{4.11}$$

$$\begin{aligned}u(X_j,t) = &\left\{\frac{-d_j^* n}{b_j^*(n+1)}\left\{2 + \left\{\tan h^2\left[\mu_2\left(x_j - ct\right)\right]\right.\right.\right.\\&\left.\left.\left.+\cot h^2\left[\mu_2\left(x_j - ct\right)\right]\right\}\right\}\right\}^{-\frac{1}{n-1}},\end{aligned} \tag{4.12}$$

where $c = \Omega, \mu_1 = 2\mu_2 = \Delta,$

However, for

$$b_j^* \langle 0, d_j^* \rangle \frac{\left(b_j^*\right)^2(3n-1)(n+1)}{16a_j^* n^2},$$

or

$$b_j^* < 0, d_j^* \quad 0,$$

we obtain the periodic solutions

$$u(X_j,t)=\left\{\frac{b_j^*(n+1)}{4d_j^*n}\cot^2\left[\mu_1(x_j-ct)\right]\right\}^{\frac{1}{n-1}}, \quad (4.13)$$

$$u(X_j,t)=\left\{\frac{b_j^*(n+1)}{4d_j^*n}\tan^2\left[\mu_1(x_j-ct)\right]\right\}^{\frac{1}{n-1}}, \quad (4.14)$$

$$u(X_j,t)=\left\{\frac{d_j^*n}{b_j^*(n+1)}\left\{2+\left\{\tan^2\left[\mu_2(x_j-ct)\right]\right.\right.\right. \\ \left.\left.\left.+\cot^2\left[\mu_2(x_j-ct)\right]\right\}\right\}\right\}^{-\frac{1}{n-1}}, \quad (4.15)$$

where $c=\Omega$, $\mu_1=2\mu_2=\Delta$.

5. Using the Rational Sinh and Cosh Functions Methods

We now substitute the rational cosh

$$v(X_j,t)=\frac{A\cosh\left[\mu(x_j-ct)\right]}{1+B\cosh\left[\mu(x_j-ct)\right]}, \quad (5.1)$$

into (4.5), where

$$u(X_j,t)=\left[v(X_j,t)\right]^{-\frac{1}{n-1}}. \quad (5.2)$$

Collecting the coefficients of the like hyperbolic functions, and proceeding as before we find

$$a=\pm 2(n-1), B=\pm 1, c=\pm\sqrt{a_j^*+\frac{4}{7(n-1)}},$$
$$\mu=2(n-1)\sqrt{\frac{-b_j^*(n-1)}{k_j^*n\left[7a_j^*(n-1)+4\right]}}, \quad (5.3)$$
$$d_j^*=-\frac{6}{7}b_j^*(n-1).$$

The results (5.2) can be easily obtained if we also use the rational sinh method. This gives the solitons solutions

$$u(X_j,t)=\left\{\frac{1\pm\operatorname{sec}h\left[\mu_1(x_j-ct)\right]}{2(n-1)}\right\}^{\frac{1}{n-1}} \quad (5.4)$$

and

$$u(X_j,t)=\left\{\frac{1\mp\operatorname{csc}h\left[\mu_1(x_j-ct)\right]}{2(n-1)}\right\}^{\frac{1}{n-1}} \quad (5.5)$$

for $b_j^*<0$, and the periodic wave solution

$$u(X_j,t)=\left\{\frac{1\pm\sec\left[\mu_2(x_j-ct)\right]}{2(n-1)}\right\}^{\frac{1}{n-1}}, \quad (5.6)$$

and the complex solution

$$u(X_j,t)=\left\{\frac{1\mp i\csc\left[\mu_2(x_j-ct)\right]}{2(n-1)}\right\}^{\frac{1}{n-1}}, \quad (5.7)$$

for $b_j^*>0$, where

$$\mu_1=2(n-1)\sqrt{\frac{-b_j^*(n-1)}{k_j^*n\left[7a_j^*(n-1)+4\right]}},$$
$$\mu_2=2(n-1)\sqrt{\frac{b_j^*(n-1)}{k_j^*n\left[7a_j^*(n-1)+4\right]}}. \quad (5.8)$$

6. Conclusion

The basic goal of this work has been to extend our work on the CH(*n*,*n*,*m*) equation in [1]. The sine-cosine method, the tanh method, and the rational hyperbolic functions method were used to investigate variants of the CH(*n*,2*n* – 1,2*n*,–*n*) equations. The study revealed compactons solutions, solitary wave solutions, solitons, and periodic wave solutions for all examined variants.

7. Acknowledgements

This research was supported by NNSF of China (110-61010).

REFERENCES

[1] S. Tang, Y. Xiao and Z. Wang, "Travelling Wave Solutions for a Class of Nonlinear Fourth Order Variant of a Generalized Camassa-Holm Equation," *Applied Mathematics and Computation*, Vol. 210, 2009, pp. 39-47.

[2] W. Malfliet, "Solitary Wave Solutions of Nonlinear Wave Equations," *American Journal of Physics*, Vol. 60, No. 7, 1992, pp. 650-654.

[3] W. Malfliet and W. Hereman, "The Tanh Method: II. Perturbation Technique for Conservative Systems," *Physica Scripta*, Vol. 54, 1996, pp. 569-575.

[4] A. M. Wazwaz, "A Class of Nonlinear Fourth Order Variant of a Generalized Camassa-Holm Equation with Compact and Noncompact Solutions," *Applied Mathematics and Computation*, Vol. 165, 2005, pp. 485-501.

[5] Z. Y. Yan, "New Explicit Travelling Wave Solutions for Two New Integrable Coupled Nonlinear Evolution Equations," *Physics Letters A*, Vol. 292, 2001, pp. 100-106.

C3SM: Information Assurance Based on Cryptographic Checksum with Clustering Security Management Protocol

Moad Mowafi[1], Lo'ai Tawalbeh[2], Walid Aljoby[1], Mohammad Al-Rousan[1]
[1]Department of Network Engineering and Security, Jordan University of Science and Technology, Irbid, Jordan
[2]Department of Computer Engineering, Jordan University of Science and Technology, Irbid, Jordan

ABSTRACT

Wireless Sensor Networks (WSNs) are resource-constrained networks in which sensor nodes operate in an aggressive and uncontrolled environment and interact with sensitive data. Traffic aggregated by sensor nodes is susceptible to attacks and, due to the nature of WSNs, security mechanisms used in wired networks and other types of wireless networks are not suitable for WSNs. In this paper, we propose a mechanism to assure information security against security attacks and particularly node capturing attacks. We propose a cluster security management protocol, called Cryptographic Checksum Clustering Security Management (C3SM), to provide an efficient decentralized security management for hierarchal networks. In C3SM, every cluster selects dynamically and alternately a node as a Cluster Security Manager (CSM) which distributes a periodic shared secrete key for all nodes in the cluster. The cluster head, then, authenticates identity of the nodes and derive a unique pairwise key for each node in the cluster. C3SM provides sufficient security regardless how many nodes are compromised, and achieves high connectivity with low memory cost and low energy consumption. Compared to existing protocols, our protocol provides stronger resilience against node capture with lower key storage overhead.

Keywords: Wireless Sensor Networks; Security; Message Authentication Code; Cryptographic; Node Capture Attack

1. Introduction

Wireless Sensor Networks (WSNs) are highly distributed and self-organized system that is based on collaborative effort of a large number of nodes, where each node has the ability of sensing, computation, and communication. WSNs suffer from various malicious attacks because the environment is open to the public. Thus, an enemy can easily listen to the wireless communication and intercept the traffic. To prevent such malicious attacks, secret keys should be used to encrypt wireless communication and establish data confidentiality, integrity and authentication among sensor nodes. An enemy can also capture a sensor node and access its data and communication keys. This type of attacks is called node capture attack, and forms a main challenge to develop a security mechanism for WSNs.

In wired and wireless networks, information assurance is attained by data encryption and authentication. Many complex security algorithms are developed such as public-key cryptography (e.g., RSA [1] and Diffie-Hellman [2]), digital signature and trusted third-party authentication schemes [3]. In WSNs, the sensor node does not have sufficient memory to store a lot of keys or support a complex public key algorithm. Moreover, the computation overhead and energy consumption make traditional security mechanisms not suitable for WSNs. Therefore, it is necessary to develop an appropriate security mechanism for WSNs to distribute secret keys among the nodes, encrypt communication and form authentication. However, the challenge does not lie in the development of a secure mechanism merely, but on how to efficiently create, distribute and manage the secret keys among the nodes.

In this paper, we introduce a new security protocol called Cryptographic Checksum Clustering Security Management (C3SM) that operates under clustered hierarchical network architecture. The proposed scheme provides sufficient security regardless of how many nodes are compromised and achieves efficient energy consumption with low key storage overhead. In C3SM, every cluster selects dynamically and alternately a node called Cluster Security Manager (CSM) which distributes a periodic shared secrete key for all nodes in the cluster. Then, the cluster head (*CH*) authenticates the identity of the cluster nodes, and establishes a unique pairwise key for each node in the cluster. The authentication is achieved by cryptographic checksum or Message Authentication Code (MAC). To enhance confidentiality between the cluster nodes and the *CH*, we design a local, random, dynamic, periodic and unique pairwise key for each path between the *CH* and sensor node. These key properties make the security in WSNs stronger, and attain high connectivity with low memory cost and low energy consumption. To enhance integrity and authenticity among nodes, we use cryptographic checksum (variable tiny segment of code) appended to control messages. Moreover, the proposed scheme has strong resilience against node capture because it has an alternating CSM that distributes keys at regular period of times in normal (safety) mode, monitors the cluster nodes for attack, and changes keys directly in case of an attack occurs (threat mode).

The rest of this paper is organized as follows. In Section 2, we provide a review of related work in key management for WSNs. In Section 3, we describe the proposed system architecture. In Section 4, we present and analyze the system model. In Section 5, we evaluate the system performance and present simulation results. Finally, we conclude the paper in Section 6.

2. Related Work

The existing approaches for solving the key distribution problem in WSNs can be classified into four categories [4]: Network-wide keys schemes, full pairwise key schemes, matrix-based schemes, polynomial-based schemes, and probabilistic schemes.

In the network-wide keys scheme, a single master key is loaded into all sensor nodes. This scheme provides perfect connectivity since all deployed nodes share the same key, and also new added nodes can be loaded with the same master key and connect simply. Several schemes have adopted this approach [5-7]. The shortcoming of the network-wide scheme is that a capturing of a single node will comprise all the nodes and their communication. Moreover, malicious nodes can be easily injected into the network.

In the full pairwise key scheme, each node from n nodes stores n-1 pairwise keys in order to communicate with every other node. This scheme provides a high level of security but its main drawback is its demand for very large memory storage.

Matrix-based schemes are originally created for establishing a pairwise key by Blom [8]. In Blom's scheme, each node i has the ith row and the ith column of secret and public matrices, respectively. By exchanging their columns, any two nodes i and j can create their pairwise key $K_{ij} = K_{ji}$. In this scheme, if no more than t nodes are compromised, no more keys are compromised. Increasing t can improve the scheme resilience; however more secret information needs to be stored. Extensions of Blom's scheme have been proposed in [9,10].

The polynomial-based key management schemes are originally initiated by Blundo [11] as a special case of Blom's scheme. In Blundo's scheme, each node i has a polynomial $f(x,y)$ over a finite filed. By evaluating their polynomials, any two nodes i and j can create their pairwise key $f(i,j) = f(j,i)$. Several schemes have adopted Blundo's scheme [12-14]. The main drawbacks of the polynomial-based approach are its demand for large memory to store the polynomials, and the computational power of the multiplication and exponentiation operations [4].

In the probabilistic approaches, the security services are divided into phases in order to offer high security as the pairwise key approach and lower storage as the network-wide key approach, and to find suitable tradeoff between security and overhead. In general, the probabilistic approaches pass through three phases [4]: Key pre-distribution, shared-key discovery, and path-key establishment. Our work belongs to such approaches and presents a security mechanism for each phase, aiming at attaining effective security, efficiency, and flexibility.

Several schemes, related to our work, have been proposed [15-20]. In [15], a random key pre-distribution scheme is proposed. It prepares a very large size key pool, chooses randomly a subset of keys, and then stores them in the node's memory before deployment. After the discovery process performed between the nodes that intend to communicate, the nodes can establish a connection if they share one or more of the common keys stored in their memories. The common key then becomes a shared key for the link between the nodes. Nodes that cannot find a shared key with each other can generate a path key through what so-called a connected secure graph. This scheme requires a large key storage in large scale networks. Moreover it does not support node authentication, and its resilience to node capture attacks is weak since any captured node can compromise other nodes keys.

In [16], a scheme called efficient pairwise key establishment and management (EPKEM) is proposed. In this scheme, each node stores randomly a row and column from a key matrix, and any two nodes create a distinct pairwise key by combining their common keys and node identities. If a node is compromised, the communication between non-compromised nodes remains secure. However, this scheme has high communication overhead in large scale networks, needs large key storage, and consumes energy when adding nodes.

A scheme for large-scale hierarchical WSNs is presented in [17]. It uses polynomial key calculations to create a distinct pairwise key between any two nodes. This approach assumes three phases for key management: key pre-distribution, inter-cluster pairwise key establishment, and intra-cluster pairwise key establishment. The scheme shows good security mechanism against node capture attacks, but the establishment of one pairwise key for each node needs the cluster head to communicate with other cluster heads to authenticate node connectivity.

In [18], a rekey-boosted security protocol in hierarchical WSNs is proposed. In this approach, clusters are formed based on LEACH, and random key pre-distribution is used to establish node-to-node security and authentication. A cluster key is used to secure the cluster head-to-node communication, and a key created by the cluster head is used to protect the cluster head-to-base station communication. In this scheme, the cluster head carries much overhead because it is used for both routing and security.

In [19], the proposed scheme stores a master key and random vector in each node, and any two nodes create a pairwise key by combining their random vector with the stored master key. In addition, each node stores a cluster key to communicate with the cluster head. The cluster key is derived from the preloaded master key and identification number of the cluster head. Hence, an enemy that knows the master key and the identification number of the cluster head can extract the cluster key and easily attack the cluster.

A protocol for securing the paths among the nodes in WSNs is proposed in [20]. In this protocol, the network area is partitioned into a virtual grid with identical cells. It is assumed that each node stores four keys: individual key to communicate with the base station, cell key to communicate with nodes inside the cell, eight pairwise keys to communicate with other cells, and broadcast keys. By capturing any of the cell nodes, the adversary can extract the key and then easily attack all the nodes inside the cell.

3. System Architecture

The system is organized in a multi-tier architecture according to the recourses and functionality. The resources variability divides the system into two-tier architecture. One tier represents the base station (BS) and another tier represents the deployed sensor nodes. The BS is assumed to have no computational, storage and communication limitations and is located far from the sensor field. The sensor nodes are assumed to be resource-constrained in energy, processing, and storage. The sensor nodes are homogenous, have the same resources, and start with the same level of energy. The sensors nodes are capable of control their power to vary their functionality.

From the functionality viewpoint, the system is divided into four-tier architecture as shown in **Figure 1**. The first tier represents the BS that will be considered as a powerful data processing unit that performs heavily operations, a storage center that collects data, and a key distribution center before deployment. The BS is assumed to be trusted and temper resistant. The second tier represents the *CH* that will be considered as a collector for sensed data from other members in the cluster, an aggregator for the collected data, and a sender for the fused data to the BS in a single-hop path, as depicted in **Figure 2**. The third tier represents the sensor nodes that sense data and report the target field states to the *CH* as depicted in **Figure 2**. The fourth tier, the lower layer of our proposed stack model, represents the contribution of what we target in this research that is the clustering security management layer. This layer appears dynamically in each cluster by targeting one of the sensor nodes other than the *CH*s that is the CSM as depicted in **Figure 2**. The CSM will manage the cluster security because it works as a key distribution center and as a guard for cluster sensor nodes against an adversary. The CSM periodically constructs a key and distributes it to its cluster members and to the *CH*.

4. System Model and Analysis

The C3SM scheme consists of two parts: The first part deals with key distribution and managing methodologies while the second one deals with network monitoring and resilience against the node capture attack and its implications.

4.1. Key Distribution and Managing Model

Before deploying the nodes in the target field, each sensor node will be assigned two types of key. One key to

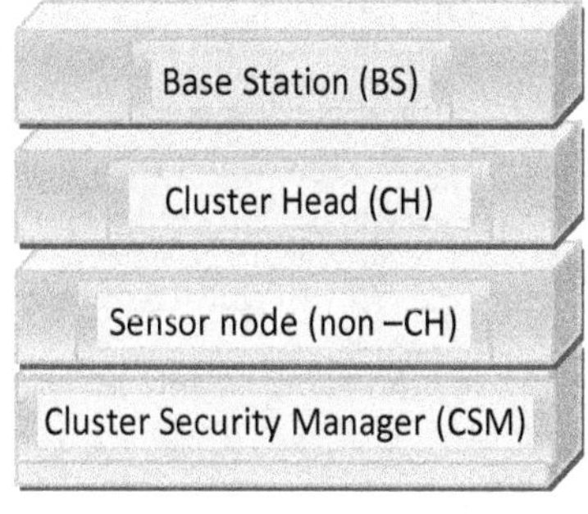

Figure 1. Four-tier clustering security model for WSNs.

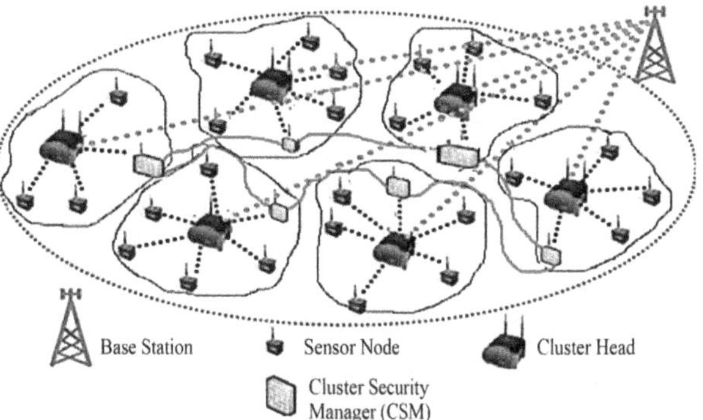

Figure 2. A clustering security architecture for WSNs.

encrypt and authenticate aggregated sensing data from a *CH* to the BS. And the other one used for a period of time after the deployment to encrypt and authenticate exchanged data between the *CH* and its sensor node members. After the deployment of sensor nodes and formation of clusters, each cluster will candidate one node to become a CSM that will protect the cluster against an adversary attacks, and distribute (re-keying) keys for the nodes in the cluster including the *CH*s. This procedure will constitute a distributed cluster among all clusters in the network with cluster members called CSMs. The key management scheme consists of two phases: key setup phase and path key establishment phase.

4.1.1. Key Setup Phase

When the nodes are deployed, each node is preloaded with an initial shared key (K_p) which assumed to be a large number symmetric key assigned for all nodes in the network. The preloaded key can be used by any sensor node to generate its master key as a function of the node *ID*. An authenticator MAC function (C-function) is used to generate the keys. For example, node *i* uses K_p and its *ID* to generate its master key (K_i) as follows:

$$K_i = C\left(K_p, ID_i\right) \tag{1}$$

The symmetric key K_p is just used after the sensor nodes deployment for a short period of time between the *CH* and cluster members to create a master key. This key is changed periodically by the CSM, thus, any attack to any node in the cluster does not affect its security.

After formation of clusters, the *CH* will broadcast its *ID* (ID_{CH}) and an advertisement message (Adv) encrypted by the preloaded key K_p to the cluster members. It is assumed that every node can know the Adv message.

$$CH \rightarrow N: \quad ID_{CH} \| C\left(K_p, \text{Adv} \| ID_{CH}\right) \tag{2}$$

After the above formatted message is broadcasted, each authorized sensor node receives the message and performs the same function, $C\left(K_p, \text{Adv} \| ID_{CH}\right)$, as the *CH* and compares with the received MAC, as depicted in **Figure 3**. Then, each member of the cluster will respond with its *ID* (ID_N), and a message contains a join signal (Ack), the *CH*'s Adv and the node *ID* (ID_N), encrypted by its preloaded key K_p, as shown in **Figure 4**.

$$N \rightarrow CH: \quad ID_N \| C\left(K_p, \text{Adv} \| ID_N \| \text{Ack}\right) \tag{3}$$

When the *CH* receives a reply from its cluster members, all of them can generate a secure master key as shown by the following equations:

$$K_{CH} = C\left(K_p, ID_{CH}\right) \tag{4}$$

$$K_N = C\left(K_p, ID_N\right) \tag{5}$$

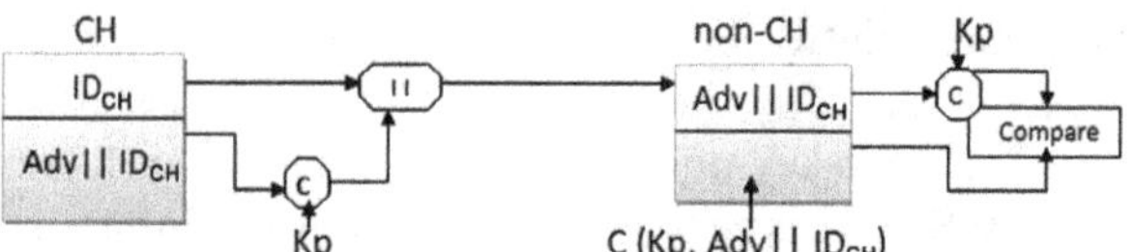

Figure 3. *CH*-to-node message authentication.

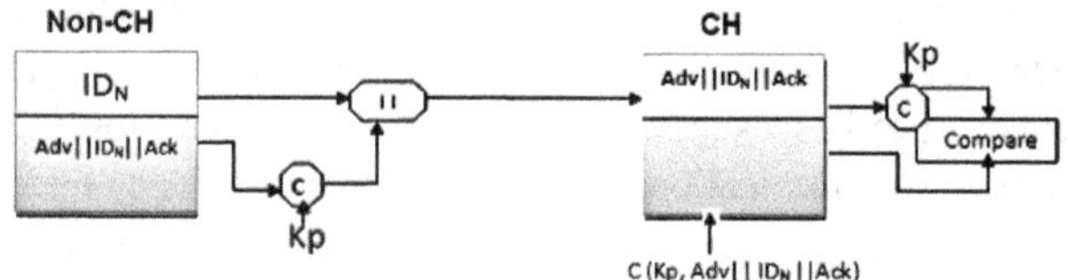

Figure 4. Node-to-*CH* message authentication.

Equation (4) represents the master key of the *CH*, and Equation (5) represents the master key of any member node *N*. After each node in the cluster generates its master key, the cluster will translate into next phase, which is called the path key establishment.

4.1.2. Path Key Establishment Phase

In this phase the pairwise key K_{CH-N} will be established between the *CH* and each cluster member node *N*. The pairwise key maintains a unique key for a path between the *CH* and each node in the cluster. Hence, it provides a sufficient security against node capture attacks since any compromised node will not affect the secure communication among non-compromised nodes. Moreover, this approach does not require a large storage for each node to store the whole pairwise keys in the network because the *CH* node just stores the pairwise keys of its cluster members. The pairwise key is derived as follows:

$$K_{CH-N} = C\left(K_N, ID_{CH}\right) \tag{6}$$

This technique can alleviate the tradeoff between the pairwise key supported security and the key storage overhead.

4.1.3. C-Function

The C-function is a cryptographic checksum function that is usually called message authentication code or MAC. However, the domain of C-function consists of a message of some arbitrary length, whereas the range consists of all possible MACs and all possible keys [21]. There are three types of MACs in our proposed system, as shown in Equations (4)-(6). The left hand side of each equation represents the generated fixed length authenticator that can be exploited to perform the following functionalities: authentication to assure that received messages are from alleged nodes, confidentiality to protect the traffic as long as the generated authenticator used as a unique pairwise key between the *CH* and its cluster members, and resiliency against node capturing because the key for each path is unique and is managed periodically by the CSM. On the other hand, the right hand side of the equation represents the variable length message which is the ID of the node and either the secret shared key between all nodes in the cluster such as K_p or the unique key between the *CH* and its cluster members such as K_N.

4.2. Clustering Security Management

After completing the formation phase for each cluster in the network, the role of security is triggered in order to protect the network against malicious attacks. The security of the network is managed by distributed nodes throughout the network, forming a security cluster.

The security cluster is a distributed cluster through all the data clusters in the network, as shown in **Figure 2**. In the safe mode, the construction of the cluster is assumed to take place at the beginning of the second half of the current data cluster cycle and remain to the ending of the first half of the next data cluster cycle.

The *CH* in each data cluster can candidate one of its cluster members to be a CSM which carries out three tasks. First, the first CSM creates a schedule in which order the cluster member nodes are elected as CSM and repeats the same process after the member nodes in the cluster are already pass the turn. The CSM checks its energy and if it is less than a threshold, the CSM will broadcast a release message to its cluster nodes. The node in schedule will take the turn and become a CSM. By this property the CSM guarantees the fairness in energy consumption among the cluster nodes. Second, the CSM can work as a key distribution center to construct and distribute periodically a shared master key for each node inside the cluster and also to the *CH* in order to re-keying them. By the master key, all the nodes in the cluster can use this key as a secrete key for establishing a new pairwise key (re-keying) between the *CH* and each sensor node in the cluster. Third, the CSM carries out monitoring and controlling the cluster member nodes against any attack. The CSM will exchange periodic messages with the cluster member nodes, and if one of the nodes does not reply, the CSM assumes an adversary captures the node, and then it will change all the keys in the cluster. In case that any CSM are captured, the nodes can tell through the disappearance of the control message sent by the captured CSM, and consequently the turn for the next appointed CSM arises to work for a period of time equals to the time of the data cluster. **Figure 5** summarizes the C3SM algorithm.

4.3. Malicious Attack and Threat Model

The malicious attacks can be divided into passive and active modes. In the passive mode, the enemy listens to the communication among the nodes to seize private data, while in the active mode it captures nodes in the network. When a node is compromised, the stored secret keys or information are revealed and, hence, false messages can be injected or the transmitted messages can be modified or dropped.

Next, we analyze the system security under node capture attacks, considering three types of sensor nodes: a cluster member, the *CH*, and the CSM.

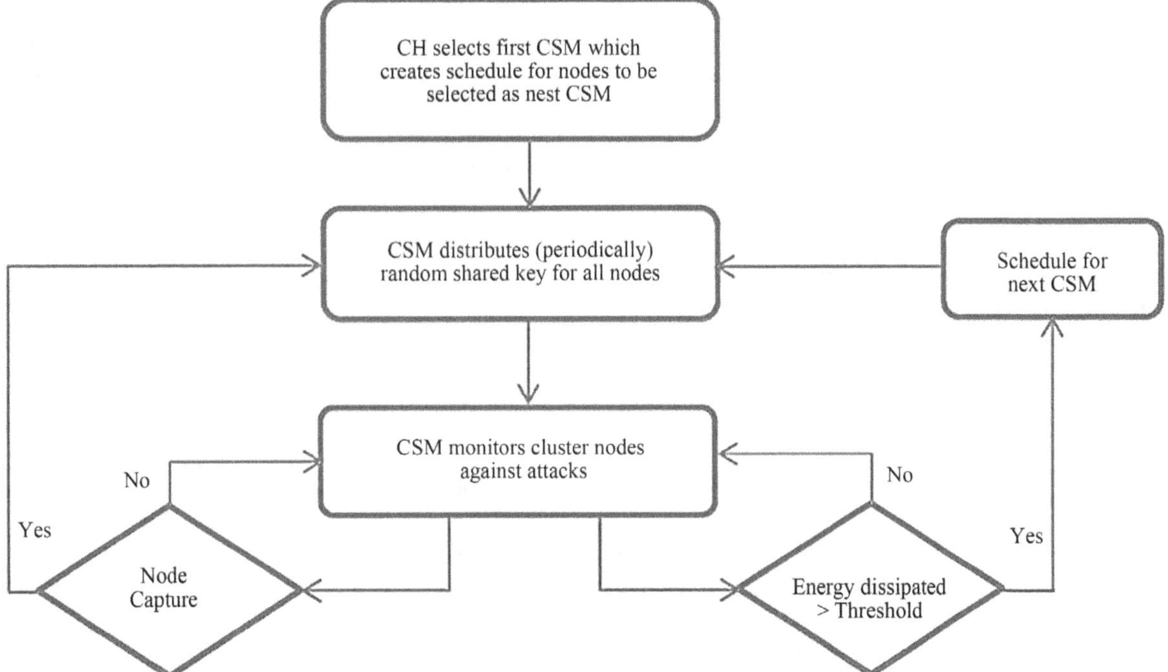

Figure 5. C3SM algorithm.

4.3.1. Sensor Node Capture Attack

In our scheme, after nodes deployment and cluster formations, in a short period of time, each *CH* will establish a unique pairwise key (K_{CH-N}) for each link with a cluster member node. In addition, after the CSM distributes a shared secrete key for the nodes in each cluster, the *CH* can also establish a unique pairwise key (K_{CH-N}) for each link with a cluster member node, and so forth. Thus, if adversaries deploy their own malicious nodes, these malicious nodes cannot be connected to the cluster because the communication with the *CH* requests from the node to know its master key (K_N) which is a cryptographic checksum or MAC from the node ID and the shared key K_p as shown in Equation (5). In case that a sensor node is physically captured, the adversary can read the contents of the node memory and discover its pairwise key with the *CH*, however it cannot compromise other non-captured nodes because the pairwise key is unique for each pair of two communicating parties. On the other hand, the CSM will lose the communication with the captured node, and distributes a new master key for the attacked cluster.

4.3.2. Cluster Head Capture Attack

In our scheme, the *CH* stores all the pairwise keys of the member nodes in the cluster. The CSM monitors the nodes in the cluster and exchanges periodic control messages with them. So, if the *CH* is captured, the CSM will detect the capture and broadcast messages to all the nodes in the cluster to set up a new round, and candidate a new *CH*. The CSM also distributes a new shared key for all the nodes in the cluster. Then, the new *CH* will use the shared key to establish a unique pairwise key with each node in the cluster. So, the adversary cannot compromise any node in the cluster because all the cluster node keys are changed and the communication is also changed to a new *CH*.

4.3.3. CSM Capture Attack

In our scheme, each elected CSM in a cluster can create a schedule to determine when each node in the cluster is elected as a CSM. In case that the CSM is captured, all nodes in the cluster lose communication with the CSM. After a short period of time the node in responsible in the schedule will take the turn to become a CSM.

5. Performance Evaluation

Security algorithms for WSNs include a tradeoff between the security level and resources consumption. In this section, we evaluate by simulation the performance of our proposed scheme, and compare it with current schemes in [15,16]. The simulation was performed by a selfdeveloped simulator using the simulation settings as follows. A deployment region of 100 × 100 m^2 is considered. The frequency of key refreshment is 5 time units, and the frequency of control messages is 1 time unit. The control message size is 50 bytes.

5.1. Communication and Computation Overhead

The communication per bit in WSNs is more costly than computation [22]. In C3SM, communication is performed inside a cluster, which means there is no longer transmission. In addition, the computational operations of key management are simple and performed locally (inside the cluster). A network of 10 clusters with 12 nodes per cluster was used. The Friis free-space model was used to estimate the communication energy consumption [23]. **Figures 6** and **7** show the energy consumed by the CSM, *CH*, and data sensor node (non-*CH*) of a randomly chosen cluster, for performing key management operations: key setup, re-keying and nodes monitoring. **Figure 6** shows the accumulated dissipated energy after completing 100 rounds, while **Figure 7** shows the dissipated energy during one round. As shown in both figures, the CSM consumes more energy compared to *CH* and non-*CH* nodes because it performs monitoring and re-keying tasks frequently while the *CH* only performs key setup and authentication with its cluster nodes.

Figures 8 and **9** show the consumed energy for each phase of key management: Setup, re-keying, and monitoring which are performed at randomly chosen cluster. **Figure 8** shows the accumulated dissipated energy during each phase at a random cluster after completing 100 rounds, while **Figure 9** shows the energy dissipated for each phase during one round. As shown in both figures, the monitoring task consumes approximately four times energy compared to re-keying task because in the monitoring task the CSM exchanges periodic messages with the cluster nodes in order to protect the network against node capture attack. On the other hand, the re-keying task consumes energy only when the CSM discovers an attack or its dissipated energy reaches a threshold. The energy consumed by the setup phase is mostly done when the *CH* performs authentication with its cluster nodes.

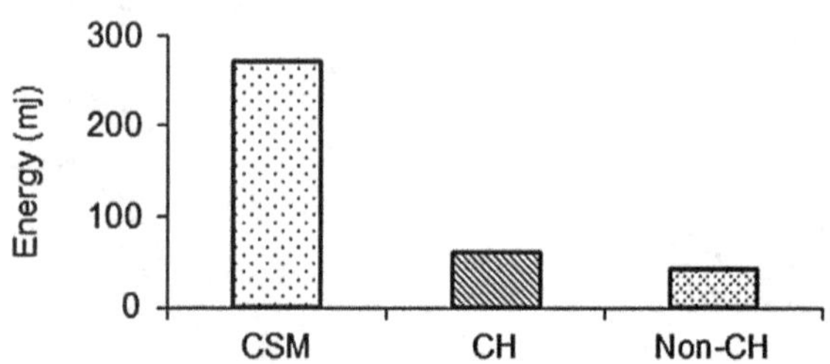

Figure 6. Consumed energy by cluster nodes of a randomly chosen cluster.

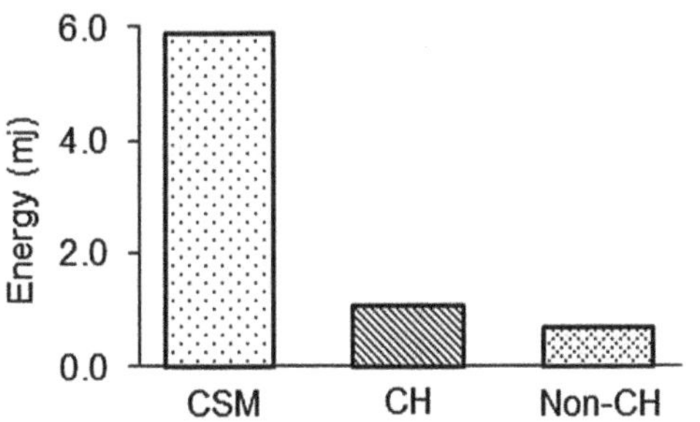

Figure 7. Consumed energy by cluster nodes of a random cluster during one round.

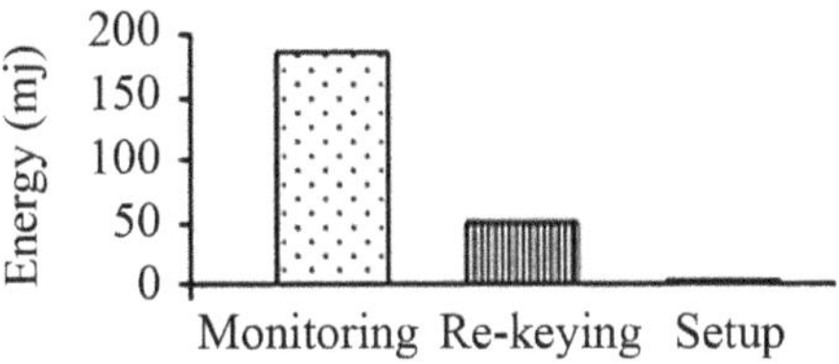

Figure 8. Consumed energy for key management phases at a randomly chosen cluster.

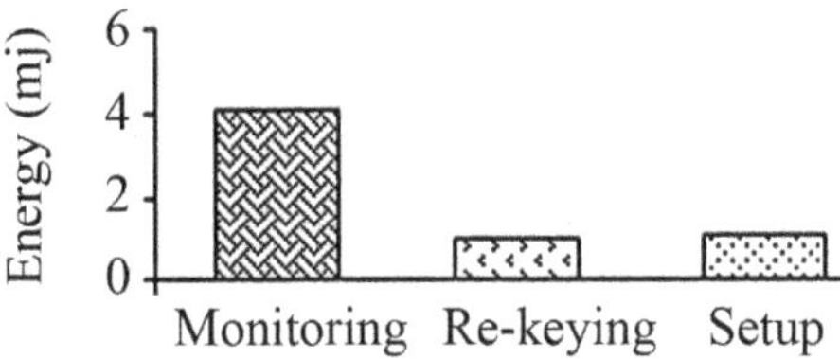

Figure 9. Consumed energy for key management phases at a random cluster during one round.

5.2. Resiliency to Node Capture

Because the resources of a sensor node are very limited, complexity of computations or long term transmission affects the lifetime of the network. Many approaches try to solve the problem of node capture attack. However, most of them still suffer from overhead or compromising nodes attack. In the random key pre-distribution scheme in [15], the same keys are used by different nodes and, hence, if a node is captured, the secure communication among other nodes is compromised. In EPKEM [16] and our proposed C3SM, pairwise keys are stored in every node and, hence, the resilience against node capture is improved. C3SM prevents key compromise for non-compromised nodes, even if many of the sensor nodes are captured. **Figure 10** shows the network resilience against node capture attacks for our C3SM scheme in addition to the random key pre-distribution scheme in [15] and the EPKEM scheme in [16]. It is shown that in the random key pre-distribution scheme, the fraction of compromised keys in non-captured nodes increases as the number of captured nodes increases, while in EP-KEM and C3SM it remains at low fraction regardless how many nodes are captured. In C3SM, each sensor node receives periodically a shared key from the CSM, and then the *CH* uses this key to establish a pairwise key with each node in the cluster. Pairwise keys are different for each path and cannot easily be derived because the MAC used is many-to-one function. Namely, there are many keys to produce the correct MAC; consequently the opponent has no way to know the correct key. Furthermore, keys are refreshed periodically.

5.3. Key Storage Overhead

In random key distribution, to achieve the required network connectivity, each sensor node is required to store a certain number of keys in its memory. **Figure 11** shows the number of keys stored in each node versus the network size for the three schemes: C3SM, EPKEM, and the random key pre-distribution scheme. It is shown that the number of keys per node increases linearly in the random key pre-distribution scheme, and increases sub-linearly in

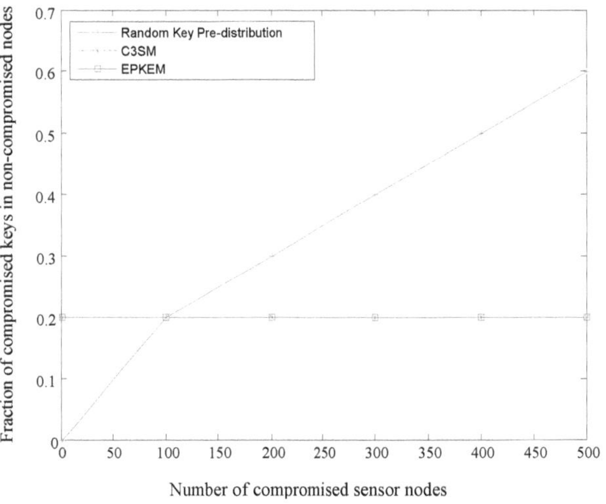

Figure 10. Network resilience against node capture attacks.

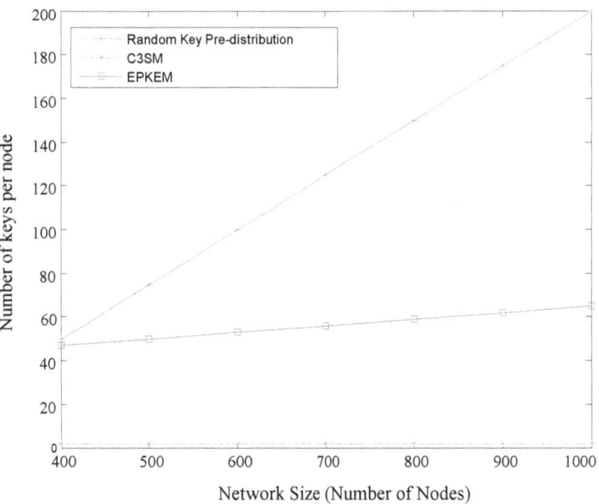

Figure 11. Key storage overhead versus network size.

EPKEM. On the other hand, C3SM has the lowest key storage overhead. In C3SM, each node only needs to store a pairwise key with the *CH* and a key with the BS in its memory no matter how many nodes are in the network.

6. Conclusions

In this work, we propose a cluster-based security protocol for WSNs, called Cryptographic Checksum Clustering Security Management (C3SM). Our protocol uses cryptographic checksum to authenticate communication among nodes. In C3SM, each node only stores two keys despite the network size, which reduces the key storage overhead especially in large scale networks.

To enhance confidentiality between the cluster nodes and the cluster head, we use a local, random, periodic and unique pairwise key for each path between the cluster head and the sensor node. These key properties make the network security stronger while achieving high connectivity with low memory cost and low energy consumption. Compared to existing schemes, C3SM achieves better network resilience against node capture attacks with lower key storage overhead.

7. Acknowledgements

The authors would like to thank Jordan University of Science and Technology, and the Scientific Research Support Fund at the Ministry of High Education in Jordan for supporting this research.

REFERENCES

[1] R. L. Rivest, A. Shamir and L. M. Adleman, "A Method for Obtaining Digital Signatures and Public-Key Cryptosystems," *Communications of the ACM*, Vol. 21, No. 2, 1978, pp. 120-126.

[2] W. Diffie and M. E. Hellman, "New Directions in Cryptography," *IEEE Transactions on Information Theory*, Vol. 22, No. 6, 1976, pp. 644-654.

[3] Y. Jararweh, L. Tawalbeh, H. Tawalbeh and A. Moh'd, "Hardware Performance Evaluation of SHA-3 Candidate Algorithms," *Journal of Information Security*, Vol. 3, No. 2, 2012, pp. 69-76.

[4] M. A. Simplício Jr., P. S. Barreto, C. B. Margi and T. C. Carvalho, "A Survey on Key Management Mechanisms for Distributed Wireless Sensor Networks," *Computer Networks*, Vol. 54, No. 15, 2010, pp. 2591-2612.

[5] B. Lai, S. Kim and I. Verbauwhede, "Scalable Session Key Construction Protocol for Wireless Sensor Networks," *IEEE Workshop on Large Scale Real-Time and Embedded Systems* (*LARTES*), Austin, December 2002, p. 6.

[6] Y. Zeng, B. Zhao, J. Su, X. Yan and Z. Shao, "A Loop-Based Key Management Scheme for Wireless Sensor Networks," *Proceedings of the* 2007 *Conference on Emerging Direction in Embedded and Ubiquitous Computing* (*EUC*'07), Taipei, 17-20 December 2007, pp. 103-114.

[7] B. Dutertre, S. Cheung and J. Levy, "Lightweight Key Management in Wireless Sensor Networks by Leveraging Initial Trust," Technical Report, System Design Laboratory, Menlo Park, 2004.

[8] R. Blom, "An Optimal Class of Symmetric Key Generation Systems," *Proceedings of the Eurocrypt* 84 *Workshop on Advances in Cryptology*, Paris, 9-11 April 1984, pp. 335-338.

[9] H. Chien, R.-C. Chen and A. Shen, "Efficient Key Pre-Distribution for Sensor Nodes with Strong Connectivity and Low Storage Space," *Proceedings of the* 22*nd International Conference on Advanced Information Networking and Applications* (*AINA*'08), Okinawa, 25-28 March 2008, pp. 327-333.

[10] W. Du, J. Deng, Y. Han, P. Varshney, J. Katz and A. Khalili, "A Pairwise Key Pre-Distribution Scheme for Wireless Sensor Networks," *ACM Transactions on Information and System Security*, Vol. 8, No. 2, 2005, pp. 228-258.

[11] C. Blundo, A. Santis, A. Herzberg, S. Kutten, U. Vaccaro and M. Yung, "Perfectly-Secure Key Distribution for Dynamic Conferences," *Proceedings of the* 12*th Annual International Cryptology Conference on Advances in Cryptology* (*CRYPTO*'92), Santa Barbara, 16-20 August 1992, pp. 471-486.

[12] H. Chan and A. Perrig, "PIKE: Peer Intermediaries for Key Establishment in Sensor Networks," *Proceedings of the* 24*th Annual Joint Conference of the IEEE Computer and Communications Societies* (*INFOCOM*'05), Miami, 13-17 March 2005, pp. 524-535.

[13] D. Liu and P. Ning, "Establishing Pairwise Keys in Distributed Sensor Networks," *Proceedings of the* 10*th ACM Conference on Computer and Communications Security* (*CCS*'03), Washington DC, 27-31 October 2003, pp. 52-61.

[14] D. Liu, P. Ning and R. Li, "Establishing Pairwise Keys in Distributed Sensor Networks," *ACM Transactions on Information and System Security*, Vol. 8, No. 1, 2005, pp. 41-77.

[15] L. Eschenauer and V. D. Gligor, "A Key-Management Scheme for Distributed Sensor Networks," *Proceedings of the 9th ACM Conference on Computer and Communications Security*, Washington DC, 17-21 November 2002, pp. 41-47.

[16] Y. Cheng and D. P. Agrawal, "Efficient Pairwise Key Establishment and Management in Static Wireless Sensor Networks," *Proceedings of the* 2*nd IEEE International Conference on Mobile Ad Hoc and Sensor Systems*, Washington DC, 7-10 November 2005, p. 7.

[17] Y. Cheng and D. Agrawal, "An Improved Key Distribution Mechanism for Large-Scale Hierarchical Wireless Sensor Networks," *Ad Hoc Networks*, Vol. 5, No. 1, 2007, pp. 35-48.

[18] Y.-Y. Zhang, W.-C. Yang, K.-B. Kim, M.-Y. Cui and M.-S. Park, "A Rekey-Boosted Security Protocol in Hierarchical Wireless Sensor Network," *Proceedings of the 2nd International Conference on Multimedia and Ubiquitous Engineering*, Seoul, 24-26 April 2008, pp. 57-61.

[19] D. P. S. E. Christina and R. J. Chitra, "Energy Efficient Secure Routing in Wireless Sensor Networks," *Proceedings of* 2011 *International Conference on Emerging Trends in Electrical and Computer Technology* (*ICETECT*), Tamil Nadu, 23-24 March 2011, pp. 982-986.

[20] S. G. Yoo, S. Kang and J. Kim, "SERA: A Secure Energy and Reliability Aware Data Gathering for Sensor Networks," *Proceedings of* 2010 *International Conference on Information Science and Applications* (*ICISA*), Seoul, 21-23 April 2010, pp. 1-11.

[21] W. Stallings, "Cryptography and Network Security: Prin ciples and Practice," 5th Edition, Pearson-Prentice Hall, Upper Saddle River, 2011.

[22] J. Hill, R. Szewczyk, A. Woo, S. Hollar, D. E. Culler and K. S. J. Pister, "System Architecture Directions for Networked Sensors," *Proceedings of the 9th International Conference on Architectural Support for Programming Languages and Operating Systems*, Cambridge, 12-15 November 2000, pp. 93-104.

[23] W. R. Heinzelman, A. Chandrakasan and H. Balakrishnan, "An Application-Specific Protocol Architecture for Wireless Microsensor Networks," *IEEE Transactions on Wireless Communications*, Vol. 1, No. 4, 2002, pp. 660-670.

23

Two Approaches on Implementation of CBR and CRM Technologies to the Spam Filtering Problem

Rasim Alguliyev, Saadat Nazirova
Institute of Information Technology, Azerbaijan National Academy of Sciences, Baku, Azerbaijan

ABSTRACT

Recently the number of undesirable messages coming to e-mail has strongly increased. As spam has changeable character the anti-spam systems should be trainable and dynamical. The machine learning technology is successfully applied in a filtration of e-mail from undesirable messages for a long time. In this paper it is offered to apply Case Based Reasoning technology to a spam filtering problem. The possibility of continuous updating of spam templates base on the bases of which new coming spam messages are compared, will raise efficiency of a filtration. Changing a combination of conditions it is possible to construct flexible filtration system adapted for different users or corporations. Also in this paper it is considered the second approach as implementation of CRM technology to spam filtration which is not applied to this area yet.

Keywords: E-Mail Spam; Unsolicited Bulk Message; Theory of Precedent; CBR; CRM

1. Introduction

The development of Internet has generated many problems the one of which is spam. Spam is undesirable message appearing in e-mail, search engines, chats, forums, IM (instant messaging). The most known and bothered kind of spam is email spam, as e-mail an effective, fast and cheap kind of communication. Almost each computer user has e-mail, and faces spam problem.

For 2010 year Symantec reports that the total amount of spam in mail traffic was 89.1%, and according to Kaspersky Lab annual report the total amount of spam in mail traffic was 90.8% [1,2]. Such a quantity for spam does electronic communication useless, and sometimes not secured. As spam grows very fast, spammers begin to send harmful software, Trojans, malicious content within it. According Symantec annual report for 2010 there has been registered more than 339,600 various viruses, which are hundreds times more than for 2009 [1]. As seen from above diagram (**Figure 1**) the numbers of registered malicious attacks increased in the summer in 2010, so that they were found in approximately 6% of all emails. According to Ferris Research estimations the worldwide cost of spam email in 2009 was roughly 130 billion dollars [3]. All these facts once again urge us to struggle with spam with most effective new methods. As spam changes too quickly (the body, subject, sender's mail and IP addresses changes) and email filtration should be individual (the message noted as spam by one user for another one may be desirable) the effective anti-spam system should be trainable and personified.

2. Related Works

Every day computer users receive in their email boxes hundreds of spam messages from new email accounts. Frequently these messages are come with different subject, body automatically generated by robot software. It is almost impossible to filter them with such traditional methods as black-white lists. Applying artificial intelligence methods to the problem of filtering email accounts from unsolicited messages it is possible to raise efficiency of a filtration of spam. Artificial intelligence methods are [4]:

- Convection—machine learning methods based on a formalism and a statistical analysis;
- Computing—methods of iterative working out and the training based on the empirical data;
- Hybrid—methods using convection and computing methods in common.

One of convection methods is Case Based Reasoning (CBR). In this paper it is considered the possibility of CBR method application to spam filtration problem. CBR is a method of reasoning based on precedents. This is a computing model which uses previous events to understand and solve new problems. In some scientific literature CBR meets as "the theory of precedents". The construction of CBR systems begins in 1982 year from

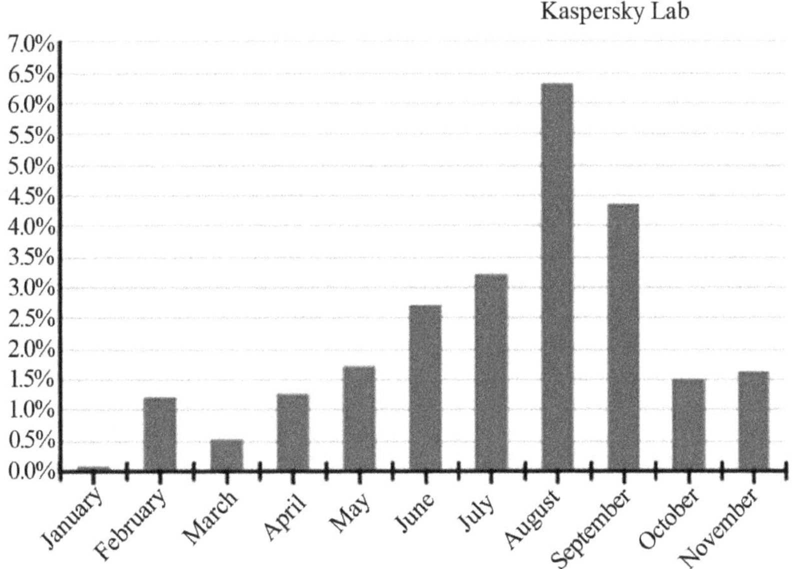

Figure 1. The percentage of email spam with malicious attachments in 2010, Kaspersky Lab [2].

Shank's arguments where the notion reminders coordinate the last events with current events to allow generalization and a prediction [5]. Further Kolodner has developed the first CBR system CYRUS expanding Shank's ideas. This CBR system is differing from expert systems. Expert systems store past experience as the generalized rules and objects, whereas CBR systems store past experience as a separate problem, solving episodes [6]. CBR systems try to solve new problem using events from earlier solved problems. So the main principele of such systems is that one can solve new problems remembering similar events of similar situations.

CBR methods are successfully applied in various areas as classification, diagnostics, forecasting, planning and designing. Independently on a problem for their solving by CBR methods, it is necessary to execute certain sequence of tasks (**Figure 2**).

The basic stages of CBR tasks cycle are considered in such sequence [7]:

1) Choice of the most similar cases of the cases saved up in base.

2) Use of the information and knowledge of this case (set of cases) for the solving new problem.

3) Revision and changes of the solution of the new problem.

4) Preservation of this experience for the solving future problems.

The application of CBR method to spam filtration problem is considered in papers [8-12]. According to these works the classifier based on CBR proves better, than Naive Bayes in spam filtering. Distributed CBR approach can unite in itself spam filtration based on content filtration and collaborative filtration.

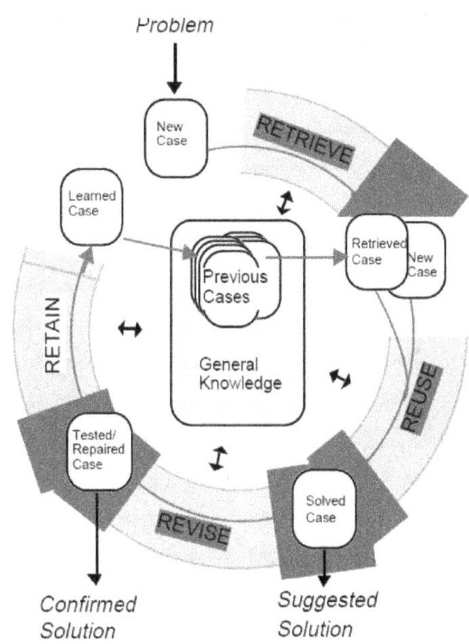

Figure 2. CBR cycle [6].

In work [13] there is described the anti-spam system ACABARASE developed on the basis of CBR which after certain training filters spam with less false-positive cases.

The spam filtration model SPAMHUNTING presented in works [14-18] also based on CBR, which applies the disjoint knowledge representation engine. This spam filter able to address the concept drift problem by combining a relevant term identification technique with an evolving sliding window strategy. The idea consists in to identify and remove the obsolete and irrelevant knowledge that has accumulated over to the passage of time.

Continuous updating technique used in SPAMHUNTING works at two various levels: 1) indexation of the knowledge base; 2) continuous search of its best representation.

Another one machine learning technology is Customer Relation Management (CRM). In spite of the fact that CRM theory has 20 year history, and the expression customer relationship management has been in use since the early 1990s, it did not applied to spam filtering problem yet. But there is great practice of implementation of CRM to different problems [19-25].

3. CBR and CRM Implementation Approaches

In this paper it is considered the centralized system of a filtration from unsolicited bulk messages, coordinating all Internet Service Providers (ISP) within country and functioning as collaborative spam filter involving e-mail users of this system and all ISP. This mechanism can be realized at ISP level continuously updating system database with new spam templates, white-black-grey lists. ISP can operatively delegate or delete the data from databases, or transfer them to Network Service Provider (NSP) which provides ISP with Internet traffic (**Figure 3**).

The offered system has the multilayered hierarchical structure consisting of three levels: state, corporate and personal. At each level of multilayered hierarchical system there are server nodes in which there exists database of spam templates. In these databases the spam templates coming from lower level nodes or from the ordinary nodes-user's of the same level are collected.

3.1. CBR

For above considered spam filtering problem we define the following cycle of tasks according to CBR theory. At the first step when the user of our multilayered hierarchical spam filtration system reports to the server about new coming spam message system indicates is as *a new case*.

This new case is compared to the previous cases which have been saved up in base of cases—database of spam templates, and the most similar gets out. Combining the chosen case with a new case we get a suggested solution. The combined case is called as *a solved case*.

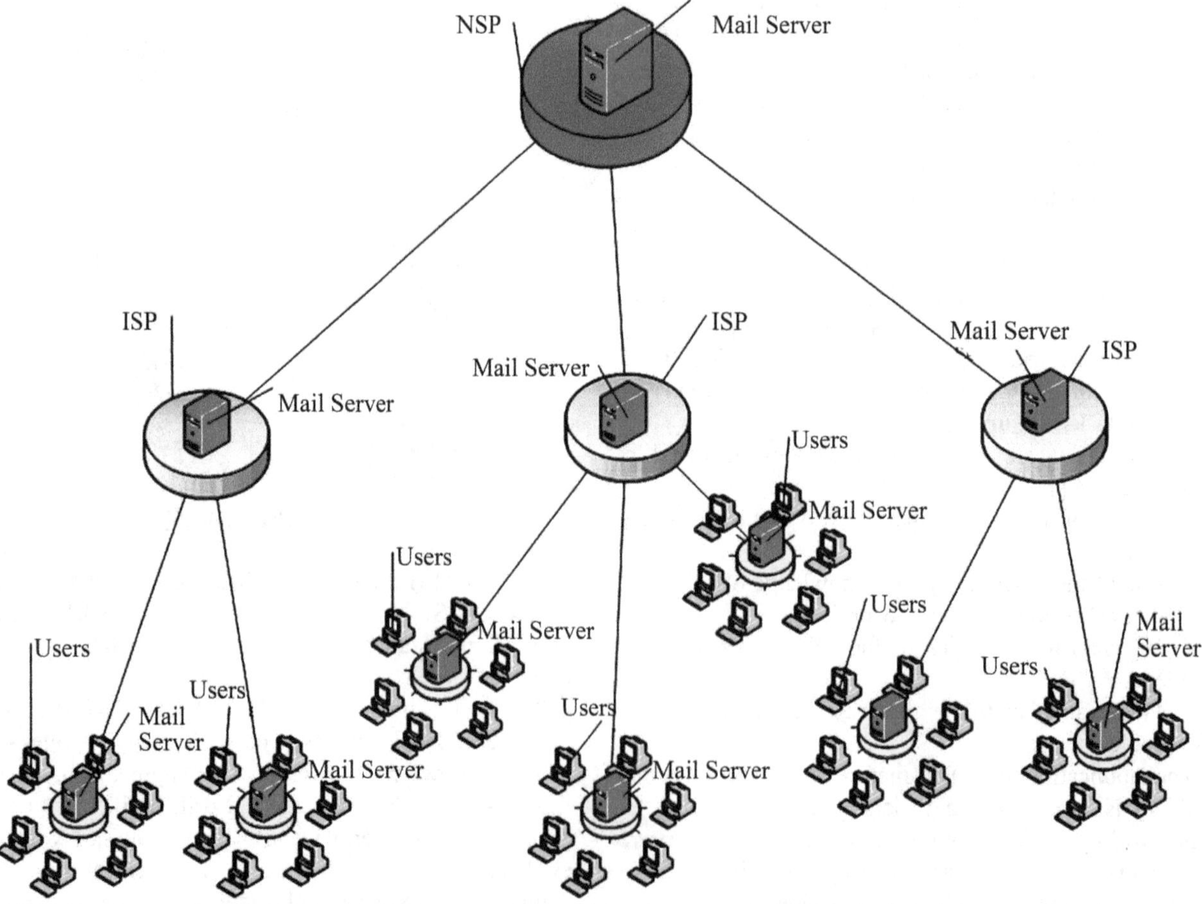

Figure 3. Architecture of multilayered hierarchical system of spam filtration.

Having reconsidered this solution, it is checked on success and applicability to the real world. The solution got at this step is confirmed solution and this case we call as *a tested case*.

In case of a failure the new more suitable case gets out. In a preservation stage the successful case with the corresponding solution registers in base for use in future and is called as *a learned case*.

There should be developed the mathematical methods for solving the tasks belonged to each step. For comparison and extraction of cases one can use the different methods described in works [26,27]. In order to compare new coming message with spam messages collected in database we define the following case parameters—set of characteristics of message:

1) Sender's e-mail address
2) Sender's IP address
3) Subject of message
4) Key words in message body
5) Key phrases in message body
6) Message body

Let's introduce some notations.

N is a number of layers of the offered multilayered system;

L_i is a number of server nodes on i th level, $i = \overline{0, N}$;

K_{l_i} is a number of nodes on i th level connected to the server node l_i, $i = \overline{0, N}$ $l_i = \overline{1, L_i}$.

Since the proposed system is assumed dynamic and trainable, and the database of spam templates gradually be updated with new templates, we introduce the parameter of time $t \in T$.

Assume we have n number case parameters, as $x_1, x_2, \cdots, x_n$. In this work $n = 6$.

$s^z_{k_{l_i}}(x_1, x_2, \cdots, x_n, t)$ is zth message coming to the node k_{l_i} as spam at a time t, with case parameters $x_1, x_2, \cdots, x_n$, where $z \in Z$, $t \in T$, $k_{l_i} = \overline{1, K_{l_i}}$. During filtering process each new message, coming to the user k_{l_i} is compared with the spam messages, previously delegated by the same user.

$U_{l_i}(t)$ is a set of spam messages delegated by user k_{l_i} to the server node l_i at a time t until delegation of z th spam message:

$$U_{l_i}(t) = \{s^1_{k_{l_i}}(x_1, x_2, \cdots, x_n, t), s^2_{k_{l_i}}(x_1, x_2, \cdots, x_n, t), \cdots, s^{z-1}_{k_{l_i}}(x_1, x_2, \cdots, x_n, t)\}$$

where $l_i = \overline{1, L_i}$, $i = \overline{0, N}$, $t \in T$, $k_{l_i} = \overline{1, K_{l_i}}$.

Spam filtration at each level is realized based on the anti-spam policy of that level. Anti-spam policy contains each user's files formed by user's official reports about spam in the received correspondence. On the basis of these official reports-cases spam filtration is realized [28].

The set of legal mails coming to the node l_i is defined by anti-spam policy $P_{l_1}(U_{l_i}(t))$ of the same node:

$$U^*_{l_i}(t) = P_{l_1}(U_{l_i}(t))$$

where $i = \overline{0, N}$, $l_i = \overline{1, L_i}$, $t \in T$.

Depending on anti-spam policy of each node, comparison can be made by one criterion or by combination of different parameters.

The number of comparisons of two spam messages is

$$N_2 = C^1_n + C^2_n + \cdots + C^n_n = 2^n - 1$$

The number of comparisons of z spam messages is

$$N_z = \frac{z(z-1)}{2}(2^n - 1)$$

In the proposed system it is allowed possibility to withdraw back (restore) the message, previously marked as spam. In this case, the message $s^z_{k_{l_i}}(x_1, x_2, \cdots, x_n, t)$ delegated by the user k_{l_i} as spam at a time t is removed from the set of spam templates $U_{l_i}(t)$. Accordingly, the set of spam templates $U_{l_i}(t+1)$ and the anti-spam policy $P_{l_1}(U_{l_i}(t+1))$ for that level $i = \overline{0, N}$ are also changed. The dynamical algorithm of the system will restore the state of a dynamical system in a real time (during the process), using the input information about the system in current discrete time.

In the absence of spam templates no decision is taken for that user. This means that either the user has recently connected to the spam filtration system, or the user is tolerant of spam messages.

3.2. CRM

The expression CRM has a variety of meanings. One of them is that CRM is an information industry term for methodologies, software and usually Internet capabilities that help an enterprise manage customer relationships in an organized way [29].

In some papers there have been identified three types of CRM: operational, analytical and collaborative. There are different approaches to these three steps. According to one of them [30]:

- Analytical CRM is responsible for analyzing customers' behavior in terms of sales, marketing or any other service provided. It utilizes data warehouse to extract appropriate data regarding different customers;
- Operational CRM is responsible for automating business processes that are related to customers like marketing and sales etc.;
- Communication/Collaborative CRM as the name implies, is responsible for efficient collaboration/association with the customers through e-mails, fax, phone, SMS or face to face communication.

The graphical interpretation of above steps according

to Liu & Zhu [31] takes place in **Figure 4**.

Xu & Walton [32] name these steps as main principles of CRM and define them as following:

- Collect information;
- Efficiently usage of collected data;
- Automation of process.

In this paper we consider CRM theory as a management of relation between customers and their choices. By learning relevant information about the customers such as; names, habits, preferences and expectations one-on-one relation can be formed [33]. Learning this information can help to make right decision. Some times during spam filtration process the legal messages indicates as spam and user lost the important mail. Almost in best anti-spam solutions there takes place some percent of false positives. The advantage of using CRM approach is to decrease the number of false positives.

In case of spam filtering problem we consider customer as e-mail user k_{l_i} and choices as messages that indicated by user k_{l_i} as spam $s^z_{k_{l_i}}(x_1, x_2, \cdots, x_n, t)$. Our approach is to use the main idea of CRM theory, that using more information about customer—user, one can increase efficiency of spam filtering. The CRM database containing data, user-profile as preferences, interests, scientific direction, and etc is in the input of our filtration system (**Figure 5**). Processing this profile can automatically manage filtration. Depending on time this profile can be changed by user himself manually or can be organized through automatic analyses of information derived from mails and/or visited Web recourses.

According to the above presented main steps of any CRM system, we can define the following consequence of tasks describing the technology framework of our CRM based spam filtering system (**Figure 6**):

- First one is the construction of analytical CRM system which focuses on data mining tools to gather, analyzes and interprets huge amount of data belonged to users. This data can be derived from e-mail and visited web resources All information belonged to user as his preferences regarding e-mail (which content he like, and which one dislike) and his profile are key points in filtration of his e-mail.

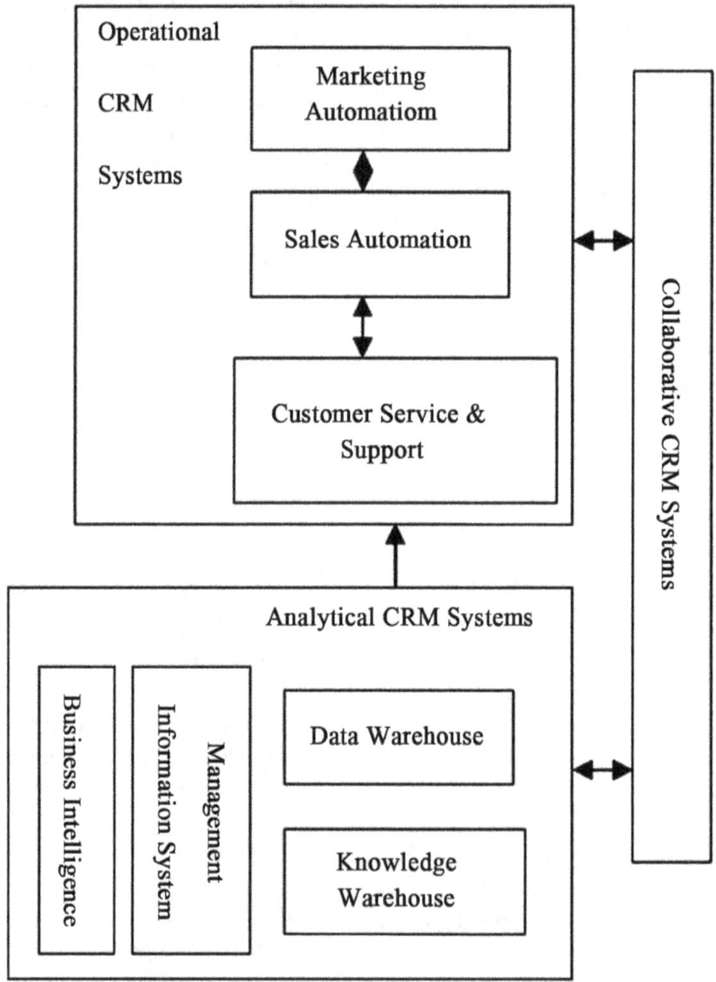

Figure 4. Technology framework of CRM [31].

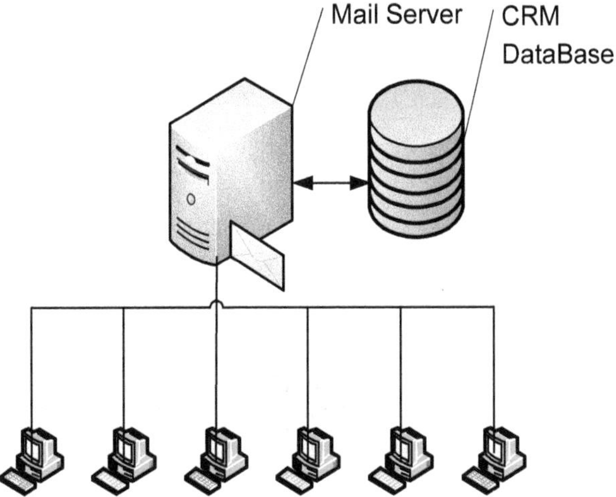

Figure 5. CRM based spam filtering.

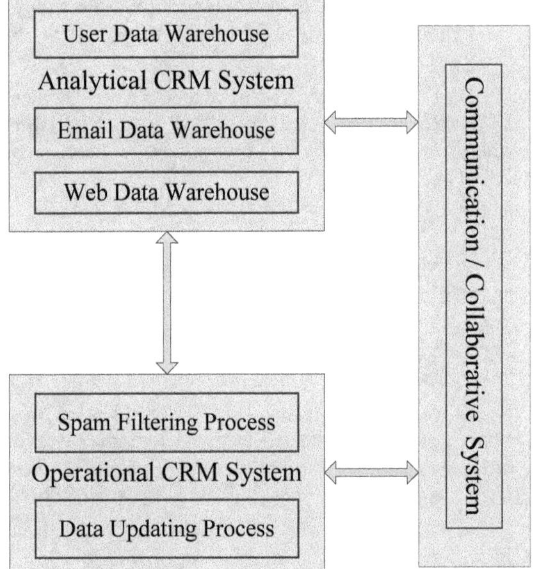

Figure 6. Technology Framework of CRM based Spam Filtering System.

- Second step is the construction of operational CRM system. After data collection it should be placed in right place—in CRM based spam filtering system database at the input of the system, also can be assessable to user himself in order to manage this data time by time.
- Third step should be the automated process of filtration. During this process the filtering system can recognize the new coming spam messages, comparing spamness signs of message with corresponding data from spam templates reported by user k_{l_i} and stored in database and also with information from profile.

The efficiency of spam filtration depends on used comparison method and the volume of collected data. So well-trained CRM based spam filtering system will show high efficiency with the less number of false positives.

4. Conclusion

In this work it is suggested conception of application of two well-known mathematical apparatus to spam filtering. One of them is CBR technology which is began to apply to spam filtering recently. Another one is CRM technology which is not applied to spam filtering problem yet. These are two machine learning concepts and could be effectively used in spam filtering. As spammers constantly change external signs of spam messages to skip spam filtering systems, there arises a need for adaptive, trainable filtering system. So development of server side personalized e-mail filtering systems that use the learning-based classification algorithms based on CBR and/or CRM technology is a very perspective direction.

5. Future Work

Future work will focused on providing methods and experiments to prove the effectiveness of implementation of CBR & CRM technologies onto spam filtration problem.

REFERENCES

[1] Symantec, "State of Spam and Phishing," *Annual Report*, 2010 http://www.symantec.com/about/news/release/article.jsp?prid=20101207_01

[2] Kaspersky Security Bulletin, "Spam Evolution 2010," 2010 http://www.securelist.com/en/analysis/204792163/Kaspersky_Security_Bulletin_Spam_Evolution_2010

[3] Ferris Research, "Cost of Spam is Flattening—Our 2009 Predictions," 2009. http://www.ferris.com/2009/01/28/cost-of-spam-is-flattening-our-2009-predictions/

[4] E. A. Razdobarina, "Historical Review of Works in Artificial Intelligence," 2009. http://www.smaut.com/main/public/AiHistoryScool.html

[5] R. Shank, "Dynamic Memory. A Theory of Learning in Computers and People," Cambridge University Press, New York, 1982.

[6] J. Kolodner, "Case-Based Reasoning," Magazin Kaufmann, San Mateo, 1993, p. 386.

[7] E. P. Aamodt, "Case-Based Reasoning: Foundational Issues, Methodological Variations, and System Approaches," *AI Communications*, Vol. 7, No. 1, 1994, pp. 39-59. http://citeseerx.ist.psu.edu/viewdoc/download?doi=10.1.1.15.9093&rep=rep1&type=pdf

[8] C. Padraig, N. Niamh, J. D. Sarah, *et al.*, "A Case-Based Approach to Spam Filtering that Can Track Concept Drift," *Proceedings of the ICCBR03 Workshop on Long-Lived CBR System*, Trondheim, June 2003.

http://citeseerx.ist.psu.edu/viewdoc/download?doi=10.1.1 14.3235&rep=rep1&type=pdf

[9] J. D. Sarah, C. Padraig, T. Alexey, *et al.*, "A Case-Based Technique for Tracking Concept Drift in Spam Filtering," *Knowledge Based Systems*, Vol. 18, No. 4-5, 2005, pp. 187-195.

[10] J. D. Sarah, C. Padraig and C. Lorcan, "An Assessment of Case-Based Reasoning for Spam Filtering," *Artificial Intelligence Review*, Vol. 24, No. 3-4, 2005, pp. 359-378.

[11] J. D. Sarah, C. Padraig, D. Dónal, *et al.*, "Generating Estimates of Classification Confidence for a Case-Based Spam Filter, Case-Based Reasoning Research and Development," *Lecture Notes in Computer Science*, Vol. 3620, 2005, pp. 177-190.

[12] J. D. Sarah and B. Derek, "Textual Case-Based Reasoning for Spam Filtering: A Comparison of Feature-Based and Feature-Free Approaches", *Artificial intelligence review*, Vol. 26, No. 1-2, 2005, pp.75-87

[13] C. Andres and M. Nunez, "ACABARASE: An Anti-Spam Case-Based Reasoning Systems," *Proceedings of 3rd International Conference on IEEE, ICONS* 08, New Delhi, 13-18 April 2008, pp. 230-234.

[14] J. R. Mendez, F. Fdez-Riverola, F. Dıaz, *et al.*, "Tracking Concept Drift at Feature Selection Stage in SPAM-HUNTING: An Anti-Spam Instance-Based Reasoning System," *Proceedings of the 8th European Conference on Case-Based Reasoning*, Fethiye, 4-7 September 2006, pp. 504-518.

[15] J. R. Mendez, C. Gonzalez, D. Glez-Pen, *et al.*, "Assessing Classification Accuracy in the Revision Stage of a CBR Spam Filtering System," *Proceedings of the 7th International Conference on Case-Based Reasoning System*, Belfast, 13-16 August 2007, pp. 374-288.

[16] F. Fdez-Riverola, E. L. Iglesias, F. Dıaz, *et al.*, "SPAM-HUNTING: An Instance-Based Reasoning System for Spam Labeling and Filtering," *Decision Support Systems*, Vol. 43, No. 3, 2007, pp. 722-736.

[17] F. Fdez-Riverola, E. L. Iglesias, F. Dıaz, *et al.*, "Applying Lazy Learning Algorithms to Tackle Concept Drift in Spam Filtering," *Expert Systems with Applications*, Vol. 33, No. 1, 2007, pp. 36-48.

[18] J. R. Mendez, D. Glez-Pena, F. Fdez-Riverola, *et al.*, "Managing Irrelevant Knowledge in CBR Models for Unsolicited E-Mail Classification," *Expert Systems with Applications*, Vol. 36, No. 2, 2009, pp. 1601-1614.

[19] W. Fang and S. Mao, "Analysis on the Application of CRM in Logistics Enterprises," *Proceedings of International Conference on E-Business and E-Government* (ICEE), Guangzhou, 7-9 May 2010, pp. 3087-3089.

[20] Y. Shen, S. L. Song and S. W. Li, "The Design and Implement of CRM Data Mining System for Medium-Small Enterprises Based on Weka," *Proceedings of International forum on Information Technology and Applications IFITA*'09, Vol. 2, 2009, pp. 596-599

[21] B. Liu, G. Zhao and Y. Su, "Research of University Employment Management System Based on CRM," *International Conference on Intelligent Computation Technology and Automation*, Vol. 2, 2010, pp. 1059-1064.

[22] L. Decai and L. Yue, "Research on Application of CRM in Fields of Network Marketing: Illustrated by the Case of Maibaobao Aveyond," *International Conference on Management Science and Electronic Commerce, Artificial Intelligence*, Zhengzhou, 8-10 August 2011, pp. 4713-4716.

[23] K. Xiong, "Study on Application of CRM in E-Government Based on Public Service," *Proceedings of International Conference on Electric Information and Control Engineering*, Wuhan, 15-17 April 2011, pp. 4511-4514.

[24] B. Liu, G. Zhao and Y. Su, "Employment Management System Based on CRM," *Proceeding of International Conference on Intelligent Computation Technology and Automation* (*ICICTA*), 11-12 May 2010, pp. 1059-1064.

[25] W. Olof, S. Christer and S. Hakan, "Trends, Topics and Under-Researched Areas in CRM Research," *International Journal of Public Information Systems*, Vol. 3, 2009, pp. 192-208. http://www.ijpis.net/issues/no3_2009/ijpis_no3_2009_p3.pdf

[26] R. M. Alguliev, R. M. Aliguliyev and S. A. Nazirova, "Classification of Textual E-Mail Spam Using Data Mining Techniques," *Applied Computational Intelligence and Soft Computing*, 2011. www.hindawi.com/journals/acisc/aip/416308.pdf

[27] S. A. Nazirova, "Mechanism of Classification of Text Spam Messages Collected in Spam Pattern Bases," *Proceedings of 3rd International Conference on Problems of Cybernetics and Informatics*, Vol. 2, 2010, pp. 206-209.

[28] R. M. Alguliev and S. A. Nazirova, "Mechanism of Forming and Realization of Anti-Spam Policy," *Telecommunications*, Vol. 12, 2009, pp. 38-43.

[29] B. Francis, "Customer Relationship Management: Concepts and Technologies," Elsevier Ltd., New York, 2009, p. 500.

[30] Basics of CRM, September 2006. http://www.Advancevoip.com/whitepapers/Basics%20of%20CRM.pdf

[31] C. N. Liu and X. W. Zhu, "A Study on CRM Technology Implementation and Application Practices," *Proceedings of International Conference on Computational Intelligence and Natural Computing*, June 2009, pp. 367-370.

[32] M. Xu and J. Walton, "Gaining Customer Knowledge through Analytical CRM Industrial Management & Data Systems," *Emerald, MCB Limited*, Vol. 105, No. 7, 2005, pp. 955-971.

[33] J. Berfenfeldt, "Customer Relationship Management," Master's Thesis, 2010, p. 104.

Unsupervised Multi-Level Non-Negative Matrix Factorization Model: Binary Data Case

Qingquan Sun[1], Peng Wu[2], Yeqing Wu[1], Mengcheng Guo[1], Jiang Lu[1]
[1]Department of Electrical and Computer Engineering, The University of Alabama, Tuscaloosa, USA
[2]School of Information Engineering, Wuhan University of Technology, Wuhan, China

ABSTRACT

Rank determination issue is one of the most significant issues in non-negative matrix factorization (NMF) research. However, rank determination problem has not received so much emphasis as sparseness regularization problem. Usually, the rank of base matrix needs to be assumed. In this paper, we propose an unsupervised multi-level non-negative matrix factorization model to extract the hidden data structure and seek the rank of base matrix. From machine learning point of view, the learning result depends on its prior knowledge. In our unsupervised multi-level model, we construct a three-level data structure for non-negative matrix factorization algorithm. Such a construction could apply more prior knowledge to the algorithm and obtain a better approximation of real data structure. The final bases selection is achieved through L_2-norm optimization. We implement our experiment via binary datasets. The results demonstrate that our approach is able to retrieve the hidden structure of data, thus determine the correct rank of base matrix.

Keywords: Non-Negative Matrix Factorization; Bayesian Model; Rank Determination; Probabilistic Model

1. Introduction

Non-negative matrix factorization (NMF) was proposed by Lee and Seung [1] in 1999. NMF has become a widely used technique over the past decade in machine learning and data mining fields. The most significant properties of NMF are non-negative, intuitive and part based representative. The specific applications of NMF algorithm include image recognition [2], audio and acoustic signal processing [3], semantic analysis and content surveillance [4]. In NMF, given a non-negative dataset $V \in R^{M\times N}$, the objective is to find two non-negative factor matrices $W \in R^{M\times K}$ and $H \in R^{K\times N}$. Here W is called base matrix and H is named feature matrix. In addition, W and H satisfy

$$V \approx WH \quad s.t. W \geq 0, H \geq 0 \tag{1}$$

K is the rank of base matrix and it satisfies the inequality $K \leq MN/(M+N)$.

For NMF research, the cost function and initialization problems of NMF are the main issues for researchers. Now the rank determination problem becomes popular. The rank of base matrix is indeed an important parameter to evaluate the accuracy of structure extraction. On the one hand, it reflects the real feature and property of data; on the other hand, more accurate learning could help us get better understanding and analyzing of data, thus improving the performance in applications: recognition [5,6] surveillance and tracking. The main challenge of rank determination problem is that it is pre-defined. Therefore, it is hard to know the correct rank of base matrix before the updating process of components. As the same as the cost function, there are no more priors added to the algorithm in previous methods. That is why the canonical NMF method and traditional probabilistic methods (*ML*, *MAP*) cannot handle the rank determination problem. Therefore in this paper, we propose an unsupervised multi-level model to automatically seek the correct rank of base matrix. Furthermore, we use L_2-norm to show the contribution of hyper-prior in correct bases learning procedure. Experimental results on two binary datasets demonstrate that our method is efficient and robust.

The rest of this paper is organized as follows: Section 2 provides a brief review of related works. In Section 3, we describe our unsupervised multi-level NMF model in details. The experimental results of two binary datasets are shown in Section 4. Section 5 concludes the paper.

2. Related Work

As we mentioned above, rank determination problem is a new popular issue in NMF research. Actually, there are few literatures discussing this issue. Although the author in [7] proposed a method based on sampler selection, it needs to pass through all the possible values of rank of base matrix to choose the best one. Obviously, this method is not impressive enough for unsupervised learning. In [8], the author proposed a rank determination method based on automatic relevance determination. In this method, a parameter is defined relevant to the columns of *W*. Then using *EM* algorithm to find a subset, however, this subset of bases is not accurate to represent true bases. Actually, the nature of this hyper-parameter is to affect the updating procedure of base matrix and feature matrix, thus affect the components' distributions.

The only feasible solution is fully Bayesian models. Such kind of methods have been proposed in [9]. In this paper, the author addresses an *EM* based fully Bayesian algorithm to discover the rank of base matrix. *EM* based methods are an approximation solution. In comparison, a little more accurate solution is Gibbs sampling based methods. Such approach is utilized to find the correct rank in [10]. Although such kinds of methods are flexible, it requires successively calculation of the marginal likelihood for each possible value of each rank *K*. The drawback is too much computation cost involved. Additionally, when such methods are applied to real time application or some large scale dataset based applications, the high computation load is impractical. Motivated by the current condition, we propose a low computation, robust multi-level model for NMF to solve rank determination problem. Our unsupervised model with multi-lever priors only calculate once of the rank of base matrix and is able to successfully find the correct rank of base matrix given a large enough rank *K*. Therefore, our method involves less computation. This will be discussed in details in next section.

3. Unsupervised Multi-Level Non-Negative Matrix Factorization Model

In our unsupervised multi-level NMF model, we introduce a hyper-prior level. Hence, there are three levels in our model: data model, prior model, hyper-prior model. The model structure is shown in **Figure 1**. We will seek

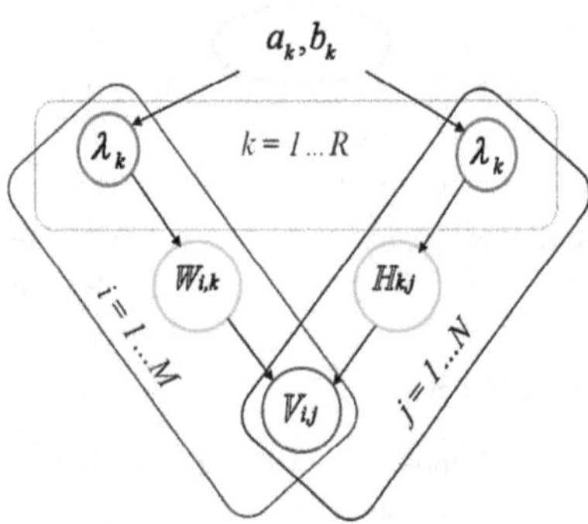

Figure 1. Unsupervised multi-level non-negative matrix factorization model.

the solutions through optimizing the maximum a posterior criterion. Our approach could be depicted by the following equation, here $=^c$ denotes equality up to a constant, $\boldsymbol{\lambda}$ is the prior of both $\boldsymbol{W}$ and $\boldsymbol{H}$.

$$MAP(\boldsymbol{W},\boldsymbol{H},\boldsymbol{\lambda}) =^c \log p(\boldsymbol{V}|\boldsymbol{WH}) + \log p(\boldsymbol{W}|\boldsymbol{\lambda}) + \log p(\boldsymbol{H}|\boldsymbol{\lambda}) + \log p(\boldsymbol{\lambda}) \quad (2)$$

The difference between our approach and the traditional *MAP* criterion is that in traditional one there is no hyper-prior added to the model. Moreover, in our model we attempt to update the hyper-priors recursively, but not just set it as a constant.

3.1. Model Construction

In NMF algorithm, the updating rules are based on the specific data model. Therefore, the first step is to set a data model for our problem. Here, in our experiment we assume that the data follows Poisson distribution. Consequently, the cost function of our model will be generalized *KL*-divergence. So given a variable *x*, which follows *Poisson* distribution with parameter λ, we have $p(x|\lambda) = e^{-\lambda} \times \lambda^x / \Gamma(x+1)$. Thus, in NMF algorithm, given dataset *V*, we have the likelihood

$$p(\boldsymbol{V}|\boldsymbol{WH}) = e^{-\boldsymbol{WH}} (\boldsymbol{WH})^{\boldsymbol{V}} / \Gamma(\boldsymbol{V}+1) \quad (3)$$

The generalized *KL*-divergence is given by:

$$D_{KL}(\boldsymbol{V}|\boldsymbol{WH}) = \sum_{mn}\left(v_{mn}\log\left(\frac{v_{mn}}{[wh]_{mn}}\right) - v_{mn} + [wh]_{mn}\right) \quad (4)$$

Thus, the log-likelihood of the dataset *V* can be rewritten as:

$$\begin{aligned} &\log p(\boldsymbol{V}|\boldsymbol{WH}) \\ &= -D_{KL}(\boldsymbol{V}|\boldsymbol{WH}) \\ &\quad -\sum_m\sum_n\left[v_{mn}(1-\log v_{mn}) + \log\Gamma(v_{mn}+1)\right] \end{aligned} \quad (5)$$

From (2) and (5) we could conclude that maximizing a posterior is equivalent to maximizing the log-likelihood, and maximizing the log-likelihood is equivalent to minimizing the *KL*-divergence. Thus, maximizing a posterior is equivalent to minimizing the *KL*-divergence. Therefore, it is possible to find a base matrix $\boldsymbol{W}$ and a feature matrix $\boldsymbol{H}$ to approximate the dataset *V* via maximizing a posterior criterion.

In data model $p(\boldsymbol{V}|\boldsymbol{WH})$ we regard $\boldsymbol{WH}$ as the parameter of data *V*. With respect to the base matrix $\boldsymbol{W}$ and the feature matrix $\boldsymbol{H}$, we also introduce a parameter $\boldsymbol{\lambda}$ as a prior to them. Moreover, we define an independent *Exponent* distribution for each column of $\boldsymbol{W}$ and each row of $\boldsymbol{H}$ with prior λ_k because exponent distribution has sharper performance. It is no doubt that we can choose other exponential family distributions such as

Gaussian distribution, Gamma distribution, etc. Therefore, the columns of $\boldsymbol{W}$ and rows of $\boldsymbol{H}$ yield:

$$p\left(w_{mk} \mid \lambda_k\right) = \lambda_k \times e^{-\lambda_k w_{mk}} \tag{6}$$

$$p\left(h_{kn} \mid \lambda_k\right) = \lambda_k \times e^{-\lambda_k h_{kn}} \tag{7}$$

Then the log-likelihood of the priors could be rewritten as:

$$\log p\left(\boldsymbol{W} \mid \boldsymbol{\lambda}\right) = \sum_m \sum_k \left(\log \lambda_k - \lambda_k \times w_{mk}\right) \tag{8}$$

$$\log p\left(\boldsymbol{H} \mid \boldsymbol{\lambda}\right) = \sum_k \sum_n \left(\log \lambda_k - \lambda_k \times h_{kn}\right) \tag{9}$$

Compare to setting λ as a constant, the diversity of λ_k and recursively updating of λ_k enable the inference procedure to converge at the stationary point. Through calculating the L_2-morm of each column of base matrix W, we could discover that the data finally emerges to two clusters. One cluster contains the points of which the L_2-norm are much larger than 0, whereas in the other cluster the L_2-norm values are 0 or almost 0.

In order to find the best value for λ_k, here we introduce hyper-prior for λ_k. Since λ_k is the parameter of *Exponent* distribution, we define λ_k follows Gamma distribution which is the conjugate prior for Exponent distribution.

$$p\left(\lambda_k \mid a_k, b_k\right) = \frac{1}{\Gamma(a) \times b_k^{a_k}} \lambda_k^{a-1} \exp\left(-\lambda_k / b_k\right) \tag{10}$$

Here a_k and b_k are the hyper-priors of λ_k. Thus, the log-likelihood of $\boldsymbol{\lambda}$ is given as:

$$\begin{aligned} &\log p(\boldsymbol{\lambda}) \\ &= \sum_k \left(-a_k \log b_k - \log \Gamma\left(a_k\right) + \left(a_k - 1\right) \log \lambda_k - \lambda_k / b_k\right) \end{aligned} \tag{11}$$

3.2. Inference

After the establishment of data model and the deduction of log-likelihood of each prior, we can gain the maximum a posterior equation:

$$\begin{aligned} &MAP(\boldsymbol{W}, \boldsymbol{H}, \boldsymbol{\lambda}) \\ &= \sum_m \sum_n \left[v_{mn} \log\left(v_{mn} - 1\right) + \log \Gamma\left(v_{mn} + 1\right)\right] \\ &\quad - \Big[D_{KL}\left(\boldsymbol{V} \mid \boldsymbol{WH}\right) + \sum_m \sum_k \left(\lambda_k w_{mk} - \log \lambda_k\right) \\ &\quad + \sum_k \sum_n \left(\lambda_k h_{kn} - \log \lambda_k\right) \\ &\quad + \sum_k \left(a_k \log b_k + \log \Gamma\left(a_k\right) + \lambda_k / b_k\right) - \left(a_k - 1\right) \log b_k \Big] \end{aligned} \tag{12}$$

Since the first factor in (12) has nothing to do with the priors, and we have discussed the relationship between the posterior probability and *KL*-divergence, here we minimize the second factor to seek the solutions for this criterion. In our paper, we choose gradient decent updating method as our updating rule. Although multiplicative method is simpler, it has no detailed deduction about why the approach works. On the contrary, gradient decent updating will give us clear deduction about the whole updating procedure. We utilize this method to infer the priors $\boldsymbol{W}$ and $\boldsymbol{H}$, as well as the hyper-priors $\boldsymbol{\lambda}$ and $\boldsymbol{b}$. First we find the gradient of the parameters:

$$\frac{\partial f}{\partial W} = -\frac{\boldsymbol{V}}{\boldsymbol{WH}} \times \boldsymbol{H}^T + \boldsymbol{H}^T + \boldsymbol{\lambda} \tag{13}$$

$$\frac{\partial f}{\partial H} = -\boldsymbol{W}^T \times \frac{\boldsymbol{V}}{\boldsymbol{WH}} + \boldsymbol{W}^T + \boldsymbol{\lambda} \tag{14}$$

$$\frac{\partial f}{\partial \lambda_k} = \sum_m w_{mk} + \sum_n h_{kn} + 1/b_k - \left(N + M + a_k - 1\right) \tag{15}$$

$$\frac{\partial f}{\partial b_k} = -\frac{\lambda_k}{b_k^2} + \frac{a_k}{b_k} \tag{16}$$

Then we utilize gradient coefficient to get rid of the subtraction operation during the updating procedure for $\boldsymbol{W}$ and $\boldsymbol{H}$ to guarantee the non-negative constrain. The parameters λ_k and b_k are updated by zeroing.

The updating rules are listed as follows:

$$w_{mk}^* = w_{mk} \times \frac{\dfrac{v_{mn}}{[wh]_{mn} + \varepsilon} \times \sum_n h_{kn}}{\sum_n h_{kn} + \lambda_k + \varepsilon} \tag{17}$$

$$h_{kn}^* = h_{kn} \times \frac{\sum_m w_{mk} \times \dfrac{v_{mn}}{[wh]_{mn} + \varepsilon}}{\sum_m w_{mk} + \lambda_k + \varepsilon} \tag{18}$$

$$\lambda_k = \frac{M + N + a_k - 1}{\sum_m w_{mk} + \sum_n h_{kn} + 1/b_k + \varepsilon} \tag{19}$$

$$b_k = \frac{a_k}{\lambda_k + \varepsilon} \tag{20}$$

Then we find the correct bases and determine the order of the data model by:

$$R = \|B\|_1 \tag{21}$$

where B is defined as

$$B \triangleq \left\{\|w_k\|_2, \|w_k\|_2 \gg 0\right\} \tag{22}$$

R is the rank of base matrix.

4. Experimental Results and Evaluation

In this section, we apply our unsupervised multi-level NMF algorithm on two binary datasets. One is fence dataset, and the other is famous swimmer dataset. Both of the experiment results demonstrate the efficacy of our method on the rank determination issue.

4.1. Fence Dataset

We first performed our experiments on fence dataset. Here I defined the data with four row bars (the size is 1 × 32) and four column bars (the size is 32 × 1). The size of each image is 32 × 32 with zero-value background, and the value of each pixel in eight bars is one. Each image is separated into five parts in both horizontal direction and vertical direction. Additionally, in each image the number of row bars and the number of column bars should be the same. For instance, there are two row bars in a sample image, then there should be two column bars in this image. Hence, the total number of the fence dataset is N = 69. The samples of Fence dataset are shown in **Figure 2**.

Here, we set the initial rank K = 16 (the initial value of rank K needs to be larger than the value of real rank of base matrix), the hyper-parameter $a = 2$, $b_k = [0.05 \cdots 0.05]_{1\times K}$. **Figure 3** shows the base matrix and feature matrix learned via our unsupervised multi-level NMF approach, we could see that the data is sparse, especially the base matrix. In both images, the color parts denote the effective bases or features, and the black parts denote irrelevant bases or features there. In addition, from image processing perspective, we can conclude that compared to the values of effective bases and features, the values of irrelevant bases and features are very small, since the color of such pixels are very dark. We could clearly find that there are eight color column vectors in the first image. Additionally, among the eight color vectors, four are composed of several separated color pixels, whereas the other four are composed of assembly pixels. Actually, the former four vectors are row bars, and the latter four vectors are column bars. We resize the dataset in columns during factorization procedure. Hence the row bars and column bars have different structures. Furthermore, there are also eight rows in the second image, which are the corresponding coefficients of the bases.

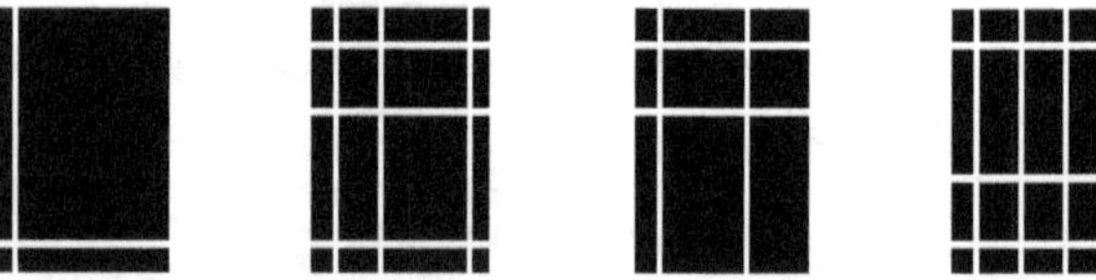

Figure 2. Sample images of fence dataset.

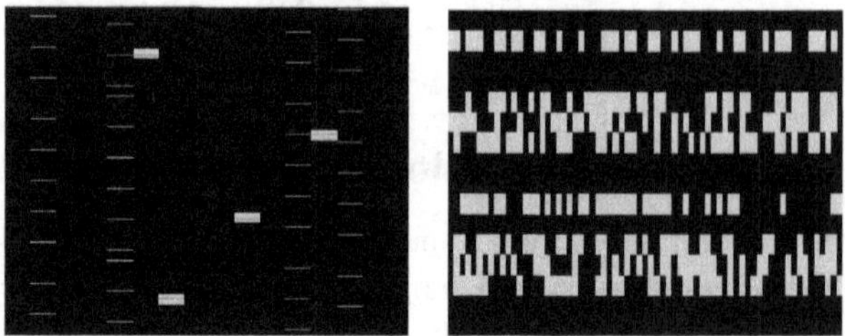

Figure 3. Base matrix W and feature matrix H learned via our algorithm.

In order to show the bases clearly, we draw the bases in **Figure 4**. Since we set the initial rank of base matrix K = 16, however, only eight images have non-zero values. Moreover, the eight images show 4 row bars and 4 column bars appearing in different positions. The results are perfectly consistent to the design of Fence dataset. Therefore, we could get the conclusion that our algorithm is very powerful and efficient to find the real basic components and the correct rank.

4.2. Swimmer Dataset

The other dataset we used is the swimmer dataset. Swimmer dataset is a typical dataset for feature extraction. Due to the clearly definition and composition of 16 dynamic parts, it is quite appropriate to the unique characteristic of NMF algorithm, which is to learn part-based data. As we know, however, the swimmer dataset is a gray-level image dataset. In our experiment, we focus on binary dataset, so first we need to convert this gray-level dataset to binary dataset. Then apply our approach to perform inference. In this swimmer dataset, there are 256 images totally, each of which depicts a swimming gesture using one torso and four dynamic limbs. The size of each image is 32 × 32. Each dynamic part could appear at four different positions. **Figure 5** shows some sample images of the swimmer dataset.

In this experiment part, the initial rank is set to $K = 25$, the initial values of hyper-parameters are $a = 2$, $b_k = [0.05 \cdots 0.05]_{1\times K}$. **Figure 6** shows the experiment

Figure 4. The bases obtained by our algorithm on fence dataset.

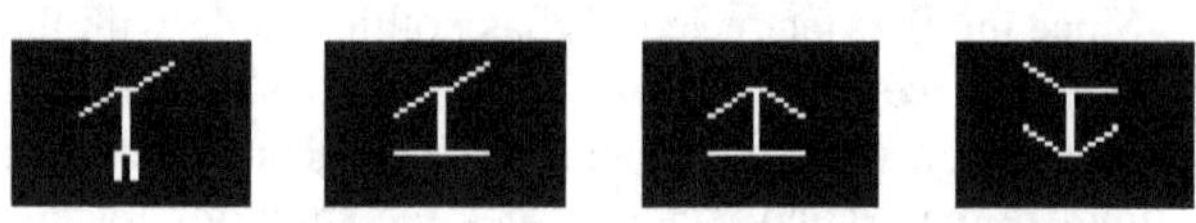

Figure 5. Sample images of the swimmer dataset.

results for the swimmer dataset. It could be observed that as for this dataset, we also could find out the correct bases via our algorithm. In this figure there are 25 base images. The black ones correspond to irrelevant bases, and the other 17 images depict the torso and the limbs at each possible position. We can see that the correct torso and limbs are discovered successfully.

The differences between the black images and the correct base images are shown in **Figure 7**. **Figure 7** depicts L_2-norm of each column of the base matrix. The total number of points in this figure is the same to the initial rank. Obviously, the points are classified into two clusters. One is zero-value cluster, and the other is larger-value cluster. Thus the rank of base matrix in swimmer dataset is $R = \|B\|_1 = 17$. The results of L_2-norm of base matrix not only tell us how we could find the correct bases, but also tell us how we could determine the correct rank of base matrix.

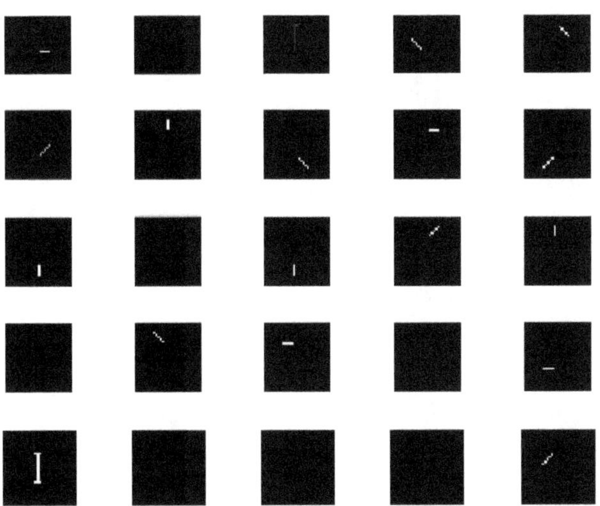

Figure 6. The bases of swimmer dataset learned by our algorithm.

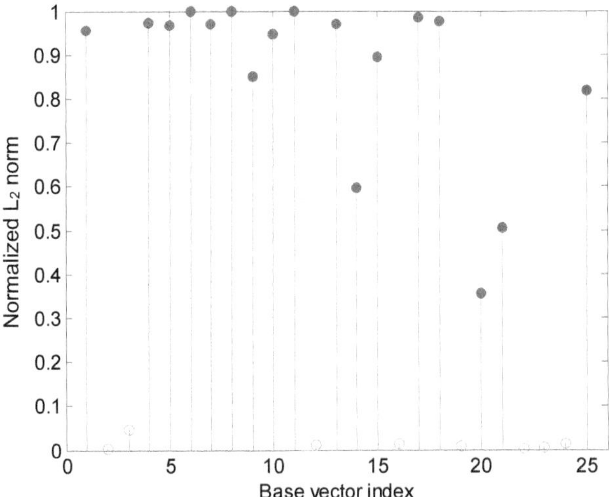

Figure 7. L_2-norm of base vectors.

5. Conclusion

We have presented an unsupervised multi-level non-negative matrix factorization algorithm which is powerful and efficient to seek the correct rank of a data model. This is achieved by introducing a multi-prior structure. The experiment results on binary datasets adequately demonstrate the efficacy of our algorithm. Compare to the fully Bayesian method, it is simpler and more convenient. The crucial points of this method are how to introduce the hyper-priors and what kind of prior is appropriate to a certain data model. This algorithm also could be extended to other data models and noise models. Although our experiment is based on binary dataset, this algorithm is suitable to other datasets such as gray-level dataset, colorful dataset, etc.

REFERENCES

[1] D. D. Lee and H. S. Seung, "Learning the Parts of Objects by Non-Negative Matrix Factorization," *Nature*, Vol. 401, No. 6755, 1999, pp. 788-791.

[2] Z. Yuan and E. Oja, "Projective Non-Negative Matrix Factorization for Image Compression and Feature Extraction," Springer, Heidelberg, 2005.

[3] C. Fevotte, N. Bertin and J. L. Durrieu, "Non-Negative Matrix Factorization with the Itakura-Saito Divergence," *With Application to Music Analysis. Neural Computation*, Vol. 21, No. 3, 2009, pp. 793-830.

[4] M. W. Berry and M. Browne, "Email Surveillance Using Non-Negative Matrix Factorization," *Computational and Mathematical Organization Theory*, Vol. 11, No. 3, 2005, pp. 249-264.

[5] Q. Sun, F. Hu and Q. Hao, "Context Awareness Emergence for Distributed Binary Pyroelectric Sensors," *Proceeding of* 2010 *IEEE Conference on Multisensor Fusion and Integration for Intelligent Systems*, Salt Lake City, 5-7 September 2010, pp. 162-167.

[6] F. Hu, Q. Sun and Q. Hao, "Mobile Targets Region-of-Interest via Distributed Pyroelectric Sensor Network: Towards a Robust, Real-Pyroelectric Sensor Network," *Proceeding of* 2010 *IEEE Conference on Sensors*, Waikoloa, 1-4 November 2010, pp. 1832-1836.

[7] Y. Xue, C. S. Tong and Y. C. W. Chen, "Clustering-Based Initialization for Non-Negative Matrix Factorization," *Applied Mathematics and Computation*, Vol. 205, No. 2, 2008, pp. 525-536.

[8] Z. Yang, Z. Zhu and E. Oja, "Automatic Rank Determination in Projective Non-Negative Matrix Factorization," *Proceedings of* 9*th International Conference on LVA/ICA*, St. Malo, 27-30 September 2010, pp. 514-521.

[9] A. T. Cemgil, "Bayesian Inference for Non-Negative Matrix Factorization Models," *Computational Intelligence and Neuroscience*, Vol. 2009, 2009, Article ID: 785152.

[10] M. Said, D. Brie, A. Mohammad-Djafari and C. Cedric,

"Separation of Nonnegative Mixture of Nonnegative Sources Using a Bayesian Approach and MCMC Sampling," *IEEE Transactions on Signal Processing*, Vol. 54, No. 11, 2006, pp. 4133-4145.

State of the Art for String Analysis and Pattern Search Using CPU and GPU Based Programming

Mario Góngora-Blandón, Miguel Vargas-Lombardo
Centro de Investigación, Desarrollo e Innovación en Tecnologías de la Información y las Comunicaciones (CIDITIC) Grupo de Investigación en Salud Electrónica y Supercomputación (GISES), Technological University of Panama, Panama City, Panama

ABSTRACT

String matching algorithms are an important piece in the network intrusion detection systems. In these systems, the chain coincidence algorithms occupy more than half the CPU process time. The GPU technology has showed in the past years to have a superior performance on these types of applications than the CPU. In this article we perform a review of the state of the art of the different string matching algorithms used in network intrusion detection systems; and also some research done about CPU and GPU on this area.

Keywords: GPU; String Matching; Pattern Matching

1. Introduction

Jack Dongarra [1,2], explains that GPU computing is the use of graphics processing unit together with a CPU to accelerate general-purpose scientific and engineering applications.

String matching algorithms allow string or pattern searching in a given text. These algorithms are used in many applications such as: word processors and in utilities like grep in UNIX [3] based operating systems.

The network based network intrusion detection systems also apply these algorithms, since most of the processing is found in pattern search.

Studies reveal that this process takes about 75% of the total CPU time in modern intrusion detection systems. For this reason the graphic processors, known as GPU, are studied to develop general purpose applications with the GPU [4]. The main reason is that the GPU are specialized in computationally intensive operations and highly parallel operations, required for graphic rendering, therefore are more adequate for data processing than for cache data storage and flow control. In this article we will be discussing different string matching algorithms and their application in intrusion detection systems in CPU as well as in GPU. The article is organized as follows: in Section II we described different string matching algorithms. In Section III we present a state of the art of the different studies in the network intrusion detection systems (NIDS) using string matching algorithms.

Section IV presents the state of the art of the studies done in the GPU field using string matching algorithms. In Section V the conclusions are presented.

2. String Matching Algorithms Used in Intrusion Detection Systems

The objective of the String Matching Algorithms is to locate and identify all the sub-strings, given a set of patterns in a specific text. To make the reading easier lets clarify the following terms when we refer to a string matching algorithm [3]:

- A string is a finite sequence of symbols.
- Where $K = \{y_1, y_2, \cdots, y_k\}$ is a finite set of strings usually called keywords.
- And x is a random string that we can call text string.

These algorithms can be classified in unique or multiple pattern algorithms. This means that if we have k patterns to search, the algorithm is repeated k times. Knuth-Morris-Pratt [5] and Boyer-Moore [6] are some of the most used unique pattern search algorithms. Multiple pattern search algorithms look simultaneously for a set of patterns in a text. This is achieved by applying preprocessing techniques to the set of patterns to get an automaton. The automaton is a state machine that's represented as a table, or a tree or a combination of both. Each text character will be searched once. Some of the multiple pattern search algorithms are: Aho-Corasick [7], Wu-Manber [8] and Commentz-Walter [9]. Next we will describe some of these algorithms.

2.1. Brute-Force Algorithm

The Brute-Force Algorithm [3] consists in comparing

two strings of characters. This algorithm compares from left to right each word the user writes with each letter of the name of the file found inside of the route the user specifies. The process that this algorithm performs is the following [3]:

- Takes the character with which the pattern starts.
- Starts to compare it with each of the text characters, until the first match is found.
- It stops in said position and from there it starts to verify if the pattern matches with the rest of the text.

If the pattern matches, it stops the comparison and then the next file in the route is reviewed. If otherwise, the pattern is not equivalent it will compare again the initial position with the rest of the text characters until a match is found again.

The outer loop is executed at most $n + m - 1$ times, and the inner loop m times, for each iteration of the outer loop. Therefore, the running time of this algorithm is in $O(nm)$ in the worst case. **Algorithm 1** shows the Brute-Force algorithm.

```
Naive-String-Matcher (T,P)
    n = T.length
    m= P.length
    for s = 0 to n – m
        if P[1..m] == T[s + 1..s + m]
        print "Pattern occurs with shift" s
```

Algorithm 1. Brute force.

2.2. Knuth-Morris-Pratt Algorithm

Knuth-Morris-Pratt [5] developed KMP, an algorithm that has the primary objective to search for the existence of a pattern inside a text string. In the algorithm it is used the information based on the previous data capture mistakes, taking in advantage the information that the search word has on it itself (a table of values is calculated about it), to determine where the next finding could be, without the need of analyzing more than once the character string where it's been searched.

The KMP locates the start position of a character string inside another. The first step is to locate a string, immediately a table of values is calculated (known as fault or error table). Next the strings are compared with each other and are used to make hops when an error is located.

For example, in a pre-calculated table, both strings start the comparison using an advance pointer for the string that is been searched (pattern), if an error occurs instead of returning to the position next to the first match, it hops the pattern and it places it aligning the character where the error occurred and then it continues verifying the matches. This process is executed until the pattern matches completely with the text. The Knuth-Morris-Pratt algorithm reaches an execution time of $O(n+m)$, which is optimal in the worst case scenario, where each text character and pattern has to be examined at least once. **Algorithm 2** shows the Knuth-Morris-Pratt algorithm.

```
KMP-Matcher(T,P)
        n = T.lenght
        m = P. lenght
        p = Compute-Prefix-Function(P)
        q = 0
        for i = 1 to n
                while q > 0 and P[q + 1] <> T[i]
                        q = p[q]
                        if P[q + 1] == T[i]
    q = q + 1
    if q == m
            print "Pattern occurs with shift"   i - m
            q = p[q]
                return p
```

Algorithm 2. Knuth-morris-pratt.

2.3. Boyer-Moore Algorithm

The Boyer-Moore algorithm [6] is considered the most efficient string processing algorithm on usual applications. A simplified version or the complete algorithm are frequently implemented on text editors for the search and replace commands.

This algorithm consists on aligning the pattern in a text window and comparing from right to left the characters in the window with the ones in the pattern. If there is a mismatch a secure displacement, is calculated, which allows the displacement of the window to in front of the text without the risk of omitting a match. If the start of the window is reached and there are no mismatches, then a match is reported and the window is displaced.

The Booyer-Moore algorithm as presented in the original paper has worst case running time of $O(n+m)$ only if the pattern does not appear in the text. When the pattern does occur in the text the running time of the original algorithm is $O(nm)$ in the worst case. In the best case the complexity of this algorithm is in $O(n/m)$. In **Algorithm 3** we present the Boyer-Moore Algorithm.

```
Boyer-Moore-Matcher(T,P,E)
        n = T.length
        m = P.length
        l = Compute-Last-Ocurrence-Function(P, m, E)
        y = Compute-Good-Suffix-Function(P, m)
        s = 0
        while s <= n – m
                do j = m
        while j > 0 and P[j] = T[s + j]
                do j = j – 1
                        if j = 0
            print "Pattern occurs at shift" s
            s = s + y[0]
                else
            s = s + max(y[j],j - l[T[s+j]])
```

Algorithm 3. Boyer-moore.

2.4. Aho-Corasick Algorithm

The Aho-Corasick [7], algorithm it's a search algorithm created by Alfred V. Aho and Margaret J. Corasick. Is a dictionary search algorithm that locates the elements of a finite set of strings (dictionary) within an input text. The complexity of the algorithm is linear to the length of the patterns, plus the length of the searched text, plus the number of matches that the output provides. It should be noted that due to the fact that all the matches are located, there can be a quadratic number of coincidences if each sub-string matches.

The algorithm builds a finite state machine that resembles to a tree with additional links between the different intern nodes. These internal links allow fast transitions between the matching patterns without the need to take steps back. When the dictionary pattern it's known beforehand the building of the automaton can be done once it's off-line and the compiled automaton stored for future use.

In this situation, its execution time is linear in the input length plus the number of matching inputs. In this way, we can conclude that the Aho-Corasick algorithm is $O(n)$ and the pre-processing of the string is linear with the size of the pattern $O(m)$. **Algorithm 4** shows the Aho-Corasick algorithm.

```
begin
        state = 0
        for i = 1 to n
                begin
                while g(state, a1) = fail do state = f(state)
                state = g(state, a1)
                if output(state) <> empty
                        begin
            print i
            print output(state)
                        end
            end
end
```

Algorithm 4. Aho-corasick.

2.5. Karp-Robin Algorithm

The Karp-Rabin algorithm [10] searches for a pattern in a text by hashing. So we preprocess p by computing its hash code, then compare that hash code to the hash code of each substring in t if we find a match in the hash codes, we go ahead and check to make sure the strings actually match (in case of collisions). The best case and average case time for this algorithm is in $O(n+m)$ (m time to compute hash (p) and n iterations through the loop). However, the worse case time is in $O(nm)$, which occurs when we have the maximum numbers of collisions. Karp-Rabin is inferior for single pattern searching to many other options because of its slow worst case behavior. However, it is excellent for multiple pattern searches. If we wish to find one of some large number, say k, fixed length patterns in a text, we can make a small modification that uses a hash table or other set to check if the hash of a given substring of t belongs to the set of hashes of the patterns we are looking for. In this way, we can find one k patterns in $O(km+m)$ time (km for hashing the patterns, n for searching). In **Algorithm 5** we present the Karp-Robin algorithm.

```
KarpRabin(T, P)
        n = T.length
        m = P.length
        hpatt = hash(P)
        htxt = hash(T[0..m–1])
        for i = 0 to n
                if(htxt == hpatt)
                        if(t[i..i + m – 1] == P
                        return i
                        htxt = hash(T[i + 1..i + m])
                print "not found"
                return -1
```

Algorithm 5. Karp-robin algorithm.

After describing each one of the algorithms in **Table 1**, the execution times of each algorithm are shown. The string matching processing time is defined for the worst case and best case respectively.

In the worst case scenario, the Aho-Corasick algorithm with a $O(n)$ runtime has the best execution time among the analyzed algorithms. Although for simple string matching cases, it does not performs very well, but when there are multiple patterns or pattern matching is done at regular expression level, it is one of the best options.

3. String Matching Algorithm Applied to Intrusion Detection Systems

String processing is a highly intensive computational process; studies demonstrate that the total processing time in a CPU reaches 75% in modern intrusion detection systems. For this reason, is necessary to count on string

Table 1. Comparison between the execution times. String matching algorithms. Where m is the length of the string, n the length of the text that is been searched, z is the amount of string matches and Σ the used alphabet.

Algorithm	Pre-processing	String matching	
		CaseWorst	BestCase
Brute force	No preprocessing	$O(nm)$	$O(n)$
KMP	$O(m)$	$O(nm)$	$O(n)$
Boyer moore	$O(m+\Sigma)$	$O(nm)$	$O(n/m)$
Aho corasick	$O(m)$	$O(n+z)$	$O(n)$
Karp rabin	$O(m)$	$O(nm)$	$O(n+m)$

matching algorithms capable of processing high amounts of information.

Most of the network intrusion detection systems use finite automata and regular expressions for string matching. Both Fisk and Vagese [11] optimized the Boyer-Moore-Horspool algorithm for it to process a set of rules (strings) simultaneously.

An innovative proposal is offered in the Set-Wise Boyer-Moore-Horspool which demonstrated to be faster than the Aho-corasick algorithm and the Boyer-Moore algorithm for pattern sets smaller than 100. At the same time, about this work, Coit, Stainford and MacAlemey [12] implemented a new version of Gunsfield in the Commentz-Wlater algorithm using suffix trees for the heuristics of good suffix. The algorithm was improved in the performance of Snort [13] combining the keyword tree of the Aho-Corasick algorithm with the hop characteristic of the Boyer-Moore algorithm.

In brief, they only measured the performance of a single set-wise algorithm, while Fisk and Vaghese [11] measured multiple algorithms and obtained better measurements without sacrificing the semantic of the rules used by Snort. Tuck [14] optimized the Aho-Corasick algorithm applying bitmap nodes and path compression.

4. State of the Art of Applications Based on String Matching in GPU

The continuous growth of traffic and signature databases make the performance of these systems increasingly more defying and important, is for this reason that the researchers are developing technologies that involve the Graphic Processing Units more every time. The main reason resides in that the GPU specializes in calculation of highly intensive and parallel operations, and therefore, are designed in such a way that more transistors are dedicated to data processing instead of cache data storage and flow control [4]. The following works [15-22], are based in GPU high performance computing.

One of the first works in the GPU field was PixelSnort [15], a version of the intrusion detection system Snort which processed the string matches with a NVIDIA GPU. The GPU programming was complicated, because this video card doesn't support general purpose programming models for GPU. The system coded the Snort rules and packages to textures and did string searches using the Knuth-Morris-Pratt algorithm. However, PixelSnort did not get satisfactory results in normal load conditions. In addition, it doesn't have any multiple pattern matching algorithms adapted to GPU. This represents a serious limitation because the multiple pattern matching algorithms are Snort's by default.

For Marziale [16] the GPU shaping tool performance was evaluated. The system was implemented in a G80 architecture [23] and the results showed that the GPU usage increased substantially in the performance of the digital forensic software analysis, which is based in binary string search. Both Nottingham and Irwin [17] designed gPF: a package classification program based in GPU. In Smith [18] a programmed signature matching system in a GPU G80 [23] based in SIMD (Simple Instruction Multiple Data) was implemented. This system outperforms a Pentium 4 until 9X and a 32 thread system based in Niagara until 2.3X demonstrating that the GPU are promising candidates for signature matching. In their work they evaluated two signatures matching mechanism based in finite automata, these are:

- Deterministic Finite Automaton (DFA [19]: it recognizes the exact type of regular expression.
- Extended Finite Automaton (XFA) [20,24], it reduces the DFA memory requirements.

On the other hand, Vasiliadis and Ioannidis developed GrAVit [21], an antivirus engine, using the architecture of an NVIDIA GPU. They designed, implemented and evaluated pattern matching algorithms, integrated their GPU implementation in the ClamAV [25], antivirus, a very popular open source antivirus. GrAVity reached an end to end performance in the 20 Gbits order, a 100 times the performance of ClamAV using only CPU.

In [4] an intrusion detection system was designed based in Snort, which potentiates the computational power of the video cards (GPU). Its prototype, called Gnort, reached maximum processing rates of traffic of 2.3 Gbits using synthetic tracks, while using an Ethernet interface; it surpassed Snort by a factor of two. Its results demonstrate that modern video cards can be used effectively to accelerate the intrusion detection systems, as well as other systems that involve string matching operations. Seaman and Alexander [22] presented ways to build a special type of regular expressions used by ClamAV in a GPU. Phar and Fernando [26] show a review of some high performance applications adapted to GPU.

This state of the art allowed us to identify string matching algorithms with better performance that the ones described previously. Also, it was demonstrated that exists a very wide research field on GPU, specifically in pattern analysis in intrusion detection systems. These researches have given evidence that the usage of GPU give better performance than the CPU.

5. Conclusion

In this article, we present a state of the art of different algorithms used for pattern matching in network intrusion detection systems. We compare the execution time of these algorithms. Also, we discuss different studies that presented proposals to improve the algorithms based in string matching. Finally, we present a state of the art on some studies on pattern search and package signing using GPU technology. We can state that in the next years the high performance application development using GPU will increase, displacing CPU eventually.

REFERENCES

[1] S. Tomov, J. Dongarra and M. Baboulin, "Towards Dense Linear Algebra for Hybrid GPU Accelerated Manycore Systems," *Parallel Computing*, Vol. 36, No. 5-6, 2010, pp. 232-240.

[2] NVIDIA, "What Is GPU Computing," 2012. http://www.nvidia.com/object/what-is-gpu-computing.html

[3] D. Gusfield, "Algorithms on Strings, Trees, and Sequences: Computer Science and Computational Biology," Cambridge University, Cambridge, 1997.

[4] G. Vasiliadis, S. Antonatos, M. Polychronakis, E. P. Markatos and S. Ioannidis, "Gnort: High Performance Network Intrusion Detection Using Graphics Processors," *Proceedings of the 11th International Symposium on Recent Advances in Intrusion Detection*, Cambridge, 15-17 September 2008, pp. 116-134.

[5] D. E. Knuth, J. H. Morris Jr. and V. R. Pratt, "Fast Pattern Matching in Strings," *SIAM Journal on Computing*, Vol. 6, No. 2, 1977, pp. 323-350.

[6] R. S. Boyer and J. S. Moore, "A Fast String Searching Algorithm," *Communications of the ACM*, Vol. 20, No. 10, 1977, pp. 762-772.

[7] A. V. Aho and M. J. Corasick, "Efficient String Matching: An Aid to Bibliographic Search," *Communications of the ACM*, Vol. 18, No. 6, 1975, pp. 333-340.

[8] S. Wu and U. Manber, "A Fast Algorithm for Multi-Pattern Searching," Technical Report TR-94-17, University of Arizona, Tucson, 1994.

[9] B. Commentz-Walter, "A String Matching Algorithm Fast on the Average," *Automata, Languages and Programming*, Vol. 71, 1979, pp. 118-132.

[10] R. M. Karp and M. O. Rabin, "Efficient Randomized Pattern-Matching Algorithms," *IBM Journal of Research and Development*, Vol. 31, No. 2, 1987, pp. 249-260.

[11] M. Fisk and G. Varghese, "Applying Fast String Matching to Intrusion Detection," University of California, San Diego, 2004.

[12] C. J. Coit, S. Staniford and J. McAlerney, "Towards Faster String Matching for Intrusion Detection or Exceeding the Speed of Snort," *DARPA Information Survivability Conference and Exposition*, Vol. 1, No. 2, 2001, pp. 367-373.

[13] M. Roesch, *et al.*, "Snort-Lightweight Intrusion Detection for Networks," *Proceedings of the 13th USENIX Conference on System Administration*, Seattle, 7-12 November 1999, pp. 229-238.

[14] N. Tuck, T. Sherwood, B. Calder and G. Varghese, "Deterministic Memory-Efficient String Matching Algorithms for Intrusion Detection," *INFOCOM*, Vol. 4, 2004, pp. 2628-2639.

[15] N. Jacob and C. Brodley, "Offloading IDS Computation to the GPU," *Proceedings of the 22nd Annual Computer Security Applications Conference*, Washington DC, 11-15 December 2006, pp. 371-380.

[16] L. Marziale, G. G. Richard III and V. Roussev, "Massive Threading: Using GPUs to Increase the Performance of Digital Forensics Tools," *Digital Investigation*, Vol. 4, 2007, pp. 73-81.

[17] A. T. Nottingham and B. Irwin, "gPF: A GPU Accelerated Packet Classification Tool," *Southern African Telecommunications Networks and Applications Conference*, Royal Swazi Spa, 30 August-2 September 2009, pp. 339-344.

[18] R. Smith, N. Goyal, J. Ormont, K. Sankaralingam and C. Estan, "Evaluating GPUs for Network Packet Signature Matching," *IEEE International Symposium on Performance Analysis of Systems and Software*, Boston, 26-28 April 2009, pp. 175-184.

[19] F. Yu, Z. Chen, Y. Diao, T. V. Lakshman and R. H. Katz, "Fast and Memory-Efficient Regular Expression Matching for Deep Packet Inspection," *Proceedings of the 2006 ACM/IEEE Symposium on Architecture for Networking and Communications Systems*, California, 4-5 December 2006, pp. 93-102.

[20] R. Smith, C. Estan, S. Jha and S. Kong, "Deflating the Big Bang: Fast and Scalable Deep Packet Inspection with Extended Finite Automata," *SIGCOMM Computer Communication Review*, Vol. 38, No. 4, 2008, pp. 207-218.

[21] G. Vasiliadis and S. Ioannidis, "Gravity: A Massively Parallel Antivirus Engine," *Recent Advances in Intrusion Detection*, Vol. 6307, 2011, pp. 79-96.

[22] E. Seamans and E. Alexander, "Fast Virus Signature Matching on the GPU," *GPU Gems*, Vol. 3, No. 1, 2007, pp. 771-783.

[23] J. Owens, "GPU Architecture Overview," *ACM SIGGRAPH*, Vol. 1, No. 2, 2007, pp. 5-9.

[24] R. Smith, C. Estan and S. Jha, "XFA: Faster Signature Matching with Extended Automata," *Proceedings of the 2008 IEEE Symposium on Security and Privacy*, Oakland, 18-21 May 2008, pp. 187-201.

[25] T. Kojm, "ClamAV," 2004. http://www. clamav. net

[26] M. Pharr and R. Fernando, "2: Programming Techniques for High-Performance Graphics and General-Purpose Computation (Gpu Gems)," Addison-Wesley Professional, Boston, 2005.

26

Category-Based Intrusion Detection Using PCA

Gholam Reza Zargar[1], Tania Baghaie[2]
[1]GIS Department, Khuzestan Electrical Power Distributed Company, Ahvaz, Iran
[2]Training Center of Applied Science and Technology, Tehran Municipality Information and Communication Technology Organization, Tehran, Iran

ABSTRACT

Existing Intrusion Detection Systems (IDS) examine all the network features to detect intrusion or misuse patterns. In feature-based intrusion detection, some selected features may found to be redundant, useless or less important than the rest. This paper proposes a category-based selection of effective parameters for intrusion detection using Principal Components Analysis (PCA). In this paper, 32 basic features from TCP/IP header, and 116 derived features from TCP dump are selected in a network traffic dataset. Attacks are categorized in four groups, Denial of Service (DoS), Remote to User attack (R2L), Remote to User attack (U2R) and Probing attack. TCP dump from DARPA 1998 dataset is used in the experiments as the selected dataset. PCA method is used to determine an optimal feature set to make the detection process faster. Experimental results show that feature reduction can improve detection rate for the category-based detection approach while maintaining the detection accuracy within an acceptable range. In this paper KNN classification method is used for the classification of the attacks. Experimental results show that feature reduction will significantly speed up the train and the testing periods for identification of the intrusion attempts.

Keywords: Intrusion Detection; Principal Components Analysis; Data Dimension Reduction; Feature Selection; Classification

1. Introduction

Intrusion Detection Systems (IDS) is designed to complement other security measures based on attack prevention (firewalls, antivirus, etc.). Amparo Alonso-Betanzos *et al.* [1] say that "The aim of the IDS is to inform the system administrator of any suspicious activities and to recommend specific actions to prevent or stop the intrusion". Intrusion can be defined as an attempt to gain unauthorized access to network resources [2]. IDS is necessary for effective computer system protection. There are two approaches for intrusion detection, *i.e.* signature-based and anomaly-based intrusion detection. In signature-based or misuse detection method, patterns of well known attacks are used to identify intrusions [3]. In anomaly-based intrusion detection, network traffic is monitored and compared versus any deviation from the established normal usage patterns to determine whether the current state of the network is anomalous. An anomalous traffic can be flagged as intrusion attempt. Misuse detection uses well defined patterns known as signatures of the attacks. Anomaly-based detection builds a normal profile and anomalous traffic is detected when the deviation from the normal model reaches a preset threshold [4].

Signature-based IDSs typically require human input to create attack signatures or to determine effective models for the normal behavior [4]. Feature selection ranking can be used in anomaly-based and signature-based intrusion detection systems. Feature selection is an important issue in intrusion detection. The reason for it is due to the large number of features that should be monitored for the intrusion detection purpose. Elimination of useless or less relevant features will maintain accuracy of the detection while speeding up its calculations. Therefore, any reduction in the number of features used for the detection will significantly improve the overall performance of the IDS. In cases where there are no useless features, concentrating on the most important ones is expected to improve the execution speed of an IDS. This increase in the detection speed will not affect accuracy of the detection in a significant way.

Incorrect selection of the features may not only reduce the speed of the operation but may also reduce detection accuracy [5].

This paper reports a work aimed on improving the intrusion detection time using a category-based intrusion detection model. In **Figure 1**, network traffic in divided into six groups, normal, DoS, R2L, U2R, Probing and Undetermined Anomalous Behavior (UAB). The main goal in a Category-Based Intrusion Detection (CBID) is

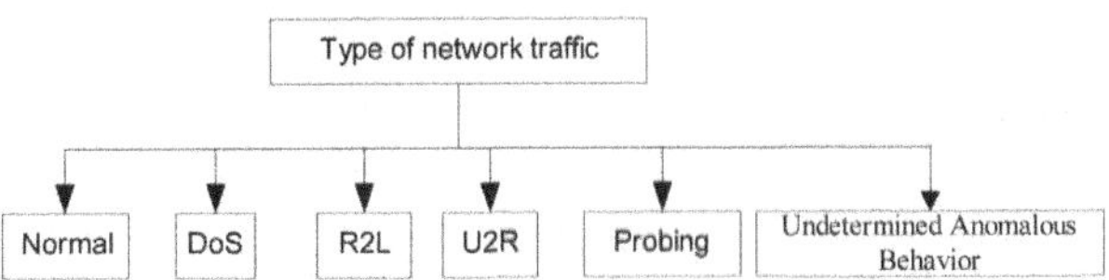

Figure 1. Category-based separation of the network traffic.

to reduce the amount of data that is less important with regard to the intrusion detection and to eliminate them.

This approach has the benefit of reducing memory requirements for storage, reducing data transfer and processing time, and improving the detection rate [6]. IDS has to examine a very large audit data in a short period of time. Therefore, any reduction in the volume of data may save the processing time [7].

Considering certain attack categorizes, some features in the traffic data are more relevant than the rest for intrusion detection.

Feature reduction can be performed in several ways [7-10]. In this paper, the category-based approach is used to find the relevance between features extracted from the network traffic. This paper also proposes a method based on TCP/IP header parameters and derived features selected from TCP dump network traffic dataset. In the proposed approach, Principal Components Analysis (PCA) is used as a dimension reduction technique. KNN classification method is used the detection of the intrusion attempts and results are reported.

2. Related Works

In a reported work, Chakraborty [11] reports that the existence of irrelevant and redundant features generally affects the performance of machine learning part of the work. Chakraborty Proves that proper selection of the feature set results in better classification performance. A. H. Sung *et al.* [8] have demonstrated that the elimination of these unimportant and irrelevant features did not significantly reduced performance of the IDS.

Chebrolu *et al.* [7], report that an important advantage for combining redundant and complementary classifiers is to increase robustness, accuracy and better overall generalization. Chebrolu *et al.* [7] have also identified important input features in building IDS that are computationally efficient and effective. In their reported work, they have investigated performance of three feature selection algorithms, *i.e.* Bayesian networks (BN), Classification and Regression Trees (CART) and an ensemble of BN and CART.

Sung and Mukkamala [8], have explored SVM and Neural Networks to identify and categorize features with respect to their importance to detect specific kinds of attacks such as probing, DoS, Remote to Local (R2L), and User to Root (U2R). They have also demonstrated that elimination of these less important and irrelevant features did not reduce the performance of IDS significantly. Mukkamala *et al.* [12] have demonstrated that use of ensemble of classifiers gave the best accuracy for each category of attack patterns. In designing a classifier, their first step was to carefully construct different connectional models to achieve best generalization performance for the classifiers. Sung and Mukkamala [13] have analyzed data from a large network traffic since it causes a prohibitively high overhead and often becomes a major problem for the IDS.

Chebrolu *et al.* [7] proposed CART-BN approach, where CART performed best for Normal, Probe and U2R and the ensemble approach worked best for R2L and DoS. Meanwhile, A. Abraham *et al.* [14] proved that ensemble of Decision Tree was suitable for Normal, LGP for Probe, DoS and R2L and Fuzzy classifier was good for R2L attacks. A. Abraham *et al.* [15] demonstrated the ability of their proposed Ensemble structure in modeling light-weight distributed IDS.

3. Data Reduction and Feature Selection Using PCA

Principal Components Analysis (PCA) is a predominant linear dimensionality reduction technique, and it has been widely applied on datasets in many different scientific domains [16]. PCA allows us to compute a linear transformation that maps data from a high dimensional space to a lower dimensional space. The first principal components have the highest contribution to the variance in the original dataset. Therefore, the rest can be disregarded with minimal loss of the information value during the dimension reduction process. Another method is to use their weights and transform data in to a new space with lower dimensions. The transformation works in the following way [17]:

$$X_{M\times N}=\begin{bmatrix} x_{11} & x_{12} & \cdots & x_{1N} \\ x_{21} & x_{22} & \cdots & x_{2N} \\ \cdots\cdots & & & \\ x_{M1} & x_{M2} & \cdots & x_{MN} \end{bmatrix}=\left[x_1, x_2, \cdots, x_M\right] \quad (1)$$

Given a set of observations $x_1, x_2, \cdots, x_M$ are $N \times 1$ vectors, where each observation is represented by a vector of length N. Thus, the dataset is presented by matrix Equation (1).

The mean value for each column is defined by the expected value. This is explained in Equation (2).

$$\bar{x}=\frac{1}{M}\sum_{i=1}^{M}x_i \quad (2)$$

Once the mean value is subtracted from the data yields expression Equation (3).

$$\varphi_i = x_i - \overline{x} \tag{3}$$

C that is correlation compute from matrix $A = [\varphi_1 \varphi_2 \cdots \varphi_M]$ ($N \times M$ Matrix), Equation (4):

$$A = [\varphi_1 \varphi_2 \cdots \varphi_M] C = \frac{1}{M} \sum_{n=1}^{M} \varphi_n \varphi_n^T = AA^T \tag{4}$$

Sampled $N \times N$ covariance matrix characterizes how data is scattered [18].

The eigenvalues of C: $\lambda_1 > \lambda_2 > \cdots > \lambda_N$ and the eigenvectors of C: $u_1, u_2, \cdots, u_N$ have to be calculated. Since C is symmetric, $u_1, u_2, \cdots, u_N$ form a basis (*i.e.* any vector x or actually $(x - \overline{x})$ can, can be written as a linear combination of the eigenvectors) Equation (5).

$$x - \overline{x} = b_1 u_1 + b_2 u_2 + \cdots + b_N u_N = \sum_{i=1}^{N} b_i u_i \tag{5}$$

During the dimensionality reduction, only the terms corresponding to the K largest eigenvalues are mentioned in Equation (6) [19].

$$\hat{x} - \overline{x} = \sum_{i=1}^{K} b_i u_i \quad \text{where } K \ll N \tag{6}$$

The representation of $\hat{x} - \overline{x}$ into the basis $u_1, u_2, \cdots, u_K$ is thus $[b_1 \; b_2 \; \cdots \; b_K]^T$.

The linear transformation $R^N \Rightarrow R^K$ by PCA that performs the dimensionality reduction is presented in Equation (7).

$$\begin{bmatrix} b_1 \\ b_2 \\ \vdots \\ b_K \end{bmatrix} = \begin{bmatrix} u_1^T \\ u_2^T \\ \vdots \\ u_K^T \end{bmatrix} (x - \overline{x}) = U^T (x - \overline{x}) \tag{7}$$

The new variables (*i.e.* b_i's) are uncorrelated. The covariance matrix for the b_i's is presented in Equation (8).

$$\mathrm{U^T}CU = \begin{bmatrix} \lambda_1 & 0 & 0 & 0 \\ 0 & \lambda_2 & 0 & 0 \\ 0 & 0 & . & 0 \\ 0 & 0 & 0 & \lambda_n \end{bmatrix} \tag{8}$$

The covariance matrix represents only second order statistics among the vector values.

Let n to be the dimensionality of the data. The covariance matrix is used to calculate $\mathrm{U^T}CU$ that is a diagonal matrix. $\mathrm{U^T}CU$ is sorted and rearranged in the form of $\lambda_1 > \lambda_2 > \cdots > \lambda_n$ so that the data exhibits maximum variance in y_1, the next largest variance in y_2 and so on, with minimum variance in y_n [20,21].

4. K-Nearest Neighbor Algorithm (KNN)

The K-nearest neighbor (KNN) decision rule has been a ubiquitous classification tool with good scalability. Experience has shown that the optimal choice of K is dependent on the data. This makes it difficult to tune the parameters for different applications.

KNN classification algorithm tries to find the K nearest neighbors of x_0 and uses a majority vote to determine the class label of x_0. Without any prior knowledge, the KNN classifier usually applies Euclidean distances as the distance metric [22].

KNN is an example of instance-based learning, in which the training data set is stored, so that, a classification for a new unclassified record may be found simply by comparing it to the most similar records in the training set.

The most common distance function is Euclidean distance, which represents the usual manner in which humans think of distance in the real world (8):

$$d_{\text{Euclidean}}(x, y) = \sqrt{\sum_i (x_i - y_i)^2} \tag{8}$$

where $x = x_1, x_2, \cdots, x_m$, and $y = y_1, y_2, \cdots, y_m$ represent the m attribute values of two records [23,24].

5. Three Way Handshake

The three-way handshake in Transmission Control Protocol (also called the three message handshake) is a method used to establish and tear down network connections. This handshaking technique is referred to as the 3-way handshake or as "SYN-SYN-ACK" (or more accurately SYN, SYN-ACK, ACK). The TCP handshaking mechanism is designed so that two computers attempting to communicate can negotiate the parameters of the network connection before beginning communication. This process is also designed so that both ends can initiate and negotiate separate connections at the same time. Below is a (very) simplified description of the TCP 3-way handshake process (**Figure 2**).

- Source sends a TCP Synchronize packet to destination;
- Destination receives source's SYN;
- Destination sends a Synchronize Acknowledgement packet;

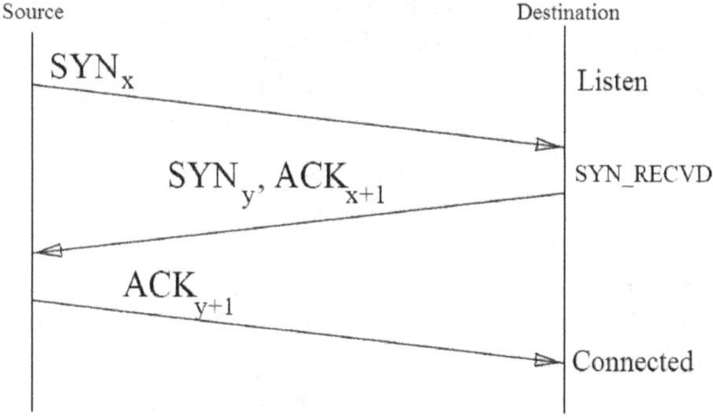

Figure 2. Three-way handshake.

- Source receives destination's SYN-ACK;
- Source sends an Acknowledgement packet;
- Destination receives an Acknowledgement packet;
- TCP connection is established.

Synchronization and Acknowledgement messages are identified by a bit inside the TCP header of the segment. TCP knows whether the network connection is opened, synchronized or established by using the Synchronization and Acknowledgement messages when establishing a network connection.

When the communication between two computers ends, another 3-way communication is performed to tear down the TCP connection. This setup and teardown of a TCP connection is part of the reason why TCP qualifies to be a reliable protocol [25].

6. The Dataset Used in This Work

The DARPA'98 dataset was used for the training dataset in the reported work. The dataset provides around 4 gigabytes of compressed TCP dump data [26] for 7 weeks of the network traffic [27]. This dataset can be processed into about 5 millions of connection records each about 100 bytes in size. Dataset contains payload of the packets transmitted between hosts inside and outside a simulated military base. BSM[1] audit data from one UNIX Solaris host for some network sessions are also provided. DARPA 1998 TCP dump dataset [28] was preprocessed and labeled using two class labels, e.g., normal and attack.

7. Pre-Processing

In this work 32 basic features are extracted from TCP/IP header protocols. These features are derived from TCP, IP, UDP and ICMP packet headers without inspecting the payload. The possible candidates for this feature category includes timestamp, source port, source IP, destination port, destination IP, flag, to name a few. In another dataset 116 derived features are selected from TCP dump network traffic dataset [28]. This dataset is intended to provide a wide variety of features characterizing flows. This includes simple statistics about packet length and inter-packet timings, and information derived from the transport protocol (TCP) such as SYN and ACK counts. This information is extracted using all the packets transmitted in both directions as well as on each direction individually (server → client and client → server).

Many packet statistics are derived directly by counting packets, and packet header-sizes. A significant number of features (such as estimates of round-trip time, size of TCP segments, and the total number of retransmissions) are derived from the TCP headers. TCP trace [29] was used for this information.

Each object within dataset represents a single flow of TCP packets between client and server.

All of the features that are extracted in this work are displayed in **Appendix 1**, **Table A.1**. Wire-shark, Editcap and TCP trace softwares are used to analyze and minimize TCP dump files and extract features [30,31].

The dataset contains 13 different types of attacks that are broadly categorized into five groups such as DoS, U2R, R2L, Probing and anomalous behavior. Goal is categorize different intrusion methods into a number of categories. This approach aims to summarize the intrusion method into a few similar approaches. Following the proposed approach, system will be able to deal with variations of the different attacks within each category. Considering the DARPA'98 dataset, there are five main categories of attacks proposed in this paper. The proposed attack categories are listed and described in the following sections.

7.1. Denial of Service (DoS) Attacks

Denial of service attacks consume a large amount of resources thus preventing legitimate users from receiving service with some minimum performance or they may prevent a computer from complying with a legitimate requests by consuming its resources [32,33]. Apache2, Back, Land, Mail bomb, SYN Flood, Ping of death, Process table, Smurf, Teardrop, Udpstorm and Neptune attacks are some examples of the Dos attack. In this work Syn flood attack is used for the experiments. Therefore, Syn flood scenario will be explained in this section: Syn flood is a DoS attack in which every TCP/IP implementtation is vulnerable to it in some degree. Each half-open TCP connection made to a machine will cause the "tcpd" server to add a record to the data structure that stores information describing all pending connections (**Figure 3**). This data structure has a size limit and it may overflow by intentionally creating too many partially-open connections. The half-open connections data structure on the victim server system will eventually fill up. Once the data structure is full, unless the table is emptied, the system will not be able to accept any new incoming con-

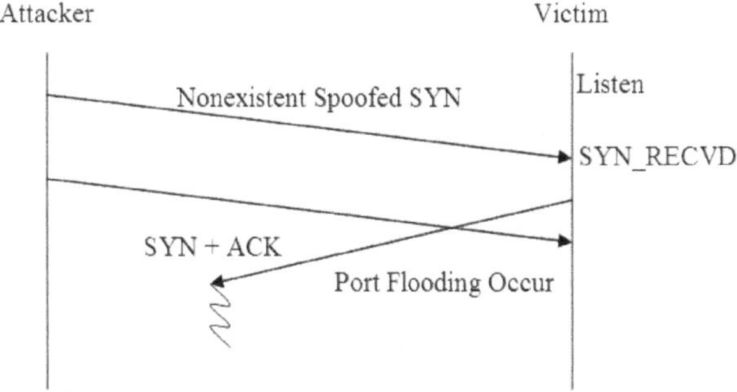

Figure 3. Attacking a victim machine with half-open connections.

[1]Basic Security Monitoring (BSM).

nections [34].

Normally, there is a time-out associated with a pending connection, so that, half-open connections will eventually expire and the victim server system will recover. However, the attacker system can simply continue sending IP-spoofed packets requesting new connections faster than the rate victim system can drop the pending connections. Christopher [35] believes that "Typical SYN flooding attacks can vary several parameters: the number of SYN packets per source address sent in a batch, the delay between successive batches, and the mode of source address allocation".

7.2. User to Root Attacks (U2R)

In this attack, an attacker starts with accessing a normal user account on the system and will end in gaining root access on that system. Regular programming mistakes and environment assumption give an attacker opportunity to exploit the vulnerabilities that may lead to a root access. An example of this type of attacks include buffer overflow, Eject, Ffbconfig, Fdformat, Loadmodule, Perl, Ps, Xterm, perlmagic and ffb attacks [36].

7.3. Remote to User Attacks (R2L)

In this attack, an attacker sends packets to a machine over a network and exploits the machine's vulnerability to gain local access as a user illegally. There are different types of R2U attacks; the most common attack in this class is carried out using social engineering. Examples for these types of attacks are Dictionary, Ftp_write, Guest, Imap, Named, Phf, Sendmail, Xlock, Xsnoop, guessing password and Dict attacks [36].

7.4. Probing Attacks

Probing is a class of attacks where an attacker scans a network to gather information for the purpose of finding known vulnerabilities. An attacker with a map of machines and services that are available on a network can manipulate the information and look for exploits. There are different types of probing, some of them abuse the computer's legitimate features; others use social engineering techniques. This class of attacks is the most common because it requires very little technical expertise. Examples are Ipsweep, Mscan, Nmap, Saint, Satan, pingsweep and Portsweep attacks [6].

7.5. Undetermined Anomalous Behavior

There are anomalous user behaviors, such as "a manager becomes (*i.e.* behaves like) a system administrator". For example, when your computer was automatically blacklisted (blocked) by the network due to the number of abnormal activities originating from your connection, it is possible that your computer is infected with a worm and/or virus.

8. Misuse Detection

Training data from the DARPA dataset includes "list files" that identify the timestamp, source host and port, destination host and port, and the name of each attack [37-40]. This information is used to select intrusion data for the purpose of pattern mining and feature construction, and to label each connection record with "normal" or "attack" label types. The final labeled training data is used for training the classifiers. Due to the large volume of audit data, connection records are stored in several data files. **Table 1** shows 43418 basic feature samples and 20095 derived feature samples that include records from both attack and normal state categories that are selected for the analysis. These data are extracted from the fifth day of the sixth week. Sequences of normal connection records are randomly extracted to create the normal dataset.

Dictionary table is used to convert text data into numeric data.

9. Experiments

Experiments were aimed on generating a categorized attacked or normal state dataset. In the experiments for basic features, 9459 normal connections and 33,959 attacks are included in the categorized attack and were randomly selected to create a dataset. As for the derived features, 10,413 normal connections and 9682 are included in the categorized attack and were randomly selected to create another dataset. With these dataset that included derived features, all experiments repeated again and selected some derived feature in attacks categorized.

Classes of the relevant features with their associated information value are reported in **Tables 2** and **3**. In these tables, all attack categories are compared versus the normal state. As it is reported in this paper, some different features were selected from attacks categories and

Table 1. Number of records that are used for the calculations in different categories.

Category	Number of basic Records	Number of derived records
DoS	19,440	8789
U2R	513	16
R2L	3798	867
Prob	10,137	10
Anomaly	71	0
Normal	9459	10,413
SUM	43,418	20,095

Table 2. List of the most effective basic features for detecting a list of attacks.

Class name	Relevant features in descending order	Total information value
DoS	28,19,5,1,16	99.75%
U2R	12,13,25,28,5	98.13%
R2L	27,25	97.69%
Probing	29,26,25,28,12,13,5,27,1,10	98.01%
Non-deterministic Anomaly	26,28,25,2,3,10,19	99.29%
Normal	27,25	98.84%

Table 3. List of the most effective derived features for detecting a class of attacks.

Class name	Relevant features in descending order	Total information value
DoS	2	99.36%
U2R	79,97,101,10,86,59,47	94.5%
R2L	36,3,77	88.5%
Probing	2,3,35,37,38,61,62,87,89,90,103,104, 102,86,47,10.83	96.24%
Normal	105,99,23,107,103,89	99.22%

normal state. A comparison between the feature importance in different attack categories and the normal state is presented in **Figures 4** and **5**. The Scree graph for the calculated PCA coefficients is depicted in **Figures 6** and 7.

10. Experimental Results

Each attack has a different consequence and effect on computer network features. Aforementioned features are used to compare each session against a normal or a known attack behavior. **Table 2** for basic and **Table 3** for derived features show relevant features in descending order for different attack categories. As reported in **Table 2**, one single feature (number 27) in normal behavior have 98.22% information value, this is maximum information.

Value in the normal dataset. Once the component number 25 is included, their total information value will rise to 98.84% of the total information value. Therefore, it can be said that the component number 25 does not have a significant effect in detecting the normal state. Comparing information value of the component number 25 versus threshold value for the normal state and R2L attack, normal state and R2L attack can be separated. In the derived features, six features *i.e.* features: 105, 99, 23, 107, 103 and 89 have 99.22% information value for the normal behavior.

As the three-way handshaking was explained in Section 5, intruder may use Syn Flag for the intrusion. The experimental result shows that component number 28 *i.e.* Syn Flag (**Appendix 1**, **Table A.1**) have the highest information value for the detection of a DoS attack. Once DoS attack scenarios are compared against the effective features presented in **Table 2**, a relation between the behaviors of their parameters can be extracted.

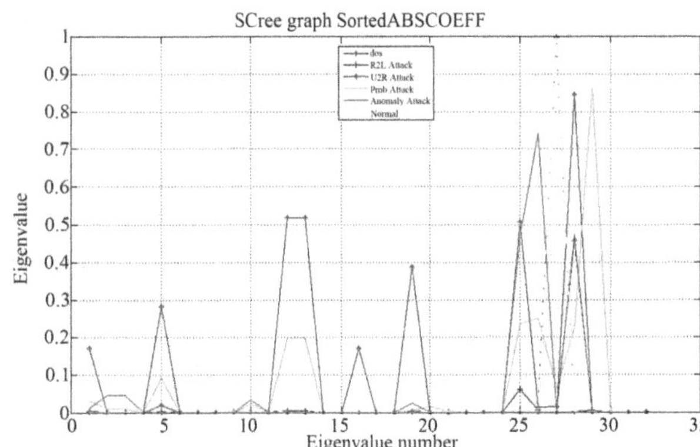

Figure 4. A comparison between the information value of different features in different states of the network operation (basic features).

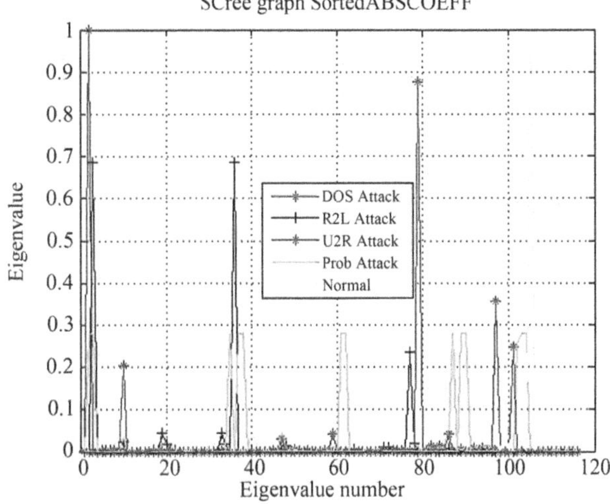

Figure 5. A comparison between the information value of different features in different states of the network operation (derived features).

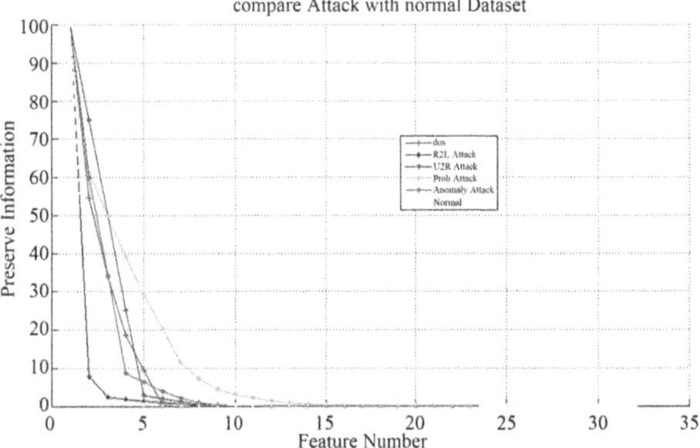

Figure 6. Comparison between Scree graphs for the different calculated PCA coefficients (basic features).

In TCP scan attack, hackers use TCP scans to identify active devices, TCP port status and their TCP-based application-layer protocols. In TCP FIN scan, that is a kind of TCP scan attack, hackers scan the network to identify TCP port numbers that are listening. The TCP packets used in this scan have only their TCP FIN flag set. Results from the experiments in **Table 2**, for probing attacks, show that the 29th component in **Table A.1** *i.e.* Fin flag has the highest information value. Hence, it is the most important component in the probing scenario attack and for the detection purpose. Comparing results of this experiment with TCP FIN scan scenario, intrusion attempt by probing attack can be detected. In **Table 2**, result of the probing attack scenario shows that the first four components are TCP flags with 70.97% of information value.

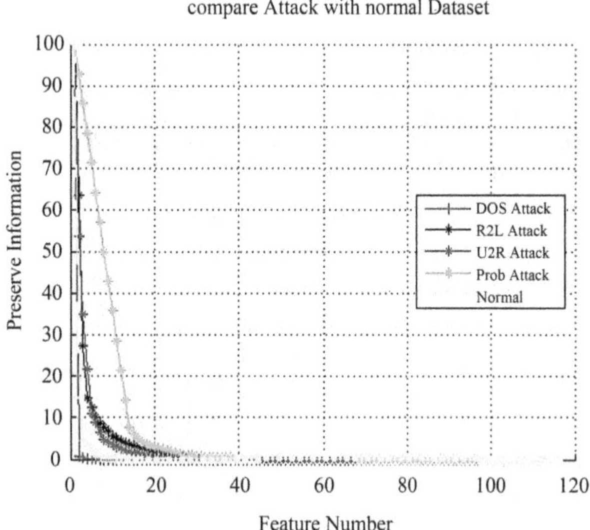

Figure 7. Comparison between Scree graphs for the different calculated PCA coefficients (derived features).

KNN classification method was implemented to show the performance of the proposed measures and to prove that feature reduction will speed up the training and the test processes for the attack identification system considerably. **Table 4** shows the confusion matrix for applying the KNN classification method. In **Table 5**, the classification time for the experiments using all the features are compared with when only effective features are used. True positive and false positive for six classes reported. Once the detection time for the two different feature sets are compared, the result shows that using effective features, the detection time is reduced without any decline in the detection accuracy. Hence, detection time can be reduced using effective features extracted by means of the PCA. In a different experiment, all the attacks in **Table 6** are categorized in an attack class and normal connections are categorized as the second category and the KNN classification method was applied. Process time in this experiment decreased as well, while the accuracy showed a small change.

Table 4. Confusion matrix resulted from implementing KNN classification.

	NOR	DoS	R2L	U2R	PROB	ANOM
NOR	8429	21	8	27	22	6
DoS	0	17,510	0	0	0	0
R2L	10	11	438	2	0	0
U2R	11	0	53	3342	12	0
PROB	40	38	0	5	9040	0
ANOM	1	0	0	2	5	55

Table 5. Comparing classification time for all the features versus when only effective features are used.

Class name	Class 1		Class 2		Class 3		Class 4		Class 5		Class 6		Process time (second)
Record type	Normal		DoS		U2R		R2L		Prob		Anomaly		
Number of record	9459		19,440		513		3798		10,137		71		
Result	TP	FP	TP	FP	TP	FP	TP	FP	TP	FP	TP	FP	
KNN classification with all feature	99.01	0.98	100	0	95.01	4.6	97.77	2.2	99.09	0.91	87.30	13.11	200.98
KNN classification with effective feature	98.35	0.84	99.78	0.2	92.03	6.9	94.98	9.0	97.04	0.44	85.2	14.21	135.98

Table 6. A comparison between classification time needed when all features are used or once only the effective features are used.

Class name	Class 1		Class 2		Process time (second)
Record type	Normal		Attack		
Number of record	9459		33,959		
Result	TP	FP	TP	FP	
KNN classification with all feature	99.01	0.99	99.82	0.17	185.32
KNN classification with effective feature	94.05	4.3	99.36	0.58	125.22

11. Conclusions

A feature selection method based on Principal Component Analysis (PCA) for CBID is proposed and implemented to provide results with a similar accuracy but with a smaller set of features. The proposed approach improved the detection speed. Feature selection reduced the total number of features in the dataset (32 basic features and 116 derived features). Due to the smaller search space, this reduction means that less data is needed for training the classifier. Paper reports a new CBID approach that can produce better and more accurate results in identifying the category of the attacks instead of the precise type of the attack. This result also indicates that there are analytical solutions for the feature selection that are not based on the trial and error. The possibility and feasibility of detecting intrusions based on characterization of different types of attacks such as DoS, probes, U2R and R2L attacks is an important goal in the reported work. Results of this investigation seem to be promising.

Results indicate that normal state of the network and category of the attacks can be identified using a small number of a carefully selected network features. On the other hand, it is proven that certain features have no contribution to intrusion detection. Experimental results show that dimension reduction and identification of effective network features for category-based selection can reduce the process time in an intrusion detection system while maintaining the detection accuracy within an acceptable range.

12. Future Work

Plan for the future work is to use different classification methods to detect intrusions. Using the results derived from the intrusion detection and comparing it versus both the full and the reduced feature sets, one can analyze the differences in their accuracy and speed. Also merging KDD Cup 99 features with 116 newly derived features to generate one single dataset and repeat all the experiment for the new dataset and to compare the result with the result reported in this paper.

REFERENCES

[1] A.-B. Amparo, S.-M. Noelia, M. C.-F. Félix, A. S.-R. Juan and P.-S. Beatriz, "Classification of Computer Intrusions Using Functional Networks—A Comparative Study," *Proceedings of European Symposium on Artificial Neural Networks* (*ESANN*), Bruges, 25-27 April 2007, pp. 579- 584.

[2] R. Heady, G. Luger, A. Maccabe and M. Servilla, "The Architecture of a Network Level Intrusion Detection System," Technical Report, University of New Mexico, Albuquerque, 1990.

[3] K. Ilgun, R. A. Kemmerer and P. A. Porras, "State Transition Analysis: A Rule-Based Intrusion Detection Approach," *IEEE Transaction on Software Engineering*, Vol. 21, No. 3, 1995, pp. 181-199.

[4] I. Guyon and A. Elisseeff, "An Introduction to Variable and Feature Selection," *Journal of Machine Learning Research*, Vol. 3, 2003, pp. 1157-1182.

[5] T. S. Chou, K. K. Yen and J. Luo, "Network Intrusion Detection Design Using Feature Selection of Soft Computing Paradigms," *International Journal of Computational Intelligence*, Vol. 4, No. 3, 2008, pp. 196-208.

[6] G. Zargar and P. Kabiri, "Identification of Effective Network Feature for Probing Attack Detection," *Proceedings of* 1*st International Conference on Network Digital Technologies*, July 2009, pp. 405-410.

[7] S. Chebrolu, A. Abraham and J. Thomas, "Feature Deduction and Ensemble Design of Intrusion Detection Systems," *Computers and Security*, *Elsevier Science*, Vol. 24, No. 4, 2005, pp. 295-307.

[8] A. H. Sung and S. Mukkamala, "Identifying Important Features for Intrusion Detection Using Support Vector Machines and Neural Networks," *Proceedings of International Symposium on Applications and the Internet* (*SAINT*), 2003, pp. 209-216.

[9] R. Agrawal, J. Gehrke, D. Gunopulos and P. Raghavan, "Automatic Subspace Clustering of High Dimensional Data for Data Mining applications," *Proceedings of Acm-sigmod International Conference on Management of Data*, Seattle, 1998, pp. 94-105.

[10] M. F. Abdollah, A. H. Yaacob, S. Sahib, I. Mohamad and M. F. Iskandar, "Revealing the Influence of Feature Selection for Fast Attack Detection," *International Journal of Computer Science and Network Security*, Vol. 8, No. 8, 2008, pp. 107-115.

[11] B. Chakraborty, "Feature Subset Selection by Neuro-Rough Hybridization," Lecture Notes in Computer Science (LNCS), Springer, Hiedelberg, 2005.

[12] S. Mukkamala, A. H. Sung and A. Abraham, "Modeling Intrusion Detection Systems Using Linear Genetic Programming Approach," Lecture Notes in Computer Science (LNCS), Springer, Hiedelberg, 2004.

[13] A. H. Sung, and S. Mukkamala, "The Feature Selection and Intrusion Detection Problems," Lecture Notes in Computer Science (LNCS), Springer, Hieldelberg, 2004.

[14] A. Abraham and R. Jain, "Soft Computing Models for Network Intrusion Detection Systems," Springer, Hiedelberg, 2004.

[15] A. Abraham, C. Grosan and C. M. Vide, "Evolutionary Design of Intrusion Detection Programs," *International Journal of Network Security*, Vol. 4, No. 3, 2007, pp. 328-339.

[16] C. Boutsidis, M. W. Mahoney and P. Drineas, "Unsupervised Feature Selection for Principal Components Analysis," *Proceedings of the* 14*th ACM Sigkdd International Conference on Knowledge Discovery and Data Mining*, Las Vegas, 2008, pp. 61-69.

[17] W. Wang and R. Battiti, "Identifying Intrusions in Com-

puter Networks Based on Principal Component Analysis," 2009. http://eprints.biblio.unitn.it/archive/00000917/

[18] R. D. Jain and J. Mao, "Statistical Pattern Recognition: A Review," *IEEE Transactions on Pattern Analysis and Machine Intelligence*, Vol. 22, No. 1, 2000, pp. 4-37.

[19] M. Turk and A. Pentland, "Eigenfaces for Recognition," *Journal of Cognitive Neuroscience*, Vol. 3, No. 1, 1991, pp. 71-86.

[20] K. Ohba and K. Ikeuchi, "Detectability, Uniqueness, and Reliability of Eigen Windows for Stable Verification of Partially Occluded Objects," *IEEE Transactions on Pattern Analysis and Machine Intelligence*, Vol. 19, No. 9, 1997, pp. 1043-1048.

[21] H. Murase and S. Nayar, "Visual Learning and Recognition of 3D Objects from Appearance," *International Journal of Computer Vision*, Vol. 14, 1995, pp. 5-24.

[22] Y. Song, J. Huang, D. Zhou, H. Y. Zha and C. L. Giles, "IKNN: Informative K-Nearest Neighbor Classification," Springer Verlag, Hieldelberg, 2007.

[23] D. Hand, H. Mannila and P. Smyth, "Principles of Data Mining," MIT Press, Cambridge, 2001.

[24] D. T. Larose, "Discovering Knowledge in Data: An Introduction to Data Mining," John Wiley and Sons Ltd., Chichester, 2005.

[25] 2009. http://support.microsoft.com/kb/172983

[26] 2009. http://www.Tcpdump.org
MIT Lincoln Laboratory, 2009.
http://www.ll.mit.edu/IST/ideval/

[27] MIT Lincoln Laboratory, Information Systems Technology Group, "The 1998 Intrusion Detection Off-Line Evaluation Plan," 1998.
http://www.11.mit.edu/IST/ideval/docs/1998/id98-eval-11.txt

[28] 2009. http://www.wireshark.org

[29] 2009. http://www.Tcptrace.org

[30] 2009.
http://www.wireshark.org/docs/man-pages/editcap.html

[31] G. R. Zargar and P. Kabiri, "Category-Based Selection of Effective Parameters for Intrusion Detection," *International Journal of Computer Science and Network Security* (*IJCSNS*), Vol. 9, No. 9, 2009.

[32] A. S. Vasilios and P. Fotini, "Application of Anomaly Detection Algorithms for Detecting SYN Flooding Attacks," *Proceedings of IEEE Globecom*, 2004, pp. 2050-2054.

[33] A.-B. Amparo, S.-M. Noelia, M. C.-F. Félix, A. S.-R. Juan and P.-S. Beatriz, "Classification of Computer Intrusions Using Functional Networks—A Comparative Study," *Proceedings—European Symposium on Artificial Neural Networks*, Bruges, 2007, pp. 579-584.

[34] A. Hassanzadeh and B. Sadeghian, "Intrusion Detection with Data Correlation Relation Graph," *3rd International Conference on Availability, Reliability and Security* (*ARES* 08), 2008, pp. 982-989.

[35] L. Christopher, I. Schuba, V. Krsul *et al.*, "Analysis of a Denial of Service Attack on TCP," *Proceedings of the IEEE Symposium on Security and Privacy*, 1997, pp. 208-223.

[36] N. B. Anuar, H. Sallehudin, A. Gani and O. Zakaria, "Identifying False Alarm for Network Intrusion Detection System Using Hybrid Data Mining and Decision Tree," *Malaysian Journal of Computer Science*, Vol. 21, No. 2, 2008, pp. 110-115.

[37] W. Lee, "A Data Mining Framework for Constructing Feature and Model for Intrusion Detection System," Ph.D. Thesis, University of Columbia, New York, 1999.

[38] W. Lee, S. J. Stolfo and K. W. Mok, "A Data Mining Framework for Building Intrusion Detection Models," *IEEE Symposium on Security and Privacy*, 1999, pp. 120-132.

[39] G. R. Zargar and P. Kabiri, "Selection of Effective Network Parameters in Attacks for Intrusion Detection," Lecture Notes in Computer Science (LNCS), Springer, Berlin, 2010.

[40] G. R. Zargar and P. Kabiri, "Identification of Effective Optimal Network Feature Set for Probing Attack Detection Using PCA Method," *International Journal of Web Application* (*IJWA*), Vol. 2, No. 3, 2010.

Table A.1. List of basic features from the TCP/IP protocol with their descriptions in this work.

No.	Feature	Description	
1	Protocol	Type of protocol	
2	Frame_lenght	Length of frame	
3	Capture_lenght	Length of capture	
4	Frame_IS_marked	Frame is marked	
5	Coloring_rule_name	Coloring rule name	
6	Ethernet_type	Type of ethernet protocol	
7	Ver_IP	IP version	
8	Header_lenght_IP	IP header length	
9	Differentiated_S	Differentiated service	
10	IP_Total_Lenght	IP total length	
11	Identification_IP	Identification IP	
12	MF_Flag_IP	More fragment flag	
13	DF_Flag_IP	Don't fragment flag	
14	Fragmentation_offset_IP	Fragmentation offset IP	
15	Time_to_live_IP	Time to live IP	
16	Protocol_no	Protocol number	**Basic feature**
17	Src_port	Source port	
18	Dst_port	Destination port	
19	Stream_index	Stream index number	
20	Sequence_number	Sequence number	
21	Ack_number	Acknowledgment number	
22	Cwr_flag	Cwr flag(status flag of the connection)	
23	Ecn_echo_flag	Ecn echo flag (status flag of the connection)	
24	Urgent_flag	Urgent flag (status flag of the connection)	
25	Ack_flag	Acknowledgment flag (status flag of the connection)	
26	Psh_flag	Push flag (status flag of the connection)	
27	Rst_flag	Reset flag (status flag of the connection)	
28	Syn_flag	Syn flag (status flag of the connection)	
29	Fin_flag	Finish flag (status flag of the connection)	
30	ICMP_Type	Specifies the format of the ICMP message such as: (8 = echo request and 0 = echo reply)	
31	ICMP_code	Further qualifies the ICMP message	
32	ICMP_data	ICMP data	

Appendix 1. Description of the basic and derived features.

No.	Feature	Description	
18	unique_byte_sent_b_a	The number of unique bytes sent the total bytes of data sent excluding retransmitted bytes and any bytes sent doing window probing (server to client)	
19	actual_data_pkts_a_b	The count of all the packets with at least a byte of TCP data payload (client to server)	
20	actual_data_pkts_b_a	The count of all the packets with at least a byte of TCP data payload (server to client)	
21	actual_data_byte_a_b	The total bytes of data seen. Note that this includes bytes from retransmissions/ window probe packets if any (client to server)	
22	actual_data_byte_b_a	The total bytes of data seen Note that this includes bytes from retransmissions/ window probe packets if any (server to client)	
23	rexmt_data_pkts_a_b	The count of all the packets found to be retransmissions (client to server)	Derived feature
24	rexm_data_pkts_b_a	The count of all the packets found to be retransmissions (server to client)	
25	rexmt_data_bytes_a_b	The total bytes of data found in the retransmitted packets (client to server)	
26	rexmt_data_bytes_b_a	The total bytes of data found in the retransmitted packets (server to client)	
27	zwnd_probe_pkts_a_b	The count of all the window probe packets seen (window probe packets are typically sent by a sender when the receiver last advertised a zero receive window to see if the window has opened up now (client to server)	
28	zwnd_probe_pkts_b_a	The count of all the window probe packets seen (window probe packets are typically sent by a sender when the receiver last advertised a zero receive window to see if the window is open now (server to client)	
29	zwnd_probe_byte_a_b	The total bytes of data sent in the window probe packets (client to server)	
30	zwnd_probe_byte_b_a	The total bytes of data sent in the window probe packets (server to client)	

Continued

31	outoforder_pkts_a_b	The count of all the packets that were seen to arrive out of order (client to server)
32	outoforder_pkts_b_a	The count of all the packets that were seen to arrive out of order (server to client)
33	pushed_data_pkts_a_b	The count of all the packets seen with the Push bit set in the TCP header (client to server)
34	pushed_data_pkts_b_a	The count of all the packets seen with the Push bit set in the TCP header (server to client)
35	SYN_pkts_sent_a_b	The count of all the packets seen with the SYN bits set in the TCP header respectively (client to server)
36	FIN_Pkts_sent_a_b	The count of all the packets seen with the FIN bits set in the TCP header respectively (client to server)
37	SYN_Pkts_sent_b_a	The count of all the packets seen with the SYN bits set in the TCP header respectively (server to client)
38	FIN_pkts_sent_b_a	The count of all the packets seen with the FIN bits set in the TCP header respectively (server to client)
39	Urgent_data_pkts_a_b	The total number of packets with the URG bit turned on in the TCP header (client to server)
40	Urgent_data_pkts_b_a	The total number of packets with the URG bit turned on in the TCP header (server to client)
41	Urgent_data_bytes_a_b	The total bytes of Urgent data sent this field is calculated by summing the urgent pointer offset values found in packets having the URG bit set in the TCP header (client to server)
42	Urgent_data_bytes_b_a	The total bytes of Urgent data sent this field is calculated by summing the urgent pointer offset values found in packets having the URG bit set in the TCP header (server to client)
43	mss_requested_a_b	The Maximum Segment Size (MSS) requested as a TCP option in the SYN packet opening the connection (client to server)
44	mss_requested_b_a	The Maximum Segment Size (MSS) requested as a TCP option in the SYN packet opening the connection (server to client)
45	max_segm_size_a_b	The maximum segment size observed during the life time of the connection (client to server)
46	max_segm_size_b_a	The maximum segment size observed during the life time of the connection (server to client)
47	min_segm_size_a_b	The minimum segment size observed during the life time of the connection (client to server)
48	min_segm_size_b_a	The minimum segment size observed during the life time of the connection (server to client)
49	avg_segm_size_a_b	The average segment size observed during the lifetime of the connection calculated as the value reported in the actual data bytes field divided by the actual data packets reported (client to server)
50	avg_segm_size_b_a	The average segment size observed during the lifetime of the connection calculated as the value reported in the actual data bytes field divided by the actual data packets reported (server to client)
51	max_win_adv_a_b	The maximum window advertisement seen if the connection is using window scaling (client to server)
52	max_win_adv_b_a	The maximum window advertisement seen if the connection is using window scaling (server to client)
53	min_win_adv_a_b	The minimum window advertisement seen this is the minimum window scaled advertisement seen if both sides negotiated window scaling (client to server)
54	min_win_adv_b_a	The minimum window advertisement seen. This is the minimum window scaled advertisement seen if both sides negotiated window scaling (server to client)
55	zero_win_adv_a_b	The number of times a zero receive window was advertised (client to server)
56	zero_win_adv_b_a	The number of times a zero receive window was advertised (server to client)
57	avg_win_adv_a_b	The average window advertisement seen, calculated as the sum of all window advertisements divided by the total number of packets seen (client to server)
58	avg_win_adv_b_a	The average window advertisement seen, calculated as the sum of all window advertisements divided by the total number of packets seen (server to client)
59	initial_window_byte_a_b	The total number of byte sent in the initial window the number of bytes seen in the initial flight of data before receiving the first ack packet from the other endpoint (client to server)
60	initial_window_byte_b_a	The total number of bytes sent in the initial window the number of bytes seen in the initial flight of data before receiving the first ack packet from the other endpoint (server to client)
61	initial_window_packets_a_b	The total number of segments (packets) sent in the initial window as explained in above (client to server)
62	initial_window_packets_b_a	The total number of segments (packets) sent in the initial window as explained in above (server to client)
63	ttl_stream_length_a_b	The theoretical stream length, this is calculated as the difference between the sequence numbers of the SYN and FIN packets giving the length of the data stream seen (client to server)
64	ttl_stream_length_b_a	The theoretical stream length, this is calculated as the difference between the sequence numbers of the SYN and FIN packets giving the length of the data stream seen (server to client)

Continued

65	missed_data_a_b	The missed data, calculated as the difference between the ttl stream length and unique bytes sent. If the connection was not complete, this calculation is invalid and an "NA" (Not Available) is printed (client to server)
66	missed_data_b_a	The missed data, calculated as the difference between the ttl stream length and unique bytes sent. If the connection was not complete, this calculation is invalid and an "NA" (Not Available) is printed (server to client)
67	truncated_data_a_b	The truncated data, calculated as the total bytes of data truncated during packet capture. For example, with Tcpdump, the sample option can be set to 64 (with -s option) so that just the headers of the packet (assuming there are no options) are captured, truncating most of the packet data. In an Ethernet with maximum segment size of 1500 bytes, this would add up to total truncated data of 1500, 64 = 1436 bytes for a packet (client to server)
68	truncated_data_b_a	The truncated data, calculated as the total bytes of data truncated during packet capture. For example, with Tcpdump, the sample option can be set to 64 (with -s option) so that just the headers of the packet (assuming there are no options) are captured, truncating most of the packet data. In an Ethernet with maximum segment size of 1500 bytes, this would add up to total truncated data of 1500, 64 = 1436 bytes for a packet (server to client)
69	truncated_packets_a_b	The total number of packets truncated as explained above (client to server)
70	truncated_packets_b_a	The total number of packets truncated as explained above (server to client)
71	data_xmit_time_a_b	Total data transmit time, calculated as the difference between the times of capture of the first and last packets carrying non-zero TCP data payload (client to server)
72	data_xmit_time_b_a	Total data transmit time, calculated as the difference between the times of capture of the first and last packets carrying non-zero TCP data payload (server to client)
73	idletime_max_a_b	Maximum idle time, calculated as the maximum time between consecutive packets seen in the direction (client to server)
74	idletime_max_b_a	Maximum idle time, calculated as the maximum time between consecutive packets seen in the direction (server to client)
75	throughtput_a_b	The average throughput calculated as the unique bytes sent divided by the elapsed time *i.e.*, the value reported in the unique bytes sent field divided by the elapsed time (the time difference between the capture of the first and last packets in the direction) (client to server)
76	throughtput_b_a	The average throughput calculated as the unique bytes sent divided by the elapsed time *i.e.*, the value reported in the unique bytes sent field divided by the elapsed time (the time difference between the capture of the first and last packets in the direction) (server to client)
77	RTT_samples_a_b	The total number of Round-Trip Time (RTT) samples found. TCP trace is pretty smart about choosing only valid RTT samples. An RTT sample is found only if an ack packet is received from the other end point for a previously transmitted packet such that the acknowledgment value is 1 greater than the last sequence number of the packet. Further, it is required that the packet being acknowledged was not retransmitted, and that no packets that came before it in the sequence space were retransmitted after the packet was transmitted. Note: The former condition invalidates RTT samples due to the retransmission ambiguity problem, and the latter condition invalidates RTT samples since it could be the case that the ack packet could be cumulatively acknowledging the retransmitted packet, and not necessarily acking the packet in question (client to server)
78	RTT_samples_b_a	(server to client)
79	RTT_min_a_b	The minimum RTT sample seen (client to server)
80	RTT_min_b_a	The minimum RTT sample seen (server to client)
81	RTT_max_a_b	The maximum RTT sample seen (client to server)
82	RTT_max_b_a	The maximum RTT sample seen (server to client)
83	RTT_avg_a_b	The average value of RTT found, calculated straightforwardly as the sum of all the RTT values found divided by the total number of RTT samples (client to server)
84	RTT_avg_b_a	The average value of RTT found, calculated straightforwardly as the sum of all the RTT values found divided by the total number of RTT samples (server to client)
85	RTT_stdv_a_b	The standard deviation of the RTT samples (client to server)
86	RTT_stdv_b_a	The standard deviation of the RTT samples (server to client)
87	RTT_from_3WHS_a_b	The RTT value calculated from the TCP 3-Way Hand-Shake (connection opening), assuming that the SYN packets of the connection were captured (client to server)
88	RTT_from_3WHS_b_a	The RTT value calculated from the TCP 3-Way Hand-Shake (connection opening), assuming that the SYN packets of the connection were captured (server to client)

Continued

89	RTT_full_sz_smpls_a_b	The total number of full-size RTT samples, calculated from the RTT samples of full-size segments. Full-size segments are defined to be the segments of the largest size seen in the connection (client to server)
90	RTT_full_sz_smpls_b_a	The total number of full-size RTT samples, calculated from the RTT samples of full-size segments. Full-size segments are defined to be the segments of the largest size seen in the connection (server to client)
91	RTT_full_sz_min_a_b	The minimum full-size RTT sample (client to server)
92	RTT_full_sz_min_b_a	The minimum full-size RTT sample (server to client)
93	RTT_full_sz_max_a_b	The maximum full-size RTT sample (client to server)
94	RTT_full_sz_max_b_a	The maximum full-size RTT sample (server to client)
95	RTT_full_sz_avg_a_b	The average full-size RTT sample (client to server)
96	RTT_full_sz_avg_b_a	The average full-size RTT sample (server to client)
97	RTT_full_sz_stdev_a_b	The standard deviation of full-size RTT samples (client to server)
98	RTT_full_sz_stdev_b_a	The standard deviation of full-size RTT samples (server to client)
99	post_loss_acks_a_b	The total number of ack packets received after losses were detected and a retransmission occurred. More precisely, a post-loss ack is found to occur when an ack packet acknowledges a packet sent (acknowledgment value in the ack packet is 1 greater than the packet's last sequence number), and at least one packet occurring before the packet acknowledged, was retransmitted later. In other words, the ack packet is received after we observed a (perceived) loss event and are recovering from it (client to server)
100	post_loss_acks_b_a	The total number of ack packets received after losses were detected and a retransmission occurred. More precisely, a post-loss ack is found to occur when an ack packet acknowledges a packet sent (acknowledgment value in the ack packet is 1 greater than the packet's last sequence number), and at least one packet occurring before the packet acknowledged, was retransmitted later. In other words, the ack packet is received after we observed a (perceived) loss event and are recovering from it (server to client)
101	segs_cum_acked_a_b	The count of the number of segments that were cumulatively acknowledged and not directly acknowledged (client to server)
102	segs_cum_acked_b_a	The count of the number of segments that were cumulatively acknowledged and not directly acknowledged (server to client)
103	duplicate_acks_a_b	The total number of duplicate acknowledgments received (client to server)
104	duplicate_acks_b_a	The total number of duplicate acknowledgments received (server to client)
105	triple_dupacks_a_b	The total number of triple duplicate acknowledgments received (three duplicate acknowledgments acknowledging the same segment), a condition commonly used to trigger the fast-retransmit/fast-recovery phase of TCP (client to server)
106	triple_dupacks_b_a	The total number of triple duplicate acknowledgments received (three duplicate acknowledgments acknowledging the same segment), a condition commonly used to trigger the fast-retransmit/fast-recovery phase of TCP (server to client)
107	max_retrans_a_b	The maximum number of retransmissions seen for any segment during the lifetime of the connection (client to server)
108	max_retrans_b_a	The maximum number of retransmissions seen for any segment during the lifetime of the connection (server to client)
109	min_retr_time_a_b	The minimum time seen between any two (re)transmissions of a segment amongst all the retransmissions seen (client to server)
110	min_retr_time_b_a	The minimum time seen between any two (re)transmissions of a segment amongst all the retransmissions seen (server to client)
111	max_retr_time_a_b	The maximum time seen between any two (re)transmissions of a segment (client to server)
112	max_retr_time_b_a	The maximum time seen between any two (re)transmissions of a segment (server to client)
113	avg_retr_time_a_b	The average time seen between any two (re)transmissions of a segment calculated from all the retransmissions (client to server)
114	avg_retr_time_b_a	The average time seen between any two (re)transmissions of a segment calculated from all the retransmissions (server to client)
115	sdv_retr_time_a_b	The standard deviation of the retransmission time samples obtained from all the retransmissions (client to server)
116	sdv_retr_time_b_a	The standard deviation of the retransmission time samples obtained from all the retransmissions (server to client)

SPCS: Secure and Privacy-Preserving Charging-Station Searching Using VANET

Tat Wing Chim[1*], Jeanno Chin Long Cheung[1], Siu Ming Yiu[1], Lucas Chi Kwong Hui[1], Victor On Kwok Li[2]

[1]Department of Computer Science, The University of Hong Kong, Hong Kong, China
[2]Department of Electrical and Electronic Engineering, The University of Hong Kong, Hong Kong, China

ABSTRACT

Electric vehicle has attracted more and more attention all around the world in recent years because of its many advantages such as low pollution to the environment. However, due to the limitation of current technology, charging remains an important issue. In this paper, we study the problem of finding and making reservation on charging stations via a vehicular ad hoc network (VANET). Our focus is on the privacy concern as drivers would not like to be traced by knowing which charging stations they have visited. Technically, we make use of the property of blind signature to achieve this goal. In brief, an electric vehicle first generates a set of anonymous credentials on its own. A trusted authority then blindly signs on them after verifying the identity of the vehicle. After that, the vehicle can make charging station searching queries and reservations by presenting those signed anonymous credentials. We implemented the scheme and show that the credential signing process (expected to be the most time consuming step) can be completed within reasonable time when the parameters are properly set. In particular, the process can be completed in 5 minutes when 1024 bits of RSA signing key is used. Moreover, we show that our scheme is secure in terms of authentication and privacy-preserving.

Keywords: Electric Vehicle; Vehicular Ad Hoc Network; Blind Signature; Anonymous Credential

1. Introduction

Electric Vehicle (EV) has attracted a lot of attention all around the world in recent years due to its many advantages such as low noise, low energy consumption and low pollution. However, the distance that can be travelled by an electric vehicle with onboard battery fully charged is usually shorter than that can be travelled by a conventional fossil fuel powered vehicle with the gas tank fully filled. Thus a driver has to search in advance the charging stations it has to visit in order for it to have enough power to complete the whole journey. On the other hand, since charging up a battery usually take much longer time than filling up a fossil fuel tank, long queues at charging stations may be resulted. Thus a reservation mechanism is desirable.

Before continuing our discussion, let us briefly talk about what a VANET is. VANET is an important element of the Intelligent Transportation Systems (ITSs) [1]. In a typical VANET, each vehicle is assumed to have an on-board unit (OBU) and there are road-side units (RSU) installed along the roads. A trusted authority (TA) and maybe some other application servers are installed in the backend. The OBUs and RSUs communicate using the Dedicated Short Range Communications (DSRC) protocol [2] over the wireless channel while the RSUs, TA, and the application servers communicate using a secure fixed network (e.g. the Internet). The basic application of a VANET is to allow arbitrary vehicles to broadcast safety messages (e.g. about vehicle speed, turning direction, road condition, traffic accident information) to other nearby vehicles (denoted as vehicle-vehicle or V2V communications) and to RSU (denoted as vehicle-infrastructure or V2I communications) regularly such that other vehicles may adjust their travelling routes and RSUs may inform the traffic control center to adjust traffic lights for avoiding possible traffic congestion. As such, a VANET can also be interpreted as a sensor network because the traffic control center or some other central servers can collect lots of useful information about road conditions from vehicles.

In this paper, we study the online charging station searching and reservation problem. We mainly focus on the security and privacy issue of the problem as most drivers may not want other to track his route down by

*Corresponding author.

learning which charging stations he visited. Based on the source and destination of a journey, the system can automatically search and suggest a set of charging stations for the driver. Reservations can also be made accordingly. Our scheme addresses two major security problems-authentication and privacy-preservation. In terms of authentication, a driver has to be properly authenticcated before it can use the searching and reservation service. This can help to avoid an attacker from making too many requests and unnecessary reservations, which in turn blocks normal users from using the service. On the other hand, it makes more sense for the searching and reservation service to be paid ones. Otherwise, a driver may simply make reservations at all charging stations around the city so that he/she can change his/her mind about where to go at the very last minute. Thus authenticcation is essential. In terms of privacy-preservation, a driver may not want others to know his/her travelling source, destination and even the route. We adopt the technique of blind signature [3] to facilitate a driver to obtain a valid anonymous credential. Then the driver can make searching and reservation queries as well as get his/her vehicle charged up at charging stations by presenting the anonymous credential. We use the term "anonymous" here because the credential can prove that the holder has been properly authenticated but no one can deduce the identity of the driver based only on the credential itself.

Privacy-preservation can then be achieved.

We provide a security analysis and we implemented the scheme to evaluate our scheme. Throughout our scheme, the most time-consuming part should be the credential signing process by the trusted authority. It may even become a bottleneck if lots of vehicles request it for signing operation at about the same time. Through our study, we show that such a credential signing process can be completed in reasonable time when the parameters are properly set. The process takes about 5 minutes when 1024 bits of RSA signing key is used.

The rest of the paper is organized as follows: related work is reviewed in Section 2. The system model, charging model, assumptions and security requirements are listed in Section 3. Our schemes are described in details in Section 4. The analysis and evaluation of our schemes are given in Sections 5-7. Finally, Section 8 concludes the paper.

2. Related Work

The idea of searching charging stations using VANET is new. However, there are some existing similar VANET applications published in recent years. For example, in [4], a VANET-based smart parking scheme for large parking lots was proposed. Though they also consider security, there are a number of differences between their scheme and ours. First, their scheme is of a small scale which covers a car park while ours is large scale to cover the whole city and beyond. Second, in their scheme a car park is monitored by three RSUs which take up the roles of determining a vehicle's location, searching for a vacant parking space and providing navigation service to guide the vehicle to go from the car park entrance to the selected parking space. In our scheme, the road system is covered by a large number of charging stations which report their status in a distributed manner. Third, our scheme allows one's identity and charging station searching query to be delinked. This feature is only interesting for wide area searching like ours. Forth, our scheme allows a driver to make a reservation at a charging station. Again, this feature is only interesting for a wide area setting like ours. Thus, the scheme provided in [4] cannot be used to solve the charging station searching problem discussed in this paper.

Other interesting VANET application recently published include [5,6]. In [5], an interesting problem about providing querying service using VANET while ensuring that queries will not be linkable to the queriers was discussed. A solution for solving the problem by using techniques of pseudo-identity, indistinguishable credentials, and oblivious transfer was then proposed. Although it also provides a way for a vehicle to anonymously obtain credentials, all credentials are assumed to be identical and so the approach cannot be adopted into our SPCS scheme in which credentials carry different times of issuance and values. In [6], a new real-time urban monitoring system using the Localizing and Handling Network Event Systems (LocHNESs) platform developed by Telecom Italia was developed. Information about urban mobility in real time, ranging from traffic conditions to the movements of pedestrians throughout the city, can be collected efficiently. However, security issues were not mentioned in this work.

In terms of security, recent efforts related to the security issues in VANET include [7-13]. In [7], a batch verification scheme known as IBV was proposed for an RSU to verify a large number of signatures at the same time using only three pairing operations. In [8], an RSU-aided inter-vehicle communications scheme was proposed. A vehicle relies on an RSU to verify the signature of another vehicle. In [9], group communications in VANETs are considered and a group key update protocol was proposed. In [10], some security and privacy-enhancing communications schemes were proposed. Of particular interest, a group communications protocol was defined. After a simple handshaking with any RSU, a group of known vehicles can verify the signature of each other without any further support from RSUs. A common group secret is also developed for secure communications among group members. [11,12] also target at driver privacy preservation but instead of using pseudo identities, the concept of group signature is adopted. The signature of any vehicle can be verified by the same group key but the actual signer can only be traced by a trusted party. Though privacy can be preserved, these schemes are rather complicated and may not be practical. In [13], a threshold anonymous announcement service using direct anonymous attestation and one-time anonymous authentication to simultaneously achieve the goals of reliability, privacy and auditability was proposed. However, it focuses on inter-vehicle message authentication in general and is not related to querying.

Our scheme is based on the idea of indistinguishable (anonymous) credential. Such a credential system was introduced by Chaum [14]. The system allows a user to obtain a credential from one organization and later show the possession of the credential to another organization while the transactions at the two organizations are not linkable. The idea of anonymous credential has been adopted in different applications. For example, [15] proposes a credential-based privacy-preserving e-learning system under which a student can show his/her progress in e-learning without leaking his/her identity information.

3. Problem Statement

3.1. System Model

Our vehicular network consists of on-board units (OBUs) installed on vehicles, road-side units (RSUs) and charging stations (CSs) along the roads, a trusted authority (TA) and a querying server (QS) in the backend for key management and for answering charging station queries and making reservations at charging stations, respecttively.

3.2. Charging Model

We assume that a client will be charged for the following instances:

- Making each charging station searching query: A driver will be charged when he/she makes charging station searching queries to the querying server. This is because the querying server operator needs to invest on facilities for the searching and scheduling service.
- Making reservation at a charging station: A driver will be charged when he/she makes reservations to charging stations and the charge is proportional to the length of the duration reserved. This is necessary because otherwise, a driver may tend to reserve a duration which is longer than necessary to ensure that he/she does not need to wait when he/she arrives at the charging station concerned.

Note that our system also supports different charging models. For example, an operator may want to charge a driver more if he/she makes reservations during peak hours.

3.3. Assumptions

We further assume the followings:

- The TA is trusted while the QS is only semi-trusted. To avoid being a single point of failure, redundant TAs and QSs which have identical functionalities are installed.
- TA, QS and RSUs communicate through a secure fixed network (e.g. Internet). Thus RSUs can help to relate messages from vehicles on the road to TA and QS.
- There exists a conventional public key infrastructure (PKI) for initial vehicle authentication. Each vehicle V_i having license plate number LP_i has a conventional public key VPK_i and a conventional private key VSK_i and is given a TA-signed certificate $VCert_i$ which contains CPK_i and LP_i. We will discuss details about the generation and verification of $Cert_i$ in Section 4.
- There also exists a conventional identity-based public key infrastructure (PKI) for authenticating TA, QS and CSs. The public keys of TA and QS are the same as their real identities, *TRID* and *QRID* respectively, and are known by *everyone*. Also any charging station CS_i broadcasts its public key which is the same as its real identity $CRID_i$ with hello messages periodically to vehicles that are travelling close to it. Thus $CRID_i$ is known by all vehicles nearby. The validity $CRID_i$ can be ensured using a certificate $CCert_i$ issued by the TA. We will discuss the details in Section 4.
- The real identity of any vehicle is only known by the TA and itself but not by others.
- We assume that there is a reasonably large number of charging station searching queries issued to QS. Otherwise, if there is only one query, the sender can be linked up with the query easily.
- Each vehicle has a tamper-proof device which is responsible for all cryptographic-related functions such as storage of keys, generation of pseudo identities, signing messages and encryption of messages (details will be given one by one in the next section). Also its output interface is limited and we will specify that in the appropriate places in the next section. Finally, it is assumed to have its own clock for generating correct time stamps and be able to run on its own battery. Note that a vehicle can also have a conventional computer device for performing the verification of RSUs' hop information (to speed up the process and details will be given in the next section). Since a tamper-proof device is always associated with a dedi-

cated vehicle, we will use these two terms interchangeably without prior notice throughout the paper.

3.4. Security Requirements

We aim at designing a scheme to provide VANET-based charging station searching and reservation service for electric vehicles. The scheme has to satisfy the following two security requirements:

- Message integrity and authentication: A vehicle should be authenticated before it can request for credential signing, issue a charging station searching query, make reservations to charging stations and receive charging service at charging stations. On the other hand, TA, QS and vehicles are able to verify that a message is indeed sent and signed by a certain party without being modified by anyone.
- Privacy-preserving: In this paper, the privacy of a driver is defined as his driving habit and travelling route. It can be preserved by two means. First, even if TA and QS collude, they cannot link up a vehicle's query (which contains the travelling source and destination) with its real identity. Thus no one can trace a driver's travelling route and driving habit easily. Second, a vehicle's query (which contains the travelling source and destination) as well as the list of charging stations returned by QS can not be eavesdropped by neighboring vehicles easily.

4. Our Solutions—SPCS

This section presents our Secure and Privacy-preserving Charging-station Searching (SPCS) scheme using VANET. Our scheme consists of five phases—setup phase, credential signature requesting phase, charging station searching and reservation phase, charging phase and reconciliation phase. Next we explain each of these phases in details.

4.1. Setup Phase

During system startup, the following steps will be carried out:

- TA assigns itself an identity *TRID* and a secret key *TSK* such that *TRID* and *TSK* form a public and private key pair. *TRID* is assumed to be known by everyone in the system.
- TA assigns QS an identity *QRID* and a secret key *QSK* such that *QRID* and *QSK* form a public and private key pair.
- For each charging station CS_i locating at CL_i an identity $CRID_i$ and a secret key CSK_i such that $CRID_i$ and CSK_i form a public and private key pair. To facilitate others to verify CS_i's identity, TA generates its certificate as $CCerti = \langle CRID_i,\ CL_i, TSIG_{TSK}\left(CRID_i \| CL_i\right)\rangle$ where $TSIG_{TSK}\left(CRID_i \| CL_i\right)$ is TA's signature on the concatenation of $CRID_i$ and CL_i. Note that any asymmetric signature scheme can be used in the above steps.
- During system setup or first registration of an electric vehicle V_i, TA assigns it a real identity $VRID_i$ and the tamper-proof device activation password $VPWD_i$. TA also assigns V_i a license plate number LP_i and generates a pair of conventional public and private keys, VPK_i and VSK_i respectively. TA then signs a certificate $VCert_i = \langle LP_i,\ VPK_i,\ TSIG_{TSK}\left(LP_i \| VPK_i\right)\rangle$ where $TSIG_{TSK}\left(LP_i \| VPK_i\right)$. TA preloads $VRID_i$, $VPWD_i$, LP_i, VSK_i and $VCert_i$ into the tamper-proof device on V_i.

Throughout the paper, conventional asymmetric and symmetric encryptions and signatures are used at some locations. To make the context concise, let us use the notations $AS\_ENC_x(M)$ and $S\_ENC_x(M), SIG_x(M)$ to denote asymmetrically encrypting, symmetrically encrypting and signing message M using the key x based on any asymmetric encryption, symmetric encryption and signature algorithms, respectively.

4.2. Credential Signature Requesting Phase

At the beginning of a charging period (say a month) or when a driver uses up all the credentials in hand, the driver triggers the tamper-proof device on his/her electric vehicle V_i to send the following credential signing request message to the TA: $\langle Cred\_Sig\_Req, VCert_i, SIG_{VSKi}(Cred\_Sig\_Req)\rangle$.
TA verifies the signature $SIG_{VSKi}(Cred\_Sig\_Req)$ using V_i's public key VPK_i as stored in $VCert_i$. If successful, TA generate a random session key *SESS_KEY* and securely transmits it to V_i's tamper-proof device. That is the transmitting message becomes

$$\langle AS\_ENC_{VPKi}(SESS\_KEY),\ TSIG_{TSK}\left(AS\_ENC_{VPKi}(SESS\_KEY)\right)\rangle$$

Upon finishing verifying TA's signature with *TRID*, the tamperproof device stores *SESS_KEY* locally for ongoing communi- cations.

Next the tamper-proof device generates a set of credentials for the TA to sign. Each credential $Cred_k$ is of the form $\langle CN_k, TOI_k, Val_k, Sig_k\rangle$ where CN_k is a unique credential number (*i.e.* different credentials have different credential numbers), TOI_k indicates the time that the credential is issued, Val_k is the duration that the electric vehicle can get charged up by presenting that credential. Sample values include 5, 10 and 15 (minutes) and the value depends on the kind of electric vehicle as well as the capacity of the onboard battery. Since a driver also needs a credential for the charging station searching service, such a credential carries a special value of 0. Sig_k represents the TA's signature on the first three fields and will be filled up later. For the credential of a certain value, the tamper-proof device generates N times more credentials than necessary (*i.e.* among every N credentials, only one credential will be used while the other (N – 1) credentials are only for checking purpose which we will describe in later context). For each credential, the tamper-proof device transforms the bit pattern of the concatenation $CN_k \| TOI_k \| Val_k$ into $CTV_k' = Trans(CN_k \| TOI_k \| Val_k)$. It then sends the transformed credentials altogether to the TA for blind signature. To avoid the credentials being stolen or tampered by eavesdroppers, all of them are encrypted symmetrically using $SESS\_KEY$ and signed using VSK_i before they are sent out.

For every N credentials with the same value, TA randomly challenges the tamper-proof device to open $(N-1)$ of them and checks whether they are of proper format (including whether any two of them have the same credential number, whether TOI_k is really close to the current time, whether all the $(N-1)$ credentials have the same value). If yes, TA blindly signs the remaining credential (*i.e.* the one that was not opened) and sends it back to the temper-proof device. Similar to the above, all communications are symmetrically encrypted using the session key $SESS\_KEY$ to resist against eavesdroppers. Also the messages from V_i and TA are signed using VSK_i and TSK respectively by the corresponding party.

After that, the tamper-proof device retrieves the actual signed credentials by removing the hiding factors. That is, for each credential, it de-transforms $SIG_{TSK}(CTV_k')$ back into $SIG_{TSK}(CN_k \| TOI_k \| Val_k)$ by performing $SIG_{TSK}(CN_k \| TOI_k \| Val_k) = DTrans(SIG_{TSK}(CTV_k'))$. At this moment, the tamper-proof device can fill up all TA signatures in all credentials. The tamper-proof device stored all credentials locally.

Finally, TA records the total number of credentials which it has blindly signed and their values into its local database (to be used in reconciliation phase).

4.3. Charging Station Searching and Reservation Phase

When a driver starts up his/her electric vehicle V_i for a journey, he/she first enters the real identity $VRID_i$ and password $VPWD_i$ (assigned by TA in Section 4.2 above) into the tamper-proof device to activate it. Here only simple hardware checking is involved. If either the real identity or the password is, or both are incorrect, the tamper-proof device refuses to perform further operations. Otherwise, the tamper-proof device prompts the driver to enter the travelling source Src_i and destination $Dest_i$. The tamper-proof device then randomly picks up a credential $Cred_k$ with value 0 (*i.e.* those for searching purpose) from its pool, composes the message $AS\_ENC_{QRID}(Cred_k \| Src \| Dest)$ and sends it to the querying server (QS). Note that no signature is required here because the tamper-proof device will hide its real identity from now on.

Upon receiving the message from V_i, QS first decrypts the message using its private key QSK. It then checks whether the attached credential $Cred_k$ is a valid one by checking the validity of TA's signature using $TRID$. If it is valid, it also checks whether the same credential (same credential number and same time of issurance) has been used before. To achieve this goal, QS maintains a local database for storing the pair (CN_k, TOI_k) of all received credentials and the checking becomes a simple linear scanning. If so unluckily the credential has been used, the QS asks the driver to present another credential by sending it the signed message

$$\langle Cred\_Used, CN_k, TOI_k, SIG_{QSK}(Cred\_Used \| CN_k \| TOI_k) \rangle.$$

The above validation process then repeats. The driver records the previous credential as unused but will not use it any more in the future. He/she also records the QS's signed message so that he/she could later present it to TA (to avoid unnecessary charging).

If the above validation is successful, based on the reservation status of the charging stations and the real-time road conditions (reported by OBUs and RSUs as discussed in [10]), QS suggests the locations of one or more charging stations together with the charging durations at each charging station to the driver. Note that the searching of charging stations is actually another non-trivial scheduling problem and we will leave it as our future work. To summarize, the searching and reservation process should guarantee that:

- The charging stations have enough power when the electric vehicle V_i arrives (since under smart grid framework, power is supplied on an on-demand manner); and
- The total delay experienced by V_i is minimized. The total delay here includes travelling delay (to be reflected by the fact that whether the chosen charging stations are close enough to the original travelling route) and queuing delay at charging stations (since an electric vehicle usually takes much longer time for charging up than for filling up the fossil fuel tank).

Since the credential number CN_k of the credential $Cred_k$ is only known by the tamper-proof device and QS, we makes use of it to develop a secure channel (*i.e.* symmetric encryption using the key CN_k) for ongoing communications between V_i and QS from now on. QS replies the tamper-proof device the set of charging stations (with identities and locations) and charging durations at each charging station via the secure channel and requests it to submit the appropriate number of credentials for reservation purpose. The tamper-proof device submits the credentials via the secure channel in return. In some cases, a driver may dislike one or more charging stations suggested. For example, the driver may have arguments with the staff at a certain charging station before. In this case, he/she can request QS to provide a replacement set of charging stations by eliminating the charging stations he/she dislikes. The above process then repeats. Similar to the above, any message sent by QS to V_i is signed using *QSK* to avoid being tampered by eavesdroppers on its way.

For simplicity, we assume that the credentials will be used in sequence. That is, the first credential in the submitted list of credentials will be used at the charging station closest to Src_i while the last credential in the submitted list of credentials will be used at the charging station closest to $Dest_i$. After validating the submitted credentials, QS distributes them to the charging stations in order. Note that QS and charging stations are connected via a fixed infrastructure and so we assume that the communications there are secure. The charging stations then record the reservations accordingly by storing the corresponding credentials. Having the credentials, a charging station can double-verify the reservation status upon V_i arrives.

4.4. Charging Phase

The driver then drives his/her electric vehicle V_i to the suggested (and reserved) charging stations in sequence. Since the credentials are being used in sequence, based on QS's suggestion (charging stations and charging durations at them), he/she knows which credential(s) should be used at which charging station and can present the credential(s) appropriately. To resist against eavesdroppers, all credentials presented are encrypted using the identity $CRID_j$ of the corresponding charging station (say CS_j).

Upon receiving the message, the charging station CS_j first decrypts using its private key CSK_j to obtain the credentials. It then checks whether it has received the same credential from QS (during reservation phase) before. If yes, it serves V_i by charging it up. For commercial purpose, an electric vehicle which has not made reservation should also be served but at a lower priority.

4.5. Reconciliation Phase

This phase is usually done at the end of each charging period (say a month). The QS sends all credentials stored in its local database to TA. Each driver also sends the credentials that have not been used (as well as QS's signed *Cred_Used* messages) to TA. For authentication and integrity purpose, a driver's tamper-proof device signs the message using VSK_i.

Since TA has recorded the number of signed credentials and their values during the credential signature requesting phase, based on the received information, it can now calculate how many times the driver has used the searching service and how many charging durations the driver has reserved. The driver is then charged accordingly.

Note that our system also supports different charging models. For example, an operator may want to charge a driver more if he/she makes reservations during peak hours. In our system, this can be done easily by requiring the driver to submit more credentials during reservation phase.

5. Security Analysis

In this section, we briefly analyze our scheme with respect to the security requirements listed in Section 3.4.

- Message integrity and authentication:

Before a vehicle can request for credential signing from the TA, it needs to authenticate itself using its signature and certificate. Thus each properly-signed credential represents the valid identity of a vehicle. Before a vehicle can issue a charging station searching query, make reservations to charging stations and receive charging service at charging stations, it needs to present one or more properly-signed credentials. Hence a vehicle is authenticated everywhere in our scheme.

Recall that in our scheme, all messages sent by TA and QS are properly signed by their private keys, *TSK* and *QSK*, respectively and their identity, *TRID* and *QRID*, are assumed to be known by everyone. Thus the actual sender of the messages concerned can be easily guaranteed.

Since our scheme relies heavily on credentials signed by the TA, next we formally prove that signatures generated by the TA is secure under the RSA assumption—given a public key (N, e) and a message m where N is a RSA modulus and e is a random number less than $\varphi(N)$, it is hard to evaluate $m^d \bmod N$ where $ed \equiv 1 \bmod \varphi(N)$.

On the other hand, since we focus on the security of TA's signature, we ignore the blind signature mechanism (in fact, a signature blindly generated by TA is equivalent to a conventional signature) and assume that all credential numbers are randomly generated by TA.

Theorem: TA's signature on any credential is secure under the RSA assumption. If there exists an adversary A who makes at most q_s signature queries and qc credential number generation queries to a random oracle and can successfully generate an existential forgery with an advantage $Adv_A \geq \varepsilon$ in time τ, we can construct a reduction

R which can make use of A to solve the RSA problem and break the RSA assumption with an advantage $Adv_R \geq \varepsilon'$ in time τ' such that $\varepsilon' \approx \varepsilon / q_c$ and $\tau' \approx \tau$.

Proof: Assume that the challenge to the reduction R is that given a public key (N, e) and a complete set of credential contents (credential value, time of issuance and value where the latter two are denoted as TV^* while all three are denoted as CTV^*, to compute CTV^* mod N where d is the private key corresponding to (N, e). R sends (N, e) to A and A can make q_s signature queries and q_c credential number generation queries (*i.e.* given time of issuance and value, to generate a credential number to complete the credential content) to R. To facilitate the execution of the game, R creates a variable i (initialized to 1) to record the number of credential number generation queries received so far. It maintains a table with entries (TV_i, CTV_i, CTV_i^d) and simulates the signature and credential number generation queries as described below. It also chooses a random $i^* \epsilon [1 \cdots q_c]$, sets $TV_{i*} = TV^*$ and sets $CTV_{i*} = CTV^*$.

We first talk about the simulation of signature queries upon given time of issuance and value (TV). If there already exists an entry in the table $(TV, *, y)$, then it returns y as the signature. If there does not exist an entry with message TV, then it picks a random number y and sets CTV to y^e and adds the entry (TV, y^e, y) to the table. Note that y is a valid signature for TV since $(y^e)^d$ mod $N = y$. It then sends y to A as a response to its signature query. If the queried time of issuance and value are TV^* (*i.e.* the i^{*th} entry), R quits since it does not know how to answer.

Next we talk about the simulation of credential number generation queries upon given time of issuance and value TV. If $i \neq i^*$, then R picks a random number y and sets CTV to y^e and adds the entry (TV, y^e, y) to the table. Note that y is a valid signature for TV since $(y^e)^d$ mod $N = y$. It then sends y^e to A as a response to its credential number generation query. But if this is the i^{*th} credential number generation query, R updates $TV_{i*} = TV$ and returns CTV^* as a response.

Finally, A is allowed to forge a signature and send to R. Since we assume that A needs R's help in generating a credential number, the signature must correspond to one of the CTV values queried before. With a probability $1/q_c$, A will forge a signature corresponding to the i^{*th} entry. R can then resolve the challenge of computing CTV^* mod N.

Therefore, $Adv_R \geq \varepsilon/q_c$. This leads to a contradiction to the RSA assumption and so we can conclude that TA's signature on any credential is secure.

- Privacy preserving:

In our scheme, the only place that a vehicle shows its real identity is when it presents its signature and certificate during credential signature requesting phase and reconciliation phase. For all other phases including charging station searching and reservation phase and charging phase, a vehicle only presents an anonymous credential signed by the TA. Since the anonymous credential does not carry any information about the vehicle's identity, even TA and QS collude, no one knows who is performing which charging station query and who will visit which charging station.

During charging station searching and reservation phase, the travelling source and destination of a driver is first encrypted using QS's public key before sending out. Thus no third party can eavesdrop them. For the searching results (*i.e.* the set of suggested charging stations and charging durations) by QS, they are encrypted using the unique credential number of the credential presented by the driver. Since that credential number is only known by the driver and QS (even TA does not know it due to the property of blind signature), no third party can obtain the results as well.

Therefore, the driver's privacy is preserved.

6. Analysis on Time Complexity

In this section, we briefly analyze the time complexity of our SPCS scheme. Note that we ignore the time complexity involved in setup phase since it can be done offline and is only done once occasionally (e.g. when TA wants to update the parameters). It is not critical to the efficiency of our scheme.

We let T_{senc}, T_{sdec}, T_{aenc}, T_{adec}, T_{sig} and T_{ver} denote the time required to perform symmetric encryption, symmetric decryption, asymmetric encryption, asymmetric decryption, signature generation and signature verification operations respectively. These operations dominate the efficiency of our scheme, so we only consider the time taken by these operations and neglect all others.

According to Section 4.2, during the credential signature requesting phase, the tamper-proof device on vehicle V_i takes T_{sig} of time to produce $SIG_{VSKi}(Cred\_Sig\_Req)$. TA then takes T_{ver} of time to verify this signature. Next TA takes T_{aenc} of time to produce $AS\_ENC_{VPKi}(SESS\_KEY)$ and T_{sig} of time to produce the signature $TSIG_{TSK}(AS\_ENC_{VPKi}(SESS\_KEY))$. Upon receiving the message, the tamper-proof device on vehicle V_i takes T_{adec} of time to decrypt $AS\_ENC_{VPKi}(SESS\_KEY)$ and takes T_{ver} of time to verify the signature $TSIG_{TSK}(AS\_ENC_{VPKi}(SESS\_KEY))$.

For each credential, the tamper-proof device on vehicle V_i takes T_{senc} of time to symmetrically encrypt it and takes T_{sig} of time to sign it. For each unopened credential, TA takes T_{sig} of time to blindly sign it. Since the credential signing process should be the most time-consuming part in our whole SPCS scheme, we will analyze its performance further using implementation in Section 7.

According to Section 4.3, during the charging station searching and reservation phase, the tamper-proof device on vehicle V_i takes T_{aenc} of time to produce $AS\_ENC_{QRID}\left(Cred_k \| Src \| Dest\right)$. QS then takes T_{adec} of time to decrypt the message and takes T_{ver} of time to check the validity of $Cred_k$ by verifying TA's signature on it. If so unluckily the credential has been used, QS takes T_{sig} of time to generate the signature $SIG_{QSK}\left(Cred\_Used \| CN_k \| TOI_k\right)$. For all ongoing communications, the tamper-proof device on V_i and QS takes T_{senc} for symmetric encryption or takes T_{sdec} of time for symmetric decryption. For any message sent by QS to V_i, QS takes T_{sig} of time to sign it while the tamper-proof device on V_i takes T_{ver} of time to verify the signature.

According to Section 4.4, during the charging phase, the tamper-proof device on vehicle V_i takes T_{aenc} of time to encrypt each credential. The charging station CS_j then takes T_{adec} to decrypt it.

According to Section 4.5, during the reconciliation phase, the tamper-proof device on vehicle V_i takes T_{sig} of time to sign all unused credentials. Accordingly, TA takes T_{ver} of time to verify the signature.

Next let us summarize the time complexity of secure taxi service scheme in **Table 1**.

7. Implementation Results

Throughout our scheme, the most time-consuming part should be the credential signing process by the trusted authority. It may even become a bottleneck if lots of vehicles request it for signing operation at about the same time. In this section, we present our implementation results and show that the credential signing process can be completed in reasonable time when the parameters are properly set.

We have written a test program in Java to measure the actual time required for the TA to sign the credentials. The TA is implemented on a laptop computer with an Intel Core 2 Duo CPU, T5870@2 GHz and all signing processes run on a single core. We assume that the TA has to sign 10,000 credentials at a certain instance. The results are shown in **Figure 1**. From the figure, we can see that longer signing time is required when the length of TA's private key (*i.e. TSK*) gets longer.

Since 512 bits RSA keys are proved to be insecure nowadays, let us compare the cases with 1024 bits and 2048 bits RSA key for *TSK* in depth. Assume that on average, an electric vehicle uses 150 credentials per day. Then for each month, each vehicle uses 4500 credentials per month. For our scheme, we set N to 10 (*i.e.* for every 10 credentials submitted by a vehicle, the TA only signs 1 of them and the other 9 are for checking purpose). This means that the TA needs to sign at least 45,000 credentials for each client. From the data we obtained from the experiment, signing 45,000 tickets using a consumer PC with 1024 bits RSA key for *TSK* needs about 5 minutes. If 2048 bits RSA key is used, it needs about 37 minutes. Assume that the TA server can run for 24 hours a day so that it can keep on signing credentials for different vehicles, about 43,200 vehicles can be supported by the system if 1024 bits RSA key is used and about 1168 vehicles can be supported if 2048 bits RSA key is used. Nevertheless, recall that the TA server is usually more powerful than a conventional laptop computer. This means that the signing process can be done much faster. It is also straight forward to apply multi-threading technique for the credential signing process and multiple TA servers can be used for this purpose.

Besides credential signing, vehicles need to prepare the binding factors which also require modular exponenttiation. However, we suggest that the exponent part of the public key can be assigned a small number. In this way, the exponentiation can be done in a much shorter time. This also allows us to use a cheaper device (*i.e.* a conventional computer or even a smart card) on the client side.

Table 1. Time complexity of spcs scheme.

Phase	Time Complexity
Credential signature requesting	$T_{sig}+T_{adec}+T_{ver}\left(V_i\right)$ $T_{ver}+T_{aenc}+T_{sig}\left(\text{TA}\right)$
Credential signing	$T_{senc}+T_{sig}\left(V_i\right)$ (for each credential) $T_{sig}\left(\text{TA}\right)$ (for each unopened credential)
Charging station searching and reservation	$T_{aenc}\left(V_i\right)$ $T_{adec}+T_{ver}\left(\text{QS}\right)$ $T_{sig}\left(\text{QS}\right)$ (if credential has been used) $T_{senc}/\left(T_{sdec}+T_{ver}\right)$ $\left(V_i\right)$ (for each ongoing communication) $T_{senc}+T_{sig}/T_{sdec}\left(\text{QS}\right)$ (for each ongoing communication)
Charging phase	$T_{aenc}\left(V_i\right)$ $T_{adec}\left(CS_j\right)$
Reconciliation	$T_{sig}\left(V_i\right)$ $T_{ver}\left(\text{TA}\right)$

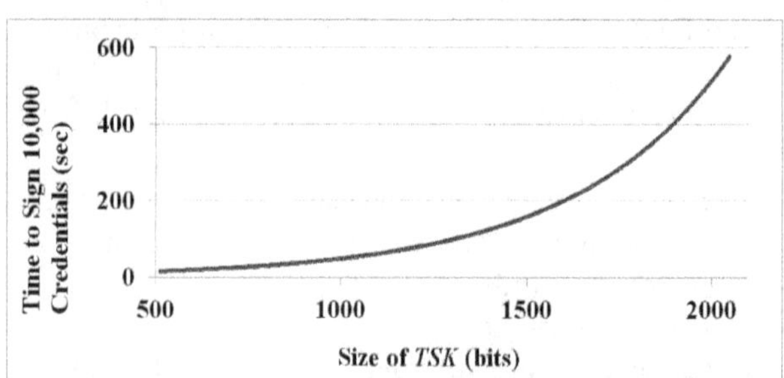

Figure 1. Time to sign 10,000 Credentials vs Size of *TSK*.

8. Conclusion

In this paper, we addressed the problem of privacy-preserving charging station searching and reservation for electric vehicles. We made use of the property of blind signature to achieve this goal. In brief, an electric vehicle first generates a set of anonymous credentials on its own. A trusted authority then blindly signs on them after verifying the identity of the vehicle. After that, the vehicle can make charging station searching queries and reservetions by presenting those signed anonymous credentials. Throughout our scheme, the most time-consuming part should be the credential signing process by the trusted authority. It may even become a bottleneck if lots of vehicles request it for signing operation at about the same time. Through implementation, we showed that such a credential signing process could be completed in reasonable time when the parameters were properly set. The process could be as quickly as 5 minutes when 1024 bits of RSA signing key was used. Moreover, we showed that our scheme is secure enough in terms of authentication and privacy-preserving. In the future, we will work out an approximate solution for the querying server to optimistically schedule electric vehicles to charging stations around the city.

REFERENCES

[1] F. Wang, D. Zeng and L. Yang, "Smart Cars on Smart Roads: An IEEE Intelligent Transportation Systems Society Update," *IEEE Pervasive Computing*, Vol. 5, No. 4, 2006, pp. 68-69.

[2] H. Oh, C. Yae, D. Ahn and H. Cho, "5.8 GHz DSRC Packet Communication System for ITS Services," *Proceedings of the IEEE VTC'99*, Amsterdam, 19-29 September 1999, pp. 2223-2227.

[3] D. Chaum, "Blind Signatures for Untraceable Payments, Advances in Cryptology," *Proceedings of the Springer-Verlag Crypto'82*, Vol. 3, 1983, pp. 199-203.

[4] R. Lu, X. Lin, H. Zhu and X. Shen, "SPARK: A New VANET-Based Smart Parking Scheme for Large Parking Lots," *Proceedings of the IEEE INFOCOM'09*, Rio de Janeiro, 19-25 April 2009, pp. 1413-1421.

[5] T. W. Chim, S. M. Yiu, L. C. K. Hui and V. O. K. Li, "OPQ: OT-Based Private Querying in VANETs," *Transactions on Intelligent Transportation Systems*, Vol. 12, No. 4, 2011, pp. 1413-1422.

[6] F. Calabrese, M. Colonna, P. Lovisolo, D. Parata and C. Ratti, "Real-Time Urban Monitoring Using Cell Phones: A Case Study in Rome," *IEEE Transactions on Intelligent Transportation Systems*, Vol. 12, No. 1, 2011, pp. 141-151.

[7] C. Zhang, R. Lu, X. Lin, P. H. Ho and X. Shen, "An Efficient Identity-Based Batch Verification Scheme for Vehicular Sensor Networks," *Proceedings of the IEEE INFOCOM'08*, Phoenix, 13-18 April 2008, pp. 816-824.

[8] C. Zhang, X. Lin, R. Lu and P. H. Ho, "RAISE: An Efficient RSU-Aided Message Authentication Scheme in Vehicular Communication Networks," *Proceedings of the IEEE ICC'08*, Beijing, 19-23 May 2008, pp. 1451-1457.

[9] A. Wasef and X. Shen, "PPGCV: Privacy Preserving Group Communications Protocol for Vehicular Ad Hoc Networks," *Proceedings of the IEEE ICC'08*, Beijing, 19-23 May 2008, pp. 1458-1463.

[10] T. W. Chim, S. M. Yiu, L. C. K. Hui and V. O. K. Li, "SPECS: Secure and Privacy Enhancing Communications for VANET," *Ad Hoc Networks*, Vol. 9, No. 2, 2011, pp. 189-203.

[11] B. K. Chaurasia, S. Verma and S. M. Bhasker, "Message Broadcast in VANETs Using Group Signature," *Proceedings of the IEEE WCSN'09*, Allahabad, 27-29 December 2008, pp. 131-136.

[12] A. Studer, E. Shi, F. Bai and A. Perrig, "TACKing Together Efficient Authentication, Revocation, and Privacy in VANETs," *Proceedings of the IEEE SECON'09*, Rome, 22-26 June 2009, pp. 1-9.

[13] L. Chan, S. L. Ng and G. Wang, "Threshold Anonymous Announcement in VANETs," *IEEE Journal on Selected Areas in Communications*, Vol. 29, No. 3, 2011, pp. 605-615.

[14] D. Chaum, "Security without Identification: Transaction Systems to Make Big Brother Obsolete," *Communications of the ACM*, Vol. 28, No. 70, 1985, pp. 1030-1044.

[15] E. Aimeur, H. Hage and F. S. M. Onana, "Anonymous Credentials for Privacy-Preserving E-learning," *Proceedings of the IEEE MCETECH'08*, Washington DC, 23-25 January 2008, pp. 70-80.

Permissions

The contributors of this book come from diverse backgrounds, making this book a truly international effort. This book will bring forth new frontiers with its revolutionizing research information and detailed analysis of the nascent developments around the world.

We would like to thank all the contributing authors for lending their expertise to make the book truly unique. They have played a crucial role in the development of this book. Without their invaluable contributions this book wouldn't have been possible. They have made vital efforts to compile up to date information on the varied aspects of this subject to make this book a valuable addition to the collection of many professionals and students.

This book was conceptualized with the vision of imparting up-to-date information and advanced data in this field. To ensure the same, a matchless editorial board was set up. Every individual on the board went through rigorous rounds of assessment to prove their worth. After which they invested a large part of their time researching and compiling the most relevant data for our readers. Conferences and sessions were held from time to time between the editorial board and the contributing authors to present the data in the most comprehensible form. The editorial team has worked tirelessly to provide valuable and valid information to help people across the globe.

Every chapter published in this book has been scrutinized by our experts. Their significance has been extensively debated. The topics covered herein carry significant findings which will fuel the growth of the discipline. They may even be implemented as practical applications or may be referred to as a beginning point for another development. Chapters in this book were first published by Scientific Research Publishing Inc.; hereby published with permission under the Creative Commons Attribution License or equivalent.

The editorial board has been involved in producing this book since its inception. They have spent rigorous hours researching and exploring the diverse topics which have resulted in the successful publishing of this book. They have passed on their knowledge of decades through this book. To expedite this challenging task, the publisher supported the team at every step. A small team of assistant editors was also appointed to further simplify the editing procedure and attain best results for the readers.

Our editorial team has been hand-picked from every corner of the world. Their multi-ethnicity adds dynamic inputs to the discussions which result in innovative outcomes. These outcomes are then further discussed with the researchers and contributors who give their valuable feedback and opinion regarding the same. The feedback is then collaborated with the researches and they are edited in a comprehensive manner to aid the understanding of the subject.

Apart from the editorial board, the designing team has also invested a significant amount of their time in understanding the subject and creating the most relevant covers. They scrutinized every image to scout for the most suitable representation of the subject and create an appropriate cover for the book.

The publishing team has been involved in this book since its early stages. They were actively engaged in every process, be it collecting the data, connecting with the contributors or procuring relevant information. The team has been an ardent support to the editorial, designing and production team. Their endless efforts to recruit the best for this project, has resulted in the accomplishment of this book. They are a veteran in the field of academics and their pool of knowledge is as vast as their experience in printing. Their expertise and guidance has proved useful at every step. Their uncompromising quality standards have made this book an exceptional effort. Their encouragement from time to time has been an inspiration for everyone.

The publisher and the editorial board hope that this book will prove to be a valuable piece of knowledge for researchers, students, practitioners and scholars across the globe.

List of Contributors

Romany F. Mansour and W. F. Awwad
Department of Computer Science, Faculty of Science, Northern Borders Univeristy, Arar, KSA

A. A. Mohammed
Department of Computer Science, Faculty of Science, South Valley University, Qena, Egypt

Adel Hammad Abusitta
College of Engeenering & IT, Al Ain University of Science and Technology, Al Ain, UAE

Shahriar Mohammadi, Vahid Allahvakil and Mojtaba Khaghani
Department of IT, Khajeh Nasir University, Tehran, Iran

Shweta Tripathi
Department of Computer Engineering, Fr. Agnel Institute of Technology, Navi Mumbai, India

Bandu Baburao Meshram
Head Department of Computer Technology, Veermata Jijabai Technological Institute, Mumbai, India

Raja Sekhar Reddy Gade and Sanjeev Kumar
Networking Research Lab, Department of Electrical/Computer Engineering, The University of Texas-Pan American, Edinburg, USA

Ming Tong, Tao Chen, Wei Zhang and Linna Dong
School of Electronic Engineering, Xidian University, Xian, China

Vladimir V. Grishachev
Russian State Geological Prospecting University (RSGPU), Moscow, Russia

Yonghong Chen and Jiancong Chen
College of Computer Science & Technology, Huaqiao University, Xiamen, China

Khalid. O. Elaalim
Department of Statistic and Computer Science, Faculty of Applied Sciences, Red Sea University, Port Sudan, Sudan
School of Computer Science and Technology, University of Science and Technology of China, Hefei, China

Shoubao Yang
School of Computer Science and Technology, University of Science and Technology of China, Hefei, China

Ahmad Bakhtiyari Shahri
Faculty of Computer Science and Information Systems, Universiti Teknologi Malaysia, Johor Bahru, Malaysia

Zuraini Ismail
Advanced Informatics School, Universiti Teknologi Malaysia, Johor Bahru, Malaysia

Yaser Jararweh and Hala Tawalbeh
Computer Science Department, Jordan University of Science and Technology (CHiS), Irbid, Jordan

Loai Tawalbeh
Cryptographic Hardware and Information Security Lab (CHiS), Computer Engineering Department, Jordan University of Science and Technology, Irbid, Jordan

Abidalrahman Mohd
Engineering Mathematics & Internetworking, Dalhousie University, Halifax, Canada

Lanfranco Lopriore
Dipartimento di Ingegneria dell Informazione: Elettronica, Informatica, Telecomunicazioni, Università di Pisa, Pisa, Italy

Archana Tiwari
Chhatrapati Shivaji Institute of Technology, Durg, India

Manisha Sharma
Bhilai Institute of Technology, Durg, India

K. K. Sindhu
Computer Engineering Department, Shah and Anchor Kutchhi Engineering College, Mumbai, India

B. B. Meshram
Computer Engineering Department, Veermata Jijabai Technological Institute, Mumbai, India

Amin Hashemi Pour
Department of Information Technology, Tehran University, Kish, Iran

Ali Payandeh
Department of Information and Communication Technology, Malekeashtar University, Tehran, Iran

Rabiah Ahmad and Zahri Yunos
Center for Advanced Computing Technology, Faculty of Information and Communication Technology, Universiti Teknikal Malaysia Melaka (UTeM), Melaka, Malaysia

Zachary Miller and Wei Hu
Department of Computer Science, Houghton College, Houghton, USA

Aziz Baayer and Mohammed Elkoutbi
Laboratory SI2M, ENSIAS, University of Mohammed-V-Souissi, Rabat, Morocco

Nourddine Enneya
Laboratory LaRIT, Faculty of Sciences, University of Ibn Tofail, Kenitra, Morocco

Usha Banerjee and Gaurav Batra
Department of Computer Science and Engineering, College of Engineering Roorkee (COER), Roorkee, India

K. V. Arya
Department of ICT, Atal Bihari Vajpayee Indian Institute of Information Technology and Management, Gwalior, India

Rabiah Ahmad, Zahri Yunos and Shahrin Sahib
Center for Advanced Computing Technology, Faculty of Information and Communication Technology, Universiti Teknikal Malaysia Melaka (UTeM), Melaka, Malaysia

Mariana Yusoff
Centre for Languages and Human Development, Universiti Teknikal Malaysia Melaka (UTeM), Melaka, Malaysia

Xinqian Lin, Shengqiang Tang and Wentao Huang
School of Mathematics and Computing Science, Guilin University of Electronic Technology, Guilin, China

Moad Mowafi, Walid Aljoby and Mohammad Al-Rousan
Department of Network Engineering and Security, Jordan University of Science and Technology, Irbid, Jordan

Loai Tawalbeh
Department of Computer Engineering, Jordan University of Science and Technology, Irbid, Jordan

Rasim Alguliyev and Saadat Nazirova
Institute of Information Technology, Azerbaijan National Academy of Sciences, Baku, Azerbaijan

Qingquan Sun, Yeqing Wu, Mengcheng Guo and Jiang Lu
Department of Electrical and Computer Engineering, The University of Alabama, Tuscaloosa, USA

Peng Wu
School of Information Engineering, Wuhan University of Technology, Wuhan, China

Mario Góngora-Blandón and Miguel Vargas-Lombardo
Centro de Investigación, Desarrollo e Innovación en Tecnologías de la Información y las Comunicaciones (CIDITIC) Grupo de
Investigación en Salud Electrónica y Supercomputación (GISES), Technological University of Panama, Panama City, Panama

Gholam Reza Zargar
GIS Department, Khuzestan Electrical Power Distributed Company, Ahvaz, Iran

Tania Baghaie
Training Center of Applied Science and Technology, Tehran Municipality Information and Communication Technology Organization, Tehran, Iran

Tat Wing Chim, Jeanno Chin Long Cheung, Siu Ming Yiu and Lucas Chi Kwong Hui
Department of Computer Science, The University of Hong Kong, Hong Kong, China

Victor On Kwok Li
Department of Electrical and Electronic Engineering, The University of Hong Kong, Hong Kong, China

Printed in the USA
CPSIA information can be obtained
at www.ICGtesting.com
JSHW052021301024
72690JS00004B/129

9 781632 403070